5029 Nunney Castle *gets a thorough grooming between turns.*

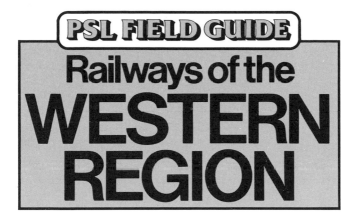

PSL FIELD GUIDE

Railways of the
WESTERN REGION

PSL FIELD GUIDE

Railways of the
WESTERN REGION

Geoffrey Body

PSL

PATRICK STEPHENS LIMITED

Title page *A typical WR branch line scene with a dmu using an open crossing, an example of the revolution in rural railway operation.*

Page 6 *Sonning Cutting, beloved of railway photographers.*

First published in 1983
Reprinted with additional material 1989

British Library Cataloguing in Publication Data

Body, Geoffrey, *1929—*
  Railways of the Western Region. — (PSL field guides)
  Rev. ed.
  1. England. Railway services: British Rail. Western Region
  385'.0942

  ISBN 0-85260-296-1

Patrick Stephens Limited is part of the Thorsons Publishing Group, Wellingborough, Northamptonshire, NN8 2RQ, England.

Printed in Great Britain by Biddles Limited, Guildford, Surrey
Typeset by MJL Limited, Hitchin, Hertfordshire

10 9 8 7 6 5 4 3 2 1

Contents

Acknowledgements

The author especially acknowledges the assistance received from the Western Region of British Rail in the preparation of this book. Without that assistance its compilation would not have been possible. Major contributions were made by R.W.N. Drummond, Public Relations Officer of the Western Region and Neil Sprinks the Divisional Public Relations Officer at Cardiff. Thanks are also due to Alan Harrison, Don Rubber, Alan Button and Chris Watts. A large number of the illustrations were provided by British Rail (Western), the maps are by Ian G. Body and other illustrations are by the Dart Valley Railway, the Forest Railroad Park, the Peco company, the Great Western Society Ltd, Roy Nash and from the author's collection.

SECTION 1

The Western Region field guide

Each of the five vast railway regions which make up the British Rail network is teeming with interesting places, equipment and practices. Many have a fascinating history or a modern significance which is not obvious to the casual observer, and most will increase in interest as more and more is known about their past and purpose. Fascinated by the journey along the Exe estuary in the trains from Exeter to Torbay and Plymouth, passengers are not likely to spot a small pond at Turf or to think much about it if they do. Yet it was once a reservoir for a set of Boulton & Watt pumping engines and is a tangible reminder of Brunel's unhappy but fascinating flirtation with atmospheric propulsion on the South Devon Railway. Similarly a train of yellow containers spotted in the Reading area may convey very little on its own, but seen as part of a pioneering activity to dispose of London's refuse in suitable tips without imposing convoys of lorries upon the countryside it becomes of much greater interest. And with 150 years of history contributing evidence from all its phases and a modern railway which thinks nothing of 125 mph running or 3,000-tonne freight trains, the interest for expert and amateur alike is almost endless.

Without attempting to be a detailed history or a highly technical treatise on the modern railway, the objective of this guide has been to provide in one volume all the information necessary to understanding the railways in a given area. Thus the main body of the book is occupied by a Gazetteer which deals alphabetically with each significant railway location and records the main items of interest associated with it. To get the flavour of the region this is preceded by a look at the 'Western' as a whole, its origins, development, routes and traffic.

In the Gazetteer section the entries, listed alphabetically by railway title, are designed to cover the present situation and role of each location together with such of its past as is relevant or interesting. There is a common standard of coverage but no rigidity of format for the intention is to give pleasure and be interesting, as well as to inform. The fact that inspections in Box Tunnel once meant a precarious hoist in a crane bucket for the unfortunate engineer may not be essential information, but it does put the task of keeping tunnels safe in a new perspective! Similar operations are not described in detail every time they occur and aspects such as services have been slightly generalised, ie, to the broad Monday to Friday pattern at the time of writing. Separate entries appear for each location of significance but some of the lesser or more general features may appear in the route descriptions.

Each main Gazetteer entry is preceded by a sub-heading designed to show its broad location. For this purpose the Western Region has been divided into a number of main sections of line and this is quoted in each case, together with a recognisable point on each side of the location to help pinpoint it more closely. Direction on British Rail lines is described as Up or Down, Up being towards London and/or the headquarters of the pre-grouping company concerned. The line sections shown in the Gazetteer sub-headings are normally described in the Down direction and on the Western Region this is away from Paddington except in such cases as: the former Midland Railway lines, eg, Bristol-Birmingham where Up was towards the MR headquarters at Derby; the Welsh valley lines where Up was generally literally away from the sea and up towards the head of the valley; the former LNWR lines where Up was towards Euston making Newport and Llanelli to Shrewsbury the Up direction.

The sub-headings also give distances, mostly from Paddington, and based on the Sectional Appendix to the Working Timetable. These distances in some cases (and indicated by an asterisk) reflect historical rather than present route factors, eg, (1) The West of England main line where (i) the distances west of Cogload reflect the original, pre cut-off, route via Bristol, and (ii) distances between Westbury and Castle Cary are those of the route via Thingley and Bradford Junctions to Weymouth. (2) South Wales where the distances are based on the old route via Gloucester.

The distances quoted refer to a signal box where one exists or otherwise to the station or other feature being described, the nearest distance to Paddington being given in such cases as tunnels. In the case of branch lines the length of the line is given and all distances are rounded to the nearest chain.

In most cases the Gazetteer deals with points of interest on a location basis but this is varied where a line is so much a single entity that the fragmentation of its description would be confusing. This applies particularly on branch lines and in parts of South Wales. The Liskeard to Looe branch, for example, has a character of its own derived from the canal in its history and a route which twice points north and requires one sharp curve and one reversal to get its diesel multiple units south to the coast.

The reference numbers for the Gazetteer entries appear again in the first of the supplementary sections which follow. Here are summary descriptions of each of the main routes of the region provided so that their physical features and function can be seen as an entity. Coupled with the table of diverging routes and branches, this section can be used to add interest to a journey in the same way that the Gazetteer will add interest to a location visit. Related to a good relief map the route data gives not only a railway working and hardware picture but a view of the countryside traversed and some insight into the way lines like the one from Yeovil to Weymouth used river valleys to avoid excessive gradients and construction costs. Other supplementary sections cover the principal closed lines, the preservation locations and the main departmental activities of the modern railway in order to cater for those interested in the whole railway panorama in a particular area or in a particular railway activity such as signalling or buildings and architecture.

Throughout the text of the book mention is made of good spots for viewing and photography but, however interesting a railway location may be, trespass is an offence under the bye laws as well as being dangerous and anti-social. The same applies in the case of private property where there is a railway interest. Although a strong regard for safety is inherent in the railway industry, British

Rail is helpful to the careful and viewing, spotting and photography are generally permitted, at the discretion of the local BR management, wherever access is free or available by platform ticket.

BR provides a comprehensive service for information on train services and fares and there are many reduced fare facilities which can be put to good use in the pursuit of a railway interest or study. The Western Region has travel centres at Barnstaple, Bath, Bristol, Exeter, Penzance, Plymouth, St Austell, Taunton, Torquay, Truro, Weston-super-Mare and Yeovil in the West, at Bridgend, Cardiff, Neath, Newport, Port Talbot and Swansea in South Wales, and at Gloucester, Oxford, Reading, Slough, Swindon, Westbury and Worcester elsewhere in the region. All are listed in the local telephone directory along with other stations able to provide passenger train service information.

In the interests of good public relations, the railway PROs at the board, region (Paddington) and division (Reading, Bristol, Cardiff) level will try to help with any special needs, but with limited time and resources they are not really in a position just to satisfy idle curiosity. Visits to the works of British Rail Engineering Limited should be pursued with the location concerned, but any request for special facilities tends to interfere with the full-time task of running the railway and visits are best achieved by means of the many open day opportunities. The railtours organised by railway societies often cover lines not normally used by passenger trains and represent another opportunity to see more of the railway network.

In preparing this book every effort has been made to ensure accuracy and account has been taken of changes known to be coming along during the interval between writing and publication. Yet the railway scene is constantly changing—new facilities being introduced, old ones abandoned, others modernised, and even new evidence of the past uncovered like the broad gauge track section unearthed in 1980—and for the benefit of future volumes the compiler would be glad to hear from readers about any additional or altered items.

Abbreviations used

CCTV	Closed circuit television.	*m*	Mile(s).
ch	Chain(s).	*MAS*	Multiple Aspect Signalling.
DGL	Down Goods Loop.	*mgr*	Merry-go-round.
dmu	Diesel multiple unit.	*UGL*	Up Goods Loop.
HST	High Speed Train.		

Key to maps

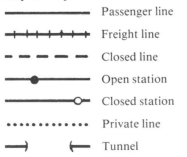

———————— Passenger line

+-+-+-+-+-+-+ Freight line

– – – – – Closed line

———●———— Open station

———○—— Closed station

············ Private line

—→)   (← Tunnel

┬┬┬┬┬┬┬┬ London Transport

——————— Original route*

—·—·—·— Cut-off lines*

* Relates only to maps on pages 14/15 where dates shown are those of opening (P—passenger, G—goods).

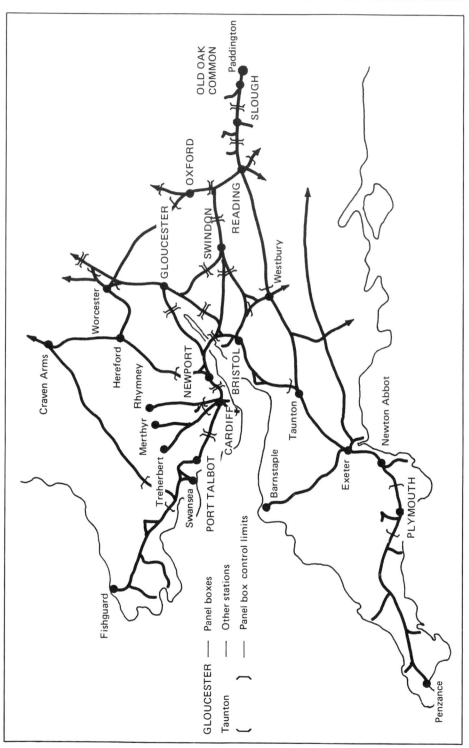

SECTION 2

The Western

The area covered by British Rail's Western Region is a geographical segment of Great Britain widening out from Paddington to embrace Berkshire and Wiltshire and then takes in most of Oxfordshire, the West Midlands and Wales below the railway boundaries at Barnt Green and Craven Arms, and the whole of the south-west peninsula beyond Gillingham (Dorset). It is an area full of modern railway interest and of evidence of the fascination of the past, brought together where High Speed Trains pass through the Severn Tunnel or massive aggregate trains start their journey from Mendip branch lines long forgotten by rail passengers.

The 'Western' area played as big a part as most in the birth of Britain's vast railway enterprise. South Wales had its first wagonway, near Neath, before the end of the 17th century and contributed the world's first line to convey fare-paying passengers when the Oystermouth Railway started carrying the good people of Swansea out to the Mumbles in 1807. Three years earlier Richard Trevithick's locomotive had won the wager that it could haul a load of iron from Penydarren to Abercynon, but the damage done to the 4 ft 2 in gauge plateway in the process soon ended this experiment.

The Midland, L&NW and L&SW companies may have probed their tentacles into South Wales and the West, but the area was always dominated by one railway name. The Great Western Railway *was* railways in the West, although many may have been guilty of the minor heresy of wondering how it came to be known as 'God's Wonderful Railway'.

When a geographical area of high interest and activity is linked with the fact that the GWR remained a large, single railway entity longer than any other, and to this is added the individualism associated with Brunel, the broad gauge, Castles and Kings, diesel hydraulics and the advent of the HSTs, some of the reasons for the Western magic become apparent. Of course, the Great Western had its failings—and lost some of its territorial battles because of them—but its standards were good, its innovation high and its management capable. The amalgam which could preserve these qualities and also spread its publicity message through one of the largest publishing activities of its day must deserve some of the high regard in which it came to be held.

So much for reason. In any view of a public enterprise there is always a subjective, personal colouring. Most memories of the Great Western are of trains along the South Devon coastal section at Dawlish, of coal trains from the valleys to Newport and Cardiff docks, of Kings at speed, branch auto-trains,

The days of the broad gauge on the Great Western.

Thames Valley railcars and ubiquitous slip coaches. Other ingredients are the steam, bustle and search for the right portion of a summer Saturday holiday train from Paddington, excursions to Weston or Weymouth, crowded market trains and the plunge into the smoky tunnel outside Snow Hill. Add essence of Swindon and the mixture becomes irresistible. Since, in the good times, dividends on ordinary shares were as high as 7½ per cent, such views of the GWR are not wholly romantic ones.

The Great Western Railway was born at a meeting of Bristol merchants in 1832 and, thanks to the energy and enterprise of men like Charles Saunders, Isambard Kingdom Brunel and Daniel Gooch, opened its first section of railway from London to Maidenhead on June 4 1838. By the end of 1845 the combined mileage of the GWR and its Bristol & Exeter Railway partner had reached 246 and trains were running from Paddington to Bristol and Exeter, as well as serving Oxford and Gloucester by branch lines.

Around the fast, flat main line, engineered to reflect the broad gauge concept of speedy and comfortable trains for the well-to-do, the GWR grew in distinct areas. South of the 'Great Way Round' (as this circuitous route to Exeter came to be called) was an area of conflict and manoeuvring reflecting the rivalries between the GWR and the London & South Western Railway. This started in 1844 with a battle for Newbury and continued in every county to the west until the rival routes to Devon and Cornwall had stabilised and the conflicts could be expressed in speed, fares and standards of comfort rather than in Parliamentary proceedings and the wooing or bullying of smaller lines. It was somehow symbolic of the differences that trains in the same direction at Exeter and Plymouth could be Up trains for one company and Down trains for the other.

Through the Wilts, Somerset & Weymouth Railway, blessed with considerably more ambition than capital, the GWR influence limped its way from Thingley Junction on the main line near Chippenham, through Westbury and Yeovil, to Weymouth. The present West of England main line section between

Reading and Taunton was a patchwork of branches until the gaps between Patney & Chirton and Westbury via Lavington and between Castle Cary and Langport were closed at the beginning of this century to take 20 m off the journey to Taunton and remove the 'Great Way Round' stigma from the GWR's image.

In 1844, as part of the thirst for expansion that was to develop into the years of the Railway Mania, the GWR had a hand in the formation of the Cornwall Railway, the South Wales Railway and the Oxford, Worcester & Wolverhampton, in addition to the Wilts, Somerset & Weymouth and several promotions of its own. The first of these, with the South Devon Railway then before Parliament, was to take the broad gauge to Falmouth. Despite the complications of the South Devon's ill-fated use of atmospheric propulsion and more in-fighting with the L&SW, the GWR had stamped its influence on the far west by 1860 and then absorbed the principal lines there in 1876 (the Bristol & Exeter), 1878 (the South Devon and West Cornwall Railways) and 1889 (the Cornwall Railway).

The Great Western chose a gauge of 7 ft and stuck to this despite early track problems and the Gauge Commission set up in 1845. Once the company's locomotive problems had been overcome, there were dividends of speed, safety and comfort deriving from the wider motive power and stock but, as the national system grew (from 1,484 m in 1840 to 6,084 m in 1850), the problems of changing trains or transhipping goods where the gauge changed led to increasing inconvenience and public outcry. Mixed gauge, ie, three rails, became significant from 1852 after a ding-dong battle with the L&NWR via the Gauge Commissioners and when 66¼ m was added to the 270 m of broad gauge routes. Two years later the addition of the Shrewsbury & Birmingham and Shrewsbury & Chester systems brought with it 77½ m of narrow gauge (ie, 4 ft 8½ in) railway and even more working and equipment problems to be surmounted.

Eventually, the Great Western conformed and completed the process of conversion to the gauge which had become standard. This took place during the weekend of May 20-22 1892 and represented a notable piece of railway history and organisation, embracing such highlights as a mammoth last train to clear the broad gauge vehicles before the changeover, a huge mobilisation of labour to carry out the work and a sad graveyard at Swindon for the old locomotives which were not to be converted. By a small piece of irony, the sidings installed at Swindon to accommodate the redundant equipment of 1892 are still in use as a graveyard. Today diesel locomotives, surplus and cannibalised, look no less forlorn than did their tiny steam predecessors in misfortune nearly a century ago.

The most bitter of all the battles fought between broad gauge and narrow gauge took place in the counties north of the original GWR main line, with the Oxford, Worcester & Wolverhampton Railway trifling dangerously with the GWR dreams of 'Broad Gauge to the Mersey' and the LNWR belief that expansion came before such old fashioned virtues as dignity and honesty. In due course the 109¼ narrow gauge miles of the 'Old Worse & Worse' were joined with the 52 m of the Newport, Abergavenny & Hereford Railway and the 9¾-mile connecting line of the Worcester & Hereford to form the West Midlands Railway in July 1860. Just over three years and several additions later the WMR became part of the Great Western.

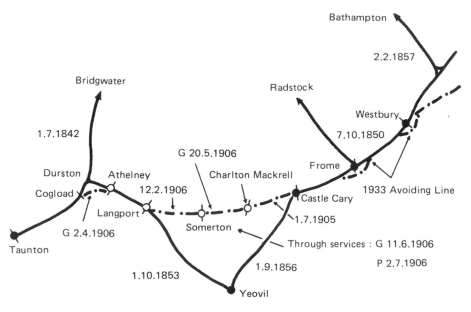

In 1862 the South Wales Railway had added 174¾ m to the GWR broad gauge network and stretched its tentacles to West Wales. Various other Welsh and Forest of Dean lines were absorbed up to 1890 but South Wales remained a complex pattern of railways serving and competing for the lucrative coal business until the tidying up brought about by the provisions of the Railways Act 1921. The year 1922 brought such lines as the Taff Vale, Rhymney and Barry Railways into the GWR fold plus several smaller Welsh systems and the 295¼ m of the Cambrian Railways. A few more systems followed in 1923 including the Forest of Dean Central and some other small companies from west of the Severn. Elsewhere the main additions of the 'grouping' year and the stabilisation of the GWR into the form in which most people remember it were the Midland & South Western Junction Railway (from Andoversford to Andover) and the Didcot, Newbury & Southampton Railway.

Acceptance of the 4 ft 8½ in gauge seemed to bring a new era to the GWR and soon came the acquisition, with the Midland, of the Severn Bridge Railway whose 1,387 yd bridge helped Forest of Dean coal move towards the lucrative markets to the east. Other enterprising developments followed, including the building up of a Fishguard-Rosslare route to Ireland, the doubling of the main line in the South-West and the opening of the first section of the direct route to Taunton on October 1 1900. After rebuilding to main line standards 23½ m of former branches and adding 33 m of new railway, the cut-off route came into full use in 1906 to allow the Cornish Riviera Express, boasting new stock and using the newly installed water troughs, to cut the journey time from Paddington to Plymouth to 4 hrs 7 mins.

These were exciting years in the GWR territory. 1903, for example, brought ten new 'openings', three of them associated with the direct route from Wootton Bassett to the Severn Tunnel. The latter, 4 m 428 yds of engineering drama kept dry by the massive Cornish beam engines in Sudbrook Pumping Station, had originated back in 1872 and been completed in 1886. Previously

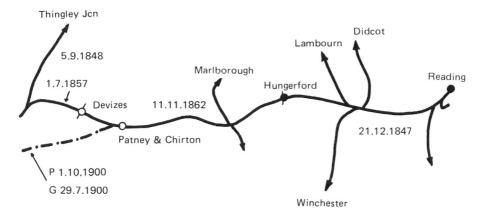

passengers had travelled up to Gloucester or used the ferry route from beside the New Passage Hotel across to Portskewett on the west bank of the estuary. The opening of the tunnel route shortened the journey time of passengers to South Wales but their trains still ran via Bath and Dr Day's Junction at Bristol until the new cut-off line direct from Wootton Bassett did for South Wales what the cut-off route to Taunton was shortly to do for the West. In the same year of 1903 the GWR started its first road motor service, between Helston and The Lizard, and followed this with the first steam rail motor service, on the Stroud Valley line between Chalford and Stonehouse. On July 14 1903 engine No 3433 *City of Bath* reached 87.4 mph at the head of a special train to Plymouth and in the following year 3440 *City of Truro* attained 102.3 mph down Whiteball bank, although the actual speed was not disclosed at the time for fear of alarming people! The GW&GC Joint lines and the route from Bristol to Birmingham via Honeybourne were opened between 1905 and 1908; 1906 brought the first use of audible cab signalling and the decade closed with the opening of the Ashendon Junction-Anyho Junction section which reduced the GWR route to Birmingham by 18½ m.

The immediate post-war period saw the GWR first rebuilding and then restarting its round of improvements. As a result of attention given to the better handling of coal flowing down the valleys to the South Wales ports the company's freight business rose by some 8 million tons overall, and some dramatic new passenger train timings—including four hours from Millbay Docks to Paddington for passengers collected by tender from the Cunard liners calling at Plymouth Sound—gave it passenger figures up to 12½ million. After the troubles of 1926 a bright spot of the following year was the advent of *King George V*, the first of a class of 4-6-0 locomotives soon to put 40,000 lb of tractive effort at the head of the GWR's crack expresses.

The economic conditions of the early '30s did little for any trading enterprise let alone the main line railways who were just beginning to feel the effects of road competition. But the GWR brightened the period with a 1931 announcement of the introduction of a Cardiff-Haldon/Roborough air service and the introduction of the first of the AEC railcars two years later. The period also saw a round of improvements deriving from 1929 legislation aimed at easing unemployment, and these included the avoiding lines at Westbury and Frome and station remodelling schemes for Paddington, Bristol, Taunton and Cardiff.

When, in 1935, a royal Jubilee and the GWR centenary coincided, that railway introduced new stock for the Cornish Riviera and put on another notable service, The Bristolian.

Heading into the years of the Second World War with 24 of its trains timed at over 60 mph, the GWR emerged from the conflict battered and weary. In between the trains, ships and workshops had given of their best but the dreams of electrification to Penzance and of 'Fair Play for the Railways' had to give way first to rebuilding and then to an acceptance of the new methods and thinking demanded by nationalisation and the establishment of the Western Region. 'Under new management' the WR followed the pattern of the wider railway system in rationalising and modernising its system but the taste for individuality showed up in the replacement of steam traction by diesel hydraulic locomotives, when everyone else was going for diesel electrics, and the taste for leadership in the introduction of the first High Speed Train services—on the original Brunel main line—in 1975.

Today, there is still no forgetting that the Western Region has GWR origins. They show in the great spans of Paddington station and the fine architecture at Bristol, the Severn Tunnel is still impressive after over a century of use, Brunel's name stands out clearly in all the photographs of the Royal Albert Bridge across the Tamar and many a route seems more spacious than average because of its broad gauge origins. But it is a slimmed down, 1980s railway with the past respected but the present paramount and the future constantly being challenged. It entered the decade with a railway system made up of 1,903 route miles (of which 427 m were freight only) and 3,507 track miles, over half laid with continuous welded rail. To serve 493 stations and depots, 33.4 million train miles were being provided annually involving such diverse activities as the serving of 9 million cups of tea and coffee and the maintenance of 7,671 bridges.

The principal Inter-City passenger routes on the WR are now worked by HST sets running between Paddington and Bristol/Taunton/Paignton via Bath, Swansea via Newport and Cardiff and on the West of England route via Westbury, Taunton, Exeter and Plymouth to Penzance. From the Penzance/

Below *One of the Kings with a 12-coach train.* **Below right** *An iron ore train exemplifies the importance of BR facilities to the heavy industries of South Wales.*

Plymouth line an Inter-City 125 service operates over the important and highly interesting cross-country route through Bristol, Gloucester (junction for the South Wales leg) and Cheltenham to Birmingham and on to the main cities of the north. Further important Inter-City services from Paddington to Oxford (then Worcester and Hereford) and on to Birmingham, from Cardiff via Newport and the old GWR trunk route to Shrewsbury and Crewe and via Bristol and Salisbury to Southampton/Portsmouth, from Exeter via Salisbury and the SR to Waterloo and from the North-West via Oxford and Reading to the south coast. Other significant through routes are the line through Bath and Yeovil to Weymouth and the 110¼ m from Llanelli, through the heart of Wales, to Shrewsbury.

The WR has a thriving commuter activity serving intermediate stations to Reading, together with the Windsor, Greenford, Marlow and Henley branches. Cross-country dmu sets provide an onward service from Reading as far as Oxford and to Bedwyn on the Taunton line, and also on the three routes to the SR via Basingstoke, Ascot and Guildford, including a service to Gatwick in addition to the Railair coach between Reading and Heathrow. There are trains from Swindon via Gloucester to Worcester and connections from the HSTs at Swansea into West Wales with a good mixture of through and local coverage for the Pembroke Dock, Milford Haven and Fishguard Harbour branches. Cardiff has its 'Valleys' services from Barry and Penarth to the south of the city and Rhymney/Merthyr/Treherbert to the north. Bristol has local services to Cardiff, Weston-super-Mare and Severn Beach and the South West a selection of seven branches—to Exmouth, Barnstaple, Gunnislake, Looe, Newquay, Falmouth and St Ives.

In common with the rest of the railway system, the Western has experienced great changes in its freight business. Gone are the small wagons and much-marshalled trains to be replaced by trainloads of high capacity wagons, often privately owned and capable of running at speeds compatible with the passenger train timetable. The Western still handles vast quantities of coal, steel, cement and chemicals from South Wales, oil products from West Wales, china clay for export or the Potteries, aggregates from the Mendips and many other bulk commodities. The region has a network of terminals for the Speedlink facility of scheduled, air-braked services and there are Freightliner depots at Bristol (West

Above *A Motorail train in Devon.* **Below right** *Bristol Parkway was opened to combat the threat of the M4 and has proved highly successful.*

Depot), Cardiff (Pengam) and Swansea (Danygraig). In addition to the Sealink services at Fishguard, the WR system exchanges traffic via the docks at Swansea, Cardiff, Newport and Avonmouth and there is a major inland distribution depot near Didcot.

To maintain the traction for hauling this passenger and freight business the WR has major running and maintenance depots at Old Oak Common, Laira (Plymouth), Bath Road (Bristol), Canton (Cardiff) and Landore (Swansea) with separate HST facilities at St Philips Marsh (Bristol) and Penzance. The locomotive fleet is made up of Class 56, 50, 47, 37 and 31 types plus Class 08 shunters and a small number of Class 03 204 hp machines, based at Landore and modified for use on the Cwmmawr and Central Wales lines. Traincrew signing on facilities exist at most of the traffic activity centres and many have fuelling facilities. Smaller depots like Gloucester provide back-up maintenance and there are strategic rolling stock servicing and maintenance points throughout the region. The diesel multiple unit fleet of cross-country units, high density suburban sets, single power cars and other items is cared for at the maintenance depots except in the London area where Reading and Southall specialise in this work. The region has 75-ton cranes at Old Oak Common, Bath Road and Canton and 45-ton cranes at Landore and Laira.

The task of the Western Region civil engineer is no easy one. On the Bristol route the Down line is maintained to 100 mph running standards as far as milepost 98¾, as is the Up line from this point to Acton. On the main line to South Wales 100 mph standards apply from Brinkworth (87 m) to Bristol Parkway (111½ m) and most of the combined 123¼ m can be used at 125 mph. It took a three-year programme, including a five-month engineer's possession of the Wootton Bassett-Westerleigh Junction section, to lift the track to this standard and it needs constant attention to maintain it. The West of England line also needed a prolonged period of track relaying and strengthening prior to the advent of the HST service, the work including track simplification at Newbury and the easing of the curves between there and Theale to lift the line speed from 90 mph to 110 mph.

Many WR lines—especially the main line in South Wales and some of the industrial routes—take a heavy pounding from freight traffic. Water is also a constant menace, not only in the several coastal and river sections but also from overground seepage and from underground springs like the one which produces up to 30 million gallons a day beneath the Severn Tunnel. Even on the branches where traffic is lighter there are usually problems of curves, gradients and clearances and, because of the tight controls on railway expenditure, track can only be maintained to the standard required by its traffic. Thus it is that some freight only routes, like the portion of the old L&SW route between Barnstaple and Meeth, have to manage with jointed track and often secondhand at that. Some idea of the costs involved can be obtained from the fact that deferring track renewal on the Central Wales line and restricting the 78½ m between Pantyffynnon and Craven Arms to use by dmus saved £½ million in 1981.

The civil engineer is also responsible for the track structures and for buildings. This includes not only the impressive items such as the Brunel viaducts in Devon and Cornwall but over 7,000 other bridges varying in size from the tall spans of the Calstock Viaduct across the Tamar to a low bridge over a former tramway route at Radstock. The WR also has six tunnels which are over a mile long—those of the Severn, Sodbury, Box, Llangyfelach, Caerphilly and Sapperton bores—as well as many smaller ones. There are ten gradients steeper than 1 in 70 to be kept in good trim, stations and depots to be cared for and thousands of mundane tasks from repairing a sleeper crossing to keeping hedges and ditches in order.

The GWR was always in the van of signalling progress and the WR signalling and telecommunications function has maintained this tradition. Some 700 route miles are covered by multiple aspect signalling and a further 107 m will be

Cement traffic is important to the WR and moves in bulk in high capacity wagons.

added when the gaps between Westbury and Totnes are filled by the completion of a current £30 million scheme for the West of England main line. Then, the addition of new panel boxes at Westbury and Exeter will bring the total up to 13. Even so, traditional semaphore signalling based on double and single line block working still serves half the region; the keen observer can still spot LMS and SR influences in some of the finials atop signal posts, while those in the GWR style are quite commonplace. In an area of 7,500 track circuits and 2,250 power points, of TV-monitored level crossings and modern data transmission systems, the past remains alive in many a piece of vintage signalling equipment and in such delightful items as the period notice boards where a hand and pointing finger emphasise the warning message about the existence of catch points.

In addition to its trains and track, stations and signalling, the WR has countless other faces. Administration is through a Paddington regional headquarters, divisional offices at Reading, Bristol and Cardiff and over 20 area manager and depot engineer locations. There are modern ticket offices and travel centres very much in the public eye, and marshalling yards, generating plant, parcels handling depots and countless other places that are not. Rolling stock ranges from the modern Mark III coaches of the Inter-City 125 trains to elderly 'Siphon' vans and from 100-tonne oil tank wagons to engineer's wagons, still bearing such telegraph code names as 'Walrus' and 'Sea Lion'.

Not all the railway within the WR geographical boundaries is BR-owned. In addition to the technical exception of the closed lines, which are the province of the BR Property Board until disposed of, there are over 300 private sidings of one sort or another and at least 20 locations of private operating railway or preservation significance.

The closed lines, many with a surprising level of interest still remaining, comprise the former SR system in North Devon and Cornwall, the Somerset & Dorset lines and the Midland & South Western Junction route, plus a host of smaller lines and branches. The industrial locations are equally varied. Some are just coal concentration depots with a single diesel shunting locomotive, others serve such activities as the massive expansion of limestone movement and are exemplified by the Foster Yeoman complex at Merehead; yet another group serves the traditional dock, power and heavy industries. South Wales, of course, is still dominated by the NCB and BSC activities, both retaining considerable track mileage and substantial locomotive fleets. Several underground systems exist and horse-worked lines are not unknown.

Variety, not unexpectedly, is also the keynote of the preservation scene. The main established lines are those of the Dart Valley enterprise (Buckfastleigh-Totnes and Paignton-Kingswear) where GWR nostalgia can be indulged to the full, the Gwili Railway and Brecon Mountain Railway in South Wales, and the Lappa Valley Railway, near Newquay. The GWR devotee can also indulge his interest in the Great Western Museum at Swindon, at the steam centres at Didcot and Hereford, and by visiting the Bristol and Cardiff industrial museums. Steam comes alive regularly at Norchard on the Dean Forest society's line, at the Bitton headquarters of the Bristol Suburban Railway Society and at the Dowty site at Ashchurch. The Swindon & Cricklade Railway Society is reviving a portion of the M&SW line and other preservation schemes exist for the Cheltenham-Honeybourne, Plym Valley, Mumbles and Lynton & Barnstaple lines. Adding further to the variety are the marvellous world of miniature railways and landscape at Pendon Museum and the 2 ft 9 in gauge tramway working out of Seaton along the trackbed of the former SR branch to Seaton Junction.

The GWR motto *Domine dirige nos virtute et industria* seems still to be appropriate in the counties of the Western.

SECTION 3

Gazetteer

A.1 Abbotswood Junction

Birmingham-Bristol line between Barnt Green and Cheltenham. 68 m 60 ch from Derby

Abbotswood Junction is the point at which the diesel multiple unit service from Worcester joins the main line from Birmingham on its way to Cheltenham and beyond. The double track from Worcester becomes single to form the connection with the Up Main Line with Down trains then passing through the crossover. The 80-wagon Up and Down Goods Loops are staggered, reflecting the Midland Railway origins of this route, the DGL lying at the junction with the UGL further north at Spetchley.

Aber—see Rhymney Branch

A.2 Abercynon

Merthyr-Cardiff line. 16 m 25 ch from Cardiff

At Abercynon the double track line from the south divides, a freight-only route veering north-west up the Cynon valley to Aberdare and beyond, while the passenger and freight route to Merthyr continues straight ahead. To the south of the station, on the Up side, are the sidings of Stormstown Yard and the connections to the Carn Parc coal stacking area with the link to Abercynon colliery opposite. At Stormstown Junction the single track line from Lady Windsor colliery trails in on the Up side.

Abercynon station itself comprises just a single face to the Merthyr line track. On the platform is a functional brick ticket office and waiting shelter and the GWR-style signal box stands at the Cardiff end. Its signals, mainly semaphore, control the double line section south to Pontypridd and the electric token single line sections to Abercwmboi on the Aberdare line and Black Lion on the Merthyr line. The box also controls Stormstown Junction where there is a train staff instrument for the Lady Windsor Colliery branch which is operated on the One Train Working system.

All lines at Abercynon were originally part of the Taff Vale Railway which was opened from Cardiff in 1840 and on to Merthyr in 1841. The Aberdare line dates from 1846 and the Lady Windsor Colliery line from 1886. Until the early 1860s the climb towards Quaker's Yard on the Merthyr line was accomplished by a ½-mile cable-worked incline rising at 1 in 19 and 1 in 22. Traces of this earlier route, which also included a tunnel, can be seen from the present line which itself has gradients of 1 in 38 and 1 in 44. At the bottom of today's gradient there is a runaway siding which passes behind the station platform and terminates in a long sand drag.

Before the TVR was built Abercynon and Merthyr were linked by the horse traction 4 ft 4 in gauge Merthyr Tramroad, built to carry iron from the various works at Merthyr to the Glamorgan Canal. It was on this line that the world's first steam locomotive, Richard Trevithick's *Penydarren* locomotive, made its historic first run on February 21 1804. A memorial to Trevithick and the locomotive is to be seen by Abercynon fire station, close to the point where the tramroad terminated. The fire station and the nearby Navigation Inn, a name with obvious links with the canal era, can be seen on the Down side as trains leave Abercynon for Merthyr.

Passenger services at Abercynon are

part of the Barry Island-Cardiff-Merthyr suburban dmu pattern, although two workings terminate here. Freight services are predominantly for coal from the various collieries mentioned, although there is a daily ballast train from the Aberdare line. Services between Radyr Yard and Lady Windsor Colliery reverse in Stormstown Yard, as do those between Merthyr Vale colliery and Abercymboi Phurnacite patent fuel plant on the Aberdare route. Occasional special coal workings operate from the Carn Parc dump and from Abercynon colliery, although the output from the latter is normally taken underground to Lady Windsor Colliery and brought to the surface there.

The former locomotive shed at Abercynon can still be seen on the Down side, behind the station platform.

Aberdare—see Hirwaun Pond Branch

A.3 Abergavenny

Shrewsbury-Newport line between Hereford and Pontypool. 22 m 75 ch from Hereford

Just 65 chains north of the station are the remains—bridge abutment and trackbed on the Up side—of Abergavenny Junction which from 1862 gave the LNWR access to the whole of South Wales via the Heads of the Valleys route of the Merthyr, Tredegar & Abergavenny Railway. Today only the West Midlands Railway/GWR station survives to serve Abergavenny and give access to the locomotive hauled trains between Newport, Hereford and Shrewsbury. Its main, stone buildings are on the Up side slightly below the level of the platform which has an extension of raised concrete slabs at the north end. There are Up and Down Goods Loops with the goods shed and yard at the Newport end of the station.

From Abergavenny the line rises at 1 in 82/95 towards Llanvihangel and the former Abergavenny Junction, which was replaced in 1870 and then lasted, on its new site 25 ch further north, until 1958. The LNWR station at Abergavenny Brecon Road also closed in 1958, although a freight spur remained until 1971. Both points regularly provided banking assistance for the heavy gradients around them, Brecon Road being a very big shed in its heyday.

Abernant Branch—see Pantyffynnon

A.4 Aberpergwm Branch

Newport-Fishguard line, branch from Neath and Brecon Junction. 8 m 7 ch

This single track route, up the valley of the Neath river to Resolven and Aberpergwm colliery, is the surviving remnant of the Vale of Neath Railway, opened in 1851-3 from Neath to Merthyr and Aberdare. It soon became part of the strategic cross-valleys route from Neath to Pontypool Road and came into GWR ownership in 1865. Two years earlier the Vale of Neath had extended its southern end to form the present route through Jersey Marine to Swansea. This closed to passengers in 1936 but trains continued to serve Aberdylais Halt, Clyne Halt, Melyncourt Halt and Resolven on the present line until 1964.

Neath and Brecon Junction (41 m 21 ch), at the site of the former Neath Riverside station, comprises a passing loop on the single line from Jersey Marine South Junction with two single lines then diverging to Onllwyn and to Aberpergwm. There used to be a connection from the South Wales main line, used by passenger trains travelling from Swansea (High Street) via Neath General, but this is now lost under the A465 'Heads of the Valleys' road.

At Resolven (35 m 73 ch) there is a siding on the Up side serving a loading point for privately-mined coal. At the end of the line the NCB layout at Aberpergwm colliery includes a run-round loop. Both are serviced by a Monday to Friday daily train taking empty wagons from Swansea Burrows Sidings and returning with loaded ones, either for shipment through the docks or transfer to other services. Apart from a down gradient of one mile at the Neath and Brecon Junction end, the line rises gently all the way to Aberpergwm (33 m 14 ch). It is operated on the One Train Working system.

Aberthaw—see Vale of Glamorgan Line

A.5 Abingdon Branch

Didcot-Birmingham line, branch from Radley. 2 m 44 ch

This short branch was built by a local company and opened to join the main line at a point near Culham on June 2 1856. After conversion from broad gauge the junction was altered to Radley in 1873 and amalgamation with the GWR took place in 1904. Passenger services on the branch, at one time totalling 18 trains each way daily, lasted until September 9 1963. Public freight facilities continued until 1980 after which the line remained open under the control of the Oxford signalman to cater for the traffic of Associated British Maltsters.

A.6   Acton

Paddington-Swindon line. 4 m 21 ch from Paddington

There is a modest station at Acton but its importance is as one of the biggest marshalling yards in the Western Region. This occupies an area north of Acton Main Line station and beyond the sidings themselves are the houses of Acton Garden Village Estate, 491 houses built by the GWR for its employees and made available at a rent of 11/3d for a non-parlour house and 13/9d for a parlour house, excluding rates. Today railwaymen can still live in one of these houses although the weekly rent has altered somewhat!

In 1932 the yard was extended to its present size. Local goods trains served stations in the Thames Valley, heavy coal trains arrived from South Wales for sorting and transfer and goods arrived from the other lines for marshalling on to Down services. Ideally situated with links north and east via the North London and Tottenham and Hampstead lines and south via Kew Bridge and Kensington, the yard sent off dozens of freight trains daily including fitted services rejoicing in such soubriquets as The High Flyer (1.05 am to Bristol) and The Leek (9.25 pm to Llanelli). At times Acton seemed more like a farmyard as wagons of horses, cattle and sheep were fed and watered before continuing their journey.

Today Acton comprises station, goods yard and marshalling yard. The Up and Down Relief line platforms of the former are reached by steps down from the small ticket office on the bridge and metal waiting shelters are provided. Up and Down Goods lines pass behind the Up platform and beyond them are the old goods yard, with goods shed and cattle dock, and the Foster Yeoman aggregate terminal with hopper siding, grab discharge facilities and aggregate storage areas.

With air-braked traffic now concentrated on Willesden, Acton's three yard complex has taken on the task of dealing with vacuum-braked movements, includ-ing some work transferred from the SR. The 13 sidings in each of the three yards can take in and out up to 190 trains each week, the east end Up Yard handling the cross-London movements, the Mason's Lane Down Yard the westbound work and the Transfer Yard the exchange movements. The goods and transfer lines are worked on a permissive basis under the control of Acton Yard box (4 m 16 ch) and Acton West (4 m 74 ch). On the London side of the station Poplar Junction marks the line rising on the Up side to Acton Wells and Willesden Junction. Friars Junction (3 m 43 ch) follows with crossovers from Down Main to Up Relief and back, and then the approaches to Old Oak Common.

A.7   Aldermaston

Reading-Taunton line between Reading and Newbury. 44 m 63 ch from Paddington

Once a quiet place with chalet-style buildings and a wooden goods shed, Aldermaston now has an important freight activity in addition to its passenger commuter traffic.

The station itself has been simplified to consist just of platforms, shelters and connecting footbridge and 12 trains of the Reading-Newbury dmu service call in each direction daily. On the Down side, in the London direction, lie successively Padworth Sidings, Ufton Down Goods Loop and the automatic half barriers at Ufton level crossing (43 m 39 ch). The two Padworth sidings act as reception and departure lines for the freight complex which comprises the overhead gantry terminal of Conoco Ltd, Goodwin's coal sidings and the Foster Yeoman stone terminal.

A.8   Alderton Tunnel

Swindon-Newport line between Wootton Bassett Junction and Westerleigh Junction. 97 m 34 ch from Paddington

The 506 yd Alderton Tunnel (97 m 34 ch to 97 m 57 ch) was part of the extensive construction programme which preceded the opening of the South Wales & Bristol Direct line in 1903. With the Chipping Sodbury bore to the west, it was used to pass the line through the Cotswold ridge and enable gradients on the route to be kept below 1 in 300. The tunnel has no ventilation shafts and is subject to a maximum speed of 110 mph.

A.9   Aller Junction

Taunton-Penzance line between Newton Abbot and Totnes. 215 m 15 ch from Paddington*

Just beyond Newton Abbot the Plymouth and Paignton lines separate at Aller Junction under the watchful eye of a typical GWR-style signal box of brick and wood. The Down Relief line becomes the Down Paignton and there are traces of the former Down Refuge Siding beyond the junction. Until 1855 the branch trains had a separate shed at Newton Abbot and a separate line from there, a position which may recur under the Exeter multiple aspect signalling scheme.

Ammanford—see Pantyffynnon

A.10   Appleford

Didcot-Birmingham line. 55 m 16 ch from Paddington

Appleford was brought into use towards the end of the GWR's second phase of opening new halts and received its first trains on September 11 1933. The short wooden platforms, each with a 'pagoda'-type shelter, are now served by the Oxford line local trains.

An interesting development on the Down side is the ARC terminal which handles stone traffic, fly ash and

* See note on page 8.

GLC refuse is conveyed in train loads from Brentford to Appleford, using the containers shown here.

containers of compacted refuse from the GLC at Brentford. The single line to the terminal leaves the main line just north of the traditional level crossing at 54 m 48 ch. It leads to a group of five sidings, two of which lie beneath a gantry crane provided to transfer the containers of refuse to road vehicles for the final tipping. Local working is under the control of the train guard who must normally ensure that a departing train leaves at least two sidings empty for the reception and running round of the next arrival.

A.11   Ascott-under-Wychwood

Oxford-Hereford line between Charlbury and Kingham. 80 m 36 ch from Paddington

The station has a romantic name and a rustic setting and trains call at the surviving Down platform only in the morning (two Up trains) and evening (two Down). Nevertheless the location is important as the end of the 14-mile single line section from Wolvercot Junction. The signal box beyond the barrier crossing at the country end of the Down platform takes over from the Oxford panel and controls the use of the remaining siding and of the section on to Shipton and Bruern (CCTV) level crossing (83 m 15 ch).

A.12   Ashchurch

Birmingham-Bristol line between Barnt Green and Cheltenham. 79 m 47 ch from Derby

Like Ambergate, Ashchurch was one of the Midland Railway's triangular stations. In addition to the main line platforms and the two branches which connected with the main line at the south end, the branches were also linked to one another by a line which crossed the main line at right angles and on the flat. From the resultant collection of platforms the traveller could make his main line journeys to Bournemouth or Sheffield, catch an 'all stations' to Bromsgrove or Birmingham, take the branch set to Tewkesbury or Malvern Wells or vary his journey to Birmingham and go by way of Evesham and Redditch.

The station closed in 1971 but the connection to the WD private siding uses the Evesham branch spur and there are both running loop and sidings on the Down side. Opposite is the old water tower and the remains of the Dowty private siding area which received a new lease of life in the hands of the Dowty Railway Preservation Society.

A.13   Athelney

Reading-Taunton line between Castle Cary and Cogload Junction. 134 m 79 ch from Paddington

The Bristol & Exeter Railway branch from Durston via Athelney to Yeovil opened in 1853 and Athelney became a main line station in 1906 when the last of the links in the cut-off route was completed. But the station closed in 1964 and is now marked officially only by the level crossing and Up Refuge siding, although the small goods shed-cum-loading platform remains on the Down side and the trackbed from Durston can still be spotted on the Up side.

A.14   Avoncliff

Westbury-Bristol line between Bradford-on-Avon and Bathampton Junction. 5 m 63 ch from Bathampton Junction

Centred among cottages of warm stone and overshadowed by the handsome bridge across the River Avon, Avoncliff came into existence as a GWR halt on July 9 1906. It comprises two tiny platforms with wooden shelters and steps to the road above and has a weekday morning and evening service totalling seven trains. The road is carried over the railway by a slightly unusual two-arch brick bridge.

Avonmouth—see Severn Beach Branch

A.15   Awre

Gloucester-Newport line. 128 m 18 ch from Paddington

Awre was the junction for the Forest of Dean Central Railway's route into the Forest but is now more significant as the boundary, at milepost 129, between the Bristol and Cardiff Divisions of the WR. There is a former signal box, ground frame and CCTV level crossing (128 m 22 ch).

A.16   Axminster

Waterloo-Exeter line between Chard and Honiton. 144 m 41 ch from Waterloo

Axminster welcomed the coming of the railway on July 19 1860 and, although now a Western Region station, it still shows traces of its LSW/SR ancestry, including a collection of vintage luggage barrows. Only the Down line and platform are now in use but the station has six weekday buffet car services to and from Waterloo plus two other through services and one evening train from Exeter which terminates at Axminster and then forms a return working.

The platform shows evidence of extension on the London side of the Honiton Road bridge which spans the site in skew. The gabled, two-storey station buildings, with attractively modernised ticket hall, originally combined station house and office functions. There is a flat canopy and a lintel date of 1859 shows that the station was ready in good time for opening.

The branch to Lyme Regis lasted from August 24 1903 to November 29 1965, trains crossing over the main line by a flyover to terminate in a bay at the Up platform. Not much evidence of this remains but the former cattle dock and pens survive opposite in the goods yard area, which had its own connection to the branch in the early years.

From Axminster the route rises steadily for ten miles towards London and there is a CCTV level crossing 26 ch on the London side of the station.

Bargoed—see Rhymney Branch

B.1 Barnstaple Branch

Taunton-Penzance line, branch from Cowley Bridge Junction, Exeter. 37 m 55 ch

Now shown in the public timetable as a 39¾ m Western Region branch from Exeter Central to Barnstaple, the section between Exeter and Coleford Junction was once part of the LSWR/Southern Railway main line and the SR ancestry is still apparent on the whole route. The section on to Barnstaple competed for the North Devon business with the GWR line from Taunton and from Barnstaple lines led on to Torrington in one direction, and to Town station (for the Lynton & Barnstaple Light Railway) and Ilfracombe in the other. Today the line is double from Cowley Bridge Junction to Crediton but then becomes two parallel single lines to Coleford Junction. The line from there to Meldon Quarry has its own entry, as does the route beyond Barnstaple to Meeth.

To minimise the gradients, the original builders followed the course of the River Taw and paid the penalty of having to bridge this widening stream many times. But for today's traveller, if not for the Area Civil Engineer at Exeter, the compensation is a scenic route meandering amid green pastures and the slopes of wooded valleys, all seen to good advantage from the three-car dmus which provide the basic service on the route. Some workings are covered by locomotive-hauled trains and the weekday total of 21 services includes some which work through to Exmouth or other points off the line and several which omit stops or stop only on request.

The route had turbulent origins, portraying all the worst aspects of railway rivalry. In its compulsion to expand in Devon the London & South Western Railway, through nominees, stopped the opening of the broad gauge Exeter & Crediton. At the northern end of the

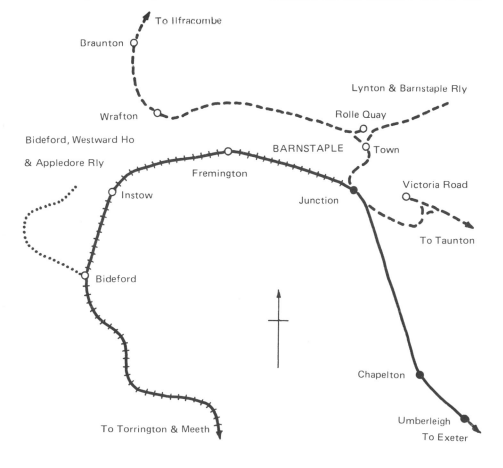

The signal box at Eggesford, passing point on the Barnstaple branch.

route the Taw Vale Extension Scheme, backed by the LSW against the broad gauge North Devon Railway, secured its authorisation by denying its parentage but then fell foul of the Gauge Commissioners. This caused the LSW to refuse to use the standard gauge tracks laid to Crediton just as had happened to the broad gauge ones. Eventually saner counsels prevailed, the Exeter & Crediton was leased to the Bristol & Exeter and the North Devon portion laid broad gauge. Opening to Crediton was on May 12 1851 and to Barnstaple on August 1 1854. The route came back into the LSWR fold in 1862/3 but it never received the priority in accommodation or services which were needed adequately to serve North Devon.

Leaving the main line east of Exeter at Cowley Bridge Junction (173 m 50 ch from Waterloo) the line is single for its crossing of the River Exe but then becomes double as it curves through flat, green farmland towards the hills ahead. Newton St Cyres (176 m 51 ch) lies on a curve and boasts only one small shelter between its two platforms. At Crediton (179 m 26 ch), for which a separate entry is provided, the double line becomes two parallel single lines, North Devon trains taking the token and the former Up track. Salmon Pool level crossing (180 m 9 ch) is followed by Yeoford (182 m 72 ch) where the wooden shelter, station house and bay are all on the Up side and there are but few reminders that this was once a busy station with an extensive yard and six holding sidings. After a simple parting of

the ways at Coleford Junction, no longer dignified by even an entry in the Sectional Appendix, the route rises through a three-bridge cutting to Copplestone (185 m 67 ch) where the first sod was cut early in 1852 and where only the Down platform is now used. Morchard Road (187 m 40 ch) is similar and the station buildings there are also in private hands, with the former dock and yard area at the Barnstaple end. Curves and cuttings along the wooded course of the river take the branch line through Lapford (189 m 65 ch) with its modest buildings, emergency loop and ground frames to complete the electric token worked section to Eggesford.

Eggesford (193 m 54 ch) provides the intermediate block post on the North Devon line and the wooden, WR-type signal box watches over the barrier crossing and the passing loop with its slightly staggered platforms. Eggesford has lost its Fox & Hounds Siding and its Mileage Road and the Down platform has only a shelter, but it is a busy and interesting little station and the substantial buildings on the Up side typify the gabled stone structures of the line. Kings Nympton (197 m 51 ch), once South Molton Road, also has gabled buildings together with a former wooden shed, a dock and a siding. The bare Down platform of Portsmouth Arms (200 m 38 ch) precedes two river crossings, Umberleigh open level crossing (204 m

Ilfracombe station, now closed but seen here with the 1.27 pm from Exeter arriving on September 15 1970.

32 ch) and Umberleigh's Down platform (204 m 52 ch), now adorned only by a metal shelter although the typical gabled stone house is still there. The Down platform, plus wooden shelter, is used again at Chapelton (207 m 2 ch) although the platform and station buildings are still in situ opposite.

More river crossings bring the line to Barnstaple, a three-span girder bridge preceding the former junction with the Taunton line whose own substantial box girder bridge was still standing in 1982. The single line runs directly to the station's Up platform on which stand the main, gabled buildings now housing a travel centre opened by the BRB chairman in 1981. At the estuary end of the station the route to Meeth veers west and a bridge reveals the direction of the former line across the river, through the town and on to Ilfracombe. The Down platform is bare and served by a runround line, with a single siding between that and the main line and a connection to the remaining sidings on the Down side. The goods yard lies behind the Up platform with the signal box (211 m 18 ch) located near the connection with the branch proper.

Barnstaple is a pleasant market town and was an important rail centre until a round of closures turned it into a railhead. The first line to go was the 1 ft 11½ in

gauge Lynton & Barnstaple, a line bought by the SR for £30,000 and closed in 1935. The first post-war victim was the Devon & Somerset Railway's route from Taunton which had reached Barnstaple in 1873 and which had become part of the GWR from 1901. The Devon & Somerset's Victoria station was linked with Barnstaple Junction from 1887 and after the Taunton line was closed in 1960 this link was to remain open to convey freight traffic to and from Victoria for another ten years. Regular passenger services on the Torrington line ended in 1965 leaving only the scenic, steeply-graded route to Ilfracombe. This had been opened as the Barnstaple & Ilfracombe Railway on July 20 1874 and doubled by the LSW, apart from the bridge between the two stations at Barnstaple and the swing bridge between Town station and the Rolles Quay branch. The round of economies in the '60s saw this once busy holiday line singled again with closure following on October 5 1970 and a brief preservation scheme foundering almost before it had got started.

B.2   Barry Branch

Newport-Fishguard line, branch from Cardiff. 9 m 33 ch

The Victorian town of Barry mushroomed in the 1880s and 1890s on the site of a small coastal village. The reason was a vast new port, opened in 1889, to cater for the rapidly expanding export trade in South Wales coal. The port, and new railways to carry coal to it, were built by a remarkable business conglomerate, the Barry Dock & Railways Company (later known simply as the Barry Railway Company), the brainchild of David Davies of Llandinam. In 1913 activity at the port reached a record level with 11 million tons of coal exported. Today only a modest amount of export coke is handled but other trades and industries have moved into the docks and surrounding areas.

By the time the Barry Railway became part of the GWR it was operating 68 busy route miles, but the great rail artery that tapped the Ely, Rhondda, Taff, Cynon and Rhymney valleys to bring coal to the port from the north via Wenvoe is now closed. However, two other routes remain, that from Cardiff which the Barry company looked upon as primarily a passenger operation, and the Vale of Glamorgan line which reaches Barry from the west and is the subject of a separate entry. Trains also continue to serve Barry Island, the resort the BR helped to create, but the extension to Barry Pier with its reminders of the company's flirtations with steamer operation closed for passengers in 1971.

The double track Barry Railway route from Cardiff leaves the ex-Taff Vale Railway Cardiff-Penarth line at Cogan Junction (2 m 29 ch), immediately before Cogan station which consists of two platforms linked by an ex-Barry Railway lattice footbridge. Each platform has a simple, modern brick shelter and on the Down side is a South Glamorgan County Council 'park and ride' car park with a new pedestrian access to the Up side and the temporary ticket kiosk staffed by a guard during peak periods. Beyond the station is the 223 yd Cogan Tunnel (2 m 75 ch to 3 m 5 ch) with the construction date 1888 inscribed above both portals. The line then cuts inland to Dinas Powys (4 m 18 ch) which consists of brick shelters, a subway and a temporary ticket office on the Up side.

On the Down side approaching Cadoxton is the site of Biglis Junction where the Taff Vale line joined until 1968. Beyond this, on the Up side, a modern housing estate now occupies the site of the former main line from Wenvoe and its extensive network of sidings which could accommodate 6,000 empty and 3,000 loaded wagons. Cadoxton station (6 m 10 ch) still has two outer platforms and a central island but uses only the Up platform and the Down face of the island, the former with modern station offices and facilities

which have had to be shuttered as a protection against vandals and the latter with a simple brick shelter. The platforms are linked by subway and alongside the southernmost is a Down Relief line leading to the docks.

The principal junction with the docks lines, now the property of the British Transport Docks Board, is immediately beyond Cadoxton station and a BTDB line runs parallel with the BR line to Barry proper. From this led the lines to the numerous coal discharge hoists on the two docks, No 2 at the Cadoxton end of the complex and which had the grain mills and coal store on its seaward side, and No 1 at the Barry end. Traces of the hoist lines can still be seen but the main activity is concentrated on the group of sidings serving the hopper parallel to No 2 dock where coke wagons are discharged and the coke passes by conveyor belt to the waiting ship. At the time of writing the trains of coke were being drawn mainly from ovens at Nantgarw. From Cadoxton a low level line, burrowing beneath the main BTDB line, descends to dock level and serves private sidings on and beyond No 2 dock, notably the sidings of BP Chemicals Ltd at which a daily train of bogie tank cars is received from the company's other plant at Baglan Bay near Port Talbot.

Barry Docks station (6 m 78 ch) consists of an island platform with modern brick shelter and ticket office, situated between the two BR tracks and reached by subway. On the Down side, beyond the BTDB lines, is the striking building of red brick and dressed stone, dating from 1898, which was the headquarters of the Barry Railway Company and now houses the local BTDB, and other, offices. The building has a clock tower and in front, facing the port he created, is a statue of David Davies (1818-90).

At Barry station (8 m 7 ch) the BTDB line rejoins the BR route. A group of sidings at the junction is known as 'High Level' and is a calling or terminating point for wagonload freight services. A line leads down to No 1 dock to serve the BR coal and freight yard within the docks and the private sidings alongside the dock. Notable among these is the yard of Woodham Bros, scrap metal merchants, who purchased many of the withdrawn steam locomotives of BR and kept them long enough for the best examples to return to active service on preserved lines. BP Chemicals at Baglan Bay forward another daily train of chemicals to the Barry area and this goes to the premises of Powell Duffryn Co Ltd on No 1 dock.

Barry station comprises a platform on the Up side with modern station offices and a South Glamorgan CC 'park and ride' car park nearby. Another ex-Barry Railway lattice footbridge links the Up platform with an island platform which is bare and which uses only the face to the Down line. Behind the station are sidings used for dmu stabling, the former loco-motive shed now used for wagon repairs, and locomotive sidings. The signal box, a distinctive ex-Barry Railway structure, stands at the Cardiff end of the island platform. At the country end the route splits into two, the Vale of Glamorgan double line to Bridgend continuing straight ahead and the route to Barry Island veer-ing off left and becoming single across the causeway and viaduct to the island.

The long platform at Barry Island (8 m 63 ch) was originally numbered 1 and 2 but now only the No 1 section is used alongside the station buildings and verandah. In the gables facing the road and the other attractions of the resort are the initials 'BR' and the date '1896'. There is also an excursion island platform reached by footbridge from the road outside the station and used at peak times, a reminder of the extensive day trip and excursion business carried by rail to enjoy the funfair and other amenities of the resort. The carriage sidings beyond the station are due for removal and the line that descended through the 280 yd tunnel to Barry Pier station (9 m 33 ch) has long since been lifted. At the other end of the station there is a signal box recently rebuilt after being damaged by fire.

Cardiff panel box controls this route as far as a point between Dinas Powys and Cadoxton, the Barry box then taking over. Track circuit block applies on the main line as far as Barry station and acceptance lever working on the remaining section, with Barry Island box switched in at busy times and Barry box controlling the single line section when only the basic passenger train service is running. The latter comprises an hourly dmu service between Treherbert, Cardiff and Barry Island with additional trains at peak periods which originate or terminate at various points on the 'Valleys' network north of Cardiff. During the winter months alternate off peak trains terminate at Barry instead of Barry Island but at summer weekends and during the main

summer school holidays additional dmu services operate to Barry Island, many of them running non-stop from Cardiff Central. Summer Saturday services include a through dmu working from Birmingham and return. Locomotive-hauled long distance excursions run to Barry Island at holiday times, the locomotive and coaches returning to Cardiff Canton during the layover period.

In addition to the block train loads mentioned and their return empty workings there is a through wagonload service each day to Plymouth mainly for cement traffic. Other wagonload move-ments, including wagons for or after repair, operate between Radyr Yard and Cardiff (Tidal Sidings) and Barry and between Barry and Aberthaw. A Class 08 locomotive is used for shunting at Barry Docks.

B.3   Bath Spa

Swindon-Bristol line between Bathampton Junction and Bristol Temple Meads. 106 m 71 ch from Paddington

From Bathampton the WR main line approaches Bath Spa parallel to but below the Kennet and Avon Canal. A retaining wall between the two heralds the stretch of railway through Sydney Gardens beneath a mixture of stone and metal bridges and through two short tunnels, Sydney Gardens East (106 m 24 ch to 106 m 28 ch) of 77 yds and Sydney Gardens West (106 m 29 ch to 106 m 33 ch) of 99 yds. The curving approach to the station is on arches, the station itself standing in a loop formed by the River Avon. The two plat-forms continue the curve, with the inner Up platform stretching from a bridge of Bath stone with a single main arch at the London end to the lattice girder bridge with central pier at the country end. The London end still reveals the former bay platform and the country end a castellated turret as part of the bridge ornamentation. The pleasant, two-storey station build-ings, surmounted by a clock, are on the Up side with ticket office and travel centre at the (lower) street level and subway/ stairs to the platforms, each of which has an arcade-style canopy. The Down plat-form, which has a rear wall of Bath stone blocks with six-pane windows, is equipped with a repeater signal because of sighting problems arising from the curve. The position of the former elevated signal box can still be spotted near the centre of the canopy.

On the Bristol side of the station the stone goods shed on the Up side still bears the faded legend 'Great Western Railway Goods Station and Bonded Store' although it is now used by Pickfords. Sundry buildings and a good example of a hand crane remain and there are more buildings in the old Down yard opposite. The two sidings remaining to the latter are reached from the Down Goods Loop which rejoins the main line just before Oldfield Park station (107 m 72 ch)—just two platforms plus a Down side shelter and the stone road bridge at the country end.

Traces remain of the point at which the Somerset & Dorset route crossed over the GWR line and of the Up side buildings of Twerton station which closed in 1917 along with Hampton Row Halt on the other side of Bath. Next come the

Above *A 1970 scene at Bath Spa before the removal of the elevated signal box.* **Below** *Sydney Gardens, Bath, showing how well the railway harmonises with its surroundings.*

ornamental Twerton Short Tunnel (108 m 70 ch to 108 m 72 ch) of 45 yds and Twerton Long Tunnel (109 m 3 ch to 109 m 15 ch) of 264 yds.

The GWR reached Bath from Bristol on August 31 1840 but the town had a much earlier railway, possibly Britain's first inclined tramway. It was part of a 3 ft 9 in gauge route constructed to carry stone from Ralph Allen's Combe Down quarry down to the growing city. Built in 1755 and passing through Allen's Prior Park estate en route to the river near the Palladian Bridge, a one-mile inclined section

remains in use as a present day roadway.

The Midland Railway also served Bath with a line from Mangotsfield, that company's Queen Square (later Green Park) station being the exchange point with the S&D system. Services ended on March 7 1966 but, after a long period of debate, it was decided to retain the attractive station frontage as part of a supermarket development. With its platforms 450 ft long, 220 ft covered by a 66 ft span roof, the station was described on opening as 'a fine structure in the classical style with a frontage set off by Ionic columns'. Although the frontage canopy with its finial-topped supports and atmosphere of the horse cab era will doubtless go, the retention of the main building with its six columns flanked by smaller-columned windows will be no small achievement.

B.4   Bathampton Junction

Swindon-Bristol line between Chippenham and Bath Spa. 104 m 45 ch from Paddington

The junction came into being with the opening of the single line up the Avon Valley on February 2 1857. Now a double line junction towards Bath, the severe curve off the route from Bradford-on-Avon dictates a speed restriction of 25 mph. There is a double crossover on the main line plus a ground frame, some railings of the former Up platform and two road bridges of different periods. In the Up direction the junction is preceded by an Up Goods Loop.

B.5   Beam Bridge

Taunton-Penzance line between Taunton and Tiverton Junction. 171 m 70 ch from Paddington*

From May 1 1843 to May 1 1844 there was a temporary railhead station here pending the completion of the Bristol & Exeter Railway's route on to Exeter. The station house is still visible on the Up side at SS 108 195.

Bedminster—see Bristol

B.6   Bedwas Branch

Newport 'Western Valleys' line, branch from Park Junction 10 m 1 ch

This single track, freight-only branch from Newport (Park Junction) to Machen and Bedwas in the lower reaches of the

Rhymney Valley is the surviving stub of the one-time Brecon & Merthyr Railway's line from Newport to Brecon. This particular section originated as part of the 4 ft 2 in gauge horse-traction Rumney Railway between Newport and Rhymney opened in 1926 and taken over in 1863 by the B&MR and converted to standard gauge operation. Passenger services, once fairly numerous at this end of the route, lasted until 1962 when the line beyond Bedwas closed completely. A line from Machen, where the B&MR had its locomotive works, to Caerphilly was open for passengers until 1956 and for freight until 1967.

The line today links the Western Valley line from Newport with the Powell Duffryn quarry at Machen, a source of railway ballast, and with the British Benzol & Coal Distillation Ltd plant at Trethomas and the NCB Bedwas colliery at the end of the line. From Park Junction the route follows that of the Western Valley line as far as the site of Bassaleg Junction (2 m 5 ch) where it veers west and where the mileage changes back to zero. Just beyond Bassaleg the line traverses two contrasting bridges. The first, completed in 1981, carries the railway over a modern by-pass route while the second, only a short distance beyond, is one of the oldest pieces of transport infrastructure in South Wales, the masonry viaduct having been built in 1826 to carry the Rumney Railway over the Ebbw River. There is an open level crossing at Rhiwderin, a former station lying between Bassaleg and Machen (5 m) and run-round loops at the latter and at Bedwas (8 m 6 ch). Trethomas (6 m 58 ch) lies between Machen and Bedwas.

The 1982 service consisted of five daily trains from Severn Tunnel Jcn East Usk, three with empty ballast hoppers going to the quarry and returning with loaded ones and the others serving Trethomas and Bedwas colliery where the bunker loading system is used. The workings are in the hands of Class 37 locomotives and the line is worked under train staff and ticket arrangements from the box at Park Junction.

B.7   Bedwyn

Reading-Taunton line, between Newbury and Westbury. 66 m 29 ch from Paddington

Although just a modest combination of Up and Down platforms plus shelter, Bedwyn originates some dozen trains daily

as part of the all-stations dmu service to
Newbury and Reading. Trains reverse
from the Down Main to the Up siding and
then into the Up platform. The home of
Sir Felix Pole, distinguished General
Manager of the Great Western Railway
from 1921 to 1929, was nearby.

Bere Alston—see Gunnislake Branch

Bere Ferrers—see Gunnislake Branch

B.8   Bicester Line

*Didcot-Birmingham line, branch from
Oxford North Junction. 12 m 9 ch to
boundary with LMR*

The line opened by the Oxford &
Bletchley Junction Railway to Oxford on
May 20 1851 lost its Oxford terminus at
Rewley Road a century later and its
passenger services in 1968. It still survives,
however, as a single line freight route for
the 10 m 58 ch from Oxford North
Junction to Bicester and for 1 m 31 ch of
double line to the regional boundary at
milepost 18.

This was an LNWR route and at one
time had seven halts between Bicester and
Oxford in addition to Islip station. The
mileages are, accordingly, reckoned from
Bletchley and Bicester, where the signal-
box which controls the entrance to the
tokenless block section, is at 19 m 31 ch.
The connection to the former Bicester
Military Railway (now MoD) is followed
by open level crossings at Langford Lane
(20 m 52 ch) and Oddington (24 m 10 ch)
and the miniature red/green light crossing
at Islip (25 m 72 ch) which also has oil and
government sidings. There is an ARC
stone terminal at Banbury Road (27 m
54 ch) followed by Oxford North Junction
at 30 m 9 ch.

B.9   Big Hill

*Links the Rhymney and Merthyr branches,
from Aber Junction to Walnut Tree
Junction. 3 m 45 ch*

'The Big Hill' is the colloquial name for
the double track, freight-only line linking
Aber Junction (Rhymney Railway main
line) and Walnut Tree Junction (at Taffs
Well, Taff Vale Railway main line). It is
the route by which the Rhymney Railway
reached Cardiff from its opening date in
1858, although from 1871 it had its own
direct route through Caerphilly Tunnel.

The name 'Big Hill' reflects the
gradients incurred as the route uses the

Nantgarw gap, a depression in the hills
separating the Rhymney and Taff valleys.
From Aber Junction the rise is gentle to
the point where the mileage changes from
79 ch to 9 m 36 ch and on to Penrhos
Stopboard (9 m 47 ch), the site of the
former Penrhos Junction. Here unfitted
or partially fitted freight trains formerly
had to stop before making the descent,
mostly at gradients of 1 in 48 to 1 in 60 to
Walnut Tree Junction (12 m 2 ch).

Until recently the line was worked on a
mixture of absolute block and permissive
block arrangements and had a 'bank
guard' at Penrhos in communication with
Aber Junction. Normal absolute block
operation now applies between the signal
boxes at Aber Junction and Walnut Tree
Junction but the route may be singled at
some time in the future.

The Big Hill is used mainly for freight
trains between the Rhymney Valley line
and its branches and Radyr Yard. Some
of the merry-go-round trains between the
collieries and opencast sites on the
Rhymney Valley branches and Aberthaw
power station also use the route,
continuing onwards via Radyr and
Penarth curve. In all some ten trains use
the line in each direction every 24 hours.

Two other routes used to cross and
connect at Penrhos Junction, that from
Pontypridd to Caerphilly and the Barry
Railway route tapping the Rhymney
Valley. At Taffs Well the ex-Rhymney
engine shed remains on the Down side,
now incorporated in the premises of an
engineering company. The sign displayed
by 'The Junction' public house outside
the station has the coat of arms of the
Rhymney Railway on one side and that of
the Taff Vale Railway on the other,
symbolising the physical junction effected
nearby.

From June 21 1982 the line was tempor-
arily taken out of use and all traffic diverted
via Cardiff.

B.10   Blackwell

*Birmingham-Bristol line, between Barnt
Green and Cheltenham. 52 m 57 ch from
Derby*

Blackwell station closed in 1966 but the
location remains important owing to its
position at the top of the Lickey incline.
Alongside the Down Goods Loop is the
accommodation for the brakesman who
authorises the descent of freight trains
which are over 160 tonnes and not fully
braked. Here, too, are stop boards,

repeater signals and the traditional notice about pinning down brakes. Banking engines from Up trains reverse on to the line between the Up and Down main lines and wait there until authorised to descend again to Bromsgrove.

Blaengarw—see Tondu

B.11   Bleadon and Uphill

Bristol-Taunton line, between Weston-super-Mare and Bridgwater. 138 m 49 ch from Paddington

Once serving the coastal village of Uphill and the Bleadon community nestled on the Mendip outcrop above, the station remains are on the Up side and are now the home of a private railway and steam collection.

B.12   Bletchington

Didcot-Birmingham line between Oxford and Banbury. 70 m 34 ch from Paddington

A short connection on the Down side serves the APCM Blue Circle cement works.

B.13   Bodmin Road

Taunton-Penzance line between Liskeard and Truro. 274 m 3 ch from Paddington*

The trains of the Cornwall Railway started serving Bodmin Road on June 27 1859. The short branch to Bodmin proper came into use in 1887 and in the following year a link to Boscarne Junction gave access to the Bodmin and Wadebridge line which the LSW owned without Parlia-

mentary sanction for 41 years and could make no physical connection with until 1895.

Bodmin Road's small signal box stands on the long, curved, Down platform which has a small shelter and a former dock at the country end. The Up island platform accommodates both the Up main line and the headshunt from a group of five sidings at the country end and has a small group of prefabricated administrative and waiting buildings. The single line from Wenford Bridge via Bodmin connects with the Up Main at the London end of the branch platform face.

An accident in 1895 between Bodmin Road and Doublebois involved the derailment of two 0-4-4 tank engines at speed and is notable in having helped bring to an end the using of tank engines for express workings.

B.14   Box Tunnel

Swindon-Bristol line between Chippenham and Bath. 99 m 12 ch from Paddington

Approached from the east by a deep cutting, Box Tunnel is 1 m 452 yds long and sited between 99 m 12 ch and 100 m 78 ch. It carries the original GWR main line under Box Hill in a straight line but on a falling gradient of 1 in 100, and is followed by an embankment leading to the short Middle Hill Tunnel of 198 yds between 101 m 39 ch and 101 m 48 ch.

Behind the water tower at Bodmin Road a Class 08 locomotive is approaching from the Wenford branch.

In this age of multiple aspect signalling and continuous track circuiting Box Tunnel holds no terrors for railway passengers, but its length and gradient came in for much hostile attention in the original Parliamentary proceedings. 'No passenger would be induced to go (through) twice,' avowed one witness, but despite water problems and the fact that the slope of the oolite terrain was opposite to that of the railway gradient the construction did not prove unduly difficult considering Box was the longest tunnel of its time. The plans for working by stationary engine proved unnecessary when this section was opened on June 30 1841 to complete the GWR's route to Bristol, but banking was used for most of the early trains.

Like most long tunnels, Box has always been the subject of special instructions in the Sectional Appendix. For many years these included the reporting of loads in the Up direction and directions for breaking the alarm wire in an emergency to set ringing the tell-tale bells in the Box and Corsham signal boxes. Nowadays eight emergency telephones and complete track circuiting provide the safety back-up plus the use of a portable locomotive headlamp for tunnel examination in the case of track circuit failure. Right from the start, when 4,000 men and 300 horses had to be put to work to get the job finished, Box Tunnel has kept the railway civil engineer on his toes and at one time his regular inspection had to be performed from the bucket of a mobile, rail-mounted crane!

The west end of the tunnel, perhaps

The ornamental western portal of Box Tunnel.

because it was visible from the old turnpike road, is highly ornamented while the eastern approach still shows traces of the small, adjacent tunnel in which the Bath & Portland Stone company's siding ended. There is a legend that the sun is at the right angle to shine through the tunnel only on Brunel's birthday on April 9 and research by O.S. Nock has done much to authenticate this delightful fragment of railway romance.

The once substantial Box station, situated to the west of Middle Hill Tunnel is now traceable only from the 19th century coal office on the Down side.

Bourne End—see Marlow Branch

B.15   Bradford Junctions

At the junction of the Thingley Junction-Westbury and Westbury-Bathampton Junction routes. 104 m 23 ch from Paddington

This triangular junction links the route of the old Wilts, Somerset & Weymouth Railway to Westbury (opened September 5 1848) with the present passenger route from Westbury to Bath (opened February 2 1857), the final leg across the top of the triangle being added in 1895. The three signal boxes at the North, South and West Junctions were replaced in the early 1930s by a single box equipped with motor points and located on the Thingley side of

South Junction. All lines are double except between the North and West Junctions and on from North to Thingley Junction, the former being worked under absolute block regulations and the latter under No Signalman Token.

The main traffic is now the passenger trains on the Westbury-Bath line, the route through Melksham to Thingley Junction being used largely for diversionary purposes. But at one time Newbury line to Bristol trains passed this way together with those from the Swindon line to Trowbridge and from Devizes to Westbury to make Bradford Junctions a very busy location.

B.16 Bradford-on-Avon

Westbury-Bristol line between Trowbridge and Bathampton Junction. 7 m 9 ch from Bath

The attractive station buildings remaining on the Up side are of warm Bath stone as is the goods shed, now isolated in the station car park. Apart from the faster Portsmouth services, the Weymouth, Salisbury and local Westbury trains all call at Bradford which, together with the 159 yd Bradford Tunnel (7 m 18 ch to 7 m 25 ch), lies in a loop of the River Avon. Beyond the tunnel is the Greenland Mill automatic half barrier level crossing (7 m 27 ch).

The old woollen town of Bradford-on-Avon was reached by the railway from the south as the end of a short branch from Staverton. Because of capital shortages following the Railway Mania the station did not see a passenger train for the first ten years of its existence and, by the time it was opened on May 2 1857, the Wilts, Somerset & Weymouth Railway had been absorbed by the GWR.

B.17 Brent

Taunton-Penzance line between Totnes and Plymouth. 229 m 60 ch from Paddington*

The branch line to Kingsbridge closed in 1963 but its route off south-east is still discernible at the former junction station at Brent. Brent lost its own passenger and freight services in the following year but a signal box building remains to mark the station site on the Down side and the former goods shed stands behind. A ground frame remains in use and there is an Up Refuge Siding.

Near the top of the long climb from Totnes to Wrangaton, Brent is a pleasant spot in summer but can become bleak and isolated in winter and at least one train has been marooned here in snowdrifts in the past.

B.18 Brentford Branch

Paddington-Swindon line, branch from Southall. 2 m 70 ch

The Brentford branch now serves a very different function from that for which it was built, the main movement being that of compacted refuse in trainloads from a GLC depot at Brentford to Appleford on the Oxford line. Each evening, Mondays to Fridays, 20 Freightliner-type 60 ft wagons, each carrying three 20 ft × 8 ft containers, are moved off the branch as a train load by a Class 47 locomotive, assisted if the rails are greasy or the declared load unduly heavy. On the way west along the main line at 55 mph the train will meet the previous day's empties returning on another of the nine-wagon sets in use (plus one being serviced).

The original 4 m branch was incorporated by the Great Western & Brentford Railway Act of 1855 to provide a broad gauge link to the Thames. Goods traffic commenced on July 18 1859 and passenger trains on May 1 1860 but freight was always the mainstay of the line with large quantities barged via the railway dock and more passing through the yard and shed at Brentford Town. The former closed in 1964 and the latter in 1970, the line now ending at 2 m 70 ch from the junction with the main line at Southall.

Originally single, later doubled and now single again, the branch is worked under Train Staff and Ticket conditions under the control of the 'person in charge' at Southall. In addition to the refuse movements the branch deals with coal and stone for Days & Sons who have a hopper discharge siding to receive stone trains from Merehead and traffic tripped down from Acton. There is also some scrap traffic.

B.19 Brewham Bank

Reading-Taunton line between Westbury and Cogload. 122 m 54 ch from Paddington

From the site of Brewham Box and the adjacent Strap Lane Halt this favourite speed stretch of the steam era drops westward for 10 m, initially at 1 in 81, 98 and 93. Still a good spot for the photographer.

B.20   Bridgend

Newport-Fishguard line between Cardiff and Port Talbot. 190 m 45 ch from Paddington*

The principal railway route through Bridgend is the east-west South Wales Railway (later GWR) main line dating from 1850. At the country end of the station is the junction with the ex-Llynfi & Ogmore Railway line northwards to Tondu and the Llynfi, Garw and Ogmore valleys, dating from 1861. At the other, London, end is the connection with the line from Barry (Vale of Glamorgan Railway/Barry Railway) opened in 1897. Deeper in history, the Bridgend-Tondu line replaced a 4 ft 7 in gauge horse-traction Bridgend Railway which followed a similar course but had its terminus in the town, away from the present station.

The South Wales main line is double track with a Down Goods Loop at Tremains (189 m 28 ch) on the approach from Cardiff. The Vale of Glamorgan junction is with the Down Main line which is then signalled for two-way working as far as the crossover at the west end of the station where two parallel single lines veer northwards from a group of Up sidings. One of these is the line to Tondu and the other accompanies it as far as the former Coity Junction and then reverses to reach Coity freight and coal depot which is actually on the stub of the former link to the Vale of Glamorgan route. At Bridgend the short bay on the Down side is now used for engineer's vehicles but is the remnant of a once-longer bay used by Barry line trains until 1964. One mile beyond the station the main line starts to rise at 1 in 132 and 163 to Stormy summit (194 m 50 ch) where there are Up and Down Goods Loops.

The station itself consists of Up and Down platforms linked by a typical GWR footbridge. The Up platform was formerly a narrow island with the outer face used by trains to and from the Tondu line but the last of these ran in 1970 and in 1978/9 a major reconstruction used up the space of this former track to produce a striking modern station with up-to-date facilities and buildings of steel and glass on both platforms. The principal buildings are adjacent to the Down side forecourt and include a travel centre but the original stone buildings, to an original Brunel design and enlarged in 1890, have been skilfully restored and now house station staff and the offices of the Area Civil Engineer. All signs at Bridgend are bilingual and include the Welsh name of the station which is Pen-y-bont.

The new station at Bridgend was officially opened by the Secretary of State for Wales on November 30 1979 and a plaque recording this event, in both languages, is to be seen in the concourse. The combination of an attractive new structure and skilful restoration of the old brought two awards in 1980 and another in the 1981 Wales in Bloom competition. The Travellers-Fare buffet, on the Up side and known as the Llynfi Buffet, is also a model of its kind and the station has a parcels office and a large car park on the Down side.

Signalling in the Bridgend area is controlled on the main line by the Port Talbot panel box and on the other lines by Cowbridge Road box on the Vale of Glamorgan line and Tondu box on the Tondu line. The principal passenger services are provided by Inter-City 125 sets on the London route plus other services to the north-east/north-west route and a few local Cardiff-Swansea dmus. The main line is also used by block trains, loads of freight and by conventional wagon load services. Other freight, including mgr trains to Aberthaw from West Glamorgan pits and the Ogmore Vale Central Washery, run via the Vale of Glamorgan line and both this and the Tondu route are sometimes used for diversionary purposes. Coity freight and coal depot is served by a Class 37-hauled trip from Margam Yard which reverses at Bridgend and Coity Junction. The line leading to the Bridgend Engine Plant of the Ford Motor Company is served from the Vale of Glamorgan line. Scheduled to cost £2.2 million, this was opened in January 1980 to receive cylinder block castings from Dagenham and despatch the output of completed engines. Half the cost, incurred mainly on the embankment and two substantial bridges, came from the Welsh Office in the form of a grant under Section 8 of the Railways Act 1974.

A pleasant touch in the modern, efficient setting of the new Bridgend travel centre is the preservation of a section of rail from the old horse-worked Bridgend Railway.

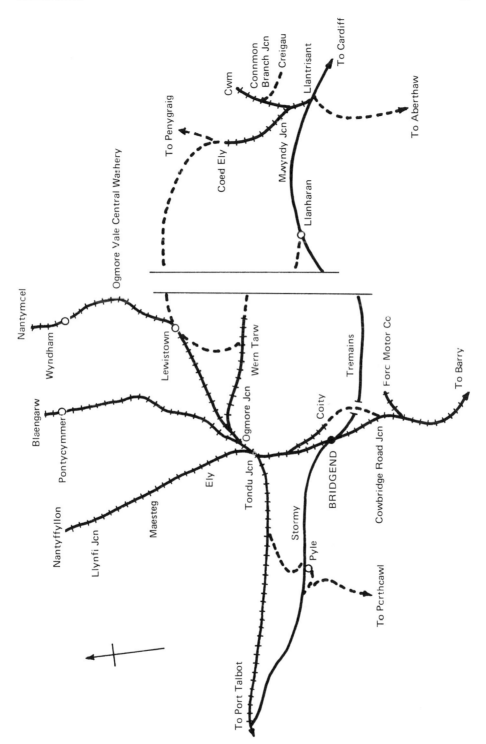

B.21   Bridgwater

Bristol-Taunton line between Weston-super-Mare and Cogload Junction. 151 m 47 ch from Paddington

1841 was a momentous year for the Somerset town of Bridgwater. Long a port, it opened new docks on March 24 of that year and was reached by the trains of the Bristol & Exeter Railway on June 14. That company also built coke ovens and carriage works, the latter eventually constructing the major part of the B&E's rolling stock requirements. A connection from the main line to a wharf on the River Parrett was obtained by taking over the Corporation's horse tramway, this line being converted for locomotive use and extended across the river into the docks after the latter had been purchased as part of the Bridgwater & Taunton Canal acquisition. The final piece of expansion came in 1890 when the Bridgwater Railway connected the town with the Somerset & Dorset at Edington Junction to give an alternative route to the Midlands and via the LSW to London.

In its heyday Bridgwater produced a large volume of goods traffic including imported coal and timber, locally manufactured bricks and other building materials. Some 70 passenger trains called

The Brunel dredger Bertha *at Bridgwater Dock in 1958.*

at the main line station plus another eight each way on the branch from Bridgwater (North) to Edington. The latter closed in 1954 when a new connection linked the former S&D goods depot to the docks branch, itself closed in 1967.

Today Bridgwater has a number of through services from the Taunton direction to Paddington and Birmingham with further connections available off its Taunton-Bristol local services. The main freight traffics are the fertiliser to the large UKF store on the Up side at the London end of the yard and wagons exchanged through the British Cellophane private siding opposite. Flasks to and from Hinckley Point atomic power station can be craned on and off their special wagons in the main goods yard where the stub of the branch to the docks is still visible. At the country end of the station the extensive sidings on the Up side are now little used except for stabling purposes.

Although the level crossing south of the station has been replaced by a bridge, the station itself has altered little and is dominated by the squat, single-storey buildings on the Up side which house the main entrance and ticket office. A footbridge connects the flat canopy section on each platform and the drinking fountains add to the atmosphere of the station. There are four ground frames, East (151 m 9 ch), Station (151 m 44 ch), Up Sidings (151 m 56 ch) and West (151 m 68 ch) and a substantial bridge where the line crosses the River Parrett south of the station.

There are some good viewing points suitable for photography and the docks area is worth a visit. The Brunel dredger which once worked there can now be seen at the Exeter Maritime Museum.

B.22   Bristol

Temple Meads is on the Swindon-Taunton line 118 m 26 ch from Paddington and Parkway on the Swindon-Newport line 111 m 62 ch from Paddington

Bristol was the birthplace of the Great Western Railway and, as the largest interchange point on the WR, remains of considerable importance. It offers much of interest in both modern and historical terms and the station area complex, comprising the 1878 main station, the 1854 Bristol & Exeter Railway offices and the original 1840 GWR station, is hard to rival for pleasing the eye and exciting the imagination. The B&E offices, constructed in a Jacobean style, lie on the right of the approach road to the station and the 1840 station on the left. The latter, with its Temple Gate frontage and bow window of the directors' board room, was constructed on arches and entered through Clock Tower Yard on the city side. Used in recent years as a car park, the office area and part of the station under a quasi-hammer beam roof, is now in the hands of the Brunel Engineering Centre Trust.

An early proposal to form a London and Bristol Rail-Road Company crystallised into the formation of a board of directors in 1833 and the Royal Assent to the Great Western Railway Bill was given on August 31 1835. The line was to commence near a 'Field called Temple Mead' in the Bristol parish of Temple. Just five years after the passage of the Act the first passenger train from Bristol (Temple Meads) to Bath left the GWR terminus, and by the middle of the following year trains were leaving via a sharp curve to reach the B&E's newly opened line to Bridgwater. In 1845 the B&E opened its own station at an angle from the GWR premises and an express platform on the curve between the two accommodated the through services. In fact, this gave little relief to the GWR station which needed to handle the trains running north to Gloucester as the dust settled on the battle which had tipped the infant Bristol

& Gloucester company into the fast-growing Midland network.

To keep pace with traffic demands some major changes were made in the 1870s. Work started in 1871 on a new joint station with the MR and to the designs of Sir Matthew Digby Wyatt, and this remains in existence as the main buildings and roofed portion of the present complex. In the same 1870s period, the GWR engine shed at Barton Hill (where it lay on the Up side with the coking plant opposite) was abandoned in favour of the B&E shed site at Bath Road. Among the buildings of the present wagon maintenance shops at Barton Hill, one still incorporates iron columns inscribed 'Wolverhampton 1871'.

There were some further changes at Temple Meads following the opening of the Severn Tunnel and the congestion there was eased by the use of the Relief Line between East Depot and Pylle Hill from April 10 1892. The major rebuild came in 1935 when widening of bridges over the Floating Harbour and the River Avon enabled platform lengthening and the purchase of additional land allowed the addition of the two outer island platforms. The provision of scissors crossings and the bay at the end of the main

Traditional signal box and level crossing gates at Ashton Junction, Bristol.

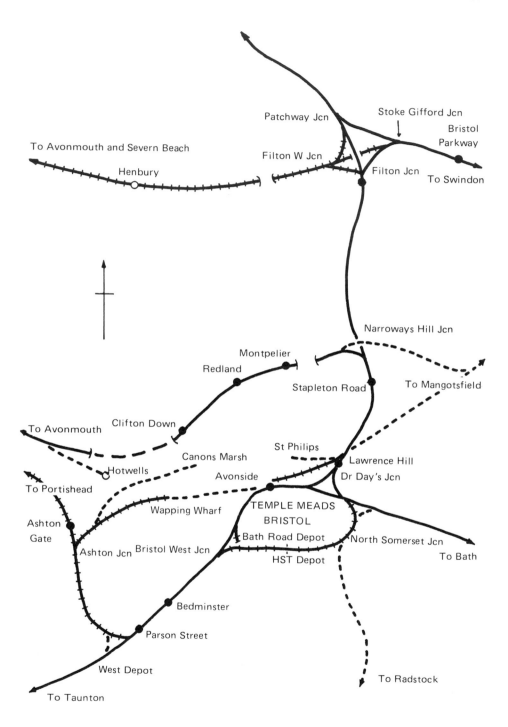

platform increased the platforms from 8 to 15, Nos 12 to 15 resulting from the division of the two long platforms in the original station which were used for the LMS and Avonmouth services.

In 1953 the services to the Mangotsfield/ Bath line were withdrawn from the single platform station at St Philips in Bristol and then ended altogether in 1966 which allowed the old station to be used as a car park. Passenger services had ended on the Radstock line in 1959 and out to Portishead in 1964. To produce the positive side of the period of change BR was going through, 1970 brought the Bristol MAS re-signalling scheme which closed the former east and west power boxes in favour of the new panel box controlling 117 route miles of railway. At the same time the entire track layout was modified to permit higher approach speeds and give easy access to and from any platform. The other major change was the routing of Birmingham line trains via Filton and Westerleigh Junction instead of via Fishponds.

Another recent development is the opening of Bristol Parkway station at Stoke Gifford on the direct South Wales-Wootton Bassett line and designed both to serve North Bristol and compete with the M4 motorway for the London-bound traveller. With a large free car park, a pleasant and efficient two-platform station and a best timing of 73 minutes to

London, Parkway has proved very popular. It has a direct service to South Wales and is also served by trains on the NE/SW route.

Temple Meads also has an excellent service to and from London and originates many of the HST workings in the Paignton/Taunton/Weston/Bristol-Paddington pattern. In addition to nearly 40 daily trains on the NE/SW route, the Cardiff-Portsmouth trains reverse at Temple Meads and there are local trains to Cardiff, Severn Beach and Weston for commuters plus stopping services on the line to Bath, Westbury and Weymouth and many extra summer services to the Bristolians' favourite resorts.

Bristol still has significant freight activity although the banana trains no longer run from Avonmouth Docks and the sensation of the Midland securing the Wills tobacco traffic from under the noses of the GWR canvassers has long since been forgotten. In addition to large movements from firms in the Avonmouth industrial complex, the freight depot at Kingsland Road is on the Speedlink network and there are coal concentration depots at Filton and Wapping Wharf. A Freightliner activity operates at West Depot using a conventional mobile crane for loading and unloading.

The extensive movement of traffic in and around Bristol requires extensive support facilities. The Bath Road traction depot lies at the country end of the station and consists of three sheds for 'daily', 'maintenance' and 'heavy lifting' work plus fuelling facilities, a booking on point

A Class 45 locomotive on the turntable at Bath Road maintenance depot at Bristol.

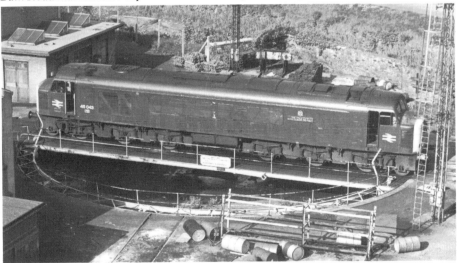

Left *Before the days of MAS schemes, a scene in the signal box at Dr Day's Bridge Junction.*

Below *Bristol Temple Meads at night.*

Right *At St Philips Marsh depot HST power car 253 011 has been lifted to allow access to its bogie.*

and administrative offices. It is also a breakdown crane base depot. On the avoiding line between North Somerset Junction and Bristol West Junction (1 m 8 ch) a new HST depot was built at St Philips Marsh when the new 125 mph trains started running on the WR and the Marsh Junction dmu maintenance depot and cleaning sidings are also reached from this line. At Malago Vale, which has given its name to a popular local ballad, there are sidings used for sleeper coaches, newspaper vans and the immaculate Royal Mail TPO vehicles. Barton Hill wagon shops, sited between the main line to Bath and the stub of the old MR route undertake wagon maintenance, especially of the fleet of stone wagons which work out of Tytherington and the Mendip quarries.

From the London direction the WR main line approaches Bristol by way of the 1,017 yd St Annes Park No 3 Tunnel (115 m 58 ch to 116 m 25 ch) and the 154 yd St Annes Park No 2 Tunnel (116 m 41 ch to 116 m 48 ch) with the site of the former station of that name following the latter, and a large stone from the original excavation still standing on the Up side of the line. No 1 Tunnel, 326 yds long, was converted into the present cutting when the marshalling yard at East Depot was opened in 1889 following the opening of the Severn Tunnel and the consequent re-routing of traffic via the Bristol Loop from Dr Day's Bridge Junction to North Somerset Junction. There is a Down Goods Loop here and a set of engineer's sidings followed by North Somerset Junction (117 m 46 ch), Kingsland Road depot (117 m 57 ch) and then Bristol East Junction (118 m 2 ch) where the main lines and the Filton lines meet. An Up Goods Loop and the outline in the red sandstone of the cutting where the raised East Depot box stood are all that remains on the Up side.

Temple Meads station has its main buildings backing platforms 3/4 and including ticket office, travel centre, buffet, motorail lounge and various administrative offices. No 1 platform is a bay used by Severn Beach and Cardiff dmus and the panel box stands behind it. From this point there is a view over to the huge former goods depot, once a pioneer of mechanised handling and now in the hands of NCL, and an opportunity to see one of the GPO mail handling terminals which link each of the three main platform areas with the GPO depot beyond the station. Two-way, permissive working lines also serve the four faces of the two islands beyond the overall roof with an Up Through line between platforms 3/4 and 5/6 and a Down Through line beyond platforms 11/12. After West Junction (118 m 58 ch) the seven lines become Up and Down Main, Up Relief and Carriage line, the latter two-way through the carriage washer and then Bedminster station (119 m 22 ch). Next follow Malago Vale (119 m 50 ch), Parson Street station (120 m 15 ch), Parson Street Junction for the line through Ashton to Portishead (120 m 15 ch) and Bristol West Depot (120 m 73 ch).

Two lines converge on Bristol from the north. From Westerleigh Junction there are traces of the closed stations at Coalpit Heath and Winterbourne before the Down Goods Loop and remaining sidings at Stoce Gifford East (111 m 38 ch). Near the Up Goods Loop at Stoke Gifford Junction (111 m 79 ch) the line heads for Filton Junction (113 m 1 ch) to unite with what was originally the Bristol & South Wales Union Railway and is still measured in miles from Bristol. There are connections between each of the routes and the line to Avonmouth via Henbury and also to the District Engineer's tip.

The approach road at Bristol Temple Meads with the station ahead and the former Bristol & Exeter building on the right.

From Filton Junction (113 m 1 ch/4 m 50 ch) there are four lines, the two on the west side being Up and Down Relief lines and Filton's spartan platforms being served by these. Past the coal concentration depot on the Up (west) side the gradient rises slightly before falling at 1 in 75 past Horfield Platform and Ashley Hill, both barely visible now, under the former MR link from the Severn Beach line to Mangotsfield, through Narroways Hill Junction (2 m 3 ch) with the Severn Beach line and into Stapleton Road. This was quite a busy station when London trains reached South Wales this way but it now serves only a modest local clientele although scrap traffic is still dealt with in the yard below and its three-span bridge is worth a second glance. Lawrence Hill (1 m 4 ch) is another drab station served by trains on the Severn Beach line. The WR line passes under the former MR route here and the goods yard is still in use for cement traffic. Behind it leads the surviving MR line down to Avonside where APCM and other traffic is dealt with. Dr Day's Junction (53 ch) perpetuates the name of a local medical man and is followed by Bristol East Junction and then Temple Meads station.

There are divisional offices at Bristol and the station deals with considerable parcels business. There is always much going on and at the right time of day one might post a letter in one of the TPO vehicles, spot a newspaper sorting train or see cars unloading from a motorail service. A plaque on the frontage commemorates the care lavished on past

railwaymen and their families by Miss Emma Saunders.

Much of past interest also exists in the Bristol area. Its first railway project dates from 1803 and was for a line to link the coal-producing area around Coalpit Heath with the port and the first successful project, the Avon & Gloucestershire Railway, was carrying coal to the River Avon before the GWR trains were running along the opposite bank. Substantial traces of the A&G line still exist along the course of the later MR line from Mangotsfield to Bitton. Further down the river, in the Avon Gorge, the portal of the Clifton Rocks Railway is still visible and the A4 has still left a few traces of the route of the Bristol Port & Pier Railway beneath the Clifton Suspension Bridge.

Bristol's once busy city docks are gradually changing into a recreational area but, in addition to the railway items in the dockside Industrial Museum, a line still serves the Wapping coal concentration depot. This originated as part of the Bristol Harbour Railway, a joint GWR, B&E and Bristol Corporation project, which eventually provided a route from behind the original station, beneath the beautiful St Mary Redcliffe church, across Bathurst Basin by means of a steam-worked bascule bridge and then into the city docks area. The route on to Ashton Junction is still operated to serve the coal concentration depot but the branch to Canon's Marsh on the opposite side of the Floating Harbour closed in 1965. A double-deck road and rail bridge once carried the joined lines across the New Cut to Ashton where a traditional GWR signal box and crossing gates still exist outside the engineer's depot. Canon's Marsh is now a car park but the long goods depot buildings are still there.

B.23   Briton Ferry

Newport-Fishguard line between Port Talbot and Neath. 206 m from Paddington*

Briton Ferry is a goods yard and former passenger station site on the South Wales main line. A little further west Court Sart Junction (206 m 58 ch) is part of the same railway complex and gives access to the line to Morlais Junction.

After the South Wales Railway main line opened in 1850 a branch to Briton Ferry Dock was added in 1861 and a connection made in 1893-4 with the Rhondda & Swansea Bay Railway which had come

down from the valleys via Port Talbot and then joined the main line at Briton Ferry from the seaward side. At Court Sart Junction the line diverged again towards the Swansea foreshore and the docks. From 1906 the RSB was worked by the GWR which, in 1915, opened a connection from the Court Sart Junction to Swansea line—at Dynevor Junction—to the new Swansea-avoiding or 'Swansea District' line. This established the Swansea District Line as linking, as it still does today, Court Sart Junction and Llandeilo Junction (Llanelli) as an alternative to the original main line route through Neath and Landore. The RSB line from the valleys is now closed but Court Sart remains important because of its link to the Swansea District route and to Swansea's docks and freight installations. The main line and the Swansea District line, both double track, are controlled by multiple aspect signalling from Port Talbot panel box. Up trains from the District line use a burrowing junction to reach the Up main line at Court Sart.

Briton Ferry yard is on the Down side and is double ended, with connections to and from the main line in both directions and others to and from the Swansea District line. From it connections lead to the private siding of Thos. W. Ward Ltd and, partially along the alignment of the old RSB route, to the huge Baglan Bay works of BP Chemicals Ltd, a significant user of company trains. Indeed Briton Ferry yard is used primarily for block train loads of chemicals and feedstocks running to and from Baglan Bay, although it is also the base for freight trips to other local sidings and for supplying the Neath freight and coal yard. A daily trip to and from Margam yard is scheduled.

Briton Ferry Dock was one of the many projects in which Brunel had an interest. He designed the lock gates and also laid out the route of the South Wales Mineral Railway which descended to the South Wales Railway by a 1½ m cable-worked incline.

B.24   Bromfield

Shrewsbury-Newport line between Craven Arms and Hereford. 25 m 20 ch from Shrewsbury

The station which served the racecourse closed in 1958 (for freight in 1964) but a signal box remains open between the old platforms and the Down Goods Loop.

B.25   Bromsgrove

Birmingham-Bristol line beween Barnt Green and Cheltenham. 55 m 30 ch from Derby

Bromsgrove lies at the foot of the Lickey incline and the banking engines are provided at the south end of the Up Goods Loop. On the Down side the existence of a Down Goods line allows descending freight trains to clear the main line for the intensive passenger service on the route. Nearby are the sad derelict buildings of the old wagon repair works.

Most of the Worcester-Birmingham trains routed via Stoke Works Junction provide a passenger service for Bromsgrove and the station is unusual in having a single platform for the use of trains in both directions. This, and the oil traffic sidings of Hallam GT Oils, lie on the Up side.

B.26   Broome

Shrewsbury-Llanelli line between Craven Arms and Llandrindod Wells. 2 m 46 ch from Craven Arms

Broome is a modest, single platform station on the former Knighton Railway now served as a conditional stop by the dmus of the Swansea-Shrewsbury service.

B.27   Bruton

Reading-Taunton line between Westbury and Castle Cary. 126 m 13 ch from Paddington*

Once a substantial little country station, Bruton lies halfway down the descent from Brewham summit towards Castle Cary and has gradients of 1 in 93/98 either side. The platforms are provided with shelters and linked by a footbridge and the signal box still exists at the country end but is normally switched out. The former dock marks the goods yard area opposite.

Weymouth line dmus provide Bruton's passenger service and halfway along the section towards the junction at Castle Cary the old S&D route crosses the main line. The abutments can still be seen and also an S&D viaduct towards the former Cole station.

B.28   Bucknell

Shrewsbury-Llanelli line between Craven Arms and Llandrindod Wells. 8 m 4 ch from Craven Arms

Another conditional stop on the former Knighton Railway route, Bucknell's simple shelters now in use contrast strongly with the former station buildings which are stately and impressive with tall gables relieving the grey of the weathered stone. There is also an open level crossing.

Bugle—see Newquay Branch

B.29   Builth Road

Shrewsbury-Llanelli line between Llandrindod Wells and Llandeilo. 37 m 40 ch from Craven Arms

The severe red brick station building looks down on its former rival Cambrian station below and the surviving Central Wales Extension Railway crosses the old Moat Lane to Brecon line on a 31 ft steel girder bridge. The approach to Builth Road from Llandrindod is past the site of Howey loop where engines which had assisted trains up the 1 in 74 gradient used to leave their trains and return to Builth. On the other side of the station lie the bridge across the Cambrian Railways route, the two wrought iron spans of the River Wye bridge and the 64 yd Rhosferig Tunnel (38 m 16 ch to 38 m 18 ch).

B.30   Burbage

Reading-Taunton line between Newbury and Westbury. 70 m 75 ch from Paddington

Served by Grafton and Burbage (M&SW) for passenger purposes, there was a goods facility on the GWR route until 1947. The wharf site just visible on the Up side was once used for railway/canal transfer traffic and Burbage had both a signal box and a station master, albeit of the lowly Class 6 variety.

B.31   Burlescombe

Taunton-Penzance line between Taunton and Tiverton Junction. 174 m 62 ch from Paddington*

Closed since 1964, Burlescombe was the last station on the climb from Exeter to Whiteball summit. Its main interest now is as the site of a loading bank on the Up side and for the route and bridge of the former Westleigh quarry tramway which led westwards from it. This short line was 3 ft gauge from 1875 to 1898 when it was converted to standard. Some old broad gauge track was recently unearthed here.

B.32 Burngullow

Taunton-Penzance line between Bodmin Road and Truro. 288 m 56 ch from Paddington*

The station closed for passenger traffic back in 1931 but the location remains of importance for the china clay traffic from the ECC works on the Up side and as the junction for the freight branch to Drinnick Mill and Parkandillack. This joins the main line in the Up direction at the London end of the former Up platform, otherwise marked by only one tiny stone building. The ECC works, with its two sets of works lines connected to the through goods siding, are located slightly nearer St Austell.

Movements are controlled from a manual signal box on a portion of the old Down platform.

B.33 Burnham

Paddington-Swindon line between Slough and Maidenhead. 20 m 77 ch from Paddington

Burnham got its station, at one time known as Burnham Beeches, in 1899. Now comprising an island platform with central red brick buildings and all round canopy, Burnham is served from the Relief lines by the Paddington-Reading dmus which serve all stations from Slough onwards.

B.34 Bynea

Shrewsbury-Llanelli line between Pantyf-fynnon and Llandeilo Junction. 1 m 7 ch from Llandeilo Junction

A conditional stop on the former Llanelly Railway portion of the Central Wales line and comprising just two bare platforms served by the Swansea-Shrewsbury dmus.

Cadoxton—see Barry Branch

Caerphilly—see Rhymney Branch

C.1 Caerwent Branch

Gloucester-Newport line, branch from Caldicot. 1 m 60 ch

This is a short, freight only, single track line running south from the military depot at Caerwent to join the main line at Caldicot Crossing (146 m 76 ch) in a junction facing towards Severn Tunnel Junction. In the process it bridges the A43 and M4 roads and the gradients of 1 in 172

and 1 in 100 falling towards the main line are followed by a final rise at 1 in 528.

The service is operated on an 'as required' basis with trains being worked by BR locomotives under the one train working system although the line is actually the property of the Ministry of Defence.

C.2 Caldicot

Gloucester-Newport line between Chepstow and Severn Tunnel Junction. 148 m 2 ch from Paddington

Caldicot Halt was opened by the GWR on September 12 1932 and it is served by the all stations dmus working between Gloucester and Cardiff. The station comprises no more than Up and Down platforms at the London end of the four track section from Severn Tunnel Junction. Caldicot Crossing and ground frame is just over a mile nearer London at 146 m 76 ch and is the point at which the short Caerwent and Sudbrook branches join the main line. There is also a Down Refuge Siding.

Calstock—see Gunnislake Branch

C.3 Camborne

Taunton-Penzance line between Truro and Penzance. 313 m 40 ch from Paddington*

At the Penzance end of the Redruth-Camborne conurbation, Camborne station has attractive, if modest, buildings on the Up side, tall chimneys surmounting the single storey structure of red brick with blue brick facings. The Down side has only a shelter, the station's other main feature being the barrier crossing at the London end. Slightly further on is Roskear Junction Crossing (313 m 19 ch) and signal box where the short siding serving Compair is of special interest as a surviving remnant of the original Hayle Railway branch to the tin mining area at Roskear.

C.4 Campden

Oxford-Hereford line between Moreton-in-Marsh and Evesham. 96 m 78 ch from Paddington

The CCTV level crossing stands at the country end of the former station area. Just 49 ch further on comes the 887 yd Campden Tunnel (97 m 47 ch to 98 m 7 ch) and the 4 m descent at 1 in 100 to Honeybourne and the Vale of Evesham. The former Mickleton Halt lay on this stretch

and the village of Mickleton gave its name
to one of the most dramatic physical con-
frontations in railway history. This
occurred during the weekend of July
20-22 1851 when Brunel and 2,000 men
tried to oust an unpaid contractor who
was holding up completion of the tunnel
contract. The manoeuvres and skirmishes
had all the atmosphere of a small war and
it took magistrates, soldiers, police armed
with cutlasses and several readings of the
Riot Act to contain the event to a series of
minor scuffles.

Carbis Bay—see St Ives Branch

C.5   Cardiff

Cardiff Central is on the Newport-Fish-
guard line 170 m 30 ch from Paddington*,
Queen Street on the Barry/Penarth-
Treherbert/Merthyr/Rhymney lines 1 m
20 ch from Central, and Bute Road is 1 m
6 ch from Queen Street

The pattern of railways in Cardiff, capital
city of Wales, reflects the classical South
Wales situation: that of the east-west
main line crossed by lines built to carry
coal from the valleys to a port. In
Cardiff's case there are additionally lines
south-west to Penarth and Barry.

When the South Wales Railway arrived
in Cardiff in 1850, the Taff Vale Railway
had been there for a decade building up its
main line to Merthyr as the foundation of
a 'valleys' network which was to add
124½ route miles at grouping. The Rhymney Railway, with 51 route miles at grouping, reached Cardiff with its own metals in
1871 after earlier beginnings inland and
after falling out with the TVR over access
to the capital. The RR had the advantage of
strong connections with the dock interests
and was the vehicle used by the LNWR
for its access to Cardiff. The dock interest,
deriving from the enterprise of the second
Marquis of Bute who was virtually the
founder of Cardiff as we know it, was in
the hands of the Bute Docks Company
which metamorphosed into the Cardiff
Railway in 1897.

There were strong rivalries and considerable competition between the various
railways in Cardiff and real co-ordination
only began when they became constituents
of the GWR as a result of the Railways
Act 1921. The Rhymney Railway had
already transferred its passenger terminus
from Adam Street to a site at Queen Street
and in 1928 this was closed in favour of a

new five-platform station on the TVR
Queen Street site. The GWR station at
Cardiff General, now Central, was
completely rebuilt in 1934 to give vastly
improved interchange and access and to
produce the present station buildings.
Work on a £638,000 scheme to modernise
the concourse was started on July 12 1982.

Approaching Cardiff from the London
direction along the four-track main line,
Cardiff's rail installations begin at the
bridge   over   the   River   Rhymney.
Immediately beyond this on the Down side
is Pengam Freightliner terminal comprising three terminal lines straddled by two
0-4-0 Morris cranes which are supplemented by a mobile crane. In 1982 there were
direct trains to Stratford (London),
Newcastle and Glasgow.

Access to the terminal is at the Cardiff
end, at Pengam Junction (168 m 20 ch)
which is also the junction for the double
track route to Tidal Sidings (4 m 20 ch)
marshalling yard and then on to the
BTDB lines and the private sidings near to
the docks, notably a Gulf Oil terminal and
the steel works of Allied Steel & Wire
Ltd. Tidal Sidings are served by trains to
and from the yards at Radyr and Severn
Tunnel Junction and they are also the
base for local trip workings. Some block
trains work to and from the local private
sidings, and on the BTDB-controlled lines
beyond movements of semi-finished steel
products, billets and rod coil take place
between the Tremorfa and Rod Mills
and Castle Works of AS&W.

On the Up side of the main line west of
Pengam Junction is Roath freight and
coal yard. Domestic fuel is the principal
traffic and there are plans to concentrate
here the coal traffic handled at two other
depots in Cardiff. Flanking the end of
Roath yard are the earthworks and bridge
abutments of the former TVR 'Roath
Line' which linked that company's main
line with the Roath and Queen Alexandra
docks.

Just before Cardiff Central comes Long
Dyke Junction (169 m 27 ch) followed by
the National Carriers depot (formerly
Newtown goods station) on the Up side
and the former Tyndall Street yard on the
Down (both at 169 m 50 ch). On the Down
side there is also an alternative route to
the AS&W's Rod Mill, on the Up side is
the remaining earthworks and bridge
abutment of the former Rhymney Railway
route to the docks.

The two bridges immediately beyond
the Tyndall Street yard area originated as

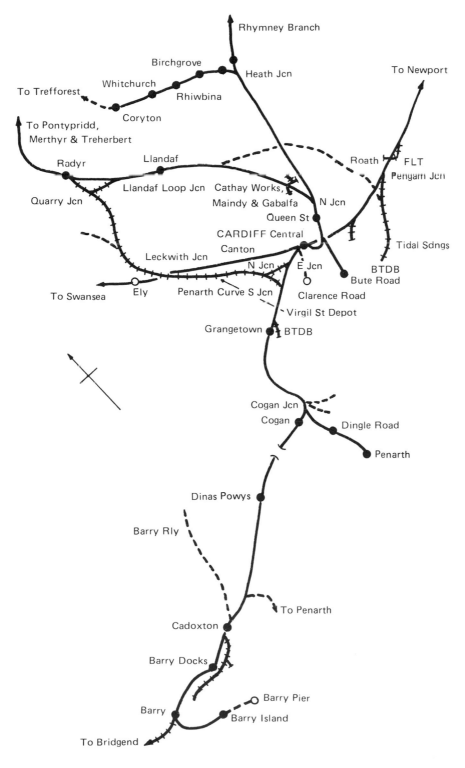

TVR routes. The first now carries the single track Queen Street-Bute Road branch and the second takes a double track line from Queen Street and its 'Valleys' passenger train service over the main line and then down to join it at Central station. The station itself consists of Up and Down main line island platforms with two through lines in between and an Up Goods Loop on the Up side. The second Down main line platform, No 4, is signalled for two-way working to allow trains to reverse there. A further island platform (Nos 6 and 7) is used by trains between the Valleys, Penarth and Barry and another (8 and 9) was, until recently, used for parcels traffic.

The Cardiff booking office, travel centre and concourse are on the Up side, with access to the platforms by subway, and are due for extensive modernisation. Outside the station is a major bus interchange depot and a small car park. The parcels and Area Manager's offices are on the Down side in the angle between the main station and the former Riverside branch. Cardiff panel box, controlling the whole station area, the branches and lines from the Valleys and the main line from Marshfield to Llantrisant, is on the Down side at the country end of the station. There are sidings for newspaper and parcels vans on the Up side and a Class 08 locomotive acts as station pilot.

After leaving the station the main line crosses the River Taff and then comes to a triangle in which lies Canton diesel depot and the dmu and carriage depot. The line to Penarth Curve South Junction and on to Penarth and Barry forms another leg of the triangle which is completed by the line from Penarth Curve South Junction to Radyr. The main triangle is then subdivided by a single track route from Penarth Curve East Junction to Penarth Curve North Junction which allows main line trains from the east to run direct to Radyr Yard and beyond. Near the North Junction is Virgil Street coal yard and beyond it is Ninian Park Halt, used for trains bringing visiting supporters to Cardiff City football ground. At this end of the Cardiff complex the four tracks of the main line are grouped by direction; east of the station they are paired by use. At Leckwith Junction (171 m 55 ch) the four merge into two and there is a single track connection to the Radyr line.

Cardiff Canton depot, the largest diesel depot in South Wales, had an allocation in 1982 of 120 main line locomotives, 20 shunting locomotives and 51 diesel multiple units. For the locomotives there are servicing and maintenance sheds, the latter incorporating lifting jacks and overhead gantries and capable of undertaking major repairs. The carriage servicing shed area includes dmu maintenance and fuelling facilities and HSTs are also serviced and fuelled overnight. At the country end

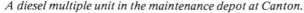

A diesel multiple unit in the maintenance depot at Canton.

of the Canton complex the civil engineer has a depot for the prefabrication and storage of switch and crossing layouts.

To the north of Cardiff Central lies Queen Street where the ex-TVR and Rhymney Railway meet. On the ex-TVR approaches Cathays Works, on the Down side, undertakes wagon repairs and the maintenance of the civil engineer's track machines while on the Up side stands the Maindy works of Powell Duffryn Wagon Co Ltd. To the north of Cathays is Gabalfa coal depot and private siding and to the south the site for the new Cathays station to serve the Welsh Office and University complexes.

Queen Street station is close to the commercial and shopping areas of the city and is used by the majority of passengers on the Valleys services. It was rebuilt in 1973/4 to the present island platform with a bay for Up trains terminating and Down trains starting. The booking office is on the Up side and opposite is the 16-floor Brunel House office block, a BR development on the site once occupied by the RR's route to the docks. The single line to Bute Street, 1 m 6 ch from Queen Street, diverges from the double track route to Central at Queen Street South Junction Bute Street itself comprises no more than a single platform but alongside is a listed building which once housed the TVR offices.

The principal main line services at

Pengam Freightliner Terminal.

Cardiff are the London-Swansea HSTs supplemented by some HSTs between London and Cardiff. There are also Inter-City services to Crewe via Hereford, to the North-East/North-West via Gloucester and to Portsmouth via Bristol. Frequent suburban dmu services connect Queen Street and Central with the Treherbert, Merthyr, Rhymney, Coryton, Penarth and Barry lines and there are peak hour services to Bute Road, mostly from Coryton, for workers in the docks area.

A great deal of freight traffic passes through Cardiff and, on the Up side opposite Canton depot, it has an Isislink facility. This is a privately owned rail/road transhipment, warehousing and distribution depot handling UK and Continental traffic via Speedlink services. The site was formerly that of Canton milk depot and beyond it is a siding with covered facilities for the transfer of newspapers from rail vans to road vehicles.

Much evidence of Cardiff's railway past still remains, especially in the docks area, and the Industrial and Maritime Museum near the main entrance to the docks in Bute Town is well worth a visit. On the main line towards Swansea the site of Ely station is visible on the Up side and further on, near the remains of St Fagans station and the busy level crossing there, are the earthworks by which the Barry Railway crossed the main line, to which it was connected by a spur on the Up side. Coal from the west to Barry used the 1889-1963 link from Peterston.

C.6   Carmarthen

Newport-Fishguard line between Llanelli and Whitland. 245 m 55 ch from Paddington*

Carmarthen is an historic county and market town and erstwhile port lying where the River Towy is bridged by road and rail before the final 6 m journey to meet the sea at Carmarthen Bay. The town was reached by the broad gauge South Wales Railway in 1852. Two years later it was pushing on towards the ultimate objective of a link to Ireland.

The original station on this main line, sited below the town with an eye on the march westwards, has long since been replaced by the present station which stands at the apex of a triangular layout of which the main line forms the base. This first station was sited at the present Carmarthen Junction (245 m 10 ch) where the through line and the station spur divide and where a modern style brick built signal box now marks the original location (which remained in subsidiary use until 1926). This box controls all movements in the area, including Carmarthen Bridge Junction at the westward point of the triangle and P&T Loop Junction at the northern point—245 m 32 ch and 245 m 30 ch respectively. Near the former is the bridge over the Towy, a bascule lifting bridge built in 1908 but now fixed.

There were originally lines north of Carmarthen to Aberaeron, Aberystwyth, Newcastle Emlyn and Llandeilo but these closed in stages between 1951 and 1973. These account for the location of the present station which was built in 1902 and which displays the typical red brick architectural style of that era of GWR expansion and cut off lines. One platform is used for all passenger trains, although

the run round line flanks a second platform which can be used in exceptional circumstances.

Between the station and P&T Loop Junction are engineer's sidings (including a modern shed for on-track maintenance machines), carriage sidings and a private siding for the Aberthaw & Bristol Channel Portland Cement Co. There are further sidings at Carmarthen Junction including, on the Up side, one leading to the United Kingdom Fertilisers depot and served by company trains from Ince, and a Down side dairy siding west of the river bridge. Beyond the station, over another Towy river bridge and along the course of the former line (part of which is now operated by the Gwili Railway preservation group), there is a goods yard (246 m 8 ch) used mainly for coal traffic. This was formerly a goods station and, before 1902, Carmarthen Town passenger station.

Carmarthen is served by Swansea-Milford Haven and Pembroke Dock trains which may be locomotive-hauled or dmus. There is a daily HST service to and from Paddington and also calls by the Milford Haven-Paddington sleeper, the Milford Haven-Bristol Travelling Post Office (TPO) train, as well as a Cardiff-Carmarthen portion off the overnight newspaper train from London. The Fishguard Harbour trains and the summer holiday trains to and from Tenby mostly use the main line and omit a Carmarthen stop and the consequent reversal. The freight position is similar although one of the two daily West Wales wagon load services calls at Carmarthen Junction for

The approach to Carmarthen, with the station lying to the right and the main line west continuing on the left.

traffic purposes. There are some prospects of a West Wales Speedlink feeder service and of a new station for Carmarthen on the main line. West of Carmarthen a CCTV crossing still exists at the site of the former Sarnau station (249 m 57 ch).

C.7   Carn Brea

*Taunton-Penzance line between Redruth and Camborne. 311 m 43 ch from Paddington**

The heyday of Cornwall's tin mining is nowhere more evident than between Redruth and Camborne. Joining the ghosts of the empty engine houses is the site of the once busy railway area at Carn Brea.

The first section of the Hayle Railway opened from Hayle to Carn Brea (then called Pool) and on to Portreath in 1837. The route of the latter and of the Crofty Branch can still be spotted east and west (respectively) of the Carn Brea site on the Up side of the main line.

The two main areas of the Carn Brea location were also on the Up side, that nearer London becoming the centre for the West Cornwall Railway's standard gauge mineral traffic locomotives when through broad gauge working commenced on the main line. Passenger services ended in 1961 but broccoli forwardings continued for a while longer.

Castle Bar Park—see Greenford Branch

C.8   Castle Cary

Reading-Taunton line between Westbury and Cogload Junction. 129 m 46 ch from Paddington

The Frome-Yeovil section of the WSWR/GWR route to Weymouth opened as a single line, with electric telegraph apparatus to control the crossing movements, on September 1 1856. Castle Cary became a junction in 1905 when the opening of a single line to Charlton Mackrell led (in 1906) to the completion of the cut-off route to Taunton and the West.

The simple station, with its principal buildings on the Up side, is preceded from the London direction by Up and Down Passenger Loops and there are two holding sidings. Beyond the platforms a crossover is provided for Up Weymouth trains, the single line of the branch then diverging from the Down Main. Opposite is the goods yard with a dock and a brick and wood shed remaining and with a severe looking signal box between it and the main line.

The station is now served by the Weymouth line dmus and by some evening trains on the main line but it has at least one more hectic event in its history. This occurred in the summer of 1970 when some 50,000 fans needed to be moved after a marathon blues festival. For two days the station yard was filled with more passengers than it normally saw in a year, trains were produced by commandeering every spare locomotive and coach and the station buildings even had their windows removed to speed up the issue of tickets.

Causeland—see Looe Branch

Cefn-on—see Rhymney Branch

C.9   Chacewater

*Taunton-Penzance line between Truro and Redruth. 306 m 9 ch from Paddington**

The station closed on October 5 1964 but the fenced off buildings on the Down side remain and the shape of the Up platform is discernible. The latter was an island and was used as the branch platform for trains on the single line to Newquay via Perranporth after the junction further west at Blackwater went out of use in 1924. Two sidings, serving a cement silo terminal, remain on the Down side.

Chacewater also gave its name to an early and important Cornish mineral line which served the rich copper mines near Redruth from 1826 to 1915 when final legal closure took place. The 4 ft gauge Redruth & Chacewater led via Lanner to the Fal River with a branch to Wheal Beacham and an uncompleted line to Chacewater.

C.10   Challow

Paddington-Swindon line between Didcot and Swindon. 63 m 20 ch from Paddington

Nowadays Challow's remaining railway significance is as the boundary point between the London and West of England divisions. Both platform faces can still be seen, together with the old dock and coal office on the Up side, but there is no reminder of the fact that this was the scene of the infant GWR's first known accident. While still the end of construction from the London direction, the night goods of October 25 1840, with *Fire King* at its head and several passengers in the leading wagon, was seen approaching at an excessive speed. Despite the shouts of Brunel and his party, who happened to be waiting for transport back to London, the train sped unchecked through the station and piled up in the engine shed beyond. The driver was killed and four others injured. At the time the station was known as Faringdon Road, the change of name coming in 1864 with the opening of the Uffington to Faringdon branch.

Chapelton—see Barnstaple branch

C.11   Chard Junction

Waterloo-Exeter line between Yeovil Junction and Honiton. 139 m 32 ch from Waterloo

Chard proper was at one time served by both LSW and GWR trains but now the railway is represented in the area only by the passing loop at Chard Junction several miles away to the south. The station closed in 1962, four years after the end of passenger services on the branch which led from Chard Junction to the joint station in the town and then on via Ilminster to Taunton.

The signal box at Chard Junction is still manned and operates the barrier crossing which it overlooks from its position at the London end of the Up platform. The gabled red brick station buildings are still intact on this platform as are the goods shed at the country end and the severe station house. On the Down side the platform face has gone and the milk depot no longer sends its output away by rail although the siding connection and ground frame remain.

C.12   Charfield

Birmingham-Bristol line between Gloucester and Westerleigh Junction. 113 m 13 ch from Derby

Closure came to Charfield in 1965 although Up and Down Goods Loops remain there and the former water tower, gabled stone house, platform buildings and goods shed can still be seen. But the name will always be remembered for the tragedy which occurred in the early hours of October 13 1928 when the bridge was piled up with blazing wreckage from a dreadful train crash which cost 15 lives.

The line was busy on the fateful night. With the 12.45 pm Leicester-Bristol parcels and the 10 pm ex-Leeds pressing on the heels of two Down goods trains, the Charfield signalman was forced to set back

the second of these into his lay-by siding. Quite properly he then accepted the speeding mail train but GWR engine No 714, to his horror, overran the signals and crashed into the reversing freight train and then bounced off it into the path of a goods train on the other line. The wreckage piled up in the cutting, reaching as high as the bridge over the line. Worse followed when the reservoirs for the coach gas lighting fractured and the wreckage of the wooden-bodied coaches became an inferno which rescuers could not get near.

C.13   Charlbury

Oxford-Hereford line between Oxford and Kingham. 76 m 60 ch from Paddington

The line through Charlbury is again single as it was on opening day and nothing remains on the Down side but a forlorn grinding wheel of the sort used by lengthmen to sharpen the tools used to keep foliage in check. The station was actively developed as a passenger railhead in the mid-1960s and is served by all Worcester line trains. This plus an active preservation group has helped to retain the Brunel chalet-style building on the Up platform where it has been sympathetically restored and is even accompanied by a period nameboard. The waiting room fire was also saved by petition.

Charlbury water troughs were sited west of the station.

C.14   Cheltenham

Birmingham-Bristol line between Barnt Green and Gloucester. 86 m 58 ch from Derby

Whereas the former GWR station is the one to survive at Gloucester, the present Cheltenham Spa is the one-time Midland Lansdown station. It comprises two platforms with canopies and connecting footbridge. The waiting room and buffet are on the Down platform from which steps lead to the ticket office at street level. It is well served by trains on the NE/SW route, which includes the Inter-City links to the North-West and to South Wales, and offers a facility for interchange between these and with the Worcester-Swindon dmus. There are still some through services to and from Paddington but the 2.30 pm Cheltenham Flyer and the later Cheltenham Spa Expresses are now but a memory.

Approaching Cheltenham from the

Gloucester direction Churchdown ground frame (86 m 49 ch) is followed by a Down Goods Loop and the gaunt brick signal box, now closed, which marks the site of the triangular connection with the former Andoversford line. The present line, now just two tracks instead of its previous four, then passes through the station on its way to Ashchurch and Birmingham. Just before reaching the Down platform the GWR trains would diverge at Lansdown Junction to that company's town centre terminus at St James' Square. This remained the main station for the London services even after Malvern Road acquired a new status when the threat of a rival M&SW scheme forced the GWR to create its new route to Birmingham via Honeybourne in 1906. Other stations at Cheltenham included Cheltenham South & Leckhampton, High Street Halt and the Racecourse Station, still visible alongside the A453 at SO 954 251.

On the Birmingham side of the passenger station, the former Midland and M&SW sidings are now Lansdown carriage sidings and Alston Coal Wharf is just marked by Alstone level crossing (86 m 21 ch). Then comes the Up Goods Loop from which access is obtained to the large coal concentration depot via High Street ground frame (86 m 4 ch). A two bay wooden shed still stands here, blackened by years of timber preservatives.

Cheltenham Lansdown station about 1906.

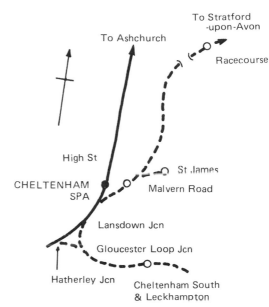

C.15 Chepstow

Gloucester-Newport line between Lydney and Severn Tunnel Junction. 144 m 33 ch from Paddington

Chepstow's first railway, from the area of the present station to Swansea, was opened on June 18 1850. The link with the GWR at Grange Court came 15 months later but only from the opposite bank of the River Wye, the bridge and the comple-

tion of the rail link not coming until July
19 1852. The bridge remains the most
interesting feature at Chepstow, a curving
embankment from the station taking the
line to the high three-section approach
bridge supported on tubular piers in sets
of three and then on to the main inverted
girder section across the river. The original
Brunel bridge used piers which cut foundations by their own weight and was
something of a model for the Royal Albert
Bridge at Saltash.

Chepstow passenger station has a
single-storey building in the Brunel chalet
style on the Up platform and just a shelter
on the Down. The connecting footbridge
gives a view of the approach of the line
along the west bank of the Wye and of the
nest of sidings on the Down side from
which a line leads down to the riverside
works below. Some of the bigger pieces of
steelwork for the modified Menai Bridge
were forwarded from the riverside works
of Fairfield Mabey.

C.16   Chetnole

*Westbury-Weymouth line between Yeovil
and Maiden Newton. 147 m 50 ch from
Paddington* *

Chetnole consists of just a short single
platform of concrete slabs lying on the
west side of the line and preceding the 1 in
53/51 climb to Evershot summit.

C.17   Chippenham

*Swindon-Bristol line between Wootton
Bassett Junction and Bath. 93 m 76 ch
from Paddington*

From the Bristol direction the approach to
Chippenham is on a long embankment
giving a view over the town. At the station
proper the main buildings, of Bath stone
and with a canopy, are on the Down side
although trains now use the island platform over the footbridge.

Skirting the cattle market on the London
side of the station is the trackbed of the
former Calne branch. This 5½ m branch
which lasted from 1863 to 1965 had a
service of 13 trains a day at one time, plus
an extra service on the third Monday of
each month for Calne Cattle Market.
Trainloads of Wiltshire sausages were a
frequent sight on the branch. On the
opposite side of the main line are three
goods sidings, a small S&T area and what
is left of the Westinghouse private sidings.

The station is well served by the
Paddington-Bristol HSTs. It has cross-

overs, two ground frames and a token
instrument for the line from Bradford
North Junction.

C.18   Chipping Sodbury

*Swindon-Newport line between Wootton
Bassett Junction and Westerleigh Junction.
104 m 40 ch from Paddington*

Passenger services were withdrawn from
Chipping Sodbury in 1961 but freight
continued for some time after. The
mineral traffic loading dock still exists but
active railway infrastructure is now confined to crossovers, ground frames and an
Up Goods Loop.

This section of line, the South Wales &
Bristol Direct, was opened in 1903 and
reduced the distance between London and
South Wales by 10 m. One of the major
works was Chipping Sodbury tunnel
(101 m 6 ch to 103 m 48 ch) which cuts
through the main ridge of the Cotswolds.
Despite the air resistance encountered by
trains in tunnels it has been possible to
allow trains through at 110 mph, partly
because the 2 m 926 yd bore has ventilation
shafts, the ornate tops of which can be
seen east of the A46 road.

C.19   Cholsey

*Paddington-Swindon line between
Reading and Didcot. 48 m 37 ch from
Paddington*

At one time, if you fancied a trip on the
river, you could change at Cholsey, take a
seven-minute journey on the 2¾ m
branch line to Wallingford and then pick
up one of Salters' Upper Thames Pleasure
Steamers for a cruise upstream to Oxford
or downstream to Henley. The branch,
opened July 2 1866 by the Wallingford &
Watlington Railway, closed in 1965
(although it continued in use in a shortened
form until 1981 as a private siding for
ABM) and Cholsey is now served only by
the Oxford-Didcot-Reading-Paddington
trains.

The station consists of an island
platform between the main and relief lines
and two further platforms outside the Up
Relief and Down Main, the latter with just
a small brick building, the main offices
being on the north side. The present station
dates from 1892 when it replaced an
earlier site 55 ch further east and called at
various times Moulsford and Wallingford
Road. There is an Up Refuge Siding at the
country end of the site.

C.20   Cilmeri

Shrewsbury-Llanelli line between Llandrindod Wells and Llandovery. 39 m 39 ch from Craven Arms

Cilmeri is a basic station and a conditional stop for the Shrewsbury-Swansea dmus. The 115 yd Cilmeri Tunnel (39 m 14 ch to 39 m 20 ch) lies to the north and there is a view to the west of the station of the stone monument to Llywelyn the Last.

Clarbeston Road—see Fishguard

C.21   Cleeve

Birmingham-Bristol line between Barnt Green and Cheltenham. 82 m 60 ch from Derby

Cleeve lies on the gentle descent from Cheltenham to Ashchurch and is marked more clearly by the surviving ground frame than by the former station. Either side are crossings at Fiddington (80 m 39 ch), Tredington (81 m 44 ch), Swindon Road (84 m 23 ch) and Morris Hill (85 m 3 ch) which include examples of the curious but attractive design of red brick crossing keepers' houses which are a feature of this section.

Clifton Down—see Severn Beach Branch

C.22   Clunderwen

Newport-Fishguard line between Whitland and Clarbeston Road Junction. 264 m 22 ch from Paddington*

Unstaffed and with waiting shelters on its staggered platforms, Clunderwen lies on a short level section preceded by a long climb from Whitland (at 1 in 101) and Clarbeston Road (at 1 in 82/3). It has intermediate block signals to break up the long block section between those two places. Marketed as a railhead for Cardigan, the station is served by most Milford Haven trains.

In its early days Clunderwen was known as Narberth Road but since 1866 Narberth has had its own station on the Pembroke Dock line. It was also the junction for the much troubled line via Rosebush to Fishguard, steeply graded and closed three times. The junction is still just discernible on the Up side west of the station.

C.23   Clydach-on-Tawe Branch

Swansea District line, branch from Felin Fran. 1 m 47 ch

This single track freight-only branch serves the Inco Europe plant at Clydach. It was originally opened in 1923 and at that time extended up the Swansea Valley to Daren colliery at Trebanos, almost 2 m beyond Clydach. This northern section was closed in 1965.

There was a project in the GWR era of expansion before the First World War to continue the line into the Amman Valley at Gwaun-cae-Gurwen. This would have provided a direct route for shipment coal from the valley to Swansea Docks but, although authorised, it was never carried out. In fact, only a 4 m gap needed to be filled, for a 2¼ m section was constructed from Gwaun-cae-Gurwen to what is now Abernant colliery, leaving just the section between Abernant and Trebanos via Pontardawe.

The branch junction faces eastwards and the line bridges the M4 at the junction end and the River Tawe at the Clydach end. The one train working (without train staff) system operates and traffic mainly consists of fuel oil and chemicals. It is carried on a trip from Swansea Burrows Sidings via Jersey Marine South and North Junctions and this also calls at Felin Fran to detach wagons of household coal.

C.24   Coaley

Birmingham-Bristol line between Gloucester and Westerleigh Junction. 105 m 36 ch from Derby

Coaley was once called Dursley Junction and later Coaley Junction to recognise the 2½ m branch built by Dursley interests to enable local mills to compete with those of the Stroud area. The junction platform is still visible on the Down side although the branch passenger service ceased in 1962, three years before the main line trains stopped calling. A short section of the former branch line runs from the Down Refuge Siding to the old goods shed. Along the Cam Valley to Dursley there was once a service of 6/8 trains a day and considerable goods traffic to and from Lister's factory but the line was finally closed in 1970 and few traces now remain.

There was a rail served cement silo at Coaley until fairly recently but now only some engineers sidings remain.

C.25   Coed Ely Branch

Newport-Fishguard line, branch from Llantrisant. 4 m 5 ch

From Llantrisant East (181 m 43 ch) on the South Wales main line this freight only branch heads northwards up the Ely Valley to the NCB colliery and the National Smokeless Fuels Ltd coking works at Coed Ely.

The line originated as the Ely Valley Railway which was worked from its inception by the GWR. At one time the railway continued on through Tonyrefail to Penygraig, 3¼ m beyond Coed Ely and high above the valley of the Rhondda Fawr. Although opened in 1860/2 the passenger train service did not begin until 1901 and was withdrawn in 1958. For freight the route stretched beyond the passenger terminating point at Penygraig to the Cambrian colliery in Clydach Vale which was also served by the Taff Vale Railway's Pwllyrhelog incline line up from Tonypandy. Beyond Coed Ely the route closed down in 1967.

The junction at Llantrisant faces Cardiff and the branch has two tracks as far as Mwyndy Junction (47 ch) where the route to Cwm diverges to the right and that to Coed Ely becomes single track and starts its climb, which includes a steepest gradient of 1 in 72. The movement of trains is controlled by the supervisor at Llantrisant with only one train allowed at a time on the single line section. Inwards traffic to Coed Ely comprises coal from nearby collieries for coke manufacture and outwards traffic coke to various destinations and in particular to a concentration depot for supplying industry at Pensnett, West Midlands. Each day Mondays to Fridays four return trips are scheduled from Llantrisant Yard to Coed Ely and back, motive power being a Class 37 locomotive.

Cogan—see Barry Branch

C.26   Cogload Junction

Bristol-Taunton line with Reading-Taunton line. 158 m 32 ch from Paddington

The last section of what is now the West of England main line was completed in April 1906 (for goods traffic only for the first three months) to make Cogload one of the GWR's most important junctions. It also brought lasting confusion to the measurement of distances which have continued to be marked via the Bristol route despite the shortening brought about by the completion of the cut-off line and the further changes resulting from the avoiding lines at Westbury and Frome. On the direct line there is a change of mileage at Cogload from 137 m 68 ch to 158 m 9 ch. Water troughs were installed at 159 m 13 ch.

The original traditional junction, coupled with the bottleneck through Taunton station, led to some nightmare delays at the busiest holiday periods. As a result the remodelling of 1930-2 led to the provision of a flyover for the Down line from Bristol to avoid it conflicting with the Up and Down West of England lines. This remains the layout with a wooden signal box on the Up side and with the flyover line carried by a lattice girder framework tied by top crossmembers.

C.27   Colnbrook Branch

Paddington-Swindon line, branch from West Drayton. 3 m 60 ch

The Staines & West Drayton Railway was authorised in 1873 but it was August 9 1884 before the single line got to the main intermediate station at Colnbrook and November 2 1885 before it reached the farmhouse which had been acquired for the station offices at Staines West. At various times this second section had halts at Poyle Estate, Poyle and Runemede Range (later Yeoveney) but it closed in 1965 and the line now terminates just beyond Colnbrook level crossing.

The single line, which is used exclusively for freight traffic, joins the main line in a junction facing towards London having passed beneath it and then round the rear of the coal concentration depot. It deals with steel and oil traffic at Colnbrook and scrap, bitumen and stone flows to Thorney Mill. Some of the traffic, like the stone from Bardon Hill in tippler wagons, works on to the line in train loads and the remainder is tripped down from West Drayton. Operation of the line is under the control of a Senior Railman (Shunter).

C.28   Colwall

Oxford-Hereford line between Great Malvern and Shelwick Junction. 131 m 72 ch from Paddington

Of the once-ample double track station only the former Up platform and its metal shelter are now used by the local dmu trains and a few through services beyond Worcester. The footbridge still exists as does the red brick goods shed although freight facilities were withdrawn in 1964.

On the London side of the station the 1,586 yd Colwall Tunnel (130 m 48 ch to 131 m 40 ch) lies on a rising gradient of 1 in 80 up to the summit between the two, having finally decided to pierce the Malvern Hills which the route has been flirting with for the previous six miles. A new tunnel, with quite a bulbous section, replaced the original bore from August 11 1926.

C.29   Combe

Oxford-Hereford line between Oxford and Kingham. 71 m 44 ch from Paddington

The modest sleeper platform, survivor of two platforms and a mill siding, is adequate for the four daily trains which serve this former halt opened in 1935.

Cookham—see Marlow Branch

Coombe—see Looe Branch

Copplestone—see Barnstaple Branch

C.30   Cornwood

Taunton-Penzance line between Totnes and Plymouth. 237 m 44 ch from Paddington*

The local trains between Exeter/Newton Abbot and Plymouth have not called here since 1959 but the station house survives on the Up side and is interesting for its South Devon Railway window style of rounded arches and higher centre section. The railway crosses the Piall River by Slade Viaduct west of Cornwood and the tiny Yealm by Blachford Viaduct just to the east. Although no longer used, the original SDR Brunel piers can still be seen.

C.31   Corsham

Swindon-Bristol line between Chippenham and Box Tunnel. 98 m 41 ch from Paddington

This was one of the original stations on the GWR's Bristol main line. Once busy with passengers and with wagons of stone quarried from Box Hill, the site is now marked by the remains of the Up platform and Down dock and by the former stone goods shed now in private hands.

Court Sart Junction—see Briton Ferry

C.32   Coryton Branch

Rhymney-Cardiff line, branch from Heath Junction. 2 m 57 ch

The branch is used for a weekdays only dmu service, mainly confined to the peak hours and linking the northern suburbs of Cardiff with Bute Road. Formed of three-car dmu sets, there are 12 services each way (10 on Saturdays) some of which go through to Central and the Barry/Penarth routes.

The line originated in the desire of the Bute Docks Company to emulate the Barry Railway in building a railway to bring coal to its own port, in this case Cardiff. Despite strong opposition, an Act of 1897 authorised a change of name to the Cardiff Railway and the construction of a line from Treforest, where it would tap the busy Taff Vale main line, through Heath, where there would be a junction with the Rhymney, and then eastwards through the Roath area of the city to the docks. The Treforest-Heath section was completed in 1909 after a great deal of money had been spent on cuttings and bridges (including £30,000 on a skew bridge of 480 ft over the River Taff) and on May 15 the inaugural train ran over the new line. It was to be the first and last service for the TVR promptly closed the junction to start a period of dispute and litigation that lasted for the next five years. A passenger service was operated from Rhydyfelin (south of Treforest Junction) to Cardiff via Heath and the RR line from 1911 but this was cut back to Coryton after only 20 years. North of Coryton the route remained open to serve Nantgarw colliery but since 1952 the colliery has been connected to the ex-TVR main line at Taffs Well. The line from Heath to the docks never did get built.

The Coryton branch commences at Heath Junction with a short stretch of double track but has been reduced to single line and the redundant platforms abandoned on the remainder of the route. The stations at Heath Low Level (29 ch), Birchgrove (1 m 37 ch), Rhiwbina (1 m 78 ch), Whitchurch (2 m 25 ch) and Coryton have simple shelters provided with the financial help of the South Glamorgan County Council and no runround facilities are provided at Coryton as the service is entirely operated by dmus. The line is controlled from Heath Junction signal box and operates on the one train working basis with train staff.

C.33   Cranmore Branch

Reading-Taunton line, branch from Witham. 5 m 47 ch

This line originally ran to Shepton Mallet

The East Somerset line from Witham to Wells is now truncated at Cranmore marooning buildings like this old goods shed at Wells.

and on to Wells where it linked up with the Cheddar Valley & Yatton Railway to give a typical GWR rural cross-country route on which through trains took 1 hour 44 minutes for the Up direction run from Yatton to Witham, a distance of 33½ m. The passenger service was withdrawn in 1963 and, after the transfer of the Dulcote despatches, the route cut back to Cranmore where the station is now part of the East Somerset Railway project.

There is a Shell Mex bitumen installation at Cranmore in addition to the padlocked connection with the ESR's private line and this end of the branch stub is, in effect, a siding extension from Merehead. From 1871 to 1946 a line ran from Waterlip Quarry to Cranmore, originally 2 ft gauge and horse-worked but later converted to standard and operated by a four-wheel Sentinel steam locomotive.

C.34   Craven Arms

Shrewsbury-Newport line between Shrewsbury and Hereford. 19 m 77 ch from Shrewsbury

Craven Arms takes its name from a former coaching inn and is the junction between the line opened by the Shrewsbury & Hereford Railway in 1852-3 and the Knighton Railway which was one of the links in the chain that today makes up

the Central Wales line through Llandrindod Wells to Llanelli. The two platform station is served by the trains on both routes.

On the Shrewsbury side of the station is the former LMS carriage shed on the Up side and also the level crossing and signal box (19 m 48 ch). Further north lies the boundary between the WR and LMR at 18 m 10 ch. Immediately south of the station is the ground frame (Station Ground Frame 20 m 1 ch) used by guards of the Central Wales line dmus to operate the junction points.

C.35   Crediton

Barnstaple branch between Cowley Bridge Junction and Coleford Junction. 179 m 26 ch from Waterloo

A line from Exeter to the flour mills at Crediton was sanctioned as early as 1832, a second scheme following in 1845 and becoming a pawn in the unsavoury rivalry between the LSW and GW interests. Crediton's first line lay derelict for four years while the battles went on and was finally opened on May 12 1851 with broad gauge trains operating on a single line and the adjoining track remaining of standard gauge!

Nowadays Crediton sees only the dmus of the Barnstaple branch service instead of the SR expresses and multiplicity of local trains which once headed for the Ilfracombe and Okehampton lines, although coal, stone and clay wagons still rattle through the station. It remains of particular interest as a junction at which

Crediton, a typical country station.

the double track route from Exeter is converted to two single lines which continue on a parallel course before diverging at Coleford Junction to serve Barnstaple and Meldon Quarry. Movements are controlled by the modest signal box which stands between the station's full barrier crossing and the two crossovers which link the double and single line sections.

Crediton's yard and main station building are now in private hands but the weighbridge remains in the former and the latter has some pleasant arches and beams to enliven its modest size and red brick construction. Substantial beams are used in the wooden shelters on each platform and there is the usual selection of gradient posts, signs and other railway 'furniture'. The station has conventional semaphore signalling and an adjoining inn, The Dartmoor Railway.

C.36 Crewkerne

Waterloo-Exeter line between Yeovil Junction and Honiton. 131 m 33 ch from Waterloo

This former SR station, now using only the Up platform and its single storey buildings, lies on a steep climb of 3 m up to milepost 133¼. After rising at 1 in 80 from the Yeovil direction the single line levels out slightly for the station site and then continues to climb at the same gradient, past the automatic half barrier crossing (132 m 3 ch) and through the

205 yd Crewkerne Tunnel (132 m 39 ch to 132 m 48 ch) to the summit. The Down platform is still in existence and the former goods shed is now in private hands.

C.37 Culham

Didcot-Birmingham line between Didcot and Oxford. 56 m 17 ch from Paddington

'Brunel station just the ticket for a rail buff' said the *Daily Telegraph* article on December 3 1981, referring to the BR Property Board's search for a sympathetic occupant for the 1844 buildings on the Up side at Culham station. With a steeply gabled roof, tall chimneys and an extensive awning, the combined booking office and waiting room is one of the few remaining examples of its type.

Culham lies in a loop of the Thames and has viaducts on each side. The service is provided by the Reading-Oxford local trains. It was known as Abingdon Road until the branch to Abingdon opened in 1856 and now comprises just the two platforms and the site of the goods yard which closed in 1965.

C.38 Cwm Branch

Newport-Fishguard line, branch from Coed Ely branch. 2 m 61 ch

The Cwm branch is similar in function to the adjacent line to Coed Ely from which it diverges at Mwyndy Junction. It links the South Wales main line at Llantrisant with the NCB colliery and NSF coking works at Cwm. Although the section as far as Cowbridge Road level crossing (16 ch) is on a down gradient, the route then climbs steeply mostly at 1 in 40 but with short sections of 1 in 34 and 1 in 36.

The lower section of the line, the 1 m 4 ch from Mwyndy Junction to the former Maesaraul Junction, was part of the Ely Valley Railway/GWR line to Brofiskin colliery. The remainder originated with the Llantrisant & Taff Vale Junction Railway, a TVR stratagem to contain GWR expansion and give the former company a route linking Treforest with Llantrisant. The L&TVJR route was opened in 1863 and later leased by and amalgamated with the Taff Vale. From 1875 to 1952 passenger trains ran between Llantrisant and Treforest (and on to Pontypridd), some of the trains working through between Cowbridge and Pontypridd. The line beyond Cwm was closed completely in 1964.

Common Branch Junction (1 m 71 ch) was the site of the connection to Creigiau until the beginning of 1981. Originally this line ran through to Waterhall Junction on the outskirts of Cardiff to give a direct route from the collieries of the Ely Valley area to Cardiff and Penarth docks. In recent years it has been truncated beyond Creigiau quarry from which limestone continued to pass to the works of the steel industry.

The movement of trains on the line between Llantrisant and Cowbridge Road is controlled by the supervisor at the former point. Control of the remainder of the single line is the responsibility of the person in charge at the level crossing and only one train is allowed on the line at any one time.

Traffic on the Cwm branch consists of coal from local collieries passing to Cwm for coking and a heavier outwards movement of coal and coke, some for coke manufacture at the nearby Coed Ely works or at the coke ovens of the BSC at Llanwern. From Monday to Friday of each week six return trips are scheduled from Llantrisant yard, each worked by a Class 37 locomotive.

C.39   Cwmmawr Branch

Newport-Fishguard line, branch from Pembrey. 12 m 43 ch

This single track, coal-carrying line started life as the Burry Port & Gwendreath Valley Railway. It is still known as the BP&GV and still has some unusual characteristics associated with its light railway past. Despite this the route fulfils an important modern traffic function in linking the South Wales main line with the NCB coal washery and opencast disposal centre at Coedbach, near Kidwelly, and then continuing up the valley of the Gwendreath Fawr to the opencast disposal centre at Cwmmawr.

The BP&GV line was opened in 1869 as a successor to early canals and a tramroad which had connected industries in the area with the now closed harbours at Kidwelly and Burry Port. In fact part of the route is laid in a canal bed. After the redoubtable Colonel Stephens had been called in as a consultant a Light Railway Order was obtained in 1909 and a passenger service started. In the years after the GWR take-over in 1922 this provided five trains each way (and an extra late train from Cwmmawr on Saturdays) for the stations at Pembrey Halt, Craiglon Bridge Halt, Pinged Halt, Trimsaran Road, Glyn Abbey, Pontyates, Ponthenry, Pontyberem and Cwmmawr (for Tumble). The passenger service ended on September 21 1953.

Legacies of the route's canal origins are low overbridges and flooding. When the passenger service was running it had to use special vehicles ranging from ex-Metropolitan stock in the early days to later GWR steel-panelled coaches with non-standard low roofs. Today the low bridges prevent the use of modern high-capacity wagons and the motive power on the line is confined to Class 03 diesel shunters with specially cut down cabs. Flooding still interrupts traffic at times and leads to other difficulties such as wet axle boxes.

The junction with the main line is on the Down side at the London end of Pembrey and Burry Port, the branch then curving sharply beneath the main line by means of one of the problem bridges. It remains on the inland side of the main line route as far as Kidwelly Branch Junction (4 m 65 ch) which it approaches by means of a former canal aqueduct which is over 100 ft in length. In addition to the loop at Kidwelly Branch Junction there is a short branch trailing in on the seaward side. This is the stub of the former Kidwelly line and the connection to Coedbach washery and opencast disposal centre.

On the remaining section of the BP&GV there are several open crossings, two operated by the trainmen and a connection, not currently in use, to Carway loading point. The line rises as it goes up the valley and has a section of 1 in 35 as it approaches Cwmmawr where there is a run-round facility and the connection to the coal loading centre. The one train working system is used.

At the end of 1981 about 8,000 tonnes of anthracite coal were passing from Cwmmawr to Coedbach for washing, nearly half then being reforwarded to the domestic smokeless fuel market or for shipment through Swansea docks. The normal service provides for three scheduled trips which average six hours for the return journey because of the maximum line speed of 25 mph and the need to shunt at Coedbach and Cwmmawr. In normal circumstances three locomotives are used, empty wagon trains up the line having two at the front and one at the rear and loaded trains all three locomotives leading. Nine of the Class 03 locomotives are allocated to Swansea Landore depot for working the BP&GV and the trips to Llandovery on the Central Wales line. All are fitted with small headlights.

Parliamentary powers sought in the 1981-2 session were followed by British Railways Board authorisation for the restoration of the Kidwelly-Coedbach link to allow closure of the section of the BP&GV between Pembrey and Burry Port and Kidwelly and the use of main line locomotives and higher capacity wagons. A new single track with a junction on the Up side facing Carmarthen is expected to be in use by 1984. The line to Cwmmawr also has a limited life expectancy for coal extraction there is coming to an end and the output from the opencast site at the lower end of the valley is likely to be moved to the washery by road.

C.40   Cynghordy

Shrewsbury-Llanelli line between Llandrindod Wells and Llandovery. 54 m 55 ch from Craven Arms

Cynghordy is just a conditional stop for the Swansea to Shrewsbury dmus before they make the 1 in 60 climb to Sugar Loaf Tunnel but the Cynghordy Viaduct which they cross on the way is a structure listed as of special architectural and historical interest. The viaduct provides the crossing of the River Bran and comprises 18 spans of 36 ft 6 in semi-circular arches on masonry piers which lift the line to 93 ft above ground level.

C.41   Cynheidre Branch

Newport-Fishguard line, branch from Llanelli West Junction. 6 m 29 ch

The single track Cynheidre branch runs

inland from the South Wales main line at Llanelli to the modern NCB colliery at Cynheidre. It is not the easiest of routes to operate for the curves are numerous and the line soon begins to rise, producing several sections at 1 in 50 and a ruling gradient of 1 in 44. It has both open level crossings with flashing warning lights and a gated crossing operated by the trainmen. These together produce a maximum line speed of 15 mph and a load of 15 wagons for a Class 37 locomotive. The one train working system applies on the line and about an hour is allowed for the trips from Llandeilo Junction yard to Cynheidre where the connection to the colliery is accompanied by a run-round facility. Up to five trips are scheduled between the normal operating hours from 06.00 to 23.00.

Despite a long history this line has never had a public passenger service although at one time a service was operated for colliery workers. The first railway on the route dates back to 1806 when the Carmarthenshire Railway, a 13 m horse tramway from Llanelli to Cross Hands, was opened. This closed in 1844 and the Llanelly & Mynydd Mawr Railway followed in 1883 and was absorbed by the GWR in 1923. At the Llanelli end the L&MMR bridged the GWR main line to reach the docks but the docks extension has now gone, as has the line beyond Cynheidre to Cross Hands.

A paradox of this line is that, in addition to the conventional situation in which locally mined coal is taken down with the gradient towards the main line and the sea, coal is also carried uphill to Cynheidre. This is coal from the new drift mine at Betws, near Ammanford, a small proportion of which moves via Pantyffynnon and Llandeilo Junction to Cynheidre because the capacity of nearer washeries is fully used. The heavy outwards movements reach 6-7,000 tonnes per week, about half of which is taken to Swansea docks for shipment with the remainder passing to inland destinations for the domestic smokeless fuel market.

D.1   Dainton

*Taunton-Penzance line between Newton Abbot and Totnes. 217 m 79 ch from Paddington**

The wooden signal box on the Down side west of the 274 yd tunnel (217 m 63 ch to 217 m 75 ch) used to be Dainton Siding box but the siding has now gone. Nor do the steep banks on either side of the tunnel—up from Aller Junction at gradients between 1 in 57 and 1 in 36 and down towards Totnes at 1 in 55 and 1 in 37—represent the problems to today's motive power that they did in the steam era. The line was built for atmospheric propulsion without much regard for gradient or curvature and this produced the 1 in 36 stretch which is the steepest gradient on a main line in Britain. The atmospheric scheme called for placing an engine house at Dainton and some remains still exist, hidden in the bushes.

D.2   Dauntsey

Swindon-Bristol line between Wootton Bassett Junction and Chippenham. 87 m 67 ch from Paddington

The trackbed of the former Malmesbury branch is still visible on the Up side although now straddled by a wooden building. The Up platform face is also discernible but little else remains of this 'demoted' junction. From 1877 to 1933 Dauntsey was the link between the main line and the abbey town of Malmesbury but the branch was then connected to the Wootton Bassett to Newport line and the southern portion abandoned. Main line trains ceased to call at Dauntsey from January 4 1965.

D.3   Dawlish

Taunton-Penzance line between Exeter and Newton Abbot. 206 m 7 ch from Paddington*

Railway stations get no nearer to the beach than at Dawlish where the Down platform is raised above the sands and all the favourite seaside activities take place alongside the railway line. This platform has only a stone shelter, the more substantial buildings being on the Up side where they have survived fires which have twice engulfed the station. The signal box, which is switched in as required, is raised above the Up platform and at one time had a mesh screen to protect it from shingle, a reminder of the winter gales which can pound the railway in this area.

No trace remains of the atmospheric era pumping station.

It is high tide at Dawlish as this Class 47 heads west with its nine-coach train.

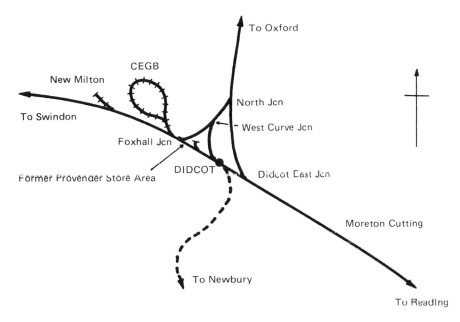

D.4 Dawlish Warren

Taunton-Penzance line between Exeter and Newton Abbot. 204 m 34 ch from Paddington*

For an unpretentious station Dawlish Warren has a slightly complicated history. There was no station at all until the GWR introduced a rail motor service between Exeter and Teignmouth in 1905 and opened Warren Halt, about ¼ m nearer Dawlish than the present station. The latter dates from 1912 but became a wartime closure victim between 1917 and 1919.

If the 1935 scheme for an inland relief route between Dawlish Warren and Newton Abbot had been realised the former might even have been a junction. As it is the two platforms are served by loops and by a local dmu service which gets very busy in the summer months. The Down platform is bare except for the tall, severe brick signal box but the wooden station buildings on the Up side include the premises of the South Devon Railway Museum. There are camping coaches in the former goods yard on the Up side and the Up Passenger Loop there is accompanied by an Up Goods Loop and an UGL extension.

Devonport—see Plymouth

D.5 Didcot

Paddington-Swindon line between Reading and Swindon. 53 m 10 ch from Paddington

Didcot was not one of the original GWR stopping points, its station of four lines and five narrow platforms being brought into use when the line to Oxford opened on June 12 1844. This cramped structure under an overall roof of two different heights lasted some 40 years until a serious fire on the Down side necessitated rebuilding. Further rebuilding came with the quadrupling of the main line to Foxhall Junction in 1932 when a new four-line shed, coaling stage and water tank were also provided.

Today Didcot has an excellent HST service and provides interchange facilities with the Oxford-Reading-Paddington local services. The station approach and main buildings are on the Down side and three platforms serve the two main lines, two relief lines and No 5 Platform Line (which, like the Up Relief, can be worked in both directions). The triangular connection with the line to Oxford lies at the country end of the station. At the other end is a second junction, used by Oxford line fast trains avoiding the station. Enclosed in the smaller triangle is the goods depot and the area of the former provender store which once fed horses all over the GWR territory. Within the larger triangle lies the former locomotive depot, now the home of the Great Western Society Ltd.

Didcot power station is served by 45-wagon coal trains from the Nottingham and Midlands coalfields. They are placed on one of the two reception lines and allowed forward by the CEGB Hopper Plant Controller on to either A or B discharge lines. The slow speed controller on the locomotive then keeps the train speed down to ½ mph at which bottom discharge of the coal is effected by a trip mechanism acting on the hopper wagons. Oil traffic is also dealt with and a 'cripple' siding provided.

West of the CEGB site the Milton Trading Estate lies on the Up side of the line. First given a rail siding in 1915, this former army depot which now occupies a 180-acre site and is provided with 1½ million square feet of covered storage space, is being developed as an inland port and storage/distribution area. A rail connection rises from the site to parallel and then join the Up Goods/Up Relief line. A serious accident occurred on this stretch of the main line in 1955 when an Up excursion train was derailed at a crossover resulting in 11 people being killed and many injured.

Didcot is a busy modern junction with a growing level of business and many ancillary functions, including its refreshment room and its trainmen's relief activities. Its past is kept alive by the adjoining GWS depot and, to some extent, by the station's wooden buildings and dark subway but the bay used by the Didcot, Newbury & Southampton Railway at the London end of No 1 platform is now part of a car park and the through coaches which once worked from it are now just a memory.

D.6   Dilton Marsh

Bristol-Portsmouth line between Westbury and Salisbury. 111 m 11 ch from Paddington*

This is one of the GWR's late halts, opened June 1 1937 and given a new lease of life by local housing developments. The two platforms, short wooden affairs with a tiny shelter, are staggered about 40 yds apart and are served by some of the Salisbury-Westbury services. At one time tickets were issued by a local resident as a GWR agent.

Dinas—see Treherbert Branch

Dinas Powys—see Barry Branch

Dingle Road—see Penarth Branch

D.7   Dinmore Tunnels

Shrewsbury-Newport line between Craven Arms and Hereford. 42 m 67 ch from Craven Arms

Curiously this is a double line route although the two 1,051 yd tunnels (42 m 67 ch to 43 m 36 ch) are both single bores and at separate levels.

The Shrewsbury & Hereford Railway was opened on November 6 1853 as a single line with provision for doubling. However, uncertainties about the geology in the area of Dinmore led to a decision that it would be safer to build a single line tunnel and add a separate one later if traffic warranted it. The second tunnel, on the Up line, was eventually added in 1893 with a 1 in 134 gradient compared with the 1 in 100 of the original, resulting in neither entrance being level with its neighbour at either end of the tunnels.

Dockyard—see Plymouth

D.8   Dolau

Shrewsbury-Llanelli line between Craven Arms and Llandrindod Wells. 25 m 26 ch from Craven Arms

Dolau is a conditional stop for the Shrewsbury to Swansea dmus after their descent from Llangynllo summit along the edge of the Radnor Forest and on to the long straight section which leads to Pen-y-bont. Of the two platforms only the Down is now used and this is preceded by an open level crossing with a 10 mph speed limit.

D.9   Dolcoath

Taunton-Penzance line between Redruth and Camborne. 312 m 52 ch from Paddington*

Comprises a ground frame for the Milk Marketing Board siding and, 10 ch west, an automatic half barrier crossing.

D.10   Dowlais Branch

Rhymney-Cardiff line, branch from Ystrad Mynach South. 11 m 43 ch

Another of the South Wales single track freight only lines, this time from Ystrad Mynach to Nelson and then up the Taff

Bargoed valley to Cwmbargoed and Dowlais (Furnace Top). It serves disposal points for NCB and privately exploited opencast coal at Cwmbargoed, sources of power station coal, and the BSC ingot moulds works at Dowlais, the one surviving remnant of the once massive iron industry of the Merthyr Tydfil-Dowlais complex. Appendix distances start at 13 m 41 ch at the junction with a change of mileage from 15 m 1 ch to 12 m 41 ch on the section to Nelson and Llancaiach (13 m 36 ch) where the line to Ocean and Taff Merthyr collieries diverges. Cwmbargoed lies at 20 m 40 ch and Dowlais Cae Harris at 22 m 44 ch.

The line was built jointly by the GW and Rhymney Railways and opened in 1876. For the GWR it was a branch to Dowlais from Nelson on their Pontypool Road-Neath line and for the Rhymney a branch from Ystrad Mynach. The 1930s train service on the former consisted of five trains each way and four Saturdays Only services and there were intermediate stops at Trelewis Platform, Bedlinog and Cwmbargoed. Passenger train services were withdrawn in 1964.

There is a gruelling climb from Nelson, largely at 1 in 35 or 1 in 62, as the line ascends the side of the valley to reach a plateau at Cwmbargoed before descending at 1 in 46: 1 in 69 to Dowlais. The junction points at Nelson are operated by train guards in liaison with the Ystrad Mynach signalman who also issues the train staff or ticket for the section as far as Cwmbargoed. Movements on to Dowlais are controlled by the BR 'person in charge' at Cwmbargoed.

At the time of writing the main traffic flow was between Cwmbargoed and Aberthaw power station with up to four trains of coal—with Class 37 traction and 35 mgr wagons—scheduled each day and more paths available at weekends. For the spasmodic inwards scrap to Dowlais and the completed moulds outwards a twice weekly trip is booked from Radyr yard.

Drayton Green—see Greenford Branch

D.11 Droitwich Spa

Worcester-Birmingham lines, junction of the routes via Bromsgrove and via Hartlebury. 126 m 10 ch from Paddington

Oxford, Worcester & Wolverhampton trains started serving Droitwich in 1852 and it still has an excellent service from trains on the two routes between Worcester and Birmingham, even if the days of main line expresses from Paddington to Shrewsbury or Wolverhampton are now just a memory. The once important salt traffic no longer passes but there is a coal concentration depot which has its own diesel shunter and still uses the old GWR weighbridge. There are also Up and Down Goods loops plus an Up Refuge Siding sited between the station and the boundary with the LMR at 130 m 40 ch.

The station lies at the Worcester end of the junction and has its main buildings on the Up side and just a simple shelter on the Down. The signal box is a large one with nearly 80 levers and stands at the junction near the point where the Worcester and Birmingham Canal crosses beneath the railway. Absolute block signalling applies on the double line to Hartlebury and track circuit block on the single line (but double junction) which leads to the main line at Stoke Works where GWR 'Down' changes to MR 'Up'.

D.12 Drump Lane

Taunton-Penzance line between Truro and Redruth. 309 m 35 ch from Paddington*

Drump Lane signal box stands on the Down side on the approach to Redruth from Truro and is now confined to signalling main line movements since the once busy goods yard closed to rail traffic. The shed still stands and there are Down Refuge sidings but the Up side private siding has gone.

D.13 Dunball

Bristol-Taunton line between Weston-super-Mare and Bridgwater. 149 m 21 ch from Paddington

On the Up side at Dunball it is still possible to spot the route of the 36 ch branch which led across the A38 to a wharf on the River Parrett. The passenger station lay between the bridge over King's Sedgemoor Drain and the cutting but has now completely disappeared.

The wharf line originated in 1844 as a horse tramway built by local coal merchants. The B&E took over operation in 1849 and later obtained powers to improve the wharf over which coal imports from South Wales were to pass for many years. At the time of closure in March 1962 access was via Dunball Pottery ground frame on the Down side and special regulations existed for crossing the main road to the wharf. These provided for a red flag to warn road traffic and limited loads to 25 wagons when propelling; only Class 1361 and 1366 locomotives plus 0-4-0T No 1338 were allowed to shunt on the wharf.

D.14   Dunhampstead

Birmingham-Bristol line between Barnt Green and Cheltenham. 62 m 12 ch from Derby

Dunhampstead, still with a level crossing, was one of two stations on the MR line avoiding Worcester. The other was Droitwich Road and both lost their passenger services as early as 1855 but continued as goods stations until 1949/1952. Both sites can still be spotted.

D.15   Durston

Bristol-Taunton line between Bridgwater and Cogload Junction. 153 m 60 ch from Paddington

The remains of the passenger station buildings at Durston date from 1853 when the Bristol & Exeter Railway opened its branch to Yeovil. The station remained quite busy for many years and even after the cut-off route linked Athelney and Cogload direct, local trains continued to work via the old single line and Lyng Halt and run into and out of Durston on the Down side at the London end. There was a bay line here and the old trackbed can still be seen although passenger services ended at Lyng Halt on June 15 1964 and at Durston on October 5 of that year.

E.1   Ealing Broadway

Paddington-Swindon line between Paddington and Southall. 5 m 56 ch from Paddington

Ealing Broadway is a modern station and a major interchange point between the WR suburban services and London Transport's Central and District lines. The former, to North Acton and then south to Wood Lane and Shepherd's Bush, originated as the Ealing & Shepherd's Bush Railway, a First World War infant planned originally to create a new GWR terminus at Shepherd's Bush. Ealing Broadway is also the starting point for services on the Greenford Branch which once continued on to Ruislip and Gerrard's Cross.

With its ticket office at street level and part of a modern development which stands on a concrete raft over the main line, the station comprises an island and (two) outer platforms with shelters. Beyond the platform serving the Up Relief line is the LT portion including the Shepherd's Bush line bay. The Greenford branch trains reverse via a siding between the main and relief lines at the London end of this busy commuter station.

Ebbw Vale—see Western Valleys

E.2   Eckington

Birmingham-Bristol line between Barnt Green and Cheltenham. 74 m 51 ch from Derby

This former station site, closed to traffic in 1965, lies between the River Avon bridge to the north and a group of interesting overbridges to the south. The hardware of the modern railway includes the Up Goods Loop, ground frame and crossovers and the remnants from the past the old goods shed, station buildings and footbridge. North of the station site an attractive stone retaining wall protects the Down line track.

Eggesford—see Barnstaple Branch

E.3   Evershot Tunnel

Westbury-Weymouth line between Yeovil Pen Mill and Dorchester West. 149 m 49 ch from Paddington*

The 308 yd tunnel (149 m 49 ch to 149 m 63 ch), at the end of the long, steepening climb from Yeovil, carries the Weymouth line through the top ridge of the Dorset Downs. The last 2 m are at 1 in 53/51 and once used to represent a stiff challenge to the steaming of heavily laden excursion trains heading for the popular seaside resort. The former station stood on a short level section at the Weymouth end of the tunnel.

E.4   Evesham

Oxford-Hereford line between Moreton-in-Marsh and Worcester. 106 m 55 ch from Paddington

A few hours at Evesham in the 1930s would have been full of fascination for the railway enthusiast. On the Great Western route there would have been the all-stations trains between Oxford and Worcester taking some 2¼ hours, the 'Kidderminster, Droitwich Spa, Hereford, Malvern and Worcester to London

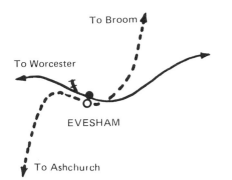

Express' services, 'one class only' locals to and from Honeybourne and such occasional excitements as a Smethwick Junction to Weston-super-Mare through service. The passenger trains running Ashchurch-Evesham-Birmingham were fairly routine on the Midland line but all sorts of freight got sent this way to avoid the Lickey incline.

The first railway to reach Evesham was that of the Oxford, Worcester & Wolverhampton company which arrived from the west on May 1 1852 and completed its route on to Wolvercot Junction and Oxford in the following year. The Midland probed up from Ashchurch in 1864 and completed 'The Loop' to Redditch (and on to Birmingham) four years later, pasenger services ending in 1963 and just failing to complete their century. Although under the pooling arrangements the LMS station master controlled both stations from 1931 onwards, there was no direct junction between the routes of the two companies serving Evesham.

The town of Evesham lies in a loop of

Evesham station looking west towards Worcester.

the River Avon which the WR route crosses by two plain girder bridges. Within the section between the two the MR route from Ashchurch crossed from the west bank of the river to a station alongside the GWR one and then passed over the main line on its way north to Broom where connections were made for the line to Stratford-on-Avon. The Midland station buildings still exist at Evesham, their simple red brick style harmonising well with that of the main WR buildings which are on the Down side. The modern design WR signal box stands at the country end of the passing loop near the entrance to the goods yard, once busy with cartage vehicles loading produce from the farms and market gardens in the Vale of Evesham to fitted vans heading for London and the provincial markets.

E.5 Exeter

Exeter St David's is on the Taunton-Penzance line 193 m 72 ch from Paddington*, Exeter St Thomas is on the same line 194 m 66 ch from Paddington* and Exeter Central lies on the route from Salisbury at 171 m 18 ch from Waterloo

Exeter is a major railway centre served by the West of England main line and by the former SR route from Waterloo via Salisbury. In addition to being the rail gateway to Devon and Cornwall it has branches to Barnstaple and Exmouth, commuter business on several of its routes and a very busy summer holiday traffic activity.

Exeter's standing as a port and as Devon's administrative centre made the building of the Bristol & Exeter Railway, to provide the link with the Great Western's route to London, a very logical development. The B&E's trains arrived on May 1 1844 and two years later, helped by

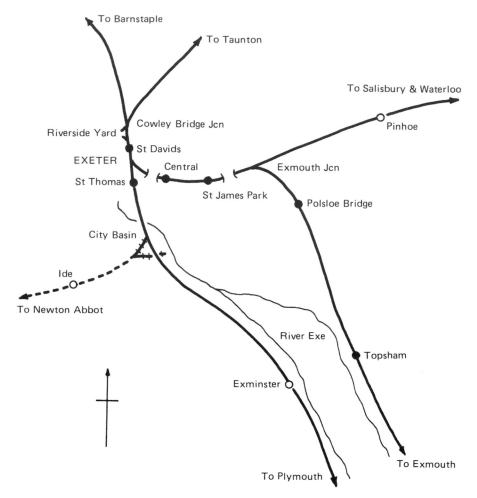

the promise of funds from the B&E, the GWR and the Bristol & Gloucester, the South Devon Railway secured its Act for a line westwards to Plymouth. In two more years the first section of this was opened but with the novelty of atmospheric propulsion which Brunel had swept into existence and which had to be abandoned amid much acrimony after another two years.

This was a period when Exeter figured in much of the railway promotion in the southern part of the country. Rival schemes planned to reach it from the London direction, and from Falmouth two different routes promised to fend off the packet port's competition from Southampton by giving a rail service to Exeter and London. It was also an era of incredible double dealing in which the

London & South Western seems frequently to have played an unsavoury part. The 'Five Kings' agreement to end the GWR/LSWR rivalries in 1845 was meaningless by 1846 when three schemes to get to Exeter were rejected by Parliament. Four more were presented in the following year but then submerged in the post Railway Mania lack of capital. When the matter surfaced again the LSW dithered between the coastal and central routes and was split by internal dissention so that 1856 had arrived before the Yeovil & Exeter got its Act and it was 1860 before LSW trains steamed into the old gloomy Queen Street station (later named Central after rebuilding in 1933).

The 1860s were another decade of railway development at Exeter. Trains from the Exmouth branch began running into Queen Street in 1861 and, to enable LSW trains to run through to the Exeter & Crediton line, the link on to St David's was opened on February 1 1862 and work started on a new station there to handle the increasing volume of traffic. This lasted until the present station was built just before the First World War and incorporated the main frontage from the station opened in July 1864.

Further developments at Exeter were the SDR branch to City Basin in 1867 and then the Exeter Railway's line opened in 1903 to complete the Teign Valley route to Newton Abbot via Heathfield. Three halts were opened east of Queen Street in 1906 and the LSW also proposed a direct route to Cowley Bridge to cut out the enforced stop at St David's. This was at a period of intense competition and high activity when the GWR expresses from Plymouth might pass a competing LSW train on the approaches to St David's, both heading for London but actually passing one another in opposite directions. The same thing might happen with a train of stone from Meldon Quarry and one of vans filled with Cornish broccoli or potatoes while, in addition to the many through services, there were trains to be divided, vehicles to be added or removed and banking engines to be worked up to the LSW station and back to the GWR one.

Although slimmed down and altered, Exeter has not sacrificed much of its railway network. All the lines are still there

A Class 46 and its train head west from Exeter in 1971. Sadly, the South Devon water tower has now gone.

with the exception of the Teign Valley route and the goods avoiding lines, and the two main stations still deal with a large volume of business, although most of it is concentrated on St David's. The biggest loss is at St Thomas which lost its overall roof but retained a portion of its SDR frontage. This was a busy station in the SDR era and passengers were encouraged to use St Thomas in preference to St David's so that the South Devon could avoid sharing its receipts with the Bristol & Exeter, but now only a few local trains stop there.

On the approach to St David's from the London direction there is a Down Goods Loop after Cowley Bridge Junction (192 m 52 ch) and then, on the Up side, the West of England Division's only marshalling yard, Exeter Riverside. Preceding the station is Exeter Middle crossing and signal box (193 m 62 ch) with the goods yard, NCL shed and locomotive stabling point lying between the main line and the River Exe which runs slightly to the west and crosses beneath the main line just beyond the station.

St David's comprises three platforms served by three Up lines, two Down lines and a Down Through line. Two of the platforms are islands, the central one generally dealing with Waterloo, Barnstaple and Exmouth line trains. All the main facilities are on the Down side and these include waiting rooms, refreshment rooms and a travel centre, one of the first of its kind to be opened. The Area Manager has his offices in the first floor accommodation, once occupied by the District Traffic Superintendent, and there

are staff signing on point offices and parcels facilities nearby. The GPO depot stands just outside the station.

Exeter Central is reached via Exeter West (where the 194 m 4 ch via Bristol mileage becomes 172 m from Waterloo) and a climb through the 184 yd St David's Tunnel (171 m 53 ch to 171 m 61 ch). The street level frontage typifies its 1933 building style and from the ticket office steps descend to the long Up and Down platforms, with a Down Passenger Loop between. Presflo wagons are dealt with in the goods yard on the Up side and the line then heads out via St James Park (originally Lion's Halt) at 170 m 72 ch, through the 262 yd Blackboy Tunnel (170 m 44 ch to 170 m 56 ch) to Exmouth Junction (170 m 21 ch) and then on past Poltimore Sidings ground frame (168 m 69 ch) to Pinhoe level crossing (168 m 39 ch) where the route becomes single line and the platforms still mark the former station site. There are grain sidings at Pinhoe, and at Exmouth Junction both wagon shops and a coal concentration depot. All along here the atmosphere is Southern, from the lattice signal posts to the almost overwhelming use of concrete.

All the freight depots in the Exeter area are serviced by trips from Riverside Yard in addition to its work of marshalling traffic to and from the west. This includes the bitumen siding and the two-line Texaco oil terminal at City Basin (195 m 16 ch) where the signal box controls the Up side connection with the stub of the

The east end of Exeter St Davids station showing the lift towers.

former Exeter Railway from which a reversal is necessary to the connection under the main line.

There is much to see at Exeter. Despite its decline from the days when it had two signal boxes and housed the offices of the SR's Western Division Superintendent, Central is full of atmosphere and can come to life again in the peaks with an Exmouth train in the bay and a main line service waiting to head down the 1 in 37 gradient to St David's. The latter's frontage is impressive and the footbridge inside makes a good way to see the canopy arcade in true perspective. South Devon reminders still exist and the Down side frontage at St Thomas is worth the difficulties of getting to see it.

E.6   Exminster

*Taunton-Penzance line between Exeter and Dawlish. 198 m 59 ch from Paddington**

Once a station served by Up and Down loops and site of one of the water troughs which made non-stop runs to Plymouth possible, Exminster is now just a block post with a Down Goods Loop. The wooden signal box stands on the Down side and opposite is the old coal yard and the station house, the latter quite a good example of South Devon Railway design. Refuge sidings exist on both sides of the line.

E.7   Exmouth Branch

Waterloo-Exeter line, branch from Exmouth Junction. 9 m 30 ch

The former SR branch to Exmouth leaves the main line east of Exeter at Exmouth Junction and is single throughout, except for the first short stretch from the junction and for the passing loop at Topsham. For the most part it follows the east bank of the broad estuary of the Exe and provides a pleasant way of viewing this attractive holiday area. The coal and freight business has now gone, and pilchard specials are no longer rushed to London, but a considerable volume of local and holiday passenger business is still catered for by the dmu service which operates in formations of up to six cars.

The route originated in an 1855 scheme for a broad gauge line from the South Devon Railway at Exminster, but LSW wooing prior to completion brought a change to narrow gauge and to using that company's Queen Street station. The new branch was opened on May 1 1861 and absorbed by the LSW in 1866. As the holiday habit caught on and Exeter expanded both commuting and holiday traffic grew. Freight and coal traffic was substantial with movements via the docks at Exmouth and over the quay and private sidings at Topsham. In the First World War the route was doubled as far as Topsham but it has now reverted to its original status and lost its freight facilities altogether at the end of 1967. A partial compensation is the new single platform station at Exmouth, on the site of the traditional four-platform station which it shares with the local bus station.

Excluding St James Park on the main line portion from Exeter Central there are five intermediate stations on the branch proper. The first, Polsloe Bridge (34 ch) still has two concrete unit platforms but only the Up one has track. Topsham (4 m 23 ch) has a level crossing and signal box and shows much of its ancestry in the station buildings and goods shed. On the winding, estuarial section Exton (5 m 67 ch), Lympstone Commando ('Only passengers having business at CTCRM may alight') (6 m 20 ch) and Lympstone (7 m 28 ch) all comprise a single platform plus shelter. Gradients are frequent but modest and

there is a substantial bridge where the River Clyst joins the estuary. Little can be seen of the Topsham quay branch or of the route on from Exmouth to Budleigh Salterton.

A summer service of over 20 trains each way is operated, most working through or having connections to Exeter St David's and some working to and from Barnstaple. The only freight is the occasional load to or from the RN depot served by Newcourt ground frame (2 m 71 ch). Acceptance lever working applies on the section to Topsham and one train working on the remainder of the route to Exmouth.

Exton—see Exmouth Branch

F.1   Falmouth Branch

Taunton-Penzance line, branch from Truro. 11 m 21 ch from Penwithers Junction

Standing on a peninsula which makes a calm estuary of Carrick Roads, Falmouth has had seafaring traditions since the earliest times and is still the largest Cornish port. It was local anxiety to protect Falmouth's status as a packet port used by the mail contract vessels that led to an early interest in railways, an interest which quickened when Southampton got a rail link with London and thus a distinct advantage in getting letters from the steamers to the capital. An early scheme of 1835 was rejected by Parliament but interest revived as the B&E reached Exeter and the South Devon scheme brought Brunel's rails further and further west.

There were two rival schemes to link Falmouth with Exeter, the 'Central' route via Launceston and the 'Coastal' to Plymouth and the SDR. The former had LSW support and the latter that of the GW and B&E interests, one was backed by the Liberals and the other by the Tories, and the factions battled with one another with all the rhetoric and manoeuvring which typified this period of Railway Mania. In the end the 'Coastal' Cornwall Railway scheme triumphed and secured its Act on August 3 1846, but Falmouth was still a long way from getting its railway. There were riots when the first sod was cut at Truro in 1847 for the local populace feared the effect of more mouths to feed when the navvies arrived, but they need not have worried for the contractor for the Falmouth to Truro section was unable to fulfil his obligations and the whole scheme went into a financial limbo.

Eventually financial support from the GW, B&E and SDR group enabled the main line to be opened as far as Truro and then fresh powers to be sought for the Falmouth section. These were obtained in 1861 and construction commenced, the southern end involving a new approach into Falmouth to afford a link to the new docks which were being built at the same period. The route at last opened on August 24 1863 as a single line from Truro, running parallel with the main line to Penwithers Junction and then across the Newham line on the level and under the protection of an early interlocking system. The dock connection at Falmouth came into use in 1864 and a new junction at Penwithers took over from the two separate lines in 1893. The link to Newham was changed to connect with the Falmouth branch instead of with the West Cornwall main line.

The country traversed by the Falmouth branch is similar to that of the main line to Truro and it necessitated eight Brunel timber viaducts, bringing the Cornwall Railway's total up to 42. From 1923 onwards the original structures were replaced, in four cases by embankments, to leave the route with four viaducts, two tunnels and four intermediate stations. The first of these is the 491 yd Sparnick Tunnel (302 m 68 ch to 303 m 10 ch), followed by the 252 yd Carnon Viaduct (304 m 26 ch) and then Perranwell station (304 m 78 ch). Still heading south-west the line passes over the 113 yd Perran Viaduct (305 m 70 ch), through the 374 yds of Perran Tunnel (306 m 23 ch to 306 m 40 ch) and over the 215 yd Ponsanooth Viaduct (306 m 74 ch) and then turns south to the modest station at Penryn (309 m 9 ch). Ponsanooth is the highest of the viaducts and College Wood (309 m 32 ch), at 318 yds, the longest. Next comes the 1925 halt at Penmere (311 m 13 ch) and then The Dell (312 m 9 ch) which was brought into use on December 7 1970 to replace Falmouth proper (at 312 m 46 ch). It was retained when the single platform Falmouth station was reopened on May 5 1975.

The branch dmu set worked ten services in each direction in the 1982-3 timetable, with a Sunday service during the holiday months only. The line operates on the basic railway principles under the one train working system and with all work carried out by the train crew. The staff is released by the Truro signalman and then taken from an auxiliary instrument on the bay platform at Truro for issue to the driver, with the procedure being reversed for Up trains. The loop and exchange siding with the dock company's premises are the only freight facilities remaining. Gradients are mostly in the 1 in 60 to 1 in 80 range and the line's two peaks are at Sparnick and milepost 307¾.

F.2   Feniton

Waterloo-Exeter line between Honiton and Exeter. 159 m 24 ch from Waterloo

Feniton consists of a Down platform plus a level crossing at the country end, both under the control of the crossing keeper. It is served by the Salisbury-Exeter trains, although some of the afternoon ones omit this stop.

Now notable for its flower display, the site was once the junction for the branch line to Sidmouth and was called Sidmouth Junction at the time of the closure of the branch and was its main line interchange point in 1967. On re-opening of the main line station in 1971 it took its original name of Feniton.

The re-opening was just a hundred years after the third attempt to give Sidmouth a railway. It succeeded to give, in 1874, a route down the Otter valley to Tipton St Johns (junction for the route to Budleigh Salterton and Exmouth) and then a series a stiff gradients before arrival at the terminus on the outskirts of Sidmouth. The trackbed of the branch is still visible at Feniton, at the London end of the station beyond the large yard area.

Ferry Road Branch—see Penarth Branch

F.3   Ferryside

Newport-Fishguard line between Llanelli and Carmarthen. 238 m 47 ch from Paddington*

Through Ferryside the South Wales main line runs alongside the scenic estuary of the River Towy, with the picturesque Llanstephan village and its castle just across the water. The station itself consists of Up and Down platforms, each with a shelter, and a signal box which also controls the barrier crossing. There is a footbridge by the crossing and also a short siding on the Up side at the Carmarthen end of the station. The service is provided by the Swansea-Carmarthen/Milford Haven/Pembroke Dock trains, but not all call at Ferryside.

F.4 Ffairfach

Shrewsbury-Llanelli line between Llandeilo and Llanelli. 17 m 19 ch from Llandeilo Junction

This single platform, conditional stop for trains of the Shrewsbury-Swansea service lies at the foot of a 1 in 105 climb which lifts the line from the narrow wooded valley of the Cennen to that of the Loughor river. It is the site of a double half barrier crossing and there is a 30 mph line speed restriction between the 15¼ and 17¼ mileposts.

Filton—see Bristol

F.5 Finstock

Oxford-Hereford line between Oxford and Kingham. 75 m 10 ch from Paddington

Long before the present sleeper platform-plus-shelter halt opened in 1934 there were sidings about 15 ch nearer Oxford for ironstone traffic transferred from the 2 ft 6 in gauge Fawler Quarry tramway. Now just four weekday trains call, two Up and two Down.

F.6 Fishguard Line

Newport-Fishguard line, section from Clarbeston Road (271 m 9 ch) to Fishguard Harbour (288 m 18 ch). 15 m 37 ch

When the South Wales Railway was authorised on August 4 1845 to extend railway communication westwards from Gloucester across South Wales, with Brunel as its engineer, Irish traffic through a port at Fishguard was one of the main goals. However, the economic consequences of the Irish famine caused a change of plan. What was to have been the Haverfordwest branch from Clarbeston Road became the main line and was extended to Neyland, on the Milford Haven seaway. The section to Fishguard, with its construction work part completed, was abandoned for over half a century.

In 1895/9 the North Pembrokeshire & Fishguard Railway was opened from Clunderwen (264 m 22 ch), some 7 m east of Clarbeston Road, to Fishguard and Goodwick, acquiring in the process a moribund railway from Clunderwen to Rosebush. The NPFR had plans for Irish traffic, but also courted the attention of the LNWR at nearby Carmarthen.

To fend off the LNWR, and to improve its own Irish services then operating out of Neyland (or New Milford as it was known at the time), the GWR took over the NPFR mainly for its section beyond

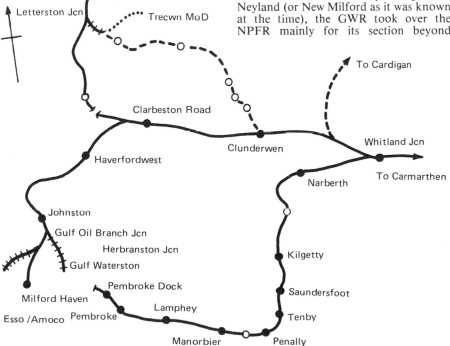

The Sealink service from Fishguard to Rosslare is provided by the Stena Normandica.

Letterston. The original Clarbeston-Fishguard project was then resurrected and the new route was opened in 1906 in conjunction with a steamer service to Rosslare, County Wexford. The final ½ m of the route, the harbour and the steamers were run by the GWR on behalf of the Fishguard & Rosslare Railways & Harbours Company, a concern which still exists today with its Welsh operations in the hands of Sealink UK Ltd. FRRH harbour and rail interests in Ireland were originally run for them by the Great Southern & Western Railway, now by Coras Iompair Eireann.

The NPFR route is no more, except for the first 20 ch (283 m 30 ch to 283 m 10 ch) at the Letterston end which leads to the 2 m 15 ch single track freight line to the Ministry of Defence establishment at Trecwn. However the change of mileage at Letterston Junction from 281 m 58 ch to 283 m 30 ch is a reminder that the NPFR was responsible for the final section of today's line. It is, in fact, made up of the original earthworks for the first mile or so, then the 1906 section to join the NPFR at Letterston Junction, then the latter's 1899 route and a final half mile to Fishguard Harbour also dating from 1906.

Clarbeston Road station is unstaffed and has platforms, with waiting accommodation, on the Up and Down lines. Reflecting Brunel's original intentions, the Fishguard line continues straight ahead (and becomes single) while the Haverfordwest and Milford Haven line, which today carries the majority of the traffic, curves off to the south west. Movements are controlled by a typical GWR 1900s style signal box with electric token working applying to Letterston Junction. The same system applies on the

section towards Fishguard and the two sections can be worked as one when the Letterston box is switched out.

Between Clarbeston Road and Letterston Junction there are signs of the former double track and of the intermediate stations at Wolf's Castle Halt, Welsh Hook Halt and Mathry Road which closed when the local train service ended in 1964. The line passes through an area of rocky outcrops, with some deep cuttings and the 242 yd Spittal Tunnel (274 m 40 ch to 274 m 51 ch). Letterston lost its passenger trains back in 1937, along with the stations on the NPFR route, and it now consists of the junction facing Fishguard, the passing loop and an Up Refuge Siding, and the timber framed, flat roof signal box. Beyond the junction there is evidence of an easier graded Up line which was planned in the early days when Fishguard Harbour cherished hopes of capturing the Atlantic liner traffic.

Beyond Letterston Junction the line climbs briefly and then drops down to Fishguard with long sections at 1 in 50. Jordanston Halt is no more but the two-platform station at Fishguard and Goodwick (287 m 50 ch) is still extant, although its only use in recent years has been for Motorail trains. There is a Car Ferry Loop here and both lines through the station are signalled for two-way working. On the Up side is a coal and goods yard, there is a catwalk for motorists alongside the car carrier vehicle siding, a GWR signal box on the Down platform and some engineer's sidings.

Fishguard Harbour station is built on a shelf of rock blasted from the steep cliff which rises behind it. The layout now consists of one face of an island platform with runround facilities and a continuation line on to the breakwater. The line along the seaward face of the platform is used as a siding for berthing the oil tank cars which fuel the Rosslare ship. Parts of the station recall the 1906 opening and a

GWR roll of honour for the First World War is still proudly displayed. Newer structures house customs and immigration facilities and a recent addition is the block containing buffet and waiting room, toilets and the Travel Centre.

In common with most other ports, Fishguard has witnessed a growth in the proportion of roadborne cargoes and its rail layout has contracted correspondingly. The regular vessel on the Sealink service to and from Rosslare is the chartered MV *Stena Normandica*, a distinctive Swedish multi-purpose ship built in 1974 and of 5,443 gross registered tons.

The final stretch of line between Fishguard and Goodwick and Fishguard Harbour, which is operated on the one train working principle, was repositioned in June/July 1982 to provide more room for road vehicle operations between the railway and the harbour.

The train service at Clarbeston Road is that applicable to the Haverfordwest-Johnston-Milford Haven section, trains on the Fishguard section being locomotive-hauled and limited, almost entirely, to connections with the two ship sailings in each 24 hours. Some of the carriage workings are advertised to carry passengers so as to provide a local service but the overall pattern is that of a Down train at 02.00 from Paddington throughout the year and connecting with the evening sailing and through trains or links with the Swansea HSTs depending upon the time of year.

There is a morning freight service from Llandeilo Junction and back, with a trip to Trecwn incorporated in the same working. Plans exist to develop this into an air braked Speedlink feeder service.

F.7   Flax Bourton

Bristol-Taunton line between Bristol and Weston-super-Mare. 124 m 38 ch from Paddington

The former station, closed to passengers on the first site in 1893 and on the second in 1963, is now just a collection of derelict passenger and freight buildings on the Up side. However, a ground frame connection still exists to the holding siding and three track oil storage depot and the trailing crossover in the main line. On the London side of the station site there is a cutting, a 110 yd tunnel (123 m 61 ch to 123 m 66 ch), five overbridges along the summit section and the modern bridge crossing of the Ashton by-pass.

F.8   Fowey (Carne Point) Branch

Taunton-Penzance line, branch from Lostwithiel. 4 m 66 ch

From the junction points at 277 m 43 ch this single, freight only, line runs to Carne Point on the outskirts of Fowey and is busy with the movements of china clay which are loaded to ship there. It did start

Unloading clay from rail wagon to ship at Fowey in 1964.

life as a mineral line to Carne Point on June 1 1869 and although a passenger service operated over a rebuilt route into Fowey proper from 1895 to 1965, the line has now reverted to its original length and purpose.

The branch plays a vital part in BR's carryings of the output of English China Clays and its use to relieve pressure on the firm's own port at Par was part of an agreement which led to the former rail route from St Blazey to Fowey via Pinnock Tunnel becoming an ECC road. The line is worked on the No Signalman Token system and has an open level crossing at the former intermediate station, Golant (281 m 11 ch). It is subject to an overall line speed restriction of 30 mph.

F.9   Freshford

Westbury-Bristol line between Bradford-on-Avon and Bathampton Junction. 4 m 70 ch from Bathampton Junction

A small station beside the River Avon and comprising just short platforms, one with a shelter, and a footbridge.

F.10   Frome

Reading-Taunton line between Westbury and Castle Cary. 115 m 44 ch from Paddington*

The Wilts, Somerset & Weymouth Railway route reached Frome from Westbury on October 7 1850 and a single line was pushed forward to Yeovil six years later. From 1906 Frome became a station on the West of England main line but was served via a loop after the short avoiding line between Clink Road Junction and Blatch-

bridge Junction was brought into use in 1933. The line from Frome to the North Somerset coalfield was opened as far as Radstock on November 14 1854.

At the London end of the loop there is a Down Refuge Siding and Frome North signal box controls access to the truncated Bristol & North Somerset line and to the engineer's and traffic sidings beyond the junction. The single line of the passenger loop, worked by acceptance lever block, then heads on to the station, built by Hannaford in the Brunel tradition. The wooden canopy covers the portion where the staggered platforms overlap to provide the last surviving example of a GWR overall roof station. The station buildings are on the Up side and mainly of wood and, happily, have recently received the benefit of a restoration programme. There was a bay at the London end and a goods yard at the country end, the dock and mixed construction shed of the latter still remaining. The small yard on the Down side of the station is a discharge point for Mobil tank wagons.

Furze Platt—see Marlow Branch

G.1   Garth

Shrewsbury-Llanelli line between Llandrindod Wells and Llandovery. 42 m 69 ch from Craven Arms

Garth was once a passing loop but is now just a conditional stop for the Shrewsbury-Swansea dmus, which use the former Up platform.

The last surviving example of a GWR overall roof, photographed at Frome as repair work starts.

Gilfach Fargoed—see Rhymney Branch

G.2   Glascoed Branch

Shrewsbury-Newport line, branch from Little Mill Junction. 1 m 64 ch

This is a single track, freight-only line serving the Royal Ordnance Factory at Glascoed. It is, in fact, the stub of the former Pontypool Road to Monmouth line opened in 1856-7 by the Coleford, Monmouth, Usk & Pontypool Railway primarily to carry iron from the Forest of Dean to the iron industry in Monmouthshire. The route was worked by the Newport, Abergavenny & Hereford Railway and eventually became part of the GWR when the section to Usk enjoyed a basic service of seven weekday trains plus two on Sundays. Passenger services between Pontypool Road and Monmouth ceased in 1955 and freight working was cut back to Usk, the further cut back to Glascoed coming ten years later. Passenger trains for the workers at ROF Glascoed had continued until 1961.

The junction at Little Mill faces Newport and the signal box there, a 'fringe' box for the Newport panel, controls train movements on the single line on which only one train is permitted at any one time. A freight working for a Class 37 locomotive is scheduled Mondays to Fridays from Severn Tunnel Junction to Glascoed and back.

G.3   Gloucester

Birmingham-Bristol line. 93 m 18 ch from Derby and 114 m 4 ch from Paddington

The first railway in Gloucester was the Gloucester & Cheltenham Railway, a horse-worked plate tramway running north from the Berkeley Canal Basin. The canal itself had been opened in 1827 to enable Gloucester to capitalise on its position on the River Severn and develop its docks by avoiding the worst effects of the estuarial tides by substituting a canal passage for the difficult portion of the river down to Sharpness.

Part of the tramway was absorbed by the Birmingham & Gloucester Railway when it opened the portion of its route from Tramway Junction to Lansdown Junction, Cheltenham, on November 4 1840. Next to arrive was the Bristol & Gloucester on July 8 1844, with the GWR completing the Cheltenham & Great Western Union's line from Swindon on May 12 1845. The latter was to have been the springboard for the advance of the broad gauge on Birmingham but when the GWR hesitated over the terms for acquiring the other two Gloucester lines the Midland jumped in and was eventually to bring its standard gauge trains to Bristol.

All this produced a highly complicated situation at Gloucester where the Great Western owned the line from Standish Junction to its own Gloucester station and to Barnwood Junction. It also owned, by repurchase of the C&GWU rights in 1845, the section between Tramway Junction and Lansdown Junction, but only as trustees for the Midland Railway at the Gloucester end! After GWR trains started running to St James' at Cheltenham in 1847, a short new line was laid from the Gloucester station to a new station on the

The diesel maintenance depot at Gloucester.

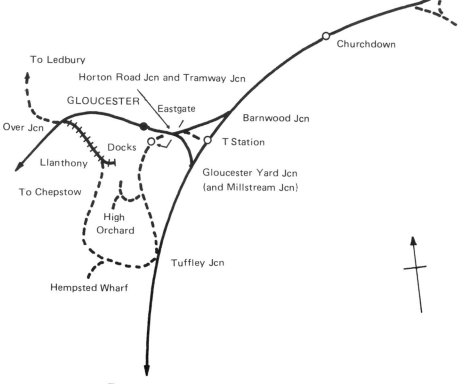

avoiding line (between Barnwood Junction and Millstream Junction) where turntables were provided to permit the transfer of through vehicles. This T Station, as it was called, ceased to be used when the line on towards Chepstow was opened in 1851, another major change following in 1854 when the MR provided its own metals between Standish Junction, Tuffley and Tramway Junction. The break of gauge added to the complications at Gloucester and gave it an unsavoury railway reputation for many years.

The lines west of Gloucester were in the hands of the Gloucester & Dean Forest, Monmouth & Hereford and South Wales companies. Although trains started running on September 19 1851, the new Gloucester station was not ready until the following year. Two years after that the connection from Over to the docks came into use, the Midland reaching the docks area by a branch from Barton Street Junction and another from Tuffley Junction to Hempsted Wharf and on to

join the GW at High Orchard. Other developments included the line to Ledbury in 1885 and the re-opening of the avoiding line after 50 years in 1901 (for passengers 1908). All this railway made Gloucester a busy and important railway junction with a host of local trains, long distance expresses and through carriages, plus a significant freight business.

As it turned out the GWR lines eventually triumphed over their Midland rivals at Gloucester for the latter's route and station have now been closed in favour of a modernisation of Gloucester Central in 1975. This was largely owing to the inconvenient level crossing on the MR section from Tuffley Junction to Eastgate station but it has meant that those trains between Bristol and the North which call at Gloucester have to reverse there.

By 1981 all but the MR platforms and one goods building had gone, including the elevated signal box and the great footbridge which had connected the two stations. After being a single platform

Right *The former Midland Railway route through Gloucester is now closed but a few reminders of its passage lingered on after closure.*

station up to 1889, the former GWR station reverted to this condition with the extension of the Down platform to accommodate two trains and the addition of new administrative buildings in 1975.

Approaching Gloucester from the Bristol direction there is a change of mileage at Tuffley (94 m 60 ch to 94 m 10 ch) where the sight of the trackbed from High Orchard/Hempsted is followed by the divergence of the trackbed to Eastgate. At Gloucester Yard Junction, where the MR mileage of 93 m 8 ch changes to the GWR 113 m 3 ch, the line for the station diverges from the avoiding line on to Barnwood Junction (92 m 21 ch) and Cheltenham and heads between the CCE/CSTE/C&W yard and the Gloucester Carriage & Wagon Company's siding to the level crossing (113 m 55 ch) adjacent to the panel box. The line from Barnwood joins at Horton Road Junction (113 m 55 ch and 92 m 75 ch) and then heads for the station, now just called Gloucester, where the platform line is authorised for two-way working. Permissive working is allowed on the adjacent Up Main and there are also Up Relief, Parcels Platform and Bay lines, the latter being used by the dmus which serve the Chepstow line.

Gloucester station enjoys a good service of trains between the Bristol and South Wales lines and the route north via Birmingham. It has its own local workings to Newport and Cardiff plus the dmus of the Worcester-Swindon service. In addition to the station facilities, including a Travellers-Fare buffet, the former locomotive depot is still in use for stabling, signing on, fuelling and minor mechanical attention. The GPO depot lies nearby on the Down side and the goods yard opposite still has a collection of period buildings that make it easy to visualise a busy past.

North of Gloucester station lie Shell Star and Foster Yeoman depots. Gloucester's other active location is reached via Over Junction ground frame (115 m 42 ch) which leads to Docks Branch Sidings, a viaduct over the waterway linking the Severn and the docks, Hempsted level crossing (75 ch) and Llanthony Yard (1 m 7 ch). This line is controlled by the travelling shunter and

serves scrap, cement and other residual traffics and docks tenancies.

G.4 Goring and Streatley

Paddington-Swindon line between Reading and Didcot. 48 m 37 ch from Paddington

Called Goring and Streatley, instead of plain Goring, from 1895 the station lost its goods facilities in 1964 and now consists of two outer, single face platforms and an island between the Main and Relief lines. The trains of the Paddington-Reading-Oxford local service use the Relief line platforms which have brick buildings with canopies.

G.5 Gorseinon Branch

Swansea District Line, branch from Gorseinon Goods Junction. 3 m 49 ch

This single track freight line runs south for 2¼ m from Grovesend Colliery Loop, near the western end of the Swansea

District Line, to the coal and freight depot at Gorseinon. Near the junction is the NCB Brynlliw colliery.

Most of the route derives from the former Llanelly Railway/LNWR/LMS Pontarddulais-Swansea (Victoria) line opened in 1866/7 and bridged by the Swansea District Line when it opened in 1913. After the former lost its passenger trains in 1964 a freight service to Gorseinon was continued via Pontarddulais (from which the branch mileage is still measured) but this was abandoned in 1974 to permit extension of the M4 and the Gorseinon service was routed via a new connection to the Swansea District line at Grovesend.

At Grovesend Colliery Loop there is a ground frame plus crossover and Down Goods Loop. The branch from Gorseinon trails in at the Swansea end of the loop and is used here for loading block coal trains at Brynlliw colliery. These consist of mgr workings to Aberthaw power station or cement works—up to four each weekday and made up of 35 mgr wagons and two Class 37 locomotives—and conventional trains to Carmarthen Bay power station. Class 37 locomotive trips from Llandeilo Junction yard bring in the empty wagons and convey household coal to the yard at Brynlliw and the depot at Gorseinon.

Swansea District Line is controlled from Port Talbot panel box and the Gorseinon branch is operated on the One Train Working system, without train staff.

G.6   Gowerton

Newport-Fishguard line between Swansea and Llanelli. 219 m 49 ch from Paddington*

This two-platform 'park and ride' station is served by the Central Wales line dmus and by some of the main line trains between Swansea and West Wales. It was renovated and redesigned for the 1980 Royal National Eisteddfod of Wales, in contrast to the forlorn abutments of the bridge which used to carry the LNWR line into Swansea (Victoria) and which can still be seen at the country end of the station.

G.7   Grampound Road

Taunton-Penzance line between St Austell and Truro. 293 m 15 ch from Paddington*

Closed in 1964, the yard gate and dock are still visible on the Down side. The minor

summit here, once provided with Up and Down Refuge Sidings, is followed by a drop at 1 in 67 towards the former Probus and Ladock platform.

G.8   Grange Court

Gloucester-Newport line between Gloucester and Lydney. 121 m 4 ch from Paddington

Despite closure of the station in 1964, Grange Court retains an operational significance because of its Up and Down Goods Loops and the emergency crossovers. A clue to its former status as a junction for the 1853-5 Hereford, Ross & Gloucester Railway's line to Hereford lies in the alignment of the Up Loop which bulges away from the main line from a point at the country end of the site where the branch trackbed is still discernible. The branch encompassed four tunnels and four substantial river bridges and was used as a test-bed for the 1892 gauge conversion.

Grange Court has Ley (120 m 20 ch) and Broken Cross (120 m 66 ch) level crossings on one side and the one at Westbury (122 m 11 ch) on the other.

Grangetown—see Penarth Branch

G.9   Great Malvern

Oxford-Hereford line between Worcester and Hereford. 129 m 6 ch from Paddington

The short level stretch on which this two-platform station stands is heralded from the London direction by three overbridges and then, at the end of the Down platform, by a private access passage which leads from the station, under the road and to the adjacent girls' school. The latter was at one time a hotel for Malvern's spa visitors and traces still remain of the boiler house which was served by a wagon turntable, the station's only freight facility.

Although minus its front canopy and soaring clock tower, the attractive Gothic-style station remains much in its 1861 form with a full range of traditional buildings and a station house still in use. The principal buildings are on the Up side and executed in mellow sandstone with rounded lintels decorated by using stone of alternately different colouring. The platform canopies, in rising corrugated form on the Down side and with leaded inverted V shape on the Up, are supported by finely decorated columns.

Above *Still largely in its original form, Great Malvern station presents a very pleasant face to the traveller.*
Right *Ornamentation on the canopy supports at Great Malvern.*

At the country end of the Down platform is the bay once used for the 14 m, 35-minute journey via Tewkesbury to Ashchurch. Opposite is the old dock.

G.10 Greenford Branch

Paddington-Swindon line, branch from West Ealing. 94 m 6 ch

The single power car and the modest suburban traffic which characterise the Greenford branch today provide little reminder of the heady origins of the line back in 1903/4. The line from West Ealing to Greenford, along with the West Ealing West Loop and the direct line from Old Oak Common to Greenford and on to High Wycombe were all part of a joint exercise with the Great Central Railway designed to give that company better access to London and the GWR a shorter route to Birmingham.

Although today's trains commence their journey at Ealing Broadway, the branch leaves the main line at West Ealing where the junction points (6 m 56 ch) are just beyond the old milk dock. The two tracks from Hanwell join those from West Ealing at Drayton Green Junction (7 m 3 ch) just before the short platforms of the

station (7 m 7 ch). A new tunnel under a housing estate leads to Castle Bar station (7 m 44 ch) and then, at an elevated level, to the one-coach wooden platforms at South Greenford (8 m 24 ch). From Greenford East (9 m 4 ch) the signal box is preceded by the single line Greenford East Loop towards Park Royal and then overlooks the connection into the Old Oak Common to Northolt Junction Down line. The branch trains pass under the

From its own bay at the end of Greenford platform a WR dmu sets off for Ealing Broadway.

Down LT line before rising to their own bay at Greenford station.

G.11   Grimstone and Frampton Tunnel

Westbury-Weymouth line between Yeovil Pen Mill and Dorchester West. 156 m 70 ch from Paddington*

This is the first of the tunnels on the descent from Evershot towards Weymouth and is of 615 yds in length (156 m 70 ch to 157 m 20 ch). The former station lay on the Weymouth side of the tunnel and Bradford Peverell and Stratton Halt two miles nearer the present Regional boundary at 160 m 20 ch.

Gulf Oil Branch—see Milford Haven

G.12   Gunnislake Branch

Taunton-Penzance line, branch from St Budeaux Junction. 11 m 61 ch

Passing through an area still relatively inaccessible by road, this is a highly scenic single line branch with delightful views of the River Tamar and of the hills of Dartmoor. It uses the former SR main line along the east bank of the river as far as Bere Alston where the trains reverse for the 4 m 44 ch section of the former Callington line as far as Gunnislake. This portion of the route includes crossing the

Tamar by the impressive Calstock viaduct and then a journey of twists, turns and climbs through the old mining area with views that are quite breathtaking.

If it were not for the remains of the engine houses it would be difficult to associate the Gunnislake area with the mining of arsenic and copper, but it was the requirements of the mines and quarries which led to the authorisation of the Callington & Calstock Railway on August 9 1869. Renamed East Cornwall Mineral Railway it opened a 3 ft 6 in gauge line on May 7 1872 with a rope-worked incline to get wagons down to the vessels waiting at Calstock Quay. Profitable years were followed by leaner times leading to the acquisition of the undertaking by the Plymouth, Devonport & South Western Union Railway which had received powers for the link from Bere Alston to Calstock in its 1883 Act. This became a light railway by virtue of an Order of July 13 1900 and, after three more Orders for amendment or time extension, was opened on March 2 1908 to give a new through route which avoided the earlier incline (although the lift to the quay did last until 1934). In the same month LSWR trains to Plymouth started using the route via Lydford, Tavistock and the PD&SWU metals.

In the 1930s the local services originating at Plymouth Friary went to Tavistock, Exeter and even Salisbury and a branch service ran from Bere Alston to Callington. The trains would then have used the SR metals in Plymouth, through Devonport, Ford and St Budeaux

(Victoria Road) but they now use the GWR route up to the latter point and then pick up the PD&SWU by crossing from the Down to the Up line and then curving beneath both. The route is now single and uses only the Down platform at St Budeaux Victoria Road (227 m 2 ch) which is 20 ch from the junction where former SR distances from Waterloo begin/end.

The route goes back beneath the West of England main line to start its journey along the east bank of the Tamar, coming first to the ground frames at Ernesettle (225 m 79 ch and 225 m 58 ch) which has an RN Armament Depot on the Down side. Tamerton Foliot station is now closed but this winding section is interesting for the eight tie-arch viaduct over the mouth of the River Tavy. With stonework approaches, the bridge is supported on cross-braced tubular iron pillars. Next is Bere Ferrers (222 m 69 ch) where trains use the Up platform which has traditional stone buildings with a wooden canopy, a similar style being used in the goods shed which survives on the Down side.

The line starts to rise at 1 in 73 to get to Bere Alston (220 m 5 ch) where the ground frame (220 m 7 ch) is preceded by an SR lattic post signal, another standing on the remaining track towards Tavistock. Only the main platform is now rail connected, although the island platform, the old goods shed and the signal box are still in existence. After the guard has set the

points for Calstock the train can set off on its 1 in 40 climb to the magnificent viaduct, 12 spans of 60 ft rising 129 ft above the water and crossed at a maximum of 10 mph. Calstock station (1 m 55 ch) lies on a curve just beyond the viaduct and consists of a single platform, a small concrete building and the old wooden dock, little enough reminder of the masses of fruit and flowers once loaded here. The position is similar at Gunnislake (4 m 48 ch) except that the old coal yard is still in use and the view is north to Dartmoor. Between the two is a steeply curving and climbing section with open level crossings at Okeltor (2 m 28 ch) and Sandways (3 m 31 ch) and a host of access crossings, 'Stop' boards and speed restrictions from 5 mph upwards. Between the huge curve clinging to the hillside beyond Sandways Crossing and Gunnislake itself there are countless signs of old mines, now succumbing to the gentler pastimes of agriculture and market gardening.

One train working is used on this branch. There is a service of eight trains each way on weekdays with freight trips to Ernesettle as required. Beyond Gunnislake the line to Callington (via various halts and sidings, including the link to the Kit Hill incline) closed in 1966.

Calstock Viaduct, used by the scenic Gunnislake branch for its crossing of the River Tamar.

The modest station at Calstock looking towards Gunnislake.

Gwaun-cae-Gurwen Branch—see Panty-ffynnon

G.13   Gwinnear Road

Taunton-Penzance line between Camborne and Penzance. 315 m 73 ch from Paddington*

Gwinnear Road became part of the railway map with the advent of the pioneer Hayle Railway in 1843 and then joined the main line system as a West Cornwall Railway station in 1852. It was a long way from Gwinnear village and of little importance until the Helston Railway came into being on May 9 1887.

The trackbed for the Helston branch, in connection with which the GWR ran its pioneer Lizard bus service, is still evident and joins the former siding area at the London end of the Gwinnear Road site. Adjacent is the old cattle dock, the modern automatic half barrier crossing and the overgrown island platform which also served the branch trains.

H.1   Hallen Marsh Branch

Swindon-Newport line, branch from Stoke Gifford Junction. 6 m 38 ch

This is a single line freight route, north of Bristol and linking the main line to South Wales with the Severn Beach branch. It was originally authorised in 1904, the year after the opening of the direct route to South Wales, and its opening effectively connected that route to Avonmouth docks without having to use the joint line through Clifton or the circuitous access via Pilning Low Level. Opening took place on May 9 1910, just a few days after the new passenger station had been opened in the Royal Edward Dock. Extensive new facilities were planned for the line to meet First World War munitions needs and, although these were not implemented as planned, the line was doubled in 1917. By that time workmen's trains were using the line and a full passenger service developed with stations at North Filton Platform, Charlton Halt, Henbury, Hallen Halt and Chittening Halt and some interesting through workings to and from Bath, Portishead and Clifton Bridge.

The passenger service on the Hallen Marsh line ended in 1964 but it continued to be used for freight to and from the large industrial works at Avonmouth. At the London end there is a ground frame link to Tip Sidings (112 m 7 ch) between Stoke Gifford Junction (112 m 4 ch) and Filton West Junction (112 m 78 ch), and connections from the latter to Filton Junction in the Bristol direction and to Patchway Junction (the Patchway Chord via Filton Tip level crossing) for services to South Wales. The route is single through North Filton (113 m 12 ch), the 302 yd Charlton Tunnel (113 m 79 ch to 114 m 12 ch) and the former station at Henbury (where a coal yard still exists) as far as Blaise ground frame (116 m 6 ch) from where it is double to Hallen Marsh and the junction points (118 m 42 ch).

H.2 Handborough

Oxford-Worcester line between Oxford and Kingham. 70 m 39 ch from Paddington

This was the Oxford, Worcester & Wolverhampton Railway's most easterly station, now quite modest despite former glories but lucky to have survived 1964/5 closure threats. In fact, freight services did end in that period and only the weighbridge and dock now mark the once extensive area of loops, sidings, goods shed and connection to wartime food depot.

During the OWW's flirtations with the LNWR Handborough achieved the distinction of a through service to Euston, the through portions being detached here for working forward by 'Wessie' engines. To go with its new status Handborough got extra sidings and a refreshment room but today the Up platform and simple shelter are more than adequate for the weekday service of two Up and two Down trains.

Handborough has another claim to a place in railway history for it was to this modest station that 4-6-2 No 34051 *Winston Churchill* brought the great man's funeral train on January 30 1965. From SR van 2464 the body was taken by hearse to the little church at Bladon for the private family burial and the station had made its own small contribution to a sad but historic occasion.

H.3 Hanwell

Paddington-Swindon line between Paddington and Southall. 7 m 29 ch from Paddington

Although not ready for opening until December 1838, Hanwell was one of the original GWR stations and until the 1981 renovation it looked the part. Now the single storey buildings on the Relief line platforms have been given a facelift for the commuter traffic into Paddington which constitutes the station's principal activity. Beyond Hanwell there is a long Up Goods Loop and also Brunel's notable Wharncliffe Viaduct spanning the Brent Valley.

H.4 Haresfield

Birmingham-Bristol line between Gloucester and Westerleigh Junction. 98 m 64 ch from Derby

Closed in 1965, Haresfield lay on the former four-track section between Tuffley and Standish junctions but was served only by the MR lines. It now has Up and Down Goods Loops as the sole reminders of a stretch on which 'racing', although forbidden, frequently took place.

H.5 Haverfordwest

Milford Haven branch. 276 m 3 ch from Paddington*

Haverfordwest is an ancient castle and market town and a seat of local government. It is also the highest point for navigation on the Western Cleddau and the point where the river is crossed by the historic road to the city of St Davids. The town was reached by the South Wales Railway from Carmarthen in 1854, the SWR by then having given up the idea of going to Fishguard and opted instead for an Irish packet port at Neyland which it reached from Haverfordwest in 1856.

Falling gradients from Clarbeston Road, through Crundale with its traditional crossing package of gates, cottage and semaphore signals, bring the double track line to Haverfordwest station where the spacious layout and the architecture testify to the reconstruction carried out between the wars. The Up and Down platforms are linked by a steel footbridge and the principal buildings on the Up side include a ticket office modernised during 1982. The station approach and forecourt is on this side and is used by buses for Fishguard and St Davids. There is an Up Goods Loop between the platform lines and a Down Goods Loop behind the Down platform. Also on the Down side there is a neat brick signal box at the London end of the platform and a goods and coal yard behind the DGL. The former goods shed is now in private hands.

Beyond the station the line curves through a short rock cutting to cross the Cleddau river by a lifting bridge. The lifting span is still in situ but is not used, the mechanism for lifting having been removed. Approaching the bridge there is a good view, on the Up side, of the town and river, dominated by the ruins of the 12th century castle.

All the Milford Haven-Swansea trains call at Haverfordwest, most now locomotive-hauled. The Monday to Friday wagonload service from Llandeilo Junction to Milford Haven also calls as required to serve the freight yard.

H.6   Hayes and Harlington

*Paddington-Swindon   line   between
Southall and Slough. 10 m 71 ch from
Paddington*

This is another of the stations serving the
WR inner suburban commuter flows and
built on the pattern of a central island plus
two outer platforms. The one adjoining
the Down Main is bare, the main
buildings and sidings being on the Up side
with the ticket office at street level above.
The station dates from 1864.

There are ground frames and Up Goods
Loops on either side of the station. The
former give access to the Tarmac Hopper
Discharge Siding at the London end and
to the EDC aggregate plant siding at the
country end.

H.7   Hayle

*Taunton-Penzance line between Camborne
and Penzance. 319 m 32 ch from Padding-
ton**

Hayle was an important trading centre of
old Cornwall with a regular steamer service to Bristol. Port for the mines of
Camborne, Redruth and beyond, it was a
place of laden pack mules, crowded
wharves and busy foundries when the
pioneer Hayle Railway was authorised in
1834. Twelve years later the West Cornwall Railway's Act provided for the
rebuilding of the mineral line and its
extension to Truro in one direction and
Penzance in the other.

The old station in Foundry Square was
replaced by the present location with the

opening of the main line on March 11
1852. The Down platform, complete with
unit ticket office, is followed immediately
by a viaduct high above the town while
opposite is the connection to the Hayle
Wharves branch, once a busy 34 ch line
but now just rusting away. The narrow-
waisted signal box stands on the Up platform, formerly an island.

Heath—see   Rhymney   and   Coryton
Branches

H.8   Heathfield Branch

*Taunton-Penzance   line,   branch   from
Newton Abbot East. 2 m 63 ch*

This freight-only single line is all that
remains of one of the GWR's Dartmoor
tourist branches and of a route to Exeter
that was to be the great alternative to the
exposed coastal main line. The Moretonhampstead & South Devon Railway
opened on July 4 1866 using part of the
earlier Haytor Tramway, a branch from
Heathfield to Ashton opened on October
9 1882 and the Exeter end was eventually
completed on July 1 1903. After closure in
1958-60, freight lingered on the original
line for some years but this is now
truncated just beyond Heathfield.

The route is under the control of the
Newton Abbot East signalman and is
subject to a speed restriction of 15 mph. A

*Serious flooding of the main line at Hele
& Bradninch in October 1960.*

scrap metal tenancy remains at Newton Abbot goods depot but there is no rail activity there and the line continues to Teignbridge Sidings (1 m 43 ch) where two major firms, English China Clays and Watts, Blake, Bearne, have sidings. The trainmen operate the level crossing at 1 m 51 ch and the line ends at 3 m 43 ch. There is a run-round facility at Heathfield, a Gulf Oil installation and another ECC siding, served by a daily trip working.

H.9   Hele and Bradninch

Taunton-Penzance line between Tiverton Junction and Exeter St Davids. 185 m 41 ch from Paddington*

This was one of the original Bristol and Exeter stations now marked by a Down Goods Loop, signal box and level crossing. A tiny portion of station building remains and a paper firm uses the Up side goods yard.

H.10   Hemerdon

Taunton-Penzance line between Totnes and Plymouth. 239 m 10 ch from Paddington*

Hemerdon Bank involves a 2 m climb for Up trains from Plympton to the former Hemerdon Siding, mainly at 1 in 42. There are Up and Down Goods Loops, the former succeeding an early private siding which at one stage was also used as a public siding with a gate dividing the two portions.

Hengoed—see Rhymney Branch

H.11   Henley-on-Thames Branch

Paddington-Swindon line, branch from Twyford. 4 m 49 ch

Although Henley waited ten years between authorisation of its railway and the opening on June 1 1857 it has been a pleasant and busy little line ever since. The terminus is near both the town and the Thames and excursion traffic used to be very heavy, especially in Regatta Week when the sidings at Henley would be full to capacity with the stock working the special trains.

Initially single and now single again, the branch runs from the junction with the main line at Twyford to the single platform face remaining in use at Henley. On the way it serves Wargrave (1 m 67 ch), opened in 1900 and comprising just a single platform, and Shiplake (2 m 65 ch) where the Up side of the island platform is used. The dmu service is generous and busy at peak periods. Operation is controlled by the Reading panel box and trains are required to stop at the open level crossing between the station at Shiplake and the former goods yard there. A 20 mph speed restriction applies on the Shiplake Viaduct which carries the railway to the north bank of the river.

Herbrandston Branch—see Milford Haven Line

Trains on the Henley branch cross the Thames by this viaduct at Shiplake.

H.12 Hereford

Shrewsbury-Newport line. 51 m 14 ch from Shrewsbury

Hereford is an ancient city, noted for its magnificent cathedral which dates from the 11th century, and long associated with the Anglo-Welsh border country. Its railway history is linked with the desires of two English companies, the London & North Western Railway and the Midland Railway, to reach the rich industrial traffic of South Wales. The rail routes at Hereford today are the 'North and West' line from Crewe and Shrewsbury to Newport and Cardiff and the line from Worcester which joins the N&W at Shelwick Junction (49 m 26 ch).

The N&W line dates from 1853 when the Shrewsbury & Hereford Railway reached the city from the north and the Newport, Abergavenny & Hereford Railway from the south. First by leasing, then by outright acquisition, the Shrewsbury & Hereford became a joint LNW/GWR line, while the line to Newport became GWR with LNW running powers. The Worcester-Hereford line was opened in 1860 and became part of the GWR via the West Midlands Railway.

Two other lines at Hereford have now closed. From 1869 the Midland Railway worked and later absorbed a line to Three Cocks Junction, 27 miles west on the way to Brecon, which gave it access to Swansea by the use of running powers over lines on either side. The other route was the 1855-1964 line to Gloucester, originating as the Hereford, Ross & Gloucester Railway and amalgamated with the GWR by virtue of an Act of 1862.

Hereford originally had three passenger stations. The present one, still referred to as 'Barrs Court', began as a Shrewsbury & Hereford Railway station. Barton on the other, west, side of the city was the NA&HR station, while the Midland had Moorfields but this closed as long ago as 1874. Barton closed to passengers in 1893 but remained open for freight until 1979 by which time it was no longer an alternative through route to that via Barrs Court.

Through Hereford station there are Up and Down Platform Lines with Up and Down Through Lines in between. The island platform on the Down side is also served by a Down Passenger Loop. The main buildings, with approach road and forecourt, are on the Up side where there is also a short bay facing Shrewsbury. On the Up side, also at the Shrewsbury end of the station, is a sizeable goods yard reached by the Brecon Curve Junction ground frame (50 m 53 ch).

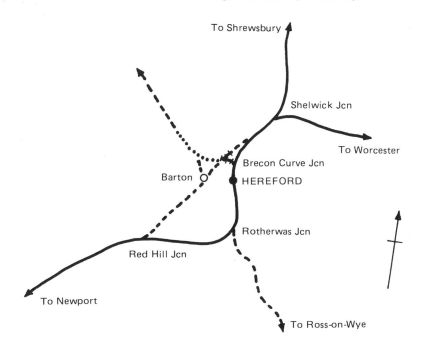

To Shrewsbury

Shelwick Jcn

To Worcester

Brecon Curve Jcn

Barton

HEREFORD

Rotherwas Jcn

Red Hill Jcn

To Newport

To Ross-on-Wye

The principal station building actually pre-dates the railway and was a private dwelling known as Barr's Court. It is a handsome brick structure with distinctive gables and window openings and is 'listed' as a Grade Two building of special architectural interest. In 1980 a new booking office and travel centre were installed, but carefully designed to harmonise with the original appearance, and the features of the platform canopies and their supporting columns and spandrels were highlighted in an imaginative colour scheme. The first floor of the station building houses the Area Manager's organisation.

At the south end of Hereford station, on the Down side, is the signal box (known as Aylston Hill when it was one of three in the area) with colour light signals and block sections to Shelwick Junction and Tram Inn. Beyond the signal box on the Up side are carriage sidings and a traction fuelling point.

Leaving Hereford southbound there is a change of mileage at Rotherwas Junction (52 m 19 ch to zero) where the line to Gloucester diverged on the Down side. Further on the former route via Barton trailed in on the opposite side at Red Hill Junction (2 m 11 ch) the section between the two, by a quirk of Hereford's complicated railway history, having belonged to the LNWR. Northbound from Hereford a single track, freight-only line diverges from the Up side at Brecon Curve Junction. Reached via the ground frame and a shunting movement through the freight yard, it is a remnant of the former route round to Barton and now serves the private sidings of Henry Wiggins & Co, Painter Bros and H.P. Bulmer Ltd and the Midlands Electricity Board private oil-fired power station opened in 1980. Immediately after the junction the line passes Burcott Road level crossing and then comes to Barton Curve where the Wiggins siding is the stub of the route from the main line to Barton. Of the former triangle beyond only the line to the power station and the Bulmer Railway Centre remains and this is privately-owned.

Hereford is served by the locomotive-hauled trains between Cardiff and Shrewsbury/Crewe and east via Worcester. It has local dmu services including accelerated trains to and from Birmingham. The route is used by summer holiday trains between the North-West and the West, by some parcels trains and Motorail and

TPO services and by occasional steam specials. The North and West line is busy at night with through freight traffic, there is a wagonload service Monday to Friday from Severn Tunnel Junction and oil trains run from Milford Haven to the MEB power station. A Class 08 shunter acts as station pilot and performs the local trips.

H.13 Heyford

Didcot-Birmingham line between Oxford and Banbury. 75 m 21 ch from Paddington

Mondays to Fridays four local trains each way daily serve this modest country station on the main line to Birmingham. Beyond its two platforms, to the north, the regional boundary with the LMR is at milepost 76½.

H.14 Highbridge

Bristol-Taunton line between Weston-super-Mare and Bridgwater. 145 m 25 ch from Paddington

From today's modest Up and Down platforms it is difficult to imagine the considerable railway activity which once went on here, although there are still some clues.

The Bristol & Exeter Railway opened its section from Bristol to Bridgwater on June 14 1841. Thirteen years later the 12 m line of Somerset Central Railway opened from Highbridge Wharf to Glastonbury, crossing the B&E route just 33 ch from its starting point. The SCR was to grow into the Somerset & Dorset and to bring Highbridge a seven-platform station, regular sailings from the wharf to other Bristol Channel and South Wales ports and a large locomotive and carriage works.

Today the WR station at Highbridge has a local dmu service and a bi-directional Up Goods Loop south of the station. The two platforms span the River Brue and are actually below sea level. The main buildings are on the Up side and one portion appears to have B&E origins. A concrete footbridge then leads to the Down platform and to the remains of the last S&D platform which makes a good vantage point for looking inland to the old works area, now back in the hands of nature apart from one forlorn building. The works closed, with the loss of 300 jobs, when separate S&D management ended in 1930. Three years later the remaining S&D cargo vessels were sold.

Despite progressive closure of the S&D system from 1951 a spur remained from Highbridge to the milk depot just beyond the overgrown single platform at Bason Bridge until the route was severed by the M5 motorway.

Looking seawards from Highbridge Down platform the route of the S&D, which crossed the GWR line on the level, can be worked out from the second arch of the veteran road bridge. It then crossed the main Bristol-Bridgwater road, also on the level, to reach Highbridge Wharf and continue to Burnham-on-Sea where the remains of the pier used for coal traffic can still be seen.

The Somerset & Dorset line from Highbridge to Burnham-on-Sea ended on the pier where Welsh coal was once landed.

H.15   Hirwaun Pond Branch

Merthyr-Cardiff line, branch from Abercynon. 12 m 7 ch

The line in the Aberdare, or Cynon, valley is freight only and now single track. It serves the NCB colliery at Penrhiwceiber (ground frames 18 m 20 ch and 18 m 66 ch), the NSF Phurnacite patent fuel plant at Abercwmboi (21 m 33 ch), a coal and freight yard plus a private siding beyond the change of mileage point (22 m to 22 m 68 ch) at Aberdare (22 m 46 ch), Robertstown Crossing (23 m 8 ch), Hirwaun (25 m 76 ch) and its interchange point with the private line to Penderyn Quarry, and then the NCB Tower colliery at the end of the line (27 m 15 ch).

As far as the change of mileage point the route is that of the Aberdare Railway opened in 1846 and later becoming part of the Taff Vale Railway. The remainder of the TVR route on to Aberdare was needed for road improvements in the 1970s so a new connection was brought into use in August 1973 to link the TVR line with the former Vale of Neath (ex-GWR Pontypool Road-Neath) line on the east side of the River Cynon. Crossing the river was effected by means of a single span girder bridge brought from Wheatley where it had previously carried the Princes Risborough-Oxford line over the A40. From Cwmbach, at the end of the bridge, the former Vale of Neath line is used and passes through Aberdare where the TVR/VoN connection had previously been made.

The former double track section between Aberdare and Robertstown has recently been singled and one train working now operates with the former signal box at Robertstown level crossing used as a ground frame. Other ground frames serve the Penrhiwceiber colliery and the NCB Locomotive Repair Shops at Mountain Ash. At Aberdare, the former goods shed on the Down side is a 'listed' building, reputedly designed by Brunel for the Vale of Neath Railway.

Inwards coal flows to the NSF plant at Abercwmboi from the other collieries on the line and from elsewhere in South Wales. With the outwards patent fuel the movements total some 30,000 tonnes per week and involve both direction services and trips from Radyr and East Usk yards. Some Class 37 locomotives are stabled at Aberdare and there is a Class 08 shunter for duties there and at Abercymboi. In addition to the coal traffic activity a ballast train is scheduled daily for the output of Penderyn quarry which provides ballast for BR track use.

Although passenger services to Aberdare and the other Cynon Valley towns had been withdrawn by 1964, locomotive-hauled excursions, using the surviving platforms of otherwise closed valley stations, continued in the '70s. These ceased in 1980 to avoid the extra expense of maintaining track to passenger-carrying standards.

H.16   Honeybourne

Oxford-Hereford line between Moreton-in-Marsh and Evesham. 101 m 48 ch from Paddington

Although Honeybourne was one of the original Worcester line stations this probably had more to do with its agricultural activity and its proximity to Stratford-upon-Avon than with the travel potential from the scattered villages of this part of the Vale of Evesham. A 9½ m branch to Stratford was, in fact, authorised before trains started serving Honeybourne in June 1853 and the latter became a junction when the branch was opened three years later.

On March 30 1908 Honeybourne was linked with Cheltenham as part of the GWR scheme for its own route from Bristol to Birmingham. It used the Westerleigh spur at Bristol, the avoiding line at Gloucester, the new line to Honeybourne, the OWW route to Stratford, on to Bearley, and a new Birmingham & North Warwickshire line to link up with the main line at Tyseley. In addition to its Worcester line trains and stopping services to and via Stratford or Cheltenham, Honeybourne saw expresses from Wolverhampton and Birmingham to Wales, Weston and the West, although these passed east of the station on the new main line beneath the old one. Curves between the two were provided in either direction on the northern side with a further curve for the Honeybourne-Cheltenham trains.

A lot of trackwork remains at Honeybourne which lost the last of its passenger services in 1969 when the link to Stratford ended. The Down platform has now been brought back into use with a limited number of Worcester line trains calling, but it is a spartan facility compared with the days of four platforms and seven signal boxes. The former box at Station South now just controls access to the Tip Sidings (ground frame) on the West Loop

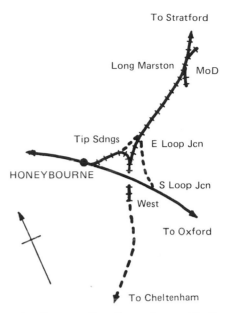

and the continuation from North Junction to West Loop Junction where the freight services for the Ministry of Defence and scrap traffic at Long Marston run round before continuing along the remaining 3 m 36 ch of the former Stratford branch.

H.17   Honiton

Waterloo-Exeter Line beween Yeovil Junction and Exeter Central. 154 m 60 ch from Waterloo

From Broad Clyst, the old LSW trains heading for Salisbury and Waterloo had nearly 14 m of rising gradients in a 1 in 100 climb to Honiton and a further stretch of 1 in 90 to the summit before descending through the 1,345 yd Honiton Tunnel (152 m 45 ch to 153 m 26 ch) and past Honiton Incline Box to Seaton Junction. Such gradients hold no terrors for the Class 50 locomotives used on the present service.

The station itself is of a modern, prefabricated design with a shelter on the Up platform and a combined ticket, waiting and staff building opposite. The red brick signal box, square and squat, controls the passing loop and Up Refuge Siding.

H.18   Hopton Heath

Shrewsbury-Llanelli line between Craven Arms and Llandrindod Wells. 5 m 9 ch from Craven Arms

Of   Hopton   Heath's   two   original

96   RAILWAYS OF THE WESTERN REGION

platforms only the Down one is now used by the Shrewsbury-Swansea dmu service. The station house stands just behind it.

H.19   Hullavington

Swindon-Newport line between Wootton Bassett Junction and Westerleigh Junction. 94 m 10 ch from Paddington

Hullavington lost its passenger service in 1961 and closed completely in 1965. It is still the site of a Down Goods Loop and also significant as the point at which the Bristol panel box takes over from the Swindon one.

H.20   Hungerford

Reading-Taunton line, between Newbury and Westbury. 61 m 47 ch from Paddington

Hungerford was originally the western extremity of the Berks & Hants Railway, incorporated in 1845, and opened from Reading in 1847, the year of its amalgamation with the GWR. The first station was planned as a temporary terminus to cater for the intention to extend the route westwards and 'the circumstance of it becoming the main line to the West of England'. In fact, the extension to Devizes waited until 1862 but Hungerford did get a new station then.

Today Hungerford consists of two long platforms, footbridge and metal shelters,

Hungerford station and its barrier crossing.

with a closed-circuit television monitored barrier crossing at the country end and an Up Goods Loop at the London end. Remains of a dock and the goods yard site are the only remaining evidence of past glories, although a station nameboard in pre-BR lettering was still managing to survive on each platform in 1981. The service is provided by the three-car dmu workings between Bedwyn and Reading.

The ground frame, emergency crossover and remaining Down siding lead are at 61 m 25 ch.

H.21   Huntspill

Bristol-Taunton line between Highbridge and Bridgwater. 137 m 5 ch from Paddington

A ground frame gives access to the Reception Sidings on the Down side of the main line, the CEGB locomotive handling traffic on the 'Factory' line which crosses over the M5 on its way to the power station.

I.1   Iver

Paddington-Swindon line between Southall and Slough. 14 m 60 ch from Paddington

Reached from a ticket office at road level below, this 1924 London suburban station comprises the standard pattern of central island and two outer platforms, those on the Relief lines having small wooden buildings of traditional design. There is an Up Goods line and an Up Refuge Siding behind the Up Relief platform.

I.2 Ivybridge

*Taunton-Penzance line between Totnes and Plymouth. 235 m 19 ch from Paddington**

The viaduct at the London end of the former station carries the line over the River Erme and was built in 1893 to take over from the original South Devon Railway structure. The Brunel-era piers of the latter can still be seen on the Up side of the line.

Ivybridge station, the existence of which may have had something to do with the convenience of railway director Lord Mildmay of Fleet, closed to passengers in 1959. The goods yard has lingered on as a clay loading facility for Watts, Blake, Bearne with access via ground frames, and the old goods shed stands behind the loop.

An earlier site at Ivybridge had been the starting point for the 3 ft gauge Redlake Tramway which used an incline to start its 7½ m climb to a lonely quarry high up on Dartmoor.

J.1 Johnston

*Milford Haven branch. 280 m 17 ch from Paddington**

Johnston lies between Haverfordwest and the terminus of the West Wales line at Milford Haven. It was a junction for the branch to the latter point when the main line ran to Neyland which (known as New Milford) was the South Wales Railway/GWR port for Ireland until eclipsed by Fishguard in 1906. Opening dates were 1856 for the Haverfordwest-Johnston-Neyland portion and 1863 for the line from Johnston to Milford Haven. Both lines were broad gauge until the 1872 conversion in South Wales. The line to Neyland closed in 1964.

From the direction of Haverfordwest the double track line rises from the valley of the Cleddau to the simple, unstaffed, two-platform Johnston station. There is a trailing crossover and Down Refuge Siding at the London end and a traditional brick and timber signal box at the country end. The line then becomes three track, the centre track being a loop and signalled for trains to reverse to the Down direction. The signals are semaphore and absolute block working applies.

Beyond Johnston, before the line descends from the open uplands of this part of Pembrokeshire, the route curves sharply south-west from the direction of the original main line straight on to Neyland. On the curve the single track section to Milford Haven commences and this is worked on the No Signalman Token system. The signalman at Johnston also controls the working of trains on the single track Gulf Oil Refinery branch which diverges from the Milford Haven route.

Johnston is served by six of the Milford Haven weekday Down trains and nine in the Up direction.

K.1 Kemble

Swindon-Gloucester line between Swindon and Stroud. 90 m 79 ch from Paddington

The Act of June 21 1836 authorising the line between Gloucester and Cheltenham on the one hand and Swindon on the other provided that the track should be in a covered way where it passed Mr Robert Gordon's Kemble House, hence the 409 yd tunnel (90 m 41 ch to 90 m 60 ch). The same protectionism pushed the first station to a site later named Coates, with only an unadvertised junction platform at the present location to allow passengers to transfer to and from the short branch to Cirencester. Kemble and Cirencester were reached from the south in 1841, with the extension to Gloucester opening in 1845 and the branch to Tetbury in 1889.

Four lightweight railbuses were put to work on the two branches from February 2 1959, three additional halts opened and ticket issue taken over by the train guards. Sadly the increase in traffic was not enough to save the services and the lines closed in 1964/5. The route of the Tetbury line can still be followed along the south side of the A419 while the terminus at Cirencester now does duty as a bus station.

At Kemble station the route of the Tetbury branch can be seen veering away from the water tank, attractive in cream and blue and supported on six columns. On the Down platform itself bay windows at the rear face on to the former Tetbury platform and there are horsehair seats in the waiting room. The main buildings are on the Up side. Attractively constructed in stone, they are L-shaped with an arcade linking the Up and Cirencester branch platforms and with a main canopy supported by decorative ironwork. The overgrown dock is at the country end on the Up side and at the London end there is a headshunt and connection between the short spur along the branch platform and

The Kemble-Cirencester branch closed in 1965 and the station at Cirencester is now used by the bus company.

the main line which becomes single before entering the tunnel.

All passenger services on the route stop at Kemble which is staffed and serves a considerable area of Wiltshire and Gloucestershire.

Keyham—see Plymouth

K.2   Keynsham

Swindon-Bristol line between Bath and Bristol. 113 m 36 ch from Paddington

The country end of Keynsham's platforms are closed and out of use, the track has been lifted from the siding which led from the London end of the Up platform to Fry's factory and the old brick goods shed is in private hands. Just the two platforms with short canopies, a road bridge across the middle of the station, two Up sidings, ground frames and a crossover remain. The commuter hours service is provided by stops in Westbury line trains.

K.3   Kidwelly

Newport-Fishguard line between Llanelli and Carmarthen. 234 m 23 ch from Paddington*

Kidwelly is an unstaffed station with shelters on each of the two platforms, an unusual design of signal box and a lifting barrier crossing at the London end. East of the station there is a user-operated level crossing at Penybedd with miniature road

warning lights, and to the west a 92 yd viaduct carries the line over the Gwendreath river, the estuary of which it then accompanies. Kidwelly is served by a number of the Milford Haven and Pembroke Dock trains.

Kidwelly will re-acquire junction status with the new connection to Coedbach Washery referred to in the Cwmmawr Branch entry. The new line will diverge on the Up side by a junction facing Carmarthen.

Kilgetty—see Pembroke Dock Branch

K.4   Kingham

Oxford-Hereford line between Oxford and Moreton-in-Marsh. 84 m 59 ch from Paddington

Within two years of the opening of its 'Cotswold Line' in 1853, the Oxford, Worcester & Wolverhampton Railway had a branch to Chipping Norton, leaving the main line at Chipping Norton Junction (called Kingham from 1909). The junction acquired a second branch when the Bourton-on-the-Water Railway opened in 1862. By 1887, arising from the Banbury & Cheltenham Direct Railway Scheme, the two branches had become part of a route from King's Sutton on the Banbury-Oxford line to Hatherley Junction at Cheltenham. A direct link between the two sections, avoiding the reversal at Chipping Norton Junction, was brought into use in 1906.

Although the B&CD carried London-Cheltenham trains and a Hull/Newcastle-South Wales through service, local traffic was rarely heavy especially after the 'Road Motor Cars' started operating between Kingham and Banbury and linking Oxford and Cheltenham. Eventually, following a round of cuts in 1962, only the original route remained and many of Kingham's loops, bays, sidings and locomotive facilities became superfluous.

The Worcester line trains now use only Kingham's Up and Down main line platforms (the latter with modern ticket office buildings), but all the trains stop there and the station serves a wide area. The derelict B&CD platform, the route of the two branches and the abutments of the bridge link can still be seen, but the station footbridge no longer extends to the Langston Hotel, built in 1870 for the railway business.

Kings Nympton—see Barnstaple Branch

K.5 Kintbury

Reading-Taunton line between Newbury and Westbury. 58 m 42 ch from Paddington

Kintbury comprises just Up and Down platforms, the latter with a small brick shelter, a barrier crossing and the old goods yard area on the Down side. It is served by the Bedwyn-Newbury dmu service.

K.6 Knighton

Shrewsbury-Llanelli line between Craven Arms and Llandrindod Wells. 12 m 23 ch from Craven Arms

With its town in Wales and station in England, Knighton has strong associations with Offa's Dyke and gave its name to the local railway from Craven Arms. The small locomotive depot has long since gone and Knighton is no longer a ticket inspection station but the station buildings of weathered stone on the remaining Down platform retain an air of distinction. South of the station the Panpunton bridge over the River Teme marks the border between England and Wales.

K.7 Knucklas

Shrewsbury-Llanelli line between Craven Arms and Llandrindod Wells. 14 m 69 ch from Craven Arms

Knucklas is just a single platform conditional stop on the Central Wales route but it gives its name to the impressive viaduct nearby. Legend has it that some of the stonework from Mortimer's castle above was used in building the viaduct which helps the 1862-5 Central Wales Railway's route towards Llangynllo summit. Certainly the two castellated turrets at each end have a martial appearance and are fitting for the whole impressive structure of 13 semi-circular stone arches, each of 35 ft 9 in span and helping to lift the track to a maximum height of 69 ft above the valley floor.

Legend has it that stones from Mortimer's Castle were used in the construction of the great viaduct at Knucklas.

Lady Windsor Colliery Branch—see Abercynon and Ynysybwl Branch

Lamphey—see Pembroke Dock Branch

L.1 Langley

Paddington-Swindon line between Southall and Slough. 16 m 18 ch from Paddington

Langley, which got its first trains in 1845, is now served by the Paddington-Slough dmus. The station comprises central island plus two outer platforms, the one on the Up side having a twin-towered building. The Dolphin Junction crossovers between Main and Relief lines lie west of the station (17 m 3 ch and 17 m 40 ch) and the three-line Total Sidings oil terminal to the east (15 m 76 ch). The latter receives regular block train loads of oil from Waterston.

L.2 Langport

Reading-Taunton line between Castle Cary and Taunton. 129 m 73 ch from Paddington

Some red brick buildings of the former Langport East station are visible on the Down side, followed by a long viaduct, a box girder bridge over the River Parrett and then the former Curry Rivell Junction where the trackbed of the closed line from Yeovil and Langport West merges with the route of today's West of England main line. The branch, closed in 1964, was prone to winter flooding and this low, marshy part of Somerset proved a considerable challenge to the railway

engineers. The ten-arch viaduct on the cut-off route link to Somerton, for example, needed foundations sunk through some 50 ft of bog peat.

Lapford—see Barnstaple Branch

L.3 Largin

Taunton-Penzance line between Liskeard and Bodmin Road. 270 m 1 ch from Paddington*

From the former station at Doublebois the Cornwall Railway route drops steeply for nine miles to Lostwithiel. The bit between Doublebois and Bodmin Road is a land of green valleys, demanding seven viaducts but contributing great colourful rhododendron hedges as if in recompense. Largin signal box on the down side controls a short single line section east over the viaduct.

L.4 Lavington

Reading-Taunton line between Hungerford and Westbury. 86 m 55 ch from Paddington

Although only the goods shed remains at the former Lavington station, the location is still important as the site, at 88 m 40 ch, of the boundary between the London and West of England Divisions of the WR.

Lawrence Hill—see Bristol

L.5 Ledbury

Oxford-Hereford line between Great Malvern and Hereford. 136 m 6 ch from Paddington

Above left *East Largin Viaduct, one of many such viaducts in Cornwall.*

Above *Ledbury, where the double line from Hereford becomes single to pass through the small bore tunnel.*

Ledbury, an attractive and growing town, lies at the country end of the single line section which takes the Worcester-Hereford line through the Malvern Hills. From the summit of the line and Colwall Tunnel the gradients steepen to 1 in 80 to pass through the 1,316 yd Ledbury Tunnel (135 m 15 ch to 135 m 75 ch) and then into Ledbury station where the line becomes double again. The first approach speed restriction, 60 mph, is marked by a GWR style round board, 40 mph then applying through the tunnel itself. The single bore had a very bad reputation for poor ventilation in steam days when Up train locomotives had to work hard and the possibility of seeing the resident headless horseman ghost at Cummins Crossing can hardly have helped.

The station comprises just platforms and shelters plus the elegant signal box which operates the 'Lock and Block' working on the single line to Malvern Wells, unique on the WR. Banking engines used to use the dock on the Up side.

There is no trace of the junction for the Newent and Gloucester line which veered off south after the viaduct west of Ledbury.

Lelant—see St Ives Branch

Lelant Saltings—see St Ives Branch

L.6 Leominster

Shrewsbury-Newport line between Craven Arms and Hereford. 38 m 60 ch from Shrewsbury.

The station buildings at Leominster now look their age and it is difficult to imagine the station as a junction with trains east to Bromyard and Worcester and west to Titley, Kington and New Radnor, with links via Titley to Eardisley and Presteign— 20 branch trains a day in the 1930s in addition to the main line services. Not that the patronage was very great; opening was late and closure early.

The Shrewsbury & Hereford Railway was opened to passenger traffic on December 6 1853 but although the Worcester, Bromyard & Leominster Railway secured its enabling Act in 1861, it was 1897 before the whole route was finally completed. The Leominster & Kington Railway did much better, being authorised in 1854 and opened in 1857.

The route of the WB&L converges on the main line well south of Leominster station although the signal box is still sited in the junction area. The branch then ran parallel with the main line to the Down platform which was once an island and now has just a footbridge, shelter and the face to the Down main line. There are two refuge sidings on the Up side south of the station and the old goods shed there is now incorporated into a factory site. North of the station, beyond the barrier crossing, the route of the Kington branch veers off to the west. This branch was closed in 1964 (to passengers 1955) and the Bromyard portion of the branch to Worcester in 1952.

L.7 Lickey Incline

Birmingham-Bristol line between Barnt Green and Stoke Works Junction. 52 m 57 ch from Derby.

In the Up direction for 2 m 4 ch between Bromsgrove and Blackwell the former Bristol-Birmingham main line of the Midland Railway rises at 1 in 37¾. Gone are the days when all but the lightest trains needed assistance and the era of *Big Emma*, the huge 0-10-0 built in 1919 to take over this role from the Johnson 0-6-0 tanks. But banking is still provided for certain Up freight trains, the bankers coming on the rear as the train concerned stands at Bromsgrove signal G71 or G171 and then giving a plunger-operated signal to the driver of the train engine. The latter similarly notifies the Gloucester signalman who then clears the signal for the ascent to begin.

There are three sets of catch points on the Up line which is bi-directional between signals G16 and B18. The bankers come off their train at the top of the incline at Blackwell where separate regulations exist for the descent based on the weight and category of the train and the number of braked vehicles it has. The banking locomotives wait in the loop between the main lines before making their descent to await the next climb.

Terence Cuneo captured the spirit of steam on the Lickey bank in one of his notable paintings. Among the footnotes he records part of a poem on the tombstone in Bromsgrove churchyard of Thomas Scaife, a driver killed as a result of a boiler explosion on the Lickey Bank in the Bristol & Gloucester days in 1840.

L.8 Limpley Stoke

Westbury-Bristol line between Bradford-on-Avon and Bathampton Junction. 4 m 28 ch from Bathampton Junction

Little remains to remind today's traveller that Limpley Stoke was once a junction for the single line branch to the Bristol & North Somerset line at Hallatrow. This line, which took over the mantle of the old Somerset Coal Canal and used its Combe Hay Tunnel, was not completed throughout until 1910. Passenger services ceased in 1925 and the line was closed in 1951 but two years later came to life again to permit the filming of *The Titfield Thunderbolt.*

A wooden station building on the Down side is still visible at Limpley Stoke and a bridge remains to mark the course of the branch route, but the loops and sidings once used for coal traffic off the latter have all gone.

L.9 Liskeard

Taunton-Penzance line between Plymouth and Bodmin Road. 264 m 66 ch from Paddington*

The Cornwall Railway opened its station at Liskeard in 1859 but the long curve to link the main line with the Looe branch was not put in until 1901. The branch trains still leave from a separate platform at right angles to the main line and connected to it by a sharp curve over

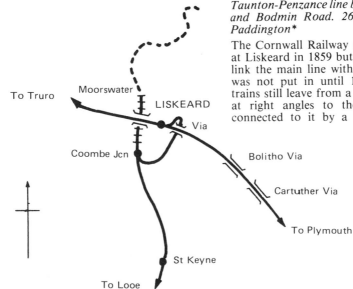

which passenger trains and long vehicles are not permitted to pass.

Once over the 150 ft viaduct which precedes Liskeard station, two short Down sidings are followed by the signal box and the Down platform—in a cutting and spanned by both a footbridge and a road overbridge. The Up side platform, with its modest buildings, is reached via a ramp from road level and a short footpath then leads from the London end to the branch station. There are further sidings off both the branch and the main line in the angle between the two.

An old coach stands at the top of the bank above the Up platform and the station is well blessed with a decoration of cotoneaster.

L.10   Llanbister Road

Shrewsbury-Llanelli line between Knighton and Llandrindod Wells. 21 m 55 ch from Craven Arms

Llanbister Road's single platform is 848 ft above sea level. From the summit at Llangynllo this section of the Central Wales Railway dips down at 1 in 122 and then up at 1 in 80, curving along the north side of the Lugg valley and through the crossing at Troidrhiwfedwen. To the south of this conditional stop for Shrewsbury-Swansea dmus the line drops steadily towards the River Aran and the Radnor Forest.

Llanbradach—see Rhymney Branch

L.11   Llandaf

Newport-Fishguard line, on the Merthyr branch from Cardiff. 4 m 27 ch from Cardiff

After Radyr Junction the main line from Merthyr to Cardiff continues as a double line plus an Up Relief line on which permissive working applies. The three tracks cross the River Taff and continue to Llandaf Loop Junction (4 m 37 ch) just north of Llandaf station.

The station has Up and Down platforms, with an ex-TVR signal box at the country end of the latter and controlling semaphore signals. The Down platform has a substantial canopy in traditional style, together with a more recent ticket office. The Up platform has a modern brick shelter and a footbridge links the two and then continues across the site of the former goods lines to the road beyond where a neat former station building, in

the distinctive TVR style, is now in private use. Officially Llandaf for Whitchurch, the station tends to be known as Llandaf North and it has a park-and-ride car park on the Up, forecourt side.

Behind the Llandaf Down platform is the space formerly occupied by the separate goods lines. Until recently a single track survived to Roath Branch Junction where a large group of sidings on the Down side was used for sorting wagons for repair at Cathays shops. From the junction a 5-mile line had curved through the eastern outskirts of Cardiff to the Roath Dock (1888-1968) and the sidings had originally been used for the storage of coal wagons using this route.

The Llandaf passenger service is as described for the Pontypridd-Taffs Well section although the station is used additionally as a turnround point for a couple of peak hour trains from the Cardiff direction on weekday mornings. The route continues as a double track from Llandaf and on this section Llandaf is a fringe box for the Cardiff panel.

L.12   Llandeilo

Shrewsbury Llanelli line between Llandovery and Llanelli. 18 m 9 ch from Llandeilo Junction

From the mountains to the north a long straight section leads through the old stations at Glanrhyd and Talley Road to Llandeilo. This was the meeting point of the LNWR and GWR influence, the junction for the route of the former to Carmarthen and its means of access to Llanelli and Swansea.

The Llanelly Railway reached Llandeilo on January 24 1857 and, by a lease of the Vale of Towy Railway, gained access to Llandovery the following year. Just ten years later the LNWR influence reached the latter and that company secured running powers over the Llanelly and a share in its VoT lease. Later this section became joint LNWR/GWR and that south of Llandeilo GWR with LNWR running powers.

The station is today a passing loop for the Swansea-Shrewsbury service of dmus with two platforms preceded in the Down direction by a red brick signal box and a goods and coal yard opposite. South of the station, which has a private refreshment room, the line crosses the River Towy before the trackbed of the former line to Carmarthen veers away to the west.

The yard at Llandeilo is serviced by a

thrice-weekly freight trip from Llandeilo Junction to Llandovery and back, worked by Class 3 locomotives to conform to current axle loading restrictions on the route.

Llandeilo Junction—see Llanelli

L.13 Llandovery

Shrewsbury-Llanelli line between Llandrindod Wells and Llandeilo. 29 m 24 ch from Llandeilo Junction

The Vale of Towy Railway reached Llandovery on April 1 1858 and the Central Wales Extension Railway on June 1 1868 to provide a through route from Craven Arms to Llanelli and a gateway for the LWNR to Swansea and West Wales. Standing at the foot of the long climb up to Sugar Loaf summit, Llandovery became the line's main engine shed and train formation point and provided the bankers for trains requiring assistance on the northbound journey.

Today Llandovery is still a passing point and block post on this 'light railway' portion of the Central Wales route. The LNWR signal box stands at the north end of the passing loop with a level crossing between it and the station. The former GWR yard was on the Up side, together with a surviving dock and refuge siding, the LMS shed and yard standing opposite. The joint interest is reflected in a signal which has an LMS post and GW arm.

On the VoT section south from Llandovery a four-span, plate girder bridge spans the Towy at Llwyn Jack and other, smaller bridges span tributaries.

L.14 Llandrindod Wells

Shrewsbury-Llanelli line between Knighton and Llandovery. 31 m 36 ch from Craven Arms

The Central Wales Railway received its enabling Act in 1859, started work at the Knighton end in 1860 and reached Llandrindod Wells in 1865. By this time a contractor had already been appointed for the Central Wales Extension Railway on to Llandovery, reached in 1868 by which time the constructing companies of both sections had been absorbed by the LNWR.

Railway access helped Llandrindod become a fashionable inland resort with Edwardian streets, Georgian-style architecture and up to 80,000 visitors in a busy season. The spa had a through service from Euston on Saturdays, taking just over five hours for the journey and usually well patronised. As many as 30 hotel porters would be on the station at the peak of the season, fully uniformed and working hard but some summer trains still needed five or ten minutes for luggage handling.

Llandrindod Wells, or Llandod as the locals call it, is still a popular and attractive town, served by the Shrewsbury-Swansea dmu service and by periodic dmu specials. It is a block post and passing loop, the signal box, the loop, a crossing and a stabling siding all lying north of the station where only the Down platform is used. This has been attractively renovated and a stone let into the platform records the first visit of HM the Queen to Wales. The Up platform has further buildings, equally pleasant and in use for permanent way staff and other BR purposes.

L.15 Llandybie

Shrewsbury-Llanelli line between Llandeilo and Llanelli. 13 m 4 ch from Llandeilo Junction

This is just a simple conditional stop on the descending section to Ammanford but it is mildly unusual in that the former station building now houses the Sheriff's Officer. North of Llandybie there is a former quarry siding on the Up side and, near the summit, the abandoned platforms at Derwydd Road.

L.16 Llanelli

Newport-Fishguard line between Swansea and Carmarthen. 225 m 20 ch from Paddington*

Llanelli stands alongside the estuary of the River Loughor which at this point forms the boundary between the counties of West Glamorgan and Dyfed. The town has important and long standing links with the coal and metal industries and is also renowned for the prowess of its rugby team. Its early industrial activity spawned local horse-worked railways: the Carmarthenshire Railway which opened in 1806 and has developed into BR's Cynheidre branch and the Llanelly Railroad & Dock Company which opened lines from 1833 onwards and provided the route for the western end of today's Swansea District and Central Wales lines. The main line opened from Landore to Carmarthen in

1852 by the South Wales Railway was thus something of a newcomer.

The two double track main line routes approaching Llanelli from the east converge at Llandeilo Junction (223 m 49 ch) where there is a marshalling yard on the Up side and on the Down, recess sidings for freight trains and a civil engineer's yard. Dominating the scene on the Up side is the BSC's Trostre tinplating plant, rail served by a connection from the Genwen Loop. This loop provides a direct link from Llandeilo Junction yard, by-passing the junction itself, to the Swansea District line at Genwen Junction. It is single track, for Up trains, but there is also a Down track from Genwen Junction to the facing connection into Trostre works and used by trains running to the BSC plant.

An Up Goods Loop, serving also as a reception line for the marshalling yard, accompanies the main line between Llanelli station and Llandeilo Junction. Between these points the modern railway cuts through the alignment of the Llanelly Railway's first line, from the docks to Dafen, opened in 1833. From 1852 until it closed in 1963 the two lines crossed on the level. Also in this area on the Up side is a coal and freight yard, locomotive holding sidings and sidings used for wagon repairs. Nearby is the former goods shed, the offices of which now house the BR Area Manager for Central

and West Wales and his staff. Opposite is the sole remnant of a once-extensive network of lines serving the docks area, the single track from the premises of a steel scrap processing company.

Operations at Llanelli station are constrained by the locally-controlled crossings at each end. There are two platforms with distinctive stone buildings, the main ones being on the Up side and

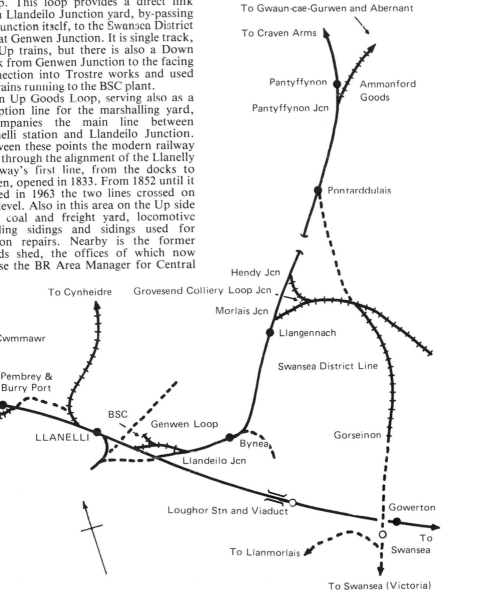

opening out into a large forecourt. Signalling on the Down line allows two trains to be in the platform together, permitting easy connections and reversal by trains on the Central Wales line service between Swansea and Shrewsbury. The station was extensively renovated in 1978-9 with the help of a grant from Dyfed County Council and received an attractive new ticket office as well as becoming the first to be signed bilingually.

West of Llanelli station is Llanelli West Junction (225 m 50 ch) where the single track Cynheidre branch diverges on the Up side by a junction facing Llanelli. Immediately beyond is Old Castle level crossing (225 m 51 ch) controlled from Llanelli West crossing box and monitored by closed-circuit television. On the Up side west of the crossing is the extensive premises of the now closed Duport Steel Company's works.

Virtually all West Wales passenger trains call at Llanelli, as do the dmus serving the Central Wales line. Through trains of oil tank cars from and to Milford Haven generally change crews at Llandeilo Junction and the marshalling yard there is the originating and terminating point for wagonload services to and from West Wales, and for the thrice weekly service to Llandeilo and Llandovery on the Central Wales line. Llandeilo Junction has services to and from Margam and Severn Tunnel Junction and the yard is also the terminal point for some inter-Regional Speedlink trains. The BSC Trostre plant is an important source of Speedlink traffic and it is also served by trains bringing vital supplies of steel coil from BSC Port Talbot via the Swansea District Line and the Genwen Loop. The bread and butter traffic at Llandeilo Junction yard is the local anthracite coal with numerous services conveying empty wagons to and bringing loaded ones away from nearby collieries. The yard also services local coal depots and the Carmarthen Bay power station and has links with the other marshalling or smaller exchange yards in the area.

L.17   Llangadog

Shrewsbury-Llanelli line between Llandovery and Llandeilo. 18 m 9 ch from Llandeilo Junction

Set amid a land of pastures, rivers and wooded hills, Llangadog's single platform lies at the end of a long straight section from Llandovery which crosses the River

Towy by the 93 yd River Towy Viaduct. The station is a condition stop for the Central Wales line dmu service.

L.18   Llangamarch

Shrewsbury-Llanelli line between Llandrindod Wells and Llandovery. 44 m 47 ch from Craven Arms

Llangamarch was formerly Llangamarch Wells, marking its link with the spa tradition of the Central Wales route. It is another of the single platform conditional stops on this line, on the descent from Sugar Loaf to Builth Road and with a 55 yd tunnel (43 m 79 ch to 44 m 1 ch) to the north. From the line, the former spa building can be seen embodied in the Lake Hotel on the east side of the track.

L.19   Llangennech

Shrewsbury-Llanelli line between Pantyffynnon and Llandeilo Junction. 3 m 1 ch from Llandeilo Junction

Llangennech is a conditional station on the double line portion common to the Central Wales line and the Swansea District line. It has just two bare platforms and is unstaffed.

L.20   Llangynllo

Shrewsbury-Llanelli line between Knighton and Llandrindod Wells. 18 m 57 ch from Craven Arms

From the Knighton direction the Central Wales line climbs at 1 in 60, through a cutting and into Llangynllo Tunnel (17 m 79 ch to 18 m 28 ch), 645 yds of curving masonry and brick-lined bore, 82 ft deep at the central air shaft. Then comes the summit, 980 ft above sea level, followed by the conditional station at Llangynllo. This was once a passing loop provided with two platforms, but only the Up platform is now used.

L.21   Llanharan

Newport-Fishguard line between Cardiff and Bridgend, 184 m 32 ch from Paddington*

The site of Llanharan station, closed in 1964, is a summit on the main line through South Wales and on the descent towards Bridgend is Llanharan opencast coal disposal point with sidings connected to the main line on the Down side. The effect of underground coal workings in this area has been to cause a cutting to sink and to maintain the correct track level the main lines have been supported by an embankment creating an interesting case of embankment within a cutting.

West from Llanharan the main line continues to Pencoed (187 m 6 ch) where there is an Up Goods Loop and a large GWR signal box controls a busy level crossing. A smaller GWR signal box survives on the Up side between Llanharan and Pencoed as a ground frame controlling Bryn-y-Gwynon level crossing. Pencoed station closed in 1964.

Llanishen—see Rhymney Branch

L.22 Llantarnam Junction

Shrewsbury-Newport line between Abergavenny and Newport. 36 m 26 ch from Hereford

The short line from Llantarnam Junction to Cwmbran Junction used to link the two routes from Newport to Pontypool. Llantarnam had trains from Newport to Hereford, Brynmawr and Blaenavon but, like its neighbours at Ponthir and Caerleon, is now only a collection of the remains of former facilities. The gaunt red brick signal box stands derelict on the Down side.

L.23 Llantrisant

Newport-Fishguard line between Cardiff and Bridgend. 181 m 43 ch from Paddington*

Actually in the township of Pontyclun, Llantrisant station closed in 1964 but the location is still important as a junction for the lines to Coed Ely and Cwm collieries and coke ovens.

Until 1952 passenger trains from Llantrisant ran to Pontypridd (an ex-Taff Vale Railway service over the line which now ends at Cwm) and until 1958 to Penygraig (an ex-GWR service on the line which now terminates at Coed Ely). South of the main line an ex-TVR service ran to the coast at Aberthaw until 1930 and there was a service as far as Cowbridge (only) on the same line until 1951. The first 1½ m continued in use, serving the Llanharry ironstone mine, until 1975 and although the track has now been lifted the route is still visible at its former junction with the main line.

From the Cardiff direction a long gentle climb precedes the approach to Llantrisant and there are Up and Down Goods Loops at Miskin (179 m 38 ch). The main line has followed the course of the Ely Valley this far but at Llantrisant the river curves northwards and the main line continues straight ahead towards the summit at Llanharan.

In addition to the junction at Llantrisant, on the Up side and facing Cardiff, there is a loop, a coal and freight yard, a locomotive stabling siding and a former goods shed. Further sidings flank the double track of the branches towards their point of separation at Mwyndy Junction. At the country end of the Up loop Llantrisant West ground frame (181 m 76 ch) controls the level crossing there. One mile further on the Cardiff panel box hands over to the Port Talbot panel.

Traffic to and from the branches is hauled on the main line by Class 37 power and linked to Radyr and Severn Tunnel Junction yards. There is also provision for services to local docks, power stations and BSC works conveying coal in block train loads, and for a through service for coke to a depot at Stourbridge Junction which then distributes to industrial users. Shunting at Llantrisant is carried out by a Class 08 locomotive.

L.24 Llanwern

Newport-Fishguard line between Severn Tunnel Junction and Newport. 153 m 5 ch from Paddington*

From the London direction the British Steel Corporation's works at Llanwern dominate the rail approach to the town of Newport. Standing between the main line and the Severn Estuary the plant fills 3½ m with its rolling mills, blast furnaces and cooling towers. It is part of the BSC's Strip Mills Division and was originally Spencer Works, a name that is still in frequent use in and around the area.

The rail service for Llanwern works is provided via the 'Service Lines', a 3 m double track loop running from one end of the site to the other. BSC property but used by BR trains, this loop diverges from the main line at Llanwern Works East Junction (153 m 5 ch), adjacent to Bishton level crossing, and rejoins it at Llanwern Works West Junction (156 m 3 ch), in each case the junction being with the Relief lines which are the southernmost pair along this stretch. The main lines and the junctions are controlled from Newport panel box, movements on the Service Lines coming under the jurisdiction of the BR signalmen who man the control centre known as Llanwern (Spencer Works) signal box.

Incoming BR trains are brought to a stand on the Service Lines and then proceed on instructions from the signalman or on hand signals. From this point movement is taken over by the BSC's own fleet of diesel shunting locomotives which undertake the positioning within the extensive network of sidings which lead to various parts of the works. At the east end, for example, are the loading bays of the slab and rolling mills and at the west end the tipplers for coal and iron ore discharge. BSC staff control all shunting operations.

Some 30-40 freight trains are scheduled to and from Llanwern each 24 hours, Mondays to Fridays, together with some light engine movements. Most services are block train loads of single commodities, primarily coking coal from the Western Valleys lines, iron ore from Port Talbot harbour, fuel oil from Llandarcy refinery, steel coil to Newport Docks and steel coil to the BSC tinplate plant at Ebbw Vale for coating. In addition trains carry semi-finished steel between Llanwern and other BSC works, eg, at Port Talbot and Shotton. Local trips link Llanwern with East Usk and Severn Tunnel Junction, the latter being used to give a connection into the Speedlink services and into a conventional wagonload service to Sheffield.

Llanwern's coking coal arrives in conventional vacuum-braked 21.5-tonne capacity wagons and these are tipped individually. The iron ore, however, comes in BSC-owned rotary tippler wagons of 101.5 tonnes gross laden weight, 30 wagons at a time, and is discharged without the wagons being uncoupled. These wagons can rotate on their couplings, enabling the train to be propelled through the tippler and each wagon to be rotated through 160 degrees, one at a time, without uncoupling. The two Class 56 engines which bring the train in wait near the Service Lines while their train is propelled through the tippler by a ram-like lineside 'positioner'. The trains which carry this iron ore from Port Talbot are the heaviest in Britain, with a payload of 2,316 tonnes and a gross trailing weight of 3,048 tonnes.

The main line infrastructure either side of Llanwern recognises the volume of traffic passing to and from the works. West of Severn Tunnel Junction the two Main lines are the centre pair of the four but at Bishton a flyover carries the Up Relief line from the north to the south side to pair the Relief lines together and allow

freight access from Llanwern without crossing the path of the intensive passenger service. At the other end, crossovers link all lines at Newport East Usk Junction. Bishton also has a level crossing, controlled from a substantial GWR signal box now acting as a ground frame.

L.25   Llanwrda

Shrewsbury-Llanelli   line   between Llandovery and Llandeilo. 25 m 40 ch from Llandeilo Junction

Another conditional call for the dmus working between Shrewsbury and Swansea. Of the previous two staggered platforms, only the Up one is now used.

L.26   Llanwrtyd

Shrewsbury-Llanelli   line   between Llandrindod Wells and Llandovery. 47 m 77 ch from Craven Arms

Llanwrtyd, once Llanwrtyd Wells, lies on the climb to Sugar Load summit. Ahead of them trains still have nearly 4 m of 1 in 70 and 1 in 80 via Berthddu Crossing, quite a stiff climb for the long summer passenger trains that used to work this way to Swansea.

The station is a passing loop and still has an LNWR atmosphere. It is 74 ch south of the LNWR signal box on the Up side at the end of the loop.

Llwynypia—see Treherbert Branch

L.27   Looe Branch

Taunton-Penzance line, branch from Liskeard. 8 m 48 ch

Distances on the Looe branch increase towards Liskeard and start at 19 ch instead of zero, giving an early clue that this is no ordinary branch line. The 33-minute journey in which the train twice points north to get south to the coast confirms this. And the fact that the name of the enterprise was the Liskeard & Looe Union Canal Company until 1895 gives some idea of the line's origins.

The canal company was authorised, by an Act of June 22 1825, to construct a 26 ft wide canal of just under 6 m from Tarras Pill to Moorswater. It was opened in 1827-8 but, with the opening in 1844 of

Right *Trains on the Looe branch must reverse at Coombe Junction, as this dmu is doing.*

the Liskeard & Caradon Railway northwards to the copper mines and granite quarries of Dartmoor, became so overburdened that powers were sought to build a railway in its place. These were granted by an Act of May 11 1858 and a line built along the route of the canal, opened for goods in 1860 and passengers in 1879. An Act of 1895 revived an old Cornwall Railway idea of making a link with the main line and this was brought into use six years later. From 1909 the GWR worked both the L&L and the L&C, closing the latter in the war years as the mines became exhausted and changing the character of the former from a busy freight line into a branch for summer visitors and tourists.

Nowadays the branch has a basic service of eight trains each way on weekdays with one extra on summer Saturdays and six trains each way on summer Sundays. Electric token working applies as far as Coombe Junction where the trains reverse and one train operation is then in force over the remaining section to Looe.

The trains for Looe, single power car dmus outside the peak periods, leave from their own separate platform at Liskeard. This is situated north of and at right angles to the main line and starts the curve that carries the branch single line through almost 360 degrees in the 2 m 14 ch to Coombe Junction (6 m 53 ch), situated beneath and south of the main line. The short remaining line north from Coombe Junction to Moorswater, where the L&L made junction with the L&C, is now used only by a freight trip working.

Coombe Junction consists of a single platform, a level crossing and the ground frame used by the trainmen to operate the points for going forward to the next station at St Keyne (5 m 3 ch). Although the station is tiny, it gives access to a museum of musical instruments and to a 'well' which promises domination to which ever marriage partner drinks before the other. The very keen eye can spot traces of the old canal on the west side of the line along this section which leads on to Causeland (3 m 58 ch) and then the slightly larger station at Sandplace (2 m 29 ch). For the final stretch into Looe the branch takes a course along the east bank of the river and terminates at the present Looe station (19 ch), a simple affair of a single platform and shelter. The line formerly continued towards the town and its original mileages were calculated from Looe Quay.

L.28 Lostwithiel

Taunton-Penzance line between Bodmin Road and Par. 277 m 34 ch from Paddington *

From Bodmin Road the main line drops through the 88 yd Brown Queen Tunnel (275 m 16 ch to 275 m 20 ch) to meet the Fowey Estuary at Lostwithiel. This is the beginning of the china clay country and much activity is usually visible on the Down side where a single line to Carne Point leads off from a junction beyond the bridge at the country end of the station. This is the route used by the trains of china clay for shipment, the lorry traffic using a new road along the route of the old line from St Blazey to Fowey. Lostwithiel's other major traffic used to be milk, still represented by the creamery siding at the London end of the railway area.

There are Up and Down Goods Loops at Lostwithiel and a double barrier crossing at the London end of the station. The latter consists of two platforms with wooden buildings and there is a wooden goods shed and sundry sidings on the Up side and a signal box on the Down platform. Behind this are further sidings for clay traffic.

L.29 Loughor

Newport-Fishguard line between Swansea and Llanelli. 221 m 49 ch from Paddington *

Loughor's ruined castle looks down upon the former station once used by the fishermen and women of the estuary to take their catch to Swansea market. The main line crosses the Loughor Estuary by the Loughor Viaduct, steel-decked and comprising 18 spans of 39 ft with timber piers supported on timber piles.

L.30 Ludlow

Shrewsbury-Newport line between Craven Arms and Hereford. 27 m 42 ch from Shrewsbury

Just two platforms with shelters and linked by a footbridge, standing in the shadow of the Shropshire hills and served by the trains of the Cardiff-Crewe service. The former goods shed stands beside the Up line at the north end of the station and a short tunnel heralds the approach from the south. The short branch to Clee Hill closed in 1960/2.

Luxulyan—see Newquay Branch

L.31   Lydney

Gloucester-Newport line between Gloucester and Chepstow. 141 m 33 ch from Paddington

The station at Lydney is a very modest affair, just Up and Down platforms plus shelters, the one on the Down side being formed from an earlier building. The service is provided by the Gloucester-Cardiff dmus and the line is also used by Inter-City trains between Birmingham and South Wales and by freight services to and from Severn Tunnel Junction. The station itself is unstaffed although the signal box—Lydney Crossing Ground Frame—is manned for the fairly constant operation of the barriers of the level crossing.

On the Gloucester side of the station are Up and Down Goods Loops, the former providing the rusting connection with the former Severn & Wye Railway system and all that is left of the fascinating network of early tramroads and later railways which once honeycombed the Forest of Dean. Lydney-Parkend was the central part of the S&W line from Berkeley Road, on the other side of the Severn, over the Severn Bridge and on through Lydney to Parkend and Lydbrook Junction. Beyond Parkend there were branches to Coleford and Cinderford and at Lydbrook Junction connection was made with the Monmouth-Ross-on-Wye line. Ownership of the S&W was finally joint LMS and GWR and although passenger trains ceased beyond Lydney Town in 1929, they continued to run from that point via Lydney Junction to Berkeley Road until the collapse of part of the Severn Bridge in 1960. General freight services from Lydney into the Forest of Dean ceased in 1967 but mineral traffic continued on the line to Parkend until 1976 after which a mineral extraction company paid BR to retain the line. This arrangement has now ceased, to allow the Dean Forest Railway Society Ltd to fulfil their ambition to acquire and operate on the branch.

The S&W route from the junction at Lydney heads through the town and crosses the main road at SO 633 033 where a shopping development has cut into the remains of the former platform of Lydney Town station. Between the two points are two groups of sidings used, at various times, for loading coal brought from the Forest by road and for stabling vans. From the same point diverged the Severn Bridge Railway's 2½ m route to the former Severn Bridge station and then the 1,387 yd bridge itself. The abutments of the bridge by which this crossed over the present line are still visible at SO 669 042 and a signal box is hidden in the woods above. In the other direction, the S&W line used to cross the main line on the level on its way to Lydney harbour where the remains of the coal loading facilities can still be seen at SO 650 014.

Lydney Harbour, where a line for unloading coal to barges and coastal vessels once occupied the foreground.

Lympstone—see Exmouth Branch

Maerdy Branch—see Treherbert Branch

M.1 Maidenhead

*Paddington-Swindon line between Slough
and Reading. 24 m 19 ch from Paddington*

Originally served by a station much nearer
Taplow which was the terminus of the first
section of the Great Western Railway,
Maidenhead got its own main line station
in 1871. Now there are three platforms
with faces to the main and relief lines and
with the northern face of the Up Relief
line platform serving the branch trains
which run to Bourne End and Marlow.
This also has a modest overall roof and a
bay at the London end. In addition there
are crossovers at Maidenhead East (23 m
58 ch), a brick shed in the goods yard and
a loading ramp for the Ford vehicle
compound.

Although subsequently widened to
accommodate four tracks, Maidenhead
Bridge on the London side of the station
still retains the elegant appearance Brunel
gave it. It aroused much controversy at
the time of its construction for the two
spans, although of 128 ft, rose only 24 ft 6
in to create one of the flattest arch shapes
that had been constructed in brick. The
premature removal of the centerings by
the contractor led to an expectation that
the whole edifice might collapse but,
complete with flood arches at each end, it
remains sound and elegant over 140 years
later.

M.2 Maiden Newton

*Westbury-Weymouth line between Yeovil
Pen Mill and Dorchester West. 154 m 12
ch from Paddington**

Maiden Newton might have been a main
line station if the GWR's Devon & Dorset
Railway had ever built its line from there
to Exeter. But the scheme was but one
more manoeuvre in the Great Western's
feuding with the London & South Western
and the station had to be content with its
status as a junction for the meandering
branch to Bridport and the extension on
to West Bay.

The station is served by the dmus to and
from Weymouth and is a passing loop
with a signal box on the Down side.
Electric token working applies on the
single line to Yeovil Pen Mill and tokenless
block in the opposite direction to the SR.
The main station buildings, a substantial

group in flint, are on the Up side where
there was also a bay for the Bridport
trains. On the same side at the country
end are the dock, coal storage area and a
refuge siding.

M.3 Malvern Link

*Oxford-Hereford line between Worcester
and Hereford. 127 m 75 ch from Paddington*

After several battles between the GWR
and LNWR camps, the Worcester &
Hereford Railway became a reality as a
result of backing from the neighbouring
Newport, Abergavenny & Hereford
concern and the first section was opened
from Henwick to Malvern Link on July 25
1859. The route was extended on to
Malvern Wells in the following year and,
apart from this brief spell as a temporary
terminus, the station has led a very
ordinary existence serving the north end
of the long Malvern township. It now
consists of just Up and Down platforms
with attractive wooden shelters on each.
The former station house, a pleasant
building of irregular sandstone blocks
with lighter stone facings, forms part of
the country end of the Down platform
and there are some fine railings amid the
foliage on the Up side.

M.4 Malvern Wells

*Oxford-Hereford line between Worcester
and Hereford. 130 m 13 ch from Paddington*

Once blessed with two stations, Malvern
Wells is now significant mainly as the
point at which the Worcester-Hereford
route singles for the passage through
Colwall Tunnel. In addition to the signal
box there is a Down Goods Loop, a refuge
siding on the Up side and a collection of
vintage catch point notices (because of the
1 in 80 gradient in the Up direction)
complete with the old symbol of hand
with pointing finger.

The Hereford route station, denoted in
some editions of Bradshaw as 'The
Common Station', was closed as a result
of a fire only a year after its opening in
1860, but reopened after three years
closing again in 1965. The Midland
station, Hanley Road, was sited about a
mile further from Great Malvern along
the line from Malvern Junction to
Tewkesbury and was closed in 1952. New
Midland Sidings were closed in 1968 but
still function as a coal depot without rail

access. They lie on the Down side just before reaching the signal box.

Manorbier—see Pembroke Dock Branch

M.5 Marazion

Taunton-Penzance line between St Erth and Penzance. 324 m 56 ch from Paddington*

Not far from St Michael's Mount, Marazion was once a passenger station and a busy loading point for Cornish broccoli. Now the only remaining railway presence is that of the West of England main line itself, but memories are kept alive by the Old Station House Restaurant and its four Pullman coaches which stand behind the remains of the old Down platform.

M.6 Margam

Newport-Fishguard line between Bridgend and Port Talbot. 198 m 35 ch from Paddington*

Margam sorting sidings and associated installations lie on former sand dunes on the seaward side of the South Wales main line as it approaches Port Talbot. The yard was completed in 1960 to provide modern sorting facilities for traffic to and from the Swansea area and West Wales and, in particular, traffic to and from the then Steel Company of Wales (now the BSC). The yard had the latest automated hump shunting facilities and was hailed as the most modern in Europe but changes in the volume and pattern of freight, and the reduced output of the BSC works, have altered Margam's role. Companion yards envisaged for Gloucester and Shrewsbury have not materialised.

Currently Margam acts as a reception and sorting yard for movements to and from BSC Port Talbot, for traffic to and from the Tondu lines reached by the Ogmore Vale Extension (OVE) route and for traffic to and from yards in the immediate vicinity of Port Talbot.

The approach to Margam from the London direction involves the double track main line in a long descent from Stormy summit, mostly at 1 in 93 and 1 in 139, to the sea level plain on which Margam yard and Port Talbot steel works stand. At Water Street Junction (197 m 14 ch) two tracks diverge on the Down side to the sorting sidings. Until 1980 the sidings were shunted by the hump system from the east end of the yard but now all

shunting is on the flat and from the west end. The hump control tower remains at the east end but this is now used just for signalling and the hump reception sidings at this end of the yard are out of use. At ground level between the hump and the main line is the Area Freight Centre and TOPS office and at the west end of the complex lie a train crew depot, diesel maintenance depot, wagon repair shops and Margam Sorting Sidings signal box (199 m 7 ch).

From the west end of Margam yard there are lines to join, at Abbey Works East Junction (199 m 30 ch), the OVE lines and lines direct to two BSC installations, viz the 'Grange' tippler at which coal is unloaded for the coke ovens and Abbey South Sidings where all other traffic (eg, outwards steel and inwards limestone) is exchanged with the BSC internal network. The signal box at Abbey Works East is located on the Down side of the main line.

Bridging the main line, more or less parallel with the west end of the yard, is the single track line from Tondu, known as the OVE line. Once over the main line it splits into lines serving the two BSC installations (Grange and Abbey South Sidings) and a line down to Abbey Works East where it is joined by the link from the Margam sorting sidings. The sidings here are used for the reversal of trains between the Tondu line and the yard and beyond them the OVE line becomes double track and runs along the Down side of the main line, over the Heol-y-Deliaid accommodation crossing, to Abbey Works West Junction now controlled by Port Talbot panel box. Here the OVE splits again into connections with the main line and a Down goods line and into the line to Port Talbot Harbour used by the iron ore trains to and from Llanwern. Beyond Abbey Works West the Up and Down Goods Lines continue to just beyond Port Talbot station.

The area where the OVE bridges the main line is known as Margam Moors. A link between the two on the Up side is now little used but the loops on this side are used for crew changing purposes by main line freight trains. On the Down side two relief lines diverge from the main line and run alongside the OVE to Abbey Works East but these and the Up Arrival Line which connects them to the yard are little used now that hump shunting has ceased. Other BR and BSC lines are out of use and awaiting recovery and further track and signalling simplifications may follow.

In addition to through passenger and freight traffic on the main line, traffic to and from Margam can be broadly classified into fuel, raw materials and steel moved for the BSC and traffic to and from the sorting sidings. Block trains of coking coal for the BSC are worked to the 'Grange' tippler sidings and other traffic is exchanged via Abbey South sidings. This comprises a regular nightly block train of limestone in covered hopper wagons from the Peak District, frequent inter-works trains of semi-finished steel between BSC Llanwern and BSC Port Talbot, trains of coil for the Velindre and Trostre tinplate works and for Shotton (and, occasionally, Ebbw Vale) and the balancing empty wagon movements.

Conventional wagonload trains link Margam with other yards at Severn Tunnel Junction, Radyr, Llandeilo Junction and Swansea Burrows Sidings and there is a nightly through service to Sheffield. Local workings are to and from collieries on or via the Tondu line and to such local yards and depots as Briton Ferry and Bridgend Coity. The Llandeilo Junction Speedlink services call at the sorting sidings and Margam occasionally originates its own Speedlink trains. Some traffic from Llandarcy oil refinery passes via Margam and there are occasional movements of empty mineral wagons between the yard and Newport.

Shunting at Margam is carried out by Class 08 locomotives, eight of which are allocated to Margam maintenance depot where servicing of main line locomotives is also undertaken. A significant activity at the wagon repair shops is the contract maintenance of the BSC bogie wagons used for the movement of iron ore from Port Talbot Harbour to Llanwern.

Movements on the main line are controlled from Port Talbot panel box and those on the freight lines from Margam Hump Tower, Margam Sorting Sidings and Abbey Works East signal boxes. Along the OVE line the electric token system of single line control applies on the section Abbey Works East-Cefn Junction signal box.

M.7   Marley Tunnels

Taunton-Penzance line between Totnes and Plymouth. 227 m 62 ch from Paddington*

These twin 867 yd tunnels (227 m 62 ch to 228 m 22 ch) lie near the top of Rattery bank. The first was provided on the South Devon Railway's single line to meet the conditions of Sir Walter Carew for the sale of the land. The separate Up line tunnel was added when the route was doubled.

M.8   Marlow Branch

Paddington-Swindon line, branch from Maidenhead. 7 m 8 ch.

This outer suburban branch line comprises 4 m 36 ch of single line to the two-platform dead end at Bourne End, with a reversal there followed by another 2 m 52 ch of single line to Marlow. After leaving the country end of Maidenhead's Up Relief line platform the route runs through the North Town housing area and then finds the open countryside as it heads through Furze Platt and Cookham for the descent to the River Thames. Bourne End is on the north bank of the river, the course of which the second section of the line follows before turning under the by-pass towards the town and terminus at Marlow.

The original route was that of the broad gauge Wycombe Railway from Maidenhead to High Wycombe, but this was closed north of Bourne End on May 4 1970 and the station layout altered to facilitate trains reversing on to the branch to Marlow. Bourne End was once Marlow Road and Marlow originally Great Marlow, the latter giving its name to the Great Marlow Railway which promoted and opened the branch (on June 28 1873). It was taken over by the GWR in 1897 and might have been part of a link with the Henley branch but for local opposition. In 1966/7 the line's goods facilities were withdrawn and a new platform built on one of the former sidings at Marlow to bring the branch to its present form.

Furze Platt (25 m 36 ch from Paddington) comprises concrete platform, ticket office and a 10 mph open level crossing but Cookham (27 m 12 ch) still has something of the air of a traditional GWR station despite the loss of one platform and the passing loop. The barrier crossing here is controlled from the former signal box and protected by traditional semaphore signals. Next comes a drop to the three-span girder bridge across the river, another traditional station at Bourne End (28 m 55 ch) and then the final stretch—at 15 mph through the open level crossings at Brooksby (18 ch from Bourne End) and Marina (21 ch)—to Marlow (2 m 54 ch).

This now consists of just a platform and a shelter, but the name 'Marlow Donkey' on a nearby public house is a reminder of the affectionate title dubbed on the branch locomotive in the more spacious days of steam traction.

The branch has enjoyed a generous service of 20 or so trains a day for some time. A single power car and trailer operate the off-peak through service and become the Bourne End-Marlow shuttle in the busier periods to allow three-car sets to work the section from Maidenhead and produce an increase in capacity and reduction in interval. Working is on the No Signalman Token system with electric tokens, One Train operation with a train staff applying beyond Bourne End.

M.9 Meeth Branch

Continuation of Barnstaple branch. 23 m 50 ch

This is a freight-only line, single apart from the passing loop at Torrington and kept open for the clay traffic tripped daily from Petrockstow and Meeth. It was part of a through route to the LSWR main line at Halwill although worked as separate portions with that south of Torrington down to two through trains each way daily, plus some local services, even before the Second World War. The service via Barnstaple to Bideford and Torrington used to be busy at holiday times but dropped steadily to the point where one-coach trains were adequate. Passenger traffic ceased altogether in 1965 although there was a brief re-opening in January 1968 when severe weather damaged the Bideford road bridge.

The origins of this route date back to the era of the North Devon scheming centred upon the Barnstaple branch. Fremington, a busy port at that time, had a horse-worked link to Barnstaple from 1848 but passenger services followed the opening to Barnstaple in 1854 and the extension to Bideford in the following year. Further extension, to Torrington, came in 1872 with the North Devon & Cornwall Junction link between there and Halwill waiting until 25 years into the present century. As far as Dunsbear Halt the ND&CJ used the route of the North Devon Clay Company's 1880 3 ft gauge tramway. The other railway in the area was the Bideford, Westward Ho! & Appledore but this ran on the opposite side of the estuary of the River Torridge and lasted only from 1901/8 to 1917.

Train Staff and Ticket working applies on the Barnstaple-Torrington section via Fremington (grounds frames at 213 m 78 ch and 214 m 3 ch), East Yelland (CEGB connection ground frame at 215 m 74 ch), the 10 mph open level crossing at Holloway (216 m 9 ch), the 83 yd Instow Tunnel (217 m 36 ch to 217 m 39 ch), Instow open level crossing (217 m 51 ch) and the 196 yd Landcross Tunnel (222 m 19 ch to 222 m 27 ch). Fremington Quay used to be busy with clay exports and coal imports and the large goods depot at Bideford included a clay siding along the wharf but all is quiet now.

Torrington (225 m 33 ch) had traditional Cattle Dock Road, Mileage Road and Shed Road with a small loco shed opposite. Until 1980 milk was forwarded from the creamery but the station's sole role is now that of a passing point and of control of movements on the remaining section of line to the English China Clays and Watts, Blake, Bearne works. The distances start again at Torrington and, once over the viaduct, there follows a

South from Torrington towards Meeth this is typical of the North Devon countryside through which the clay line passes.

Torrington station.

winding stretch with 5 mph open crossings at Watergate (1 m 58 ch), Vinney Copse (3 m 24 ch), Yarde (4 m 41 ch), Dunsbear (5 m 47 ch) and Petrockstow (7 m 62 ch). The clay traffic originates at substantial underground and surface works between the former Petrockstow station (7 m 67 ch) and the Meeth Clay Co's Siding (9 m 42 ch) which precedes the old Meeth Halt.

M.10   Meldon Quarry Branch

Barnstaple line, branch from Crediton. 19 m 55 ch

In 1862 the Okehampton Railway was authorised to build a line from Coleford Junction on the North Devon Railway. This was eventually to grow into the backbone of the LSWR network in Devon and Cornwall and to carry thousands of passengers to and from Bude, others to the Cornish resorts around Wadebridge and Padstow, and yet more over Dartmoor to reach Plymouth via the Tamar Valley. In the era of BR contraction this became known as 'The Withered Arm' and eventually lost its passenger services when the Exeter-Okehampton passenger trains made their last journey in 1972 and the intermediate stations at Bow, North Tawton and Sampford Courtenay closed down.

Today the line remains open to a point between Okehampton and the former Meldon Junction to serve the 245-acre Meldon Quarry which produces 200,000 tons annually of excellent igneous rock ballast for the permanent way activities on the Western and Southern Regions. Although the route separates from the North Devon line at Crediton, the two single lines run parallel as far as the former Coleford Junction and then part. The Meldon line, worked on the one train basis, continues through Okehampton (197 m 25 ch) with its once substantial layout which included a small locomotive shed and turntable, five-siding goods yard and the military sidings and dock. Meldon Quarry ground frame stands at 198 m 76 ch and the running line ends at 199 m 7 ch.

Two of the three quarry faces are worked and 400,000 tons of rock are blasted each year for the primary and secondary crushers to convert not only to ballast but also to smaller stone for cesses, surfaces and sale locally. Blasting takes place at 12.30 pm daily under strict safety precautions, including the movement of any train locomotive, the trainmen and the train staff to a designated safety point once the pneuphonic horn has sounded the advance warning signal. Extensive landscaping in 1979 gave the quarry a screen of a 100 ft hill and 8,000 young trees.

M.11   Melksham

Swindon-Bristol line between Thingley Junction and Bradford Junctions on diversionary route via Bradford-on-Avon/ Trowbridge. 99 m 77 ch from Paddington

Melksham was opened with the first section of the Wilts, Somerset & Weymouth Railway on September 5 1848. Although it lost its freight status in 1964 and passenger trains in 1966 a few sidings remain for the oil storage and seasonal

Some activity still remained at Melksham in 1981, the single line from Thingley Junction being used as a diversionary route.

fertiliser business. The route itself is retained for diversionary use and is worked on the No Signalman Token system. It is single, although the former Down line remains through Melksham station and is used for wagon storage.

M.12   Menheniot

Taunton-Penzance line between Plymouth and Liskeard. 261 m 61 ch from Paddington*

On weekdays four local trains in each direction call at this quiet, simple Cornish station which still has its SDR chalet-style buildings plus the brick building of a signal box on the Down side.

M.13   Merehead Quarry Junction Branch

Reading-Taunton line, branch from Witham. 3 m 50 ch

Where tank engines whistled and milk churns once clattered huge stone trains have now taken over, conveying the production from Foster Yeoman's quarry to terminals around London and in the counties of the South East. What is now a short branch from the West of England main line originally ran to Shepton Mallet and on to Wells where it linked up with the Cheddar Valley & Yatton Railway but the passenger service ended in 1963 and, after the closure of Foster Yeoman's Dulcote Quarry siding, the route was cut

Merehead Quarry soon after opening and before the installation of the overhead loading system.

Foster Yeoman's Merehead Quarry stone terminal.

back to Cranmore. The Merehead-Cranmore section is now, in effect, a siding extension from Merehead to serve the Shell-Mex bitumen installation and, at the same time, retain rail access to David Shepherd's East Somerset Railway.

The practice of moving Mendip limestone aggregates in block train loads developed in the 1960s and accelerated after the Merehead rail access facilities had been rebuilt. Now this short branch, worked on the No Signalman Token basis, handles up to 20 stone trains daily. Empty wagons, both BR and Foster Yeoman, pass via the Chord Line from which they are accepted on to the arrival sidings; outwards stone is transferred from the Exchange Sidings to the BR outward siding. The overall layout, which can be seen from the A361, comprises a triangle with a base line linking Witham and Cranmore and the apex leading to the crossing of the main road and into the quarry where movements are handled by Foster Yeoman motive power.

M.14 Merthyr Branch

Newport-Fishguard line, branch from Cardiff Central. 24 m 63 ch

Abercynon and the branch south thereof are covered in other entries, this one covering the northern portion of the branch, from Abercynon (exclusive) to Merthyr Tydfil. This was the uppermost section of the original main line of the Taff Vale Railway, engineered with the advice of Brunel (although standard gauge) and the pioneer main line steam locomotive railway in Wales. Today the route has two prime functions: as a passenger railway linking Merthyr Tydfil and the upper Taff valley with Pontypridd and Cardiff, and as a coal-carrying railway for the output from Merthyr Vale colliery, 5 m south of the town.

The Merthyr Tydfil-Abercynon line opened in 1841, Abercynon having been reached from Cardiff the previous year. However, it closely parallels an earlier 'rail way', the horse-traction Merthyr Tramroad which connected the vast iron works of the Merthyr Tydfil/Dowlais area with the Glamorganshire Canal at Abercynon. It was over this tramroad that Richard Trevithick's pioneer steam locomotive had made its first, historic journey back in 1804. In that early part of the last century Merthyr came to be the largest iron making centre in the world. By 1831 its population exceeded that of Newport, Cardiff and Swansea combined and it later became a magnet for railways, evidence of which can still be seen from the one line which remains.

The present island platform terminus at Merthyr Tydfil has modern station offices and was completed in 1971. Located in the centre of the town, it occupies the site of a larger, Brunel-style High Street station opened by the Vale of Neath Railway in

1853 for its branch from Hirwaun in the adjacent Cynon valley, and used by the TVR from 1877. There are run-round facilities and a former freight and coal yard on the Down side. The Merthyr Tydfil mileage of 24 m 51 ch is from a change of mileage point between Central and Queen Street stations and 12 ch from the former. A 1982 addition was a mural on the Up side, portraying the history of the town since 480 AD and prepared by the pupils of Pen-y-dre school.

Just south of the terminus, on the Up side, is the site of the original TVR terminus, Plymouth Street, which was used as a goods station until 1967. Further on is the site of Mardy Junction and the

Above and below *The old station at Merthyr as it was in 1947, and as it is to-day, modernised and simplified.*

trackbed of a line diverging on the Up side and which led to three others: the GWR/ Rhymney Railway joint line parallel to the TVR but on the west side of the River Taff and leading to the Neath-Pontypool line at Quakers Yard; the ex-Vale of Neath line which tunnelled through the hills to Hirwaun, also on the line to Neath; and the ex-Brecon & Merthyr line curving north towards Brecon and used by the LNWR/LMS trains to Abergavenny. The last of these lines closed to freight in 1966 but the name of Rhydycar Junction

120										RAILWAYS OF THE WESTERN REGION

with the B&M is perpetuated in the naming of the Rhydycar Leisure Centre, visible from the railway.

Between Merthyr Tydfil and Black Lion signal box (19 m 41 ch) the route is operated under the No Signalman Token system from the latter. There are intermediate stations, each unstaffed and comprising just platform and waiting shelter, at Pentre-bach (23 m 3 ch), Troed-y-rhiw (21 m 69 ch) and Merthyr Vale (19 m 77 ch), all showing evidence of the second platform of double-track days. Merthyr Vale colliery lies north of the station of that name and on the Up side but the junction with the NCB lines is further south near the modern, timber-framed Black Lion signal box and its loops. Black Lion is also the point at which the course of the TVR intersected that of the Merthyr Tramroad. The latter lay to the east of the line above Black Lion and then descended, by a course still discernible, on the west side of the TVR line towards the level of the Taff river.

From Black Lion to Abercynon the single line is controlled by the Electric Token system. Quaker's Yard station (17 m 73 ch), also unstaffed and with single platform and waiting shelter, is reached by a series of footbridges which span the trackbed of the former Neath-Pontypool Road line and its connection with the present line. North of the station are the abutments of bridges which carried that line and the GWR/RR line from Merthyr. Beyond Quaker's Yard the present railway crosses the river (and the course of the Merthyr Tramroad) by a viaduct and then pierces a rock cutting to drop down steeply to Abercynon. The gradient has previously not exceeded 1 in 75 except for a 1 in 38 section between the terminus and Pentre-bach.

The passenger service comprises 15 three-car dmu trains each way Mondays to Fridays (14 on Saturdays, 7 on Sundays). In the evenings and on Sundays these run to Pontypridd and connect there with the Treherbert-Cardiff trains but at other times there is a through service between Cardiff Central and Merthyr Tydfil, extended to/from Barry Island at peak hours and in the holiday season.

The key freight services are two block trains each way Mondays to Fridays between Abercwmboi Phurnacite Plant in the Cynon Valley and Merthyr Vale colliery, reversing at Stormstown Yard. Class 37-hauled, they bring empties in and take loaded wagons away. There are occasional mgr trains between the colliery and Aberthaw power station while an overnight Radyr yard to Merthyr working drops the empty wagons and further coal trainloads operate to other destinations from time to time and depending on the conditions of market and demand.

Merthyr Vale—see Merthyr Branch

M.15 Midgham

Reading-Taunton line between Reading and Newbury. 46 m 56 ch from Paddington

Called after the village of Woolhampton until 1873, and for a period Midgham Halt, Midgham station now consists simply of Up and Down platforms and a CCTV crossing at the London end. The station nameboards do give a small touch of the unusual. In addition to period and modern styles, the station is still proclaimed as 'Midgham for Douai School' and serves the former French college which transferred to this peaceful part of Berkshire before the First World War.

Most of the Reading-Bedwyn dmus call at Midgham.

M.16 Milford Haven

Newport-Fishguard line, branch from Clarbeston Road. 284 m 70 ch from Paddington*

The town of Milford Haven dates from the late 18th century when a dockyard and fishing port were developed on the north side of the deep Milford Haven inlet, described by Nelson as one of the best harbours in the world.

The single track from Johnston, opened in 1863, drops mostly at 1 in 82/88 and approaches Milford Haven—at a maximum speed of 20 mph—along one side of a deep, wooded inlet from the Haven and docks. This section is controlled from Johnston signal box using the No Signalman Token system and a ground frame is provided for operating the layout at Milford Haven itself.

Before reaching the station, a long loop and run-round line diverges on the Up side and rejoins the main running line beyond the platform. This is on the Down

Right *A Class 47 locomotive pulls away from the Gulf Oil refinery at Waterston with a block train load of tank cars.*

side and on a curve and is provided with a simple brick shelter. Although the station is unstaffed, a BR-accredited Travel Agent occupies premises alongside the platform and provides ticket and enquiry facilities. On the Down side is the car park, a coal and freight yard and a carriage siding used for the daytime stabling of the Paddington-Milford Haven sleeping car.

From the Up side loop, opposite the passenger platform, are the overgrown lines to the Milford Docks Company's private rail layout. The company has its own locomotive and the lines continue, beyond the large concrete road bridge, to the quays on either side of the docks. The line along the northern quay then continues further to a Ministry of Defence establishment but this has an alternative access by a line direct from the BR coal and freight depot.

Milford Haven has a weekday service of nine trains to and from Swansea and an overnight sleeper service link with Paddington. Its wagonload freight service is provided from Llandeilo Junction. It also has rail links to the three great oil refineries on the north side of the Haven which take their supplies of crude oil from giant oil tankers of over 350,000 tonnes.

From Gulf Oil Branch Junction (282 m) a single track runs to the Gulf Oil Refinery at Waterston (2 m 35 ch). Controlled by colour light signals in the Down direction and semaphore signals in the Up, the branch diverges on the Down side and dates from 1968. Operations on the line are under the control of the Johnston signalman and it has a modest summit, approached at 1 in 75 from Johnston and 1 in 100 from Waterston.

The gently rising single track route to the Esso and Amoco refineries diverges from the main line on the Up side at Herbrandston Junction (283 m 12 ch). The junction faces Johnston and is controlled by coloured light signals from the box there, operation on the branch itself being on the No Signalman Token system. There is a passing loop and siding just after the junction and the line then continues via the Amoco Sidings (1 m 6 ch) at Robeston on the north side of the branch and St Botolphs (1 m 60 ch) to the Esso Refinery at Herbrandston (2 m 34 ch). The branch was opened in 1962 and the Amoco sidings added in 1973.

Each of the refineries has its own internal rail layout handing over block trains of oil and petroleum products to BR for movement to locations in Wales and the southern half of England, and receiving the empty tank cars on inwards services. In 1982 the oil traffic required the provision of nine daily paths for oil trains and the wagonload working from Llandeilo Junction also served the refineries when required.

M.17   Minety

Swindon-Gloucester line between Swindon and Stroud. 86 m 74 ch from Paddington

Minety closed in 1964 although a level crossing remains.

Montpelier—see Severn Beach Branch

M.18   Moorswater

Taunton-Penzance line and connection from Looe Branch

From Moorswater Viaduct (265 m 38 ch*) on the main line just west of Liskeard station passengers can look down to the site of the Moorswater terminus of the Liskeard & Caradon Railway which opened to South Caradon in 1844 and to the Cheesewring Quarries two years later. The original route included a gravity incline and, at one period, passengers were carried without charge provided they paid for a piece of luggage as a way of ensuring that the obligations of a normal passenger-carrying railway did not have to be observed. An extension south of Looe was opened in 1860 and the Moorswater station closed following the opening of the link between the branch and the main line in 1901. The Caradon system north of the main line closed in 1916.

Moorswater is now a siding serving English China Clays and reached from the Looe branch via Coombe Junction. A daily trip is booked to deal with empty inwards wagons and loaded traffic outwards.

Morchard Road—see Barnstaple Branch

M.19   Moreton Cutting

Paddington-Swindon line between Reading and Didcot. 51 m 20 ch from Paddington

Between 51 m 20 ch and 51 m 55 ch lies a three-crossover junction between the main and relief lines, recently relaid to allow the previous 40 mph restriction to be raised to 70 mph.

M.20 Moreton-in-Marsh

Oxford-Hereford line between Kingham and Evesham. 91 m 56 ch from Paddington

Moreton-in-Marsh was one of the original stations on the Oxford, Worcester & Wolverhampton Railway but that company was not the town's first railway. That honour was held by a William James scheme to link the Midlands canals at Stratford with the Thames and London by means of a tramway, although this petered out by the time it reached Moreton. This 1826 horse-worked line was purchased by the OWW and some sections survived as a branch to Shipston-on-Stour.

The station now comprises two platforms, the Down housing the main buildings and the Up being an island with a shelter. Beyond it is the Up Refuge Siding and the route of the former branch. The original tramway terminated on the Down side near the road overbridge at the country end of the station and where the old coal offices now stand. The former docks and goods shed were also on the Down side and there is a Down Refuge Siding beyond the second overbridge.

All the Worcester line services call at Moreton and the station originates two morning stopping trains to Oxford. Standing on the summit of the Cotswold ridge, it serves an extensive area. The standard brick base, wooden uppers signal box stands at the London end of the island platform and controls the entrance to the single line section towards Evesham.

The summit of this part of the route lies half a mile beyond Moreton and the line then drops past the site of Aston Magna Siding to Blockley where a level crossing (CCTV) survives the former station at 94 m 77 ch. It is controlled by Moreton signal box.

M.21 Moreton-on-Lugg

Shrewsbury-Newport line between Ludlow and Hereford. 46 m 65 ch from Shrewsbury

There is a story that a hollow oak once served as a waiting room for Moreton-on-Lugg station, never very busy and closed to passengers in 1958. The site is still marked by a half barrier level crossing, a Down Goods Loop and signal box and, opposite, a long siding and connection to a Ministry of Defence depot.

M.22 Morris Cowley Branch

Didcot-Birmingham line, branch from Kennington Junction. 2 m 53 ch

This is all that remains active of the former Wycombe Railway line to Thame and Princes Risborough. It owes its survival to the existence of the British Leyland works at Morris Cowley and to a small oil depot at Littlemore, just beyond the former station. Worked from Oxford panel and with local freight trips, the electric token is issued and returned at signals OX 12, 29/79/99.

N.1 Nailsea and Backwell

Bristol-Taunton line between Bristol and Weston-super-Mare. 126 m 33 ch from Paddington

Like its neighbour, Yatton, Nailsea was one of the original Bristol & Exeter stations and the railway even had hopes of stimulating the revival of the local coalfield. Nowadays, the raised station with its simple shelters exists to serve the rapidly growing Bristol commuter belt area and is served by local dmu workings plus stops in a few longer distance trains.

N.2 Nantgarw Branch

Merthyr-Cardiff line, branch from Walnut Tree Junction. 2 m 23 ch

Another of the South Wales single track, freight-only branches, this one runs from the ex-Taff Vale Railway main line at Taffs Well to the Nantgarw colliery and coke ovens. The junction actually lies north of Taffs Well station although movements over the branch are under the control of Walnut Tree Junction box.

The branch dates only from 1952. Until then rail access to Nantgarw was over the ex-Cardiff Railway line beyond Coryton and a short section of this is still used at the Nantgarw end, including a bridge over the A4054 road.

There is an extensive internal NCB rail network at Nantgarw colliery which takes inwards coal for the coke ovens and despatches more coal, plus large quantities of coke. The outwards coal comes not only from Nantgarw, but also by underground link from Windsor colliery which was formerly served by the ex-Rhymney Railway Senghennydd branch from Aber Junction. To convey this traffic three trips are scheduled from Monday to Friday and run from Radyr Yard and back in charge of a Class 37 locomotive.

A maximum speed of 20 mph applies on the branch with a restriction to 5 mph at the open level crossing over a private road just beyond the junction at Taffs Well.

Nantymoel Branch—see Tondu

Narberth—see Pembroke Dock Branch

N.3   Neath

Newport-Fishguard line between Port Talbot and Swansea. 208 m 20 ch from Paddington*

There are three distinct sections of railway at Neath: the South Wales main line through the passenger station, the ex-Rhondda & Swansea Bay Railway 'Canalside' branch, and the ex-Vale of Neath and Neath & Brecon lines which merge and pass beneath the main line.

The double track main line was opened as far as Swansea in 1850, making a sharp detour inland to serve Neath, now the last station before Swansea. The station itself—two platforms but with evidence of a previous line between the present Up and Down lines—is well located for the town and almost entirely new, having been completely reconstructed in 1976-8. There was some regret and protest when the 1877 Neath General was demolished

but the new structure is very attractive and has been well received. It is of brick and glass, with a steeply pitched roof to the main building, giving a spacious air to the main circulating area adjoining which are the travel centre, ticket and parcels offices, and a very pleasant Travellers-Fare buffet. A plaque of Welsh slate records the official opening on March 6 1978 and there are bus stop and car parking facilities outside. The footbridge links the two platforms.

Behind the Down platform at Neath is a freight and coal yard, joined to the main line at the London end at Neath East ground frame. The layout includes a run-round facility and a siding for the Area Signal Engineer whose premises are on the opposite, Up, side of the line. The yard is served by a trip from Briton Ferry Yard, worked by a Class 08 locomotive. The station is served by the main line passenger trains with the Swansea-Paddington Inter-City 125 sets providing an hourly service on weekdays and giving a journey time of around 2½ hours.

Immediately beyond the station the line on to Swansea curves sharply as it crosses the Neath river, the A465 trunk road and the ex-Vale of Neath line. It then begins a 2½ m climb at a ruling gradient of 1 in 88 to Skewen summit, all controlled from Port Talbot panel box.

Station frontage and travel centre, in modern style, at Neath.

The freight-only branch to the premises of the Metal Box Co Ltd, Neath runs from Canal Side Ground Frame (18 m 44 ch) to 19 m 10 ch. It is the stub of the former Rhondda & Swansea Bay Railway branch to Neath Canalside station which carried passengers from its opening in 1894 until 1935. The present branch is operated on the One Train Working system but is currently out of use and its future is uncertain.

Of the two other former railway companies in the Neath area, the ex-Vale of Neath line now comprises a freight-only line from Aberpergwm colliery (33 m 14 ch) and Resolven in the Neath valley, to Neath and Brecon Junction (41 m 21 ch) and on to Jersey Marine and the freight installations (including the docks) at Swansea. The route dates from 1851 (above Neath) and 1863 (below Neath) and formed part of the GWR Pontypool Road-Neath line closed in 1964, when the connection with the main line to allow Pontypool Road trains to run into the station from the west also ended. The ex-Neath and Brecon line is now the freight branch from Onllwyn, described separately.

The two single lines merge at Neath and Brecon Junction (41 m 17 ch) and then pass beneath the main line to the signal box of that name (41 m 21 ch) and the site of the former Neath (Riverside) station. South of the signal box is a passing loop after which the line becomes single again

to Jersey Marine South Junction. This section is controlled by Track Circuit Block, mainly using colour light signals and with the South Junction supervised from Port Talbot panel box.

N.4 Newbury

Reading-Taunton line between Reading and Westbury. 53 m 6 ch from Paddington

No longer a junction at which the Didcot, Newbury & Southampton Railway trains connected with the West of England main line and the auto trains along the Lambourn Valley, Newbury is nevertheless an attractive and substantial station. A few Plymouth and Penzance services call but Newbury's main role is catering for the substantial commuter business which fills the morning trains for Reading and Paddington, one covering the 53 m in 55 minutes.

After both GWR and LSWR branch proposals had been rejected by Parliament in 1844, the former brought the first railway to Newbury when its Berks & Hants Railway Act was passed in the following year, with opening from Reading to Hungerford on December 21 1847. The second line to arrive, the DN&S, received its Act in 1873 and provoked one more row in the GW/LSW battle,

The coal and freight yard at Newbury.

including plans by the latter to assault Bristol. However, the new route reached Newbury in 1882 and opened forward from Enborne Junction to Winchester in 1885, eventually becoming part of the GWR at grouping. Finally came the Lamborne Valley Railway, authorised in 1883 but 15 years before opening and only then by courtesy of the light railway legislation. It was purchased by the GWR in 1905 and its trackbed, like that from Enborne Junction, is still visible to the west of Newbury.

Newbury station has long platforms served by bi-directional loops off the main line. The buildings are of red brick with stone facings and end gables, the main group being on the Up side and including both the ticket office and the former refreshment room. Although closed some time ago the latter still retains the solid wooden counter, massive fireplace and ageing mirror as well as a gaudy display of stained glass mixing purple, green and buff. Evidence of bay facilities remains at the country end of the station and the Up bay is still in use. A good view of the station can be obtained from the adjacent overbridge carrying the A343 road, that to the east embracing the once busy shed, yard and remaining freight facilities.

Between Newbury and Newbury Racecourse station (52 m 39 ch) the route of the line to Didcot can be seen veering off north. At the latter the main lines pass between the northern and island platforms which are linked by a long footbridge to the southern platform and the racecourse on the Down side of the line. The Down Passenger loop starts east of the Shell siding ground frame and the Racecourse Sidings ground frame and continues as far as the main station. Special trains still run on race days but the era of the Members' Special and the trains of horse boxes back to Lambourn is now just a colourful memory.

N.5   Newland

Oxford-Hereford line between Worcester and Great Malvern. 126 m 22 ch from Paddington

The engineer's permanent way pre-assembly depot lies on the Up side of the line. There is also a Down Refuge Siding, the signal box, a level crossing and a crossover, plus two period 'Catch Points' notices.

N.6   Newnham

Gloucester-Newport line between Gloucester and Lydney. 125 m 8 ch from Paddington

Passing by train through Newnham today conveys little of its former railway significance and the imagination has to work hard to see the township with its own local service to Gloucester or as a stopping point for a Newcastle-Barry 'Thro Restaurant Car Exp', as the timetable put it. Running close to the Severn on either side of Newnham, the railway loops behind it via the old station site (closed in 1964), a couple of bridges and the 235 yd Newnham Tunnel (125 m 8 ch to 125 m 19 ch).

On towards Chepstow, the route of the Cinderford branch climbs from the site of the sidings at the former Bullo Pill Junction. Opposite used to be the short line down to Bullo Pill Harbour, like Newnham a port serving the mining and industry of Dean. In the area between Newnham and Bullo Pill an early tunnel was started beneath the Severn but was inundated after the completion of 226 yds.

N.7   Newport

*Newport-Fishguard line. 158 m 47 ch from Paddington**

Newport is a town, commercial and industrial centre and port with a long history. It stands where the Usk and Ebbw rivers join the Severn Estuary and the ruins of its castle on the banks of the Usk and dating back to the 12th century are visible on the rail approach to Newport station from the east. The development of Newport and its hinterland from the 1790s was notably assisted by the Monmouthshire Canal Company which also operated early tramroads destined to develop into railways. Through its successor, the Monmouthshire Railway & Canal Company, this early transport enterprise was to become part of the Great Western Railway in 1880 and its importance is recognised in a mural at the Old Green road interchange near the station. Another interesting feature of Newport is the Transporter Bridge over the Usk, one of only two such bridges in Britain.

The basic elements of Newport's railway geography are the east-west South Wales main line and its two, north-pointing triangular junctions, one at each end of the town. At the east end the junction is with the 'North and West' line to Pontypool, Hereford and Shrewsbury and to the west the junction is with the 'Western Valleys' freight lines into the Ebbw and adjoining valleys. Also significant are short freight lines south of the main line, particularly to Uskmouth power station and into the docks, which lie between the mouths of the two rivers.

Approaching from the Llanwern direction the four track main line has the pair of relief lines on the south side to facilitate freight movements between the BSC plant and Newport docks. Then, at East Usk Junction (157 m 2 ch), the double track, freight-only East Usk Branch joins on the Down side with a junction facing Newport. Immediately following is East Usk Yard, a strategic examination, repair and sorting point for mineral wagons. A modern signal box here controls movements off the main line, the latter being under the control of the Newport panel box.

The East Usk branch dates from 1898 and may soon be altered to single track. It runs via the former Corporation Road box (1 m 8 ch) to Uskmouth signal box (2 m 79 ch) and serves several private sidings in addition to the power station at the end of the line. The latter is fed by trainloads of coal plus a weekly oil train from Milford Haven and the private sidings by Monday to Friday trips from East Usk. Permissive block working operates.

East Usk yard receives trains of empty mineral wagons from yards and coal concentration depots, together with empties from Llanwern and Uskmouth power station. After examination and, if

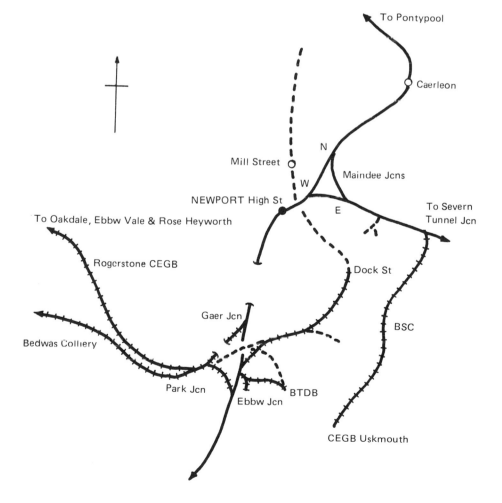

necessary, repair these are sent to coal despatch points for loading again, local movements also being made between East Usk yard and those at Severn Tunnel Junction and Alexandra Dock Junction and to and from the BR installations on the east side of Newport station.

As the main line curves to cross the River Usk and reach Newport station it provides a double line connection from each direction with the 'North and West' line. On the main line are Maindee East Junction (157 m 74 ch) and Maindee West Junction (158 m 16 ch) with 32 and 33 ch links to Maindee North Junction (41 m 33 ch from Hereford) where there are Up and Down Goods Loops and the line goes on to pass beneath the M4 and then over the Usk. In the Maindee triangle there are sidings serving a Civil Engineer's Department bridge depot. Maindee East curve is used mainly by freight trains and the West curve by the Cardiff-Newport-Shrewsbury-Crewe passenger service.

Whereas the South Wales main line through Newport dates from 1850 the N&W line, as the Newport, Abergavenny & Hereford Railway, arrived three years later although until the present route to Pontypool was opened in 1874 its access to Newport was over the Monmouthshire Railway to Mill Street station. The Mill Street site now lies beneath the modern road network crossed by the main line just east of the main station.

Freight train at Newport.

Newport station, at one time Newport High Street and still known colloquially as such, is well situated for the town. Its tall 1930s building has a spacious concourse and a modern ticket office and travel centre opened in 1973. This leads on to the Down platform but, as a result of remodelling of the layout, most trains use the island platform which is reached via the footbridge and houses the combined waiting room and Powys buffet bar. The track layout, from north to south, consists of an Up Goods Loop, Up and Down Main Lines flanking the island platform and signalled for two-way working, Up and Down Relief Lines and the Down Platform Line. At the London end on the Up side are carriage and engineer's sidings and, opposite, a parcels bay and another engineer's siding. Near the car park on the Up side are the headquarters of the Divisional Civil Engineer and the Area Signalling Engineer's depot, the Area Manager occupying premises in the main Down side building.

At the east end of the Down platform at Newport is the panel box which controls the main line from Awre and Pilning to the east and for 5 m west to Marshfield. Fringe boxes are Little Mill Junction on the N&W and Park Junction on the Western Valleys line. West of the station are the twin Newport tunnels. The 748 yd Old Tunnel (158 m 71 ch to 159 m 25 ch) taking the relief lines and the 770 yd New Tunnel (158 m 70 ch to 159 m 25 ch), which dates from 1911, the main lines.

Beyond the tunnels westward is Gaer Junction (159 m 33 ch) from which a line, single since November 1981, leads to Park Junction. The line back from the Western Valleys route at Park Junction to the main line at Ebbw Junction (160 m 7 ch) is double track and known as the 'Cardiff Curve'. The connection to Ebbw Junction diesel depot is from the Cardiff Curve although the depot itself lies alongside the main line and west of Ebbw Junction. It had an allocation of 20 Class 08 locomotives and undertook back-up servicing of main locomotives until 1982 when its exact future became uncertain.

Between Gaer Junction and Ebbw Junction on the Down side of the main line are lines to the docks, from Waterloo Loop Junction (159 m 57 ch) to Dock Street coal concentration depot and from Alexandra Dock Junction (159 m 60 ch) to Newport docks, with Alexandra Dock Junction marshalling yard lying between them and the main line. The yard now serves as a terminal yard for traffic to and from the Newport area and as an exchange point for movements to and from the docks, and has local workings to Severn Tunnel Junction, East Usk and Radyr yards.

On each side of the main line between Alexandra Dock and Ebbw junctions are the abutments of bridges which used to carry the Alexandra (Newport & South

Newport West was among the early electric signal boxes.

Wales) Docks and Railway Company's route into the docks. The original dock at Newport was Town Dock which dates from 1842 but the main development started in 1875 on the strip of land between the Usk and Ebbw rivers. The opening of the South Lock in 1914 completed the main works and these came into the hands of the GWR when that company took over the AD&RC as a result of the 1921 Railways Act. In addition to the dock railway system and its link with the Western Valleys line the Great Western became responsible for 125 acres of deep water area plus extensive crane, hoist, warehousing and other facilities.

The branch to Dock Street is almost 1½ m long and one train is scheduled daily to serve the coal concentration depot there. Alongside the branch adjacent to Waterloo Loop Junction is Waterloo Loop signal box, a modern style WR manual box controlling the local movements. Just beyond it the double track becomes single and from a headshunt nearby there is access to Eastern Valleys sidings. Further on is the site of Courtybella Junction where the recently closed line from Park Junction and the Western Valleys trailed in—the Monmouthshire Railway's original approach route. Two level crossings precede the Dock Street depot where there is a run-round facility. Until 1966 this line ran through to Mill Street and the Monmouthshire's access from the valleys east of Newport.

The line from Alexandra Dock Junction to Newport docks curves sharply and is double track. Alongside the portion in BR ownership are groups of sidings known as Low Level, New and Eastern Valleys sidings and which converge on the docks line at Eastern Valleys Sidings Junction. At East Mendalief Junction, by the boundary with the BTDB, are the Monmouthshire Bank sidings now much reduced but still serving as a tip for spent ballast. The route from Park Junction and the Western Valleys used to join at this junction. Docks traffic by 1982 had become principally block loads of export coal from South Wales pits and export steel from Llanwern. Class 08 locomotives work in Alexandra Dock Junction yard and shunt in the docks area but train engines are increasingly taking their loads on to the docks proper.

In addition to its own local traffic, Newport is also busy with freight traffic off the Western Valleys route and to and from Llanwern. The station is also one of South Wales' leading Inter-City stations with an excellent service to Paddington, via Gloucester to Birmingham and beyond and via the North and West to Shrewsbury. There is a local dmu service between Newport and Gloucester, those units not working through to Cardiff being stabled in the Up side sidings at the station between trips. There are morning peak hour services from Cardiff to Chepstow and back and trains to Bristol and the Portsmouth line add to the station's facilities.

Locomotive 47 229 heads east from Newport with a train of steel coil on bogie wagons.

In the forecourt alongside Newport station is a controversial piece of sculpture entitled 'Archform'. It consists of an 18 ft high arch of steel plate, the shapes of which are intended to symbolise features of Newport's industrial and railway heritage, the arch itself linking the past and the present conceptually. This sculpture was commissioned by BR with funds from the Welsh Arts Council. It was designed by Harvey Hood and erected in October 1981.

Along the mainline west towards Cardiff is the site of Marshfield station, the boundary between the Cardiff and Newport panels. The passenger service was withdrawn in 1959 and public freight facilities in 1965 but milk traffic continued from a siding on the Up side until relatively recently.

N.8   Newquay Branch

Taunton-Penzance line, branch from Par. 20 m 61 ch

Although only just over 20 m long, this single line climbs to the height of Bodmin Moor, passes through the heart of the china clay country and finally comes upon the North Cornwall resort of Newquay by way of an elegant viaduct over a delightful park. It is a journey high in interest, through deep cuttings, over the wild moor and past a skyline of china clay sand pyramids.

Along the route, near Luxulyan, the railway passes under the magnificent ten-arch Treffry Viaduct which takes its name from the original builder of the lines north from Ponts Mill and south from Newquay harbour. Although the present route takes a less steeply graded course along this first section, the original route can still be traced and the viaduct still carries the leat which fed the water wheel for the Carmears incline. These first sections, horse-worked and with rope inclines, became part of a wider network put together in record time by the Cornwall Minerals Railway Company in the year preceding opening on June 1 1874. The central gap was filled in, routes altered to avoid the Carmears incline, Treffry Viaduct and Toldish Tunnel, branches provided to Carbis, Retew, Drinnick Mill and Treamble Mill (extension) and locomotive working introduced. Largely to compensate for diminishing tonnages from the mines, a Fowey-Newquay passenger service commenced in 1876, one year prior to working being taken over by the GWR with whose main line a connection was made at Par in 1879.

The three-car dmus which provide the weekday branch line service traverse the Par loop to reach the St Blazey complex where a Down side signal box (282 m 19 ch) stands between the clay sidings pointing towards Fowey and the former station platforms. Here the double line ends and the crossings at Middleway (282 m 31 ch) and St Blazey Bridge (282 m 74 ch) precede the Pontsmill ground frame (283 m 15 ch) where a short line at a lower level provides a reminder of the original, Treffry alignment. To avoid the Carmears incline the 1874 line has to climb and twist, over its own viaducts and beneath Treffry, and through the naked, dripping rock of the 52 yd Luxulyan Tunnel (285 m 45 ch to 285 m 47 ch) to reach the Down face of the simple island platform of the station of the same name (285 m 78 ch).

The first crossing loop comes at Goonbarrow Junction (287 m 40 ch) where the signal box is again on the Down side, with the loop and Up Refuge Siding before it and extensive clay works and sidings behind. The rusting Carbis branch then parallels the Newquay line, over Molinnis open level crossing (287 m 76 ch), to Bugle (288 m 3 ch) where it veers off west after passing the island platform and its modest wooden shelter. The gradient is still rising as the line continues towards Roche (290 m 40 ch) where the Down platform remains in use. Then comes an open, moor stretch via Tregoss Moor open crossing (292 m 32 ch) to St Dennis Junction (294 m 17 ch), once Bodmin Road Junction. Once more the signal box is on the Down side, standing between the crossing loop and the sidings towards Meledor Mill.

The next section to St Columb Road (296 m 11 ch) is an 1874 alignment avoiding Toldish Tunnel. At the station only the Up platform is used, the Down platform and dock/yard behind now

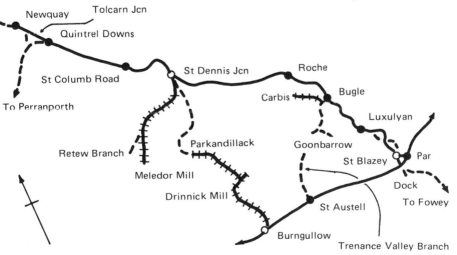

Bugle station, with the line to the Wheal Rose and Carbis branches to the left.

looking very neglected. Through Halloon level crossing (296 m 22 ch) and the open crossing at Coswarth (298 m 48 ch) the line drops steadily and the 44 yd Coswarth Tunnel (299 m 23 ch to 299 m 25 ch) disposes of one more barrier from the sea. Quintrel Downs level crossing and station (300 m 16 ch), with its one platform and corrugated shelter, precede the final stretch via Chapel (300 m 56 ch) and Trencreek (301 m 35 ch) crossings to Newquay.

Tolcarn Junction, where the original East Wheal Rose and subsequent Perranporth line diverged, is no longer apparent but the surviving branch makes a grand entrance into Newquay by way of Trenance Viaduct. Treffry's original structure was modelled on the Brunel pattern of stone piers and a timber superstructure but this was replaced in 1874, the present double track masonry viaduct dating from 1939. The branch line now ends at a two-platform terminus comprising the main platform with a single face and grey stone buildings behind and a second platform with two faces, a canopy linking the two around the buffer stops and crossover points. The signal box stands at the Par end of this second platform and the combined ticket and information office at the town end. Two stabling sidings remain in the adjacent goods yard but the former harbour line is marked only by the route of a footpath.

The basic weekday service consists of seven trains daily in each direction and calling at all stations, although Luxulyan,

Bugle and Roche are request stops. Clay traffic is worked from the line to St Blazey and there are extra passenger services in the peak season.

N.9   Newton Abbot

Taunton-Penzance line between Exeter and Plymouth. 214 m 6 ch from Paddington*

The South Devon Railway reached Newton Abbot in 1846 and just over a year later, on January 10 1848, atmospheric trains were conveying passengers forward from Exeter. But, instead of a saving of £8,000 per annum in locomotive costs, the system involved problem after problem and even Brunel's enthusiasm was eventually quenched. After eight exasperating months conventional haulage took over from the leaky pipes and labouring engines and Newton Abbot's own engine, located on the Down side between the end of the estuary and the station, gradually became just a memory now marked only by traces of the engine pond.

In the early tradition, the original station at Newton Abbot had separate Up and Down sheds in tandem on the north side of the line. A third shed was provided for Torquay branch trains but all were brought under one roof in 1861. A further major reconstruction came in 1927 when the present arrangement of two long island platforms was ceremonially brought into use on April 11. There was a separate platform for trains on Newton's other branch, the Moretonhampstead & South Devon Railway which climbed 12½ m along the course of the River Bovey and an early granite tramway. From July 1 1903 Exeter could also be reached via the Teign Valley route which left the Moretonhampstead branch at Heathfield (now the terminus).

Today's passengers at Newton Abbot obtain tickets in a building which was formerly the office of the District Locomotive Superintendent whose sheds, complete with SDR-style windows, can still be seen at the country end of the station of the Down side. From the ticket office a footbridge leads to the two island platforms, one serving the Up Relief and Up Main lines and the other the Down Main and Down Relief. Up and Down

Through lines pass outside these and there is an Up Refuge Siding at Newton Abbot West (214 m 18 ch). The other signal box, Newton Abbot East (213 m 65 ch) controls the access to the Heathfield branch but there is little activity at the goods depot which lies a short distance along it or in the former Hackney marshalling yard. Nor is there any longer carriage cleaning, maintenance or locomotive stabling in the extensive sidings south of the station platforms.

Newton Abbot's passenger traffic has not declined in the way its other activities have although the train pattern has changed a number of times. All Paignton line services stop at Newton Abbot plus some of the trains on the Plymouth line to give a good service to London and to Birmingham and beyond. The station is also a Motorail terminal and the control and stores point for Motorail services.

Newton St Cyres—see Barnstaple Branch

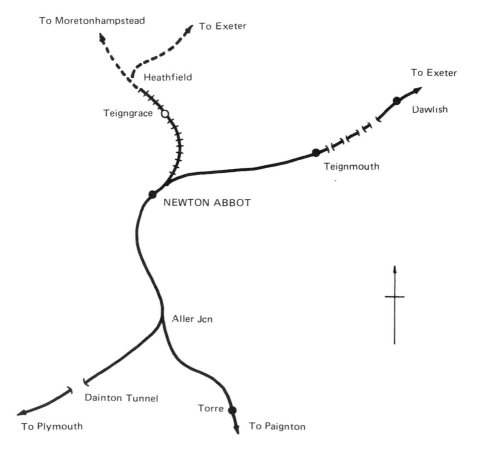

N.10   Northway

Birmingham-Bristol line between Barnt Green and Cheltenham. 78 m 76 ch from Derby

Consists of a level crossing with an attractive period, red brick house, and a Down Goods Loop on the Cheltenham side.

N.11   Norton Fitzwarren

Taunton-Penzance line between Taunton and Tiverton Junction. 165 m 10 ch from Paddington*

The original West Somerset Railway gave Norton Fitzwarren its first status, albeit as Watchet Junction, with the opening of its line to Watchet on March 31 1862. The first section of the Devon & Somerset's route to Barnstaple added to its importance from June 8 1871 and although these lines, Norton Fitzwarren's station and the signal box have all closed, the completion of the new West Somerset Railway's revival of the Minehead line may one day bring back steam to this well known railway location.

Norton Fitzwarren is well known partly as a place of railway tragedy. There were two very serious accidents in GWR days, and the recent sleeper fire has also made its mark on railway history partly by its influence on the design of the new Mark III sleeper coaches.

A sad moment in Norton Fitzwarren's past occurred in the early hours of November 11 1890 when ten people died and nine were seriously injured in a dramatic head-on collision. A Down goods train had been crossed to the Up line to allow a following train to run through and was then overlooked when the signalman cleared his signals for a lightweight 'special' conveying liner passengers from Plymouth. The use of lever collars as a reminder device for signalmen stemmed directly from the resultant head-on collision between the speeding special and the standing goods train. In a more recent drama, on a wet and windy night in November 1940, the night sleeper to Penzance was put down the relief line from Taunton West for a newspaper train to pass. The driver mistook the clear main line signals for his own and opened the regulator. Running at speed through the trap points protecting the main line 6028 *King George VI* ploughed into the ground, telescoping the leading six vehicles and causing a terrible toll of 27 killed and 75 injured.

The four tracks at Norton Fitzwarren, provided under the quadrupling programme of the 1930s, have now reverted to two and the Sectional Appendix records no railway locations between Silk Mill box and crossing to the east (164 m 35 ch) and the automatic half barrier crossings to the west at Victory (166 m 4 ch) and Bradford (167 m 55 ch). But the branch line is still there and runs through to Silk Mill and one day, who knows?

Oakdale Branch—see Western Valleys

O.1 Ocean and Taff Merthyr Collieries Branch

Rhymney-Cardiff line, branch from Ystrad Mynach. 3 m 56 ch.

The busy single track, freight-only line from Ystrad Mynach, on the Rhymney Valley line, via Nelson (junction with the line to Cwmbargoed and Dowlais) serves the complex of Deep Navigation, Trelewis and Taff Merthyr collieries in the Treharris area. The main purpose of the line is the movement of coal from this complex but it also carries a limited amount of colliery waste, a unique movement for BR in South Wales. Below Nelson there is also coal traffic from Cwmbargoed and some steel to and from Dowlais.

From Ystrad Mynach South Junction (13 m 14 ch), where the junction faces Cardiff, the lines passes behind the station's Up platform and forecourt and then starts to climb at 1 in 85. To the change of mile point (from 15 m 1 ch to 12 m 41 ch) the route is that of the Rhymney Railway's 1871 line to the GWR Pontypool Road-Neath line. At the former Penallta Junction there is now, on the north side of the line, the NCB's private Nelson East siding serving a colliery waste tip where incoming hopper wagons are discharged by gravity to an under-line conveyor belt. Coal blending is also carried out here.

On from Penallta Junction and Nelson East the line falls gently to Nelson across the watershed dividing the Rhymney and Taff river systems and then continues to descend at a ruling gradient of 1 in 165. This portion of the line is a remnant of the Pontypool Road-Neath route, dating from 1858, coming into GWR ownership

in 1863 and closing as a cross-valleys through route 101 years later. The line now ends near the site of the former Treharris station.

At Nelson (13 m 36 ch), site of the former Nelson and Llancaiach station, the line to Cwmbargoed and Dowlais diverges north, and until 1939 an ex-TVR line from Pontypridd trailed in on the Up, south, side. The site of a closed goods yard follows and then (14 m 9/27 ch) the point of divergence of a 2 m long NCB line into the Taff Bargoed valley to Taff Merthyr colliery. This line uses the same valley as the route to Cwmbargoed and Dowlais but keeps to the valley floor. It is traversed by BR trains to pick up the output of Taff Merthyr colliery and of Trelewis drift mine. At the end of the BR line proper (14 m 57 ch) there is a loading point for coal from Deep Navigation colliery going by mgr trains, and also connections to the NCB rail system on which trains of conventional wagons are loaded.

On the branch movements between Ystrad Mynach and Nelson are controlled by the signalman at Ystrad Mynach South Junction signal box but beyond Nelson they are the responsibility of the local BR supervisor. The principal movements are of mgr trains feeding Aberthaw power station and up to 12 paths are available every 24 hours for these services, with provision for weekend services as required. Loading from Deep Navigation is by lineside rapid loading equipment but at Taff Merthyr there is a modern overhead bunker capable of loading 1,100

Colliery waste is discharged from a train at Nelson Bog.

A merry-go-round train being loaded with coal at Taff Merthyr colliery.

tonnes of coal into a 35-wagon mgr train in 15 minutes. Each of these collieries also loads a daily train of colliery waste to Nelson East and the latter receives a train of coal from Trelewis for blending, an Aberthaw mgr train then picking up the blended product. There are other movements too, but the pattern constantly fluctuates. All trains are normally worked by Class 37 locomotives, the mgr trains being double headed.

O.2   Oddingley

Birmingham-Bristol line between Barnt Green and Cheltenham. 62 m 60 ch from Derby

Just gates, cabin, level crossing, crossover and ground frame on the main line between Stoke Works Junction and Abbotswood Junction.

Oldfield Park—see Bath

O.3   Old Oak Common

Paddington-Swindon line between Paddington and Southall. 2 m 64 ch from Paddington

Old Oak Common is the WR's main traction maintenance depot in the London area. It occupies a large site north of the main line between Old Oak Common panel box and Old Oak Common West (3 m 20 ch) where the Park Royal line diverges. At the country end are Up and Down Goods Loops and there is a Down Avoiding Line opposite the traction depot. At the London end the main line is crossed by the Kensington-Willesden line to which there is a double line connection to North Pole Junction of which the first 25 ch lies in the WR. Further on towards Paddington is Ladbroke Grove (1 m 73 ch) and the flyover which lifts the Up and Down Engine & Carriage Lines from one side of the main line to the other. Beyond Ladbroke Grove come North Carriage Lines 1 and 2 and the carriage washing and cleaning point on the Down side and then Portobello Junction (1 m 33 ch) where, in addition to the crossovers, the four Relief and Main lines are supplemented by a second Down Relief, an Up and Down Goods and the Up Carriage Line.

The original engine shed at Old Oak Common was opened in 1906 and replaced sheds at Westbourne Park where the Gooch broad gauge engines such as *Lord of the Isles* and Brunel's *North Star* had been maintained. Even in 1906, 14 years after the last broad gauge train ran, the two sheds there were still known as the NG (narrow gauge) and BG (broad gauge). When it was built Old Oak was the largest shed of its type in Britain, and probably the world. It had four 65 ft turntables, each with 28 radiating tracks, all electrically powered. Accommodation was provided for 56 tender and 56 tank engines and the repair facilities embraced a shop with 12 52 ft pits, a 30-ton overhead crane, and a traversing table capable of carrying 80 tons. The water tank held 290,000 gallons and the coaling stage, in the words of the *Great Western Railway Magazine*, was regarded as 'the height of perfection in the practice of coaling engines as obtaining in this country'. The steam shed at Old Oak lasted until 1964 and had a regular allocation of about 200 engines covering all the notable Great Western types.

On its site between the main line and the Grand Union Canal, Old Oak depot today is a complex involving about a hundred sidings and more than 20 m of

The control panel in Old Oak Common signal box.

track. Its functions consist of locomotive maintenance and repair work, coaching stock maintenance, the repair, maintenance and servicing of HSTs and fuelling and daily preparation work for the passenger services to and from Paddington. In addition to its own depot allocation of 46 locomotives, 12 diesel shunters and 20 Inter-City 125 sets, a considerable amount of work is done on locomotives from other depots and regions and over half of the 450-500 locomotives serviced each week are not locals. The Area Maintenance Engineer's responsibility also covers breakdown work and the Area Manager has a carriage cleaning activity within the depot.

The main locations within Old Oak Common include the heavy maintenance depot (known as 'The Factory') which can undertake everything but serious collision damage. Eight 25-ton jacks allow the largest locomotives to be lifted and all seven tracks are spanned by the 50-ton capacity overhead crane. Traction motors can be lifted out and wheel sets and bogies replaced.

Primary examinations, attention to brake blocks and similar jobs take place in the servicing shed, while the carriage lifting shed undertakes a variety of special jobs plus examination work on some 40 sets. Nearest to the main line is the HST depot where the night shift fuel the Inter-City 125s and carry out the full servicing which is scheduled every two days, the days being devoted to six-weekly major examinations.

Old Oak Common is a varied, fascinating and busy railway location exhibiting

many facets of the BR activity from the modern panel signal box to sophisticated testing and repair machinery. It is also a driver signing on point and is responsible for a considerable volume of small plant and machinery in the surrounding area.

O.4   Onibury

Shrewsbury-Newport line between Craven Arms and Hereford. 22 m 68 ch from Shrewsbury

The station at Onibury closed in 1958 and only the signal box now remains operational.

O.5   Onllwyn Branch

Newport-Fishguard line, branch from Neath and Brecon Junction via Jersey Marine South Junction. 10 m 20 ch

Now a single track freight line up the Dulais valley, this branch is the stub of the former Neath & Brecon Railway's main line which opened from Neath to Onllwyn in 1864 and was completed through to Brecon three years later. Even in 1938 there were only three through trains each way daily and closure to passengers in 1962 was no great surprise. Today what is left of the route serves Blaenant colliery (3 m 75 ch) and, at Onllwyn at the end of the line, the NCB coal washery and the nearby Banwen opencast anthracite coal site.

After freight closure, the section on to Craig-y-Nos (14 m 23 ch) had been re-opened in 1964 to serve a limestone quarry there but this traffic eventually ceased and the line beyond Onllwyn closed again in 1981. On this section had stood Colbren Junction from which a branch ran south west to link up with the lines acquired by the MR in the Swansea Valley, part of the Midland's Worcester-Hereford-Brecon-Swansea 'tentacle'. The line was also used for the railway scenes in the film *The Young Winston* and its station at Craig-y-Nos (Penwyllt) had a private waiting room for the use of singer Adelina Patti who lived nearby.

The climb from Neath to the slopes of the Brecon Beacons at Onllwyn is steep, the ruling gradient being 1 in 57. There are signal boxes at Neath & Brecon Junction, Blaenant and Onllwyn and movements over the two sections either side of Blaenant are made on the written authority of the signalmen at the first two.

Blaenant has a bi-directional loop and connections to a rapid loading overhead coal bunker from which mgr trains are despatched to Aberthaw power station. They reverse at Jersey Marine South Junction and are made up of two Class 37 locomotives and 35 wagons. Nearly 40 paths are required in an average week. The Onwllyn/Banwen coal also requires 24-hour working, although only Mondays to Fridays. Over half goes to Swansea Docks for shipment, most of the balance passing to domestic market yards and depots via Swansea Burrows Siding and Radyr yards. Class 37 locomotives are used on the four scheduled trips and haul conventional wagons.

The former passenger stations on the lower section of the line were Neath (Riverside), Cadoxton Terrace Halt, Penscynor Halt, Cilfrew, Cefn Coed Colliery Halt, Crynant, Seven Sisters, Pantyffordd Halt and Onllwyn.

O.6   Oxford

Didcot-Birmingham line between Didcot and Banbury, 63 m 41 ch from Paddington

A branch to Oxford was envisaged in the original GWR proposals but the opposition to firm plans as they crystallised kept the town dependent upon a coach service connecting with the main line trains at Steventon until 1844. On June 12 of that year the GWR-backed Oxford Railway, having provided the colleges with sufficient protections to enable them to control their (apparently) wayward undergraduates, opened its branch from Didcot to a wooden station on the south side of the river. This lasted until a new station, on the present site west of the town, was brought into use in 1852 following the opening of the line to Banbury. For another 20 years the old station lingered on as a goods depot reached via Millstream Junction (between the Hinksey Reception line ground frame at 61 m 22 ch and the Goods Depot ground frame at 62 m 25 ch and near the former GWR ballast pit), but it finally closed on November 26 1872, broad gauge to the last.

Oxford's geographical position made it inevitable that it should be in the centre of a clash between broad and standard gauge interests, especially in the Mark Huish era on the LNWR. No sooner had the GWR camp poked north as far as Banbury in September 1850 than the Euston interests were planning a service to Oxford via Verney Junction, and trains duly started running eight months later. 1852 brought a GWR service to Birmingham and a new Oxford station adjacent to Rewley Road LNW, and although the link with the Oxford, Worcester & Wolverhampton Railway via Wolvercot Junction followed on June 4 1853, the GWR could not have enjoyed seeing Euston-Worcester carriages passing to the OWW at the same point. Later additions to the railway network in the Oxford area were the Witney Railway (1861) and the Wycombe Railway line in from Thame (1864).

The same position that made Oxford a key point in the gauge and traffic rivalries led to its increasing importance as a passenger and freight centre and interchange point. In the 1930s passengers could make a through journey to such distant places as Birkenhead, Bradford, Barmouth and Bournemouth, or come from Deal, Newcastle or Manchester and catch one of the seven trains to Fairford, a

through service to Blenheim or a railcar to Thame. Freight queued up to get through the bottleneck at Oxford, especially during the war years when the Yarnton Loop became even more important and a new, more direct connection was put in between the former GW and LNW lines. Yarnton also figured in a mid-1950s plan to develop a new freight route avoiding London and using the Bletchley flyover and the Yarnton curve. Ten years later the curve had gone, along with the Thame and Fairford services, and the Oxford-Cambridge service ended in 1968.

Approaching from the south, the Oxford complex begins as the single line from Morris Cowley joins the main line at Kennington Junction (61 m 8 ch). Up and Down Goods Loops follow, with a ground frame serving the once busy Hinksey Yard. Its headshunt on the Down side is, in turn, followed by the bridging of the Isis and then Becket Street Goods

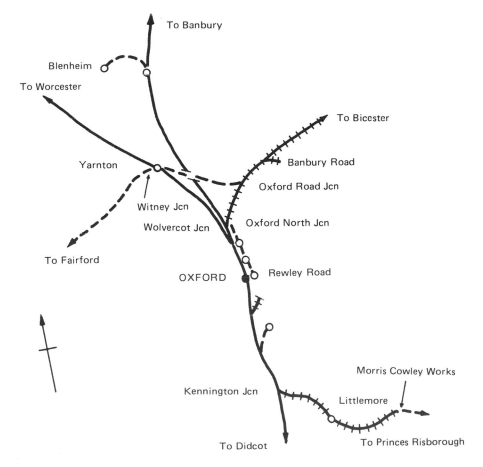

The old LNWR station at Oxford (Rewley Road), still there in 1981 but in use as a tyre centre.

on the Up side and complete with brick and corrugated goods shed and a scrap metal activity. Opposite are carriage sidings and a dock.

The station at Oxford is preceded by a narrow overbridge and a level crossing which is not normally in use. The bi-directional goods line on the Up side gives way to main and loop lines through the station. Each platform has single storey buildings of modern design, officially opened in 1972 and contrasting strongly with the remains of Rewley Road

whose ironwork came from the Great Exhibition in Hyde Park. The ticket office, taxi, parking and bus interchange facilities are on the Up side of the station, as is the parcels depot, complete with rail loading bay at the country end. The platforms are connected by subway.

Heading north from Oxford there are ground frames serving the loco depot (now mainly dmu fuelling) and carriage sidings, and Down, then Up, goods lines. At Oxford North Junction (64 m 45 ch) the freight only single line to Bicester rises and veers off east. Wolvercot Junction (66 m 32 ch) sees the separation of the Banbury and Worcester routes and the course of the Yarnton curve and of the Witney trackbed are still visible nearby.

Oxford enjoys a good Inter-City passenger train service to and from Paddington with the faster trains taking an hour for the 63½ m. Some Down trains continue on to Birmingham and there are through services from Weymouth, Poole and Brighton to the North East and North West. The local dmu service gives connections to Wales and the West at Didcot and the Hereford line trains also contribute to Oxford's continued importance in the WR activity. Freight activity includes the BL works and a small oil terminal on the Morris Cowley branch and an ARC stone terminal at Banbury Road on the Bicester line. All movements are controlled from the panel box and the signalling is by colour lights.

Left *A view north from Oxford; the former LNWR line is on the extreme right.*

P.1 Paddington

Several sites were proposed for the Great Western Railway's London terminus, including sharing Euston with the London & Birmingham Railway, but Paddington was eventually selected and the diversion of the line thereto authorised by an Act of Parliament passed on July 3 1837. The new station was ready by the time the main line was opened throughout to Bristol on June 30 1841 and consisted of two arrival and two departure platforms linked by traversers, an engine shed roundhouse and engine and carriage turntables. The entrance was by an inclined roadway from the junction of Praed Street and London Street with the station offices located in the arches of the Bishops Road bridge. A 330 ft long goods shed was built on the site of the present passenger station and began handling merchandise traffic from September 1839.

As the GWR network and traffic expanded it became clear that the original station could not cope and work on a new one, on the present site, began in 1851. Design and construction were under the control of Brunel and his friend, architect Digby Wyatt, helped with the ornamentation. Further increases in traffic brought additions and alterations, especially in the 1878-84 period when the lines, turntables and horse and carriage landing were cleared to make room for the present main concourse, long known as 'The Lawn'. Other major changes took place in the 1907-15, 1922-3 and 1930-3 periods, with the present layout dating from a 1967-8 remodelling.

Paddington stands on 13 acres of land and has 16 platforms ranging in length from 600 ft to 1,160 ft, two used exclusively by London Transport's Metropolitan line trains. The concourse fronts platforms 1 to 8 and was enlarged in 1968 by shortening these platforms by 40 ft. It is surrounded by passenger facilities, including refreshment rooms and bars, the entrances to the LT lines and the rear of the Great Western Hotel, and the ticket and information offices. These continue along platform 1 behind which stand the Western Region's headquarters offices. Train departures and arrivals are shown on the indicators over the concourse and operated from a central control room at the rear, housing the station announcers and other staff responsible for the running of the station. The station's main approach road is alongside the general offices, parallel to platform 1, with a second access descending from Bishops Bridge Road to the taxi rank between platforms 8 and 9 and exiting to Praed Street.

The architectural glory of Paddington is the great, cathedral-like roof arches. The original construction was considerably influenced by the Crystal Palace and divided the station into three spans of 68 ft, 102 ft and 68 ft over its 700 ft length. Two rows of columns rose to wrought iron arched ribs with a covering of Paxton glass roof lights. The columns lasted until

The Red Dragon express stands waiting to leave Paddington in June 1959 in the charge of a Britannia locomotive.

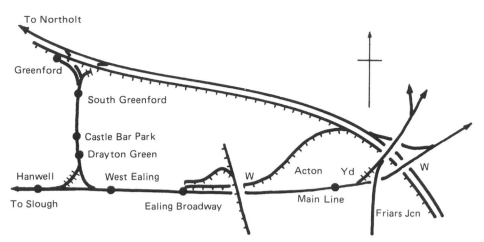

replacement of the ones on platform 2/3 in 1922 and those on platforms 7/8 in the following year and subsequent care and tasteful painting have retained their character, and that of the whole roof, without detracting from the work of a busy station. The Great Western Hotel, which fronts the station in Praed Street, is another attractive part of the Paddington complex. Built in 1851-2, the hotel was designed by Philip Charles Hardwick in Louis XIV style and with towers seven storeys high. Although modernised to keep abreast of modern tastes, the hotel is still a place of style and distinction.

Colour light signals have been used at Paddington since 1922 and new Arrival and Departure signal boxes in 1933 were worked electrically. The latest techniques were again used in the remodelling of 1967 when the manually-worked boxes were closed and all movements transferred to the Old Oak Common panel. Track simplification brought the ability to work into or out of any platform with the minimum of conflicting movements. Combined with the ease of operation deriving from diesel traction and multiple unit trains, and the progressive movement of locomotive and carriage servicing work away from the terminal, the revised layout has produced a large station which is efficient and simple to work.

Not that Paddington is not busy. Nearly 400 trains are dealt with daily, about half main line and half commuter, compared with 20 in 1855 and 201 in 1931. Some 9,000 passengers arrive between 08.00 and 09.00 Mondays to Fridays, part of a total of 48,000 passing through the station in a typical day. There is also a great deal of parcels and mail business, the station taking on a different character at night when the mail and newspaper trains are being loaded. The 220 tons of newspapers handled in an ordinary night rises to a staggering 550 tons on Saturday nights.

The main line passenger services from Paddington run to South Wales, Bristol/ Taunton/Paignton, Penzance and via Oxford to Birmingham and Hereford, or intermediately. There are other long-distance services like those to Fishguard Harbour and Cheltenham via Stroud, and a busy local service covering the intermediate stations to Reading and their branches and also station on towards Newbury, Didcot and Oxford. The strong separations of the past have diminished as the track layout and traffic patterns have changed but many West of England line trains go from No 1 platform and many of the via Oxford trains from 8, 9 and 10, with the HSTs for Bristol and South Wales using the platforms between and the suburban services the higher numbered group.

The influence of Paddington spreads well beyond the station proper and most of the railway activity in the immediate area is devoted to its efficient functioning. Immediately following the crossovers which serve the platform lines the route takes up a six-line pattern comprising Up and Down Main and Relief lines plus an Up Engine & Carriage line on the south side and a second Down Relief on the north side. From the former goods area on the Up side, now Paddington NCL, Up and Down Goods lines commence to create an eight-line pattern through

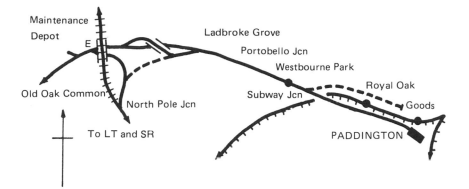

Subway Junction (61 ch) which reduces to seven through Westbourne Park (1 m 20 ch) where the Up and Down Goods lines are combined in a single bi-directional line. After Portobello Junction (1 m 33 ch) the four main and relief lines are flanked on the Down side by Up and Down Engine and Carriage lines and, opposite, by North Carriage Lines 1 and 2. The new carriage servicing and flushing apron platforms are located here, at Kensal Green, before the flyover line which links the Down side with the maintenance depot and carriage sidings at Old Oak Common. The whole section is notable for the huge, but decorative, bridges which carry the roads of the area across the WR main line.

Like all large stations, Paddington has much to offer the keen observer, from little touches like the balconies which afford a good view of the station from the offices above platform 1 to the intricacies of day to day working. As main line trains come and go and commuters hurry to and from their tubes and buses, there is always something to see whether it be the practical operation of running a large station or the happy marriage of an 1854 beginning with a 1982 function.

Behind the scenes at Paddington.

Although a busy main line station, Paddington retains a great deal of character.

P.2   Paignton

Newton Abbot-Paignton line. 222 m 12 ch from Paddington*

The Dartmouth & Torbay Railway reached Paignton from Torquay on August 1 1859 and opened on to Churston on March 15 1861. Before completion of the route to Kingswear in 1864 the concern had been acquired by the South Devon Railway and thus eventually became part of the Great Western empire, together with the ferry service operated across the mouth of the River Dart to Kingswear. Following discussions between British Rail, the local authorities and the Dart Valley Light Railway company, the route south of Paignton was taken over by the latter following its formal closure by BR in October 1972. This section, known as the Torbay & Dartmouth Railway, has its own station adjoining the BR Down platform at Paignton.

Approaching Paignton from Torquay the signal box (222 m 4 ch) and its scissors crossover precede the busy level crossing in the centre of the resort. The Up and Down platforms then follow with the main buildings on the former and including ticket and information facilities. Alongside the Down platform gates bearing the GWR insignia lead to the booking office, sales facilities and then platform of the preserved railway enterprise in the area that used to be BR carriage sidings. Beyond the station Paignton South signal box is still BR manned, the main line ending at Paignton South level crossing (222 m 22 ch) and specific Appendix instructions covering the exchange of traffic from BR to the T&DR line.

The growth in popularity of the Torbay resorts before and after the Second World War meant a hectic summer season for the stations along the Paignton line. The peak has now eased considerably and seat reservation arrangements, along with the increasing availability of HST sets, have made the summer working at Paignton much easier. Even so the normal service of trains to Newton Abbot/Exeter, Birmingham and beyond and Paddington is supplemented during the summer to total some 30 departures on a peak Saturday.

P.3   Pangbourne

Paddington-Swindon line between Reading and Didcot. 41 m 43 ch from Paddington

The chalk cutting at Pangbourne is one of the few significant topographical features of the main line stretch between Reading and Swindon. The former goods yard was sited here on the Up side, the station standing at the London end and comprising platforms serving the Relief lines only. Served by the Paddington-Reading-Oxford trains, Pangbourne was one of the original GWR station sites.

P.4   Pantyffynnon

Shrewsbury-Llanelli line between Llandeilo and Llanelli. 10 m 8 ch from Llandeilo Junction.

Pantyffynnon, centre of a group of lines near Ammanford, overshadows the town in railway terms. It is a junction and traffic centre of some significance while the town itself has always been served by adjacent 'wayside' stations.

The principal line through Pantyffynnon is the single track Llanelly Railway route from Llanelli to Llandeilo opened in stages from 1839 to 1857 and from 1868 forming part of the Central Wales route from Swansea to Shrewsbury. From Pantyffynnon Junction there is a coal traffic branch to Gwaun-cae-Gurwen and Abernant and to the south the triangular connection with the Swansea District Line. Until 1964 there was also a direct line from Pontarddulais, the next station south of Pantyffynnon, to Swansea (Victoria).

The single track Central Wales route towards Pantyffynnon leaves the Swansea District line at a triangular junction recently straddled by an M4 motorway bridge. At Morlais Junction (3 m 48 ch) the double Swansea District Line continues towards Grovesend Colliery Loop Junction, the single track of the Central Wales line heading north to Hendy Junction (4 m 56 ch) where it is joined by the double line third leg of the triangle from Grovesend Colliery Loop Junction. There are signs of an earlier second track on the single track leg and of the burrowing junction route of the former Down line.

Beyond Hendy Junction is the 88 yd Pontarddulais Tunnel (5 m 13 ch to 5 m 17 ch), its narrowness dating from the horse-traction origins of the Llanelly Railway. The tunnel also suffers from poor drainage and may become a pioneer site for the installation of slab track. Pontarddulais station (5 m 26 ch) now

A train of coal, double-headed with two Class 37 locomotives, heads for Pantyffynnon and the Swansea District Line.

consists of just a single platform and functional shelter although the platform was originally a larger affair in the vee of the junction with the line from Swansea (Victoria) which trailed in on the Down side.

Pantyffynnon station (10 m 1 ch) is also in the vee of a junction, this time with the coal line eastwards to Gwaun-cae-Gurwen—GcG as it is known—and Abernant. Only the Down Central Wales line platform is used, the station buildings there housing the train crew depot and supervisory staff for the coal traffic operations. A signal box, controlling semaphore signals, stands south of the junction and this is a 'fringe box' to the Port Talbot panel. Parallel to the Central Wales passenger line and passing the former Up platform face is the single track siding to Wernos colliery and coal washery. This fans out into a set of sidings after the two lines have passed over the level crossing beyond the station.

The branch from Pantyffynnon into the Amman Valley was also started by the Llanelly Railway and opened in 1840 as far as Garnant. An 1841 extension on to GcG was replaced by the present alignment in 1907. The spur to Abernant is the stub of a line authorised in 1911 to connect the coalfield with the Swansea District Line then being built. The southern stub also exists as the Clydach branch but the centre section was never completed. The Abernant line opened in 1922 and although it never carried a passenger service, stations were constructed and some of the buildings remain to this day.

From the sidings at the Pantyffynnon end the GcG branch passes over a crossing to the small freight and coal yard and then heads for another crossing at the site of Ammanford station (11 m 27 ch). Between the two is a group of sidings known as 'New Sidings' and which are the base for the local coal traffic workings in the area. These sidings are also connected to the site of the former Ammanford colliery where coal from the NCB's new Betws drift mine is loaded to rail. This new mine was opened in 1978 and a system of conveyor belts brings the coal from the faces, up one of the drifts (or inclined planes) to the surface, and then to the rail loading site.

Passenger trains through Ammanford up to Brynamman ceased in 1958 and Tirydail, next north of Pantyffynnon on the Central Wales line then became Ammanford & Tirydail. Now known as Ammanford (11 m 21 ch), to add to the complications it was at one time Dyffryn Lodge and the signal box still bears the name Tirydail! Back at the site of the 'proper' Ammanford, the signal box there controls movements to and from the New Sidings in conjunction with Pantyffynnon and the yard supervisor, also the operation of the level crossing and, in conjunction with the shunter accompanying each train, the movements towards GcG and Abernant.

There is a 30 mph speed limit on the two single line branches. To GcG the route climbs steeply at between 1 in 75 and 1 in 116 but with a one mile section of 1 in 40 after the 1907 alignment is joined at Garnant; there are several level crossings and a tunnel en route. At Abernant Junction (15 m 78 ch) the route divides, one leg going on to the GcG loading site for opencast coal (16 m 67 ch) and the other to the NCB colliery at Abernant (2m 23 ch).

Services in the Pantyffynnon area consist of the five daily dmu passenger trains on weekdays in each direction between Swansea and Shrewsbury and a thrice-weekly freight trip from Llandeilo Junction to Llandeilo and Llandovery. On the branch the coal moves either for shipment through Swansea or to the domestic market, that from Betws needing washing which is undertaken at Wernos, Abernant or Cynheidre. Local trips are undertaken by Class 08 locomotives and the workings of GcG and Abernant trains to Pantyffynnon and then on to Swansea Docks or Severn Tunnel Junction are all handled by Class 37 machines; these work in pairs, front and rear on the climb to GcG and Abernant and at the head of returning trains. Two Class 08s and three Class 37s are normally outbased at Pantyffynnon.

P.5 Par

Taunton-Penzance line between Bodmin Road and St Austell. 281 m 69 ch from Paddington*

J.R. Treffry, later to become chairman of the Cornwall Railway, gave Par its first railway well before the main line appeared. His combined canal and horse-worked railway route to Bugle began a development of transport for the clay industry which grew into the Cornwall Minerals Railway of which many remnants still exist in the area.

The china clay industry still dominates Par and vessels can be seen loading at the ECC port on the Down side of the WR main line. This crosses over the access line from St Blazey as it used to cross the CMR route to Fowey via Pinnock Tunnel, now an ECC road route.

At Par station the station buildings are on the Down side, modest and of grey stone. A row of railway letter boxes stands beneath the canopy and there is also a goods loop on this side. On the Up side an island platform is provided and serves not only the fairly extensive pattern of main line trains but also the dmus to and from Newquay, both controlled by the semaphore signals of the wooden signal box on the platform.

P.6 Parkandillack Branch

Taunton-Penzance line, branch from Burngullow. 5 m 8 ch

Another of the Cornish china clay branches runs from the main line at Burn-

A Class 37 locomotive and a clay train wait for access to the main line at Par.

gullow, through Lanjeth open level crossing (289 m 28 ch) and Drinnick Mill (291 m 31 ch) to Parkandillack (293 m 60 ch). The first of the two single line sections, to Drinnick Mill, is under the control of the Burngullow signalman and the remainder is the responsibility of the Drinnick Mill shunter.

The two sections of the line also originated with different companies, the southern half being opened by the Newquay & Cornwall Junction Railway in 1869 and the other portion by the Cornwall Minerals Railway in 1874. After the GWR took over the railway had to close for three-quarters of a mile south of Drinnick Mill from 1909 to 1922 while the Carpella United Clay Company exercised its mineral rights over the land on which the track lay, the 'Carpella Break' as it came to be known.

A daily train path exists for supplying empties and removing clay wagons from the line.

Parson Street—see Bristol

P.7   Patchway

Swindon-Newport line between Bristol (Parkway) and Severn Tunnel. 5 m 77 ch from Bristol (Temple Meads)

In October 1858 work began on the Bristol & South Wales Union Railway line from Bristol to New Passage and part of the civil engineering work involved was the 1,246 yd Patchway Old Tunnel (6 m 68 ch to 7 m 45 ch). Patchway New Tunnel, exactly 1 m long (6 m 56 ch to 7 m 56 ch), was built 22 years later when the route was doubled to cope with the additional traffic arising from the opening of the Severn Tunnel. This tunnel was on the Up line which was given an easier gradient than the original line which also had an additional 62 yd tunnel, Patchway Short Tunnel (7 m 53 ch to 7 m 56 ch).

The tunnels are preceded by Patchway station (5 m 77 ch) and Patchway Junction where the direct line from Swindon joins the route from Bristol (112 m 72 ch and 5 m 64 ch). The station, consisting of just two platforms linked by a footbridge, is served by three Down and four Up trains on weekdays. There is still a coal activity, not rail served, in the old yard on the Up side where the weighbridge and weighbridge office survive.

P.8   Patney and Chirton

Reading-Taunton line between Hungerford and Westbury. 81 m 7 ch from Paddington

Patney and Chirton originally lay on the Hungerford-Devizes line of the Berks & Hants Extension Railway, authorised in 1859 and opened 13 years later. After it became a main line station on the 'cut off' route Patney and Chirton became a junction of some significance, originating some local services via Devizes and dealing with a few Bristol-Paddington 'slows' in addition to the non-stop trains which passed through.

The area is still marked by the overgrown dock on the Down side, the trackbed of the line for Devizes and a long footbridge spanning the station area which once included a single-sided 'Military' platform dating from the First World War.

P.9   Pembrey and Burry Port

Newport-Fishguard line between Llanelli and Carmarthen. 228 m 70 ch from Paddington*

The town of Burry Port—these days its one-time industrial harbour is used for yachting—is 4 m west of Llanelli and marks the end of the industrial belt of South Wales. Its station is right alongside the town's shopping area and also serves the smaller township of Pembrey 1½ m further west. Unstaffed, the station consists of Up and Down platforms with shelters, a travel agency in the prefabricated timber building on the Up side also being used as a booking office for the station.

The approach to Pembrey and Burry Port is along the Loughor estuary, with views across to the Gower Peninsula and large boulders to break up the force of heavy seas. A loop alongside the Down Main line gives access to the Carmarthen Bay coal-fired power station and its extensive private layout of sidings, all three lines being crossed by a barrier level crossing controlled from the adjacent GWR-style signal box.

On the station side of the level crossing, diverging from the loop, is the start of the BPGV branch to Coedbach and Cwmmawr. This curves away ultimately to swing round beneath the main line beyond the station but will be closed when the Kidwelly-Coedbach link is re-established. Alongside the branch line is a group of exchange sidings, also sidings forming the coal and freight yard behind the Down platform of the passenger station, and a connection to the premises of a private wagon repair company.

In view of the urban nature of the area, nearly all the West Wales trains call at Pembrey and Burry Port, although the Fishguard boat trains and summer Saturday extras are exceptions. On the freight side, Class 03 204 hp diesel shunters based at Landore work to and from Llanelli to deal with the Cwmmawr branch traffic and a number of freight workings link Pembrey and Burry Port with Llandeilo Junction yard. Others serve the power station or carry shipment coal to Swansea Docks.

P.10   Pembroke Dock Branch

Newport-Fishguard line, branch from Whitland. 25 m 69 ch

Freight services on the Pembroke Dock branch, latterly only for domestic coal to Pembroke Dock, ceased at the end of 1978 and apart from occasional special trains the line is now a single track, passenger-only route. It leaves the South Wales main line at Whitland, heads south for the coastal resort of Tenby and then turns west to Pembroke, eventually terminating at the former naval dockyard town of Pembroke Dock on the southern shore of Milford Haven.

The line started off as a self contained railway opened in 1863 between Pembroke and Tenby. The extension west to Pembroke Dock came in the following year and that to the GWR at Whitland in 1866. Its origins as the Pembroke & Tenby are remembered in the term 'P&T' by which the line is still known. As a standard gauge line isolated by the broad gauge of the GWR the P&T at one time courted other 4 ft 8½ in gauge lines, including the Manchester & Milford and the LNWR at Carmarthen. As a precursor to the South Wales gauge conversion in 1872 the GWR helped to relieve the P&T's isolation by converting the Up line between Whitland and Carmarthen to standard gauge while leaving the Down line at 7 ft. The GWR leased the P&T in 1896 and absorbed it in the following year.

On the branch today electric token operation applies between Whitland and Tenby and the No Signalman Token system from the latter point to Pembroke Dock. There is a signal box at Tenby but the token instruments are in the ticket and parcels office to facilitate one-man operation of the station.

Between Whitland and Tenby there are unstaffed stations at Narberth (264 m 8 ch), Kilgetty (269 m 62 ch) and Saundersfoot (270 m 41 ch). The former, like most

The old station building at Pembroke Dock, carefully renovated and modernised.

Manorbier station where the trainmen operate the level crossing gates.

stations on the line, was once a passing point and the Up platform is the one now in use. The original canopy provides shelter but the station building is now in private hands. Immediately beyond the station is the 273 yd Narberth Tunnel (264 m 16 ch to 264 m 28 ch) followed by a summit just before the remains of the closed station at Templeton. Kilgetty and Saundersfoot have modern, stone block shelters and there are several curves along this section as well as some 1 in 47 and 1 in 52 sections on the stretch from Whitland.

Tenby station (274 m 58 ch) is approached over a viaduct, along which there is also a refuge siding. The two-platform station has a passing loop and an Up bay, and the 1950s alterations blend well with the basic, pleasant architecture of the station buildings. The modern signal box dates from 1956 and on an isolated section of track four ex-GWR corridor coaches are in use as camping coaches. At a lower level, on the Up side, the site of the original 1863 terminus is discernible.

Forward from Tenby, the line, briefly with a glimpse of the sea, descends at 1 in 62 to the level of the line to the earlier station and then heads for Pembroke Dock via unstaffed stations at Penally (275 m 71 ch), Manorbier (279 m 9 ch), Lamphey (282 m 50 ch) and Pembroke (284 m 11 ch). Penally is unusual in having closed in 1964, opened again for the summers of 1970 and 1971, and then re-opened permanently in February 1972. Its station buildings, like those at Manorbier and Lamphey, are now in private use but a shelter is provided for passengers. From Penally the line climbs to a summit at Manorbier which has a trainmen-operated level crossing, two open level crossings then preceding Lamphey. At Pembroke there are still some disused sidings although the station consists of only a platform and shelter. There is a minor summit before the end of the line and also the 460 yd Pembroke Tunnel (285 m 5 ch to 285 m 26 ch).

Pembroke Dock (286 m 26 ch) is preceded by another open crossing. There is a run-round facility, some disused sidings and evidence of the former freight branch to Hobbs Point Pier and the extension of the line into the dockyard. The station was extensively renovated following the Irish B&I Line switching its

Cork-Swansea ferry service to the new ferry terminal at Pembroke Dock in 1979. Modern ticket, waiting and toilet facilities have been embodied in the previous stone buildings and coaches link the station with the ferryport. Interestingly, the new facilities were partly financed by Dyfed County Council, Wales Tourist Board, British & Irish Steam Packet Company Ltd and the European Regional Development Fund.

The train service on the line was further revised with the opening of the B&I Rosslare route in 1980 and now comprises a basic pattern of seven trains in each direction, mostly dmus. Some trains do not serve all stations and most of the intermediate ones, other than Tenby and Pembroke, are request stops. Additional trains operate at peak periods in connection with the B&I service, for summer visitors to and from Tenby and for excursion traffic to that resort. Occasional military specials run in connection with the training establishments near the Pembrokeshire coast.

P.11   Penallta Colliery Branch

Rhymney-Cardiff line, branch from Ystrad Mynach North. 1 m 16 ch

This single line branch links the Rhymney Valley line at Ystrad Mynach North Junction (13 m 72 ch) with Penallta colliery (14 m 60 ch). Opened by the Rhymney Railway in 1906, the line is also known as the Cylla Branch and it used to extend for a further 2 m to Penrhiwfelin until the track was removed in 1958. Shortly beyond the junction the branch used to pass under the GWR Pontypool Road-Neath line and the bridge which carried the latter is still in existence.

Ystrad Mynach North Junction faces Cardiff and is worked from Ystrad Mynach South Junction signal box, half a mile away. The latter also controls movements on the branch, using the One Train Working system. The turnout to the branch at North junction is on the Up line only and Down trains use the Up line as far as the crossover at South junction. The branch climbs at a gradient of 1 in 48 towards Penallta.

Trains over the Penallta Colliery Branch are mgr workings to and from Aberthaw and consist of the standard Aberthaw formation of two Class 37 locomotives and 35 mgr wagons.

Penally—see Pembroke Dock Branch

P.12   Penarth Branch

Newport-Fishguard line, branch from Cogan Junction, Cardiff. 1 m 12 ch

Two short lines with common origins diverge from the Cardiff-Barry line after it heads south from the Penarth Curves layout west of Cardiff. One is the short, freight-only single line from Grangetown to Ferry Road and the other the single track passenger suburban line from Cogan Junction to Penarth.

Inadequate capacity at Cardiff Docks for expanding exports of coal led the Taff Vale Railway to sponsor the building, by the Penarth Harbour Dock & Railway Company, of a line from the TVR main line at Radyr to a new Ely Tidal Harbour on the north side of the mouth of the Ely river and to new docks at Penarth on the opposite side. The latter came to provide 80 acres of water space and handle a significant volume of wood pulp imports in addition to the exported coal.

The line to Ely Tidal Harbour, now surviving as the Ferry Road Branch, dates from 1859, while that to Penarth Docks was opened in 1865. The line from Cogan Junction to Penarth (Town) opened in 1878, ten years before the Barry Railway's line to Barry and the TVR coastal extension from Penarth to join it at Cadoxton. Although leased by the TVR, the Penarth HD&R company survived to be absorbed into the GWR in 1922.

Grangetown, 73 ch along the Barry branch and an unstaffed station, comprises a wide island platform reached by dingy stairs from the road below. To shelter passengers on the exposed embankment there is a large, gaunt canopy and a brick windbreak.

The junction with the Ferry Road branch is alongside the platform, on the Down side, facing Cardiff and controlled by a ground frame. The run-round is at this end and the branch continues via the old junction to Ferry Road Low Level (1 m 26 ch) to the boundary with the BTDB (2 m 3 ch). Falling traffic and plans for a new road give the line an uncertain future but in 1982 Class 08 trips served the several private sidings reached via the line, notably an oil depot on BTDB property near the Ely river.

The Ely river is crossed by the Barry line on its way from Grangetown to Cogan Junction, long Up and Down Goods Loops lying between the river bridge and the junction (2 m 41 ch). Until 1918 there was also a halt here, called Llandough

Platform and all along this stretch from Penarth Curve South Junction the width of the embankment bears witness to the additional track and sidings once necessary to deal with coal passing to Penarth and Barry docks. On the Down side at Cogan Junction the route of the lines into the now closed Penarth Docks is also clearly visible.

As the double track Barry line curves sharply west to Cogan station, the single track to Penarth continues straight ahead, through the site of Penarth Dock station (closed in 1962) and on to Dingle Road (57 ch). Like the terminus at Penarth (1 m 12 ch), Dingle Road is now a single platform on the Up side of the line with a modern brick station building although at the former the Down side TVR buildings survive in private commercial use. This final section of the line rises steeply from Dingle Road.

With its docks closed, Penarth is now a cliff top residential town on the widening estuary of the Severn and complete with pier, sea front and gardens. Mondays to Fridays the branch is served by 23 trains in each direction, using dmus and with the basic pattern formed by services to and from the Rhymney Valley. Grangetown is also served by Barry line trains and HSTs requiring reversing at Canton occasionally use the Penarth Curves triangle and the branch crossover at Cogan Junction.

P.13   Pencoed

Newport-Fishguard line between Cardiff and Bridgend. 187 m 6 ch from Paddington*

The modest local station has been closed since 1965 although there is still an Up Goods Loop here.

Pengam—see Cardiff and Rhymney Branch

Penryn—see Falmouth Branch

Pentre-bach—see Merthyr Branch

P.14   Pen-y-bont

Shrewsbury-Llanelli line between Craven Arms and Llandrindod Wells. 28 m 21 ch from Craven Arms

Pen-y-bont is another of the conditional stops on the Central Wales line, first reached from the Knighton direction in 1864. Only the Up Platform is now in use but four columns in the platform garden provide a reminder of the LNWR origins in the virtuous inscriptions 'Efficiency', 'Comfort', 'Speed' and 'Safety'. The 404 yd Pen-y-bont Tunnel (27 m 70 ch to 28 m 8 ch), lined partly in brick and partly in masonry, stands north of the station.

P.15   Penzance

Taunton-Penzance line. 326 m 50 ch from Paddington*

The important and busy terminus at the Cornish end of the West of England main line began its contribution to the railway network and to the development of Penzance as a resort, port and railhead on March 11 1852. Through services from London did not arrive until 1867 for the West Cornwall Railway was originally standard gauge and passengers had to change from the trains of the broad gauge Cornwall Railway at Truro. However, even though the early journeys to London took over 24 hours they gave the South-West realistic communications with the capital for the first time and contributed to the development of the region. The railway passenger service is still, in fact, doing this but now the Cornish Riviera reaches Paddington in five hours and there are through HST services over the North East/South West route to such places as Leeds and Newcastle.

The approach to Penzance is along the shore of Mount's Bay and over a short single line section into a four-platform terminus. The low stone embankment was originally a viaduct and suffered badly from storm damage in the early years of the line. The station buildings, with street access at both ground and first floor level, include the ticket office, travel centre, buffet and waiting facilities. The Motorail terminal and parcels train sidings are adjacent and beyond them is the bus station and the harbour. A shipping service sails from here to the Scilly Isles, the steamship company also being the railway's agent in the islands from which some of the earliest supplies of cut spring flowers originate. The station at Penzance carries a plaque dated November 28 1980, commemorating the centenary of rebuilding, and England's most westerly milepost, 326½, stands against the retaining wall, 10 ch from the end of platform 1.

I ne traffic movements at Penzance are controlled by a traditional manual signal box at the London end of the Up platform and there are CCTV level crossings at Ponsandane (325 m 75 ch) and Long Rock

The end of the line; Penzance station from the most westerly buffer stops on the WR.

(325 m 12 ch), both formerly signal box locations. Between the two the Up side is occupied formerly by the loading bank, goods depot, goods shed and latterly by the carriage sidings, carriage washing and servicing plant and the modern HST maintenance depot. The surviving dock and shed act as reminders of the once considerable goods traffic which included coal, potatoes, broccoli, fish and flowers.

P.16   Pershore

Oxford-Hereford line between Evesham and Worcester. 112 m 50 ch from Paddington

Pershore was an original OW&W station opened in May 1852. The single line was doubled in the following July but is now single again and the once extensive layout has been reduced to a single Down platform remaining in use, adorned only by a metal waiting shelter. But this rationalisation is better than the complete closure suffered by Fladbury and Stoulton on either side of Pershore and now only just discernible. At least Pershore still has a service of five trains each way Monday to Friday.

P.17   Pewsey

Reading-Taunton line between Hungerford and Westbury. 75 m 26 ch from Paddington

The Down side yard was closed in 1964 to leave just a simple station with modest single storey buildings on the Down side and a shelter on the Up. The weekday service is only four trains each way daily but this is provided mainly by stops in main line trains to put Paddington only about an hour's travelling time away.

P.18   Pilning

Swindon-Newport line between Bristol (Parkway) and Severn Tunnel. 9 m 43 ch from Bristol (Temple Meads)

Pilning's first station, later Pilning Low Level, was on the single line of the Bristol & South Wales Union Railway to New Passage and the ferry across the Severn. It closed in 1886 when the Severn Tunnel was brought into use and then opened from 1900 to 1964 to serve the line round to Severn Beach and Avonmouth. The route can still be seen on the Up side near the main line station.

The extra traffic generated by the Severn Tunnel brought, first a double line from Bristol and later the direct route via Badminton. It also led to the operation of a car ferry service between Pilning and Severn Tunnel Junction, initially using four-wheel vehicles and later bogie car flats. The car dock was on the Up side, adjacent to the cattle dock and goods shed, and the car ferry train—usually worked by a 61XX 2-6-2T—included a single coach for the car drivers and passengers.

Today Pilning station is just two platforms on the main line, with waiting shelters and a footbridge and served by stops in the peak hour Bristol-Cardiff local trains. There is a group of rusting sidings at the London end and a Down Goods line passes behind the Down platform. The Severn Tunnel emergency train of flat, tank and low wagons is stabled on the Up side.

P.19   Pirton

Birmingham-Bristol line between Barnt Green and Cheltenham. 70 m 51 ch from Derby

Pirton barrier crossing, ground frame and signal box site mark the very early passenger station, later to function as a goods depot for the agricultural activity of this fertile area.

P.20   Plymouth

Taunton-Penzance line. 245 m 75 ch from Paddington*

Plymouth has a fascinating and complex railway history. Its first line was the 4 ft 6 in gauge Plymouth & Dartmoor, born of Sir Thomas Tyrwhitt's ambition to open up the bleak acres of Dartmoor to trade and settlement. After much difficulty a line was opened on September 26 1823 from Sutton Pool via Crabtree to King's Tor

but it was more often in difficulties than not and ceased working around the turn of the century. Portions of the Plymouth & Dartmoor were incorporated in the Princetown branch and in the Lee Moor Tramway. Its route crossed the main line railway near the new road bridge at Crabtree, following the line of the road's eastbound carriageway and then veering off north near the Bass Charrington depot.

At the time of the P&D Plymouth was not the attractive place it is today. It was not even the largest of the 'Three Towns'; this was Devonport, Stonehouse lying in third place for size. However, the advent of the railway was to help the development of the area, the South Devon's line getting to Laira on the eastern outskirts on May 5 1848 and being carried on to Millbay on April 2 of the following year after a period of confusion about the link with the Cornwall Railway. In fact it was to be another ten years before the opening of the Royal Albert Bridge connected the line from Cornwall Junction with Saltash on the other side of the Tamar. In that same year, 1859, the Tavistock branch was opened.

The London & South Western Railway had watched the building of the 13-acre Great Western Dock and had plans for lines to both Sutton Harbour and Falmouth. It was 1876 before it reached Plymouth with a link via Lydford and Marsh Mills to a new, impressive terminus at Devonport, the present site at North Road getting its first station soon after. This joint GWR and LSWR running arrangement was not very satisfactory to the latter and the LSW got its own route from June 2 1890 via the Plymouth, Devonport & South Western Junction

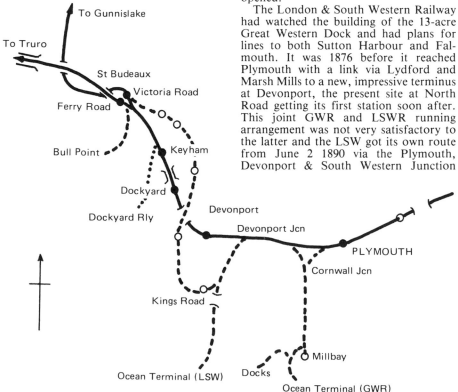

*The tunnel at Devonport which led to the
L&SWR's Ocean Quay at Plymouth.*

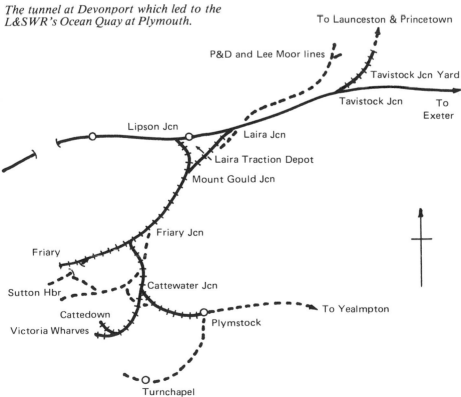

Railway line along the east bank of the Tamar, via tunnels under Devonport, and turning the station there into a through one. LSW services were extended to a new station at Friary which became a centre of competition on the two lines and produced some splendid services on the Turnchapel and Yealmpton branches.

The years around the turn of the century were full of activity. First the LSW and then the GW developed a pattern of suburban services, the latter opening new halts and introducing steam rail cars in 1904. There was also much rivalry over the traffic from the ocean liners with trains speeding towards London from the GWR's ocean terminal at Millbay and the LSW's at Stonehouse Pool. The racing period ended sadly in 1906 when 24 passengers died in a bad collision involving an 'ocean special' at Salisbury and on the very day that the GWR's Castle Cary cut-off route opened. Subsequent competition was centred more on comfort and this colourful activity continued until relatively recently, the operation of WR tender vessels ceasing in 1963 and the boat trains in 1971.

Plymouth is still a busy railway centre but its network is much slimmer these days. The high line round from North Road to Millbay has gone, between it and St Budeaux the LSW empire is marked by a few embankments and structures but no lines, and on the eastern side the lines to Yealmpton and Sutton Harbour have long since closed. But, in compensation, there is a modern station complex at North Road with HST services to

Paddington and via Bristol and local services into Cornwall and on to the Gunnislake branch. Friary remains in use for freight purposes, the branches to Plymstock and Cattewater survive and the diesel maintenance depot at Laira has been fully remodelled to cope with the expanding use of Inter-City 125 sets on the North-East/South-West route.

From the curves and gradients of South Dartmoor the West of England main line approaches Plymouth via Plympton, where the old signal box still exists on the Down side. Tavistock Junction marshalling yard (242 m 69 ch) now only deals with local and engineer's traffic, the former including ECC clay from Marsh Mills on the stub of the old Launceston branch. This is tripped to the yard by the Class 08 pilot for attaching to the air-braked service from Cornwall to the Potteries or for despatch to Fowey for shipment. Crabtree Siding ground frame (243 m 19 ch) gives access to the private siding serving Bass Charrington.

At Laira Junction (244 m 2 ch) is the access to the maintenance depot, with the through freight single line passing around it and a group of sidings beyond. From east to west the depot comprises ten stabling sidings, the fuelling line, the new carriage shed and the main diesel depot. It has access to Mount Gould Junction (244 m 39 ch) from which point the line continues, via the carriage washing machines,

Plymouth North Road station showing the clean lines of its modern architecture.

to Friary station (245 m 52 ch). From Mount Gould Junction there is a 37 ch link, completing the triangle, back to the main line at Lipson Junction (244 m 35 ch).

Friary station has been closed to passengers since 1958 and no longer despatches 27 trains a day to Turnchapel or services via Lipson Vale Halt, Mutley, North Road, Devonport, Albert Road Halt, Ford and Camel's Head Halt to St Budeaux. At the end of 1981 it was still a full load freight yard and the location of both the Area Freight Centre and a TOPS office. The route from Friary via Cattewater Junction (43 ch) to Plymstock (1 m 29 ch) remains open for cement traffic from the latter and to Cattewater for inwards oil trains ex-Fawley and outwards oil to BR depots. The Cattewater line runs via Maxwell Road trainmen-operated level crossing (1 m 16 ch), through the 48 yd Cattedown Tunnel (1 m 24 ch to 1 m 26 ch) and Cattedown open level crossing (1 m 30 ch) to the two trainmen-operated level crossings at Conoco East (1 m 43 ch) and Conoco West (1 m 49 ch) and then to Cattewater Harbour (1 m 59 ch). Both are serviced by the Class 08 Friary pilot.

Back on the main line, North Road is approached via the 317 yd Mutley Tunnel (245 m 32 ch to 245 m 46 ch) and Plymouth East ground frame (245 m 56 ch). In addition to the Up and Down Main lines there are four platform lines and a through line, all bi-directional and all but the latter

authorised for permissive working for both passenger and freight trains. The administrative offices, ticket office, travel centre and refreshment rooms are on the Down side with the other platforms reached by subway. The panel box at the country end of the station controls the area from Totnes to St Germans (exclusive). This was formerly a parcels and small goods handling area with No 1 platform a short terminal goods platform, No 2 the main passenger platform and a set of offices in mock Elizabethan style.

Beyond North Road the Cornwall Junction triangle led to Millbay and the line on into the docks and the GWR Ocean Terminal but only the bridge abutments now remain above the infilling process. There is a mileage change here (from 246 m 29 ch to 247 m 42 ch) recognising that the route was initially into Millbay and out again, and then comes the site of Devonport Junction where the curve round towards Kings Road, and via the 530 yd tunnel to the Ocean Terminal at Stonehouse Pool, is now a repository for dumped rubbish. A siding formerly joined the main line, again on the Down side, before Devonport station which comprises just shortened platforms plus shelter (248 m 28 ch) and is followed by the 117 yd Devonport Tunnel (248 m 37 ch to 248 m 42 ch).

After Dockyard station (248 m 60 ch) the route is at a higher level overlooking the naval dockyard and passing over the 161 yd Keyham Viaduct to reach Keyham station (249 m 30 ch) whose brick buildings are now closed and shuttered. Immediately

An HST power car receiving attention at Laira maintenance depot.

beyond the station the rusting connection from the dockyard area trails in at Keyham West ground frame (249 m 38 ch). A considerable volume of traffic passed this way at one time, including passenger trains to Naval Barracks Platform and trains with stores to the Exchange Sidings. For movements on from the latter to the entrance to *HMS Drake* a wooden train staff exists.

The 376 yd Weston Mill Viaduct carries the main line on to St Budeaux Junction (250 m) where the single line to Gunnislake leaves on the Up side to pass via St Budeaux Victoria Road and two crossings beneath the WR route before reaching the bank of the Tamar and turning north there. Between St Budeaux Junction and the GWR station at St Budeaux Ferry Road (250 m 15 ch) is the ground frame for the private siding at Bull Point and the main line then continues its high route to the Royal Albert Bridge. Apart from the main line trains and the dmus to Gunnislake, which take up the former SR route after serving the stations to Keyham, there is not much freight traffic this side of North Road. Explosives traffic is dealt with at Ernesettle on the Gunnislake route and there are occasional loads to or from the naval installations but the volume is not great and all movements are handled by a Class 08 shunting locomotive.

P.21   Polperro Tunnel

Taunton-Penzance line between St Austell and Truro. 297 m 50 ch from Paddington*

Two modest ridges east of Truro follow Tregeagle Viaduct and are pierced by the 581 yd Polperro Tunnel (297 m 50 ch to 297 m 76 ch) and the 320 yd Buckshead Tunnel (299 m 10 ch to 299 m 25 ch).

Polsloe Bridge—see Exmouth Branch

Pontarddulais—see Pantyffynnon

Pontlottyn—see Rhymney Branch

P.22   Pontrilas

Shrewsbury-Newport line between Hereford and Abergavenny. 11 m 14 ch from Hereford

Pontrilas closed to passengers in 1958 and to freight in 1964 but is still the site of Up and Down Goods Loops and of a block post. The wooden signal box is situated on the Up side near the old stone station buildings. At the north end of the site, still on the Down side, can be seen the track-

bed of the 18¾ m branch to Hay, closed since 1953.

P.23   Pontypool

Shrewsbury-Newport line between Abergavenny and Newport. 32 m 19 ch from Hereford

The Monmouthshire Railway & Canal Company opened a single line to Pontypool on July 1 1852, the Hereford connection came in the following year and the line from Crane Street to Blaenavon, with three colliery branches radiating from Pontnewynydd, in 1854. In the fourth year of this development cycle Pontypool was linked with the Taff Vale Railway to begin the route that was eventually to reach Neath via Aberdare and Hirwaun. With the opening of the Pontypool, Caerleon & Newport Railway in 1874 trains started using High Street station Newport instead of Mill Street.

The Cardiff/Newport-Shrewsbury/Crewe trains call at the surviving GWR station, formerly Pontypool Road, but all the other routes have gone and the 1,200 ft island platform is bare save for a small shelter. The severe, sizeable station buildings remain on the Down side along with a couple of sidings but Pontypool Station South box is closed and new roadworks overlay the former mass of sidings and junctions south of the station.

The roadworks continue south of Pontypool almost to Panteg where Up and Down loops remain, the former with a connection to the BSC works. There is also a connection on the Down side to a fibreglass works.

P.24   Pontypridd (and to Radyr)

Newport-Fishguard line, junction of Merthyr and Treherbert branches. 12 m 69 ch from Cardiff

This 7½ m of railway down the valley of the Taff is the core of the former Taff Vale Railway system, part of that company's original main line of 1840. The lines from the Rhondda and Taff valleys join at the north end of Pontypridd station, while at Radyr, in the boom days of the coal trade, the traffic split into flows to Cardiff or Penarth docks. Nowadays Pontypridd is still a busy and impressive station and the marshalling yard at Radyr is still the heart of the valleys' rail freight—mainly coal—operations.

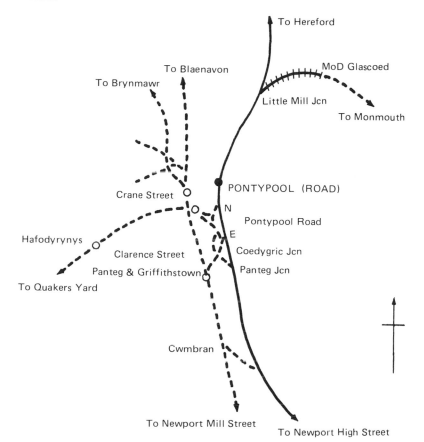

The line from the Rhondda valleys carries the passenger service from Treherbert and coal traffic from Maerdy. The one from the upper reaches of the Taff valley is used by the Merthyr passenger trains and freight traffic, mainly coal from the Cynon Valley line which joins at Abercynon. On the Down side of the line between the latter and the now closed Pontypridd freight depot can be seen the trackbed of the ex-TVR Nelson branch, the bridge which carried this line over the River Taff also being extant.

Both the line from Treherbert and that from Merthyr bridge the Rhondda river and then, in the angle of the junction between them, is Pontypridd signal box, a TVR structure now controlling colour light signals. The deep cutting used by the now-closed third leg of the triangle is still visible.

Pontypridd station (12 m 69 ch), immediately south of the junction is a vast structure standing on a shelf on the hillside with the main part of the town below. With substantial buildings of red Ruabon brick and extensive canopies supported by columns with massive, decorated bases, the station was built in 1907 as a long island platform with seven faces, staggered and using inset bays. Some 1,500 ft long with 3,452 ft of platform face, the 8,205 sq yds of platform area had 7,370 sq yds under cover until a reconstruction in 1974 provided a modern street-level facade and replaced the dim, cavernous booking office there with a modern ticket office in one of the platform buildings.

There are many interesting features at Pontypridd. Above the canopy at the street level entrance to the station is a 6 ft × 5 ft fibreglass replica of the principal part of the TVR crest built into the original terra cotta facade. Two small lions from the original crest are incorporated in the wall of the new ticket office on the platform and the marble

frontage below the ticket windows is made
up from the counter top from the station's
former 'Third Class Refreshment Room'
which previously occupied the site. The
heavy wooden framed windows on the
platform still include panels bearing the
station name and in the modern decor of
the 'Rhondda' waiting room and bar. A

place has still been kept for the intricately
decorated Victorian display case which
was carefully brought from a local pub
when the station was first built. Unfort-
unately, this fascinating station is
subjected to extensive graffiti.

Alongside the through goods lines at
Pontypridd is an engineer's siding used

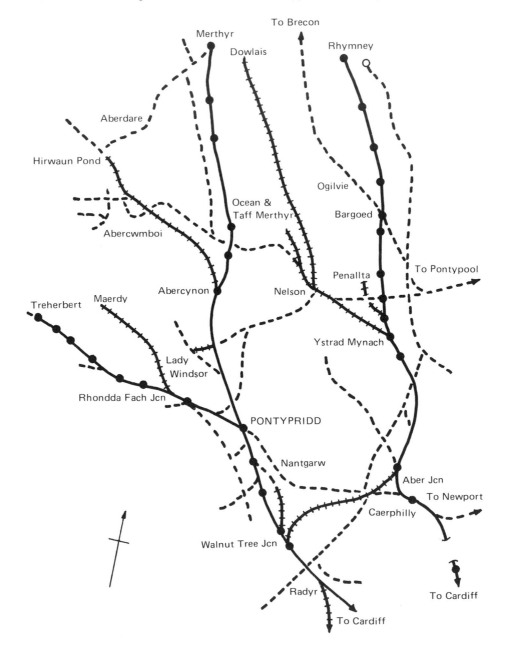

for stabling track maintenance machines. Once through the station, the single two-direction passenger line on the Up side of the island platform becomes double. The track to the now-closed freight and coal yard at Trefforest is on the Up side and opposite are the earthworks of the erstwhile Pontypridd, Caerphilly & Newport Railway's line to Caerphilly and beyond (1884-1967).

Trefforest station (12 m), just below Pontypridd, has two platforms linked by a footbridge, each with a modern brick shelter, and including a ticket office on the Down side. On the Up side, in the space formerly taken up by the extra running lines for freight, is a large Mid-Glamorgan County Council 'park-and-ride' car park and beyond it the old yard. Signs advise passengers to alight here for the nearby Polytechnic of Wales.

There have been as many as three junctions below Trefforest, all facing Pontypridd. On the Down side was the short-lived connection with the Cardiff Railway to Cardiff docks where, after carrying a ceremonial opening train in 1909, the junction was taken up in a dispute between the TVR and Cardiff companies. On the Up side, nearer to Trefforest station was an 1889 spur to the Barry Railway main line to Barry Docks, and farther south a junction (1863-1930) with the TVR line to Llantrisant. After closure of the latter, trains used the Barry route and a connection between the two lines at Tonteg. Some buildings in typical GWR signal box style on the Up side identify an S&T depot.

Maesmawr signal box (10 m 57 ch), a GWR structure on the Down side, is still a block post but the Down side connection to Trefforest Industrial Estate and the Down Loop are now out of use. Here, as elsewhere along this route, evidence remains of the former freight tracks on the Up side, that between Maesmawr and Taffs Well being the last to go.

Trefforest Estate station (9 m 53 ch), following Maesmawr, has a narrow island platform reached by a subway and dates only from 1942. On this section the gradients are gentle, mostly one in two or three hundred, no doubt reflecting the skill of the TVR's engineer, one I.K. Brunel.

The line curves before crossing the Taff on the approach to Taffs Well (7 m 24 ch) beneath the steep side of the 1,007 ft Garth Mountain and immediately before the station the 1952 freight single line from Nantgarw trails in on the Down side. The station itself has two platforms with substantial TVR buildings, reminiscent of Pontypridd but on a much smaller scale. These are now bricked up and may be replaced by modern shelters. There is a ticket office on the Up side, linked to the Down by a footbridge with TVR 'roundels' in its decorated ironwork.

At the south end of the Taffs Well station the double track freight line from Aber Junction trails in on the Down side and the two tracks become four. The junction is controlled by Walnut Tree Junction signal box (7 m 20 ch), a tall TVR structure on the south end of the platform and which completes the three absolute block sections, viz, Pontypridd-Maesmawr, Maesmawr-Walnut Tree Junction, Walnut Tree Junction-Radyr. Permissive working applies on the Relief lines on the southernmost section.

Immediately beyond Taffs Well on the Up side is the one remaining pier of the Barry Railway's Walnut Tree Viaduct (in use 1901-67, removed 1969-73), once a 120 ft high, 1,548 ft long landmark and carrying the BR's tentacle into the Rhymney Valley. The third railway through this narrow Tongwynlais gap, the ill-fated Cardiff Railway, has now largely disappeared beneath the route of the adjacent A470 trunk road.

After crossing the winding Taff once again, and overlooked by William Burgess' fairy tale Castell Coch (Red Castle), the four-track line reaches Pentyrch crossing where a distinctive white building on the Down side is part of the old station which closed as long ago as 1863. Here, also, an early industrial tramroad which pre-dated the TVR made a level crossing of the railway until 1962. A crossing of a more modern type is that by the M4 which precedes a curving approach to Radyr station (5 m 32 ch), with the river now by the side of the line and its waters pouring over a spectacular weir.

The passenger train service totals 33 dmu workings in each direction (32 on Saturdays, 8 on Sundays), mainly three-car formations to or from Merthyr or Treherbert. The off-peak pattern is hourly between Treherbert and Barry Island and between Merthyr or Abercynon and Cardiff Central. There are some variations at peak times and trains call at all stations except Trefforest Estate which is served mainly at change of shift times.

Freight traffic is monopolised by the Class 37s and is mainly coal although there is a daily ballast train from Penderyn Quarry via Hirwaun and Abercynon. Most trains originate or terminate at Radyr yard with the exception of the Aberthaw mgr trains fromerly via the Big Hill and some coal workings to Severn Tunnel Junction yard or Newport docks. Most trains, also, are loaded coming down and empty going up but there are loaded flows to Nantgarw coke ovens and Abercwmboi phurnacite plant for processing. One flow, from Maerdy colliery to Abercwmboi, involves reversal on the goods lines at Pontypridd station. There are also wagonload workings serving coal depots in the Valleys and the BSC at Dowlais.

Porth—see Treherbert Branch

P.25   Portishead Branch

Bristol-Taunton line, branch from Parson Street Junction. 9 m 37 ch

So far something of a white elephant, Bristol's Royal Portbury Dock could produce considerable business for BR. For this reason the Portishead branch, although not used, is kept intact as it could be used to link the dock area, along the south bank of the Avon, to the main line at Parson Street.

The single line was built by the Bristol & Portishead Pier & Railway Company as part of a plan to improve Bristol's shipping facilities and although maintained by the constructing company until 1884, it was worked by the GWR from opening on April 18 1867. Originally broad gauge, the single line had a crossing place added at Clifton Bridge in 1880 and the section to Ashton Junction doubled three years later.

On its route from Parson Street Junction (120 m 28 ch), Ashton Junction level crossing (121 m 18 ch) and Ashton Gate (121 m 30 ch), the line passes through the dramatic Avon Gorge and beneath Brunel's Clifton Suspension Bridge. There are four tunnels—the 56 yd Clifton Bridge No 1 (122 m 23 ch to 122 m 26 ch), the 232 yd Clifton Bridge No 2 (122 m 53 ch to 122 m 63 ch), the 88 yd Sandstone (123 m 77 ch to 124 m 1 ch) and the 665 yd Pill Tunnel (125 m 33 ch to 125 m 63 ch)—and, at various times, stations at Clifton Bridge, Ham Green Halt, Pill (traditional home of the Bristol Channel pilots), then Portbury and Portbury Shipyard. At Portishead a new station was provided in 1954 but the site is now

occupied by a petrol station. After the closure in 1967 the line was cut back to end in the docks and power station but its final traffic flow, cement in Presflo wagons, has now been moved to Lawrence Hill, Bristol and the line is unused.

P.26   Portskewett

Gloucester-Newport line between Chepstow and Severn Tunnel Junction. 145 m 77 ch from Paddington

Only an ageing footbridge, too wide for the Gloucester-Chepstow line it spans, marks the closed Portskewett station, but the route to Black Rock can still be traced providing a reminder of the ferry route across the Severn before the opening of the tunnel.

Portsmouth Arms—see Barnstaple Branch

P.27   Port Talbot

Newport-Fishguard line between Bridgend and Neath. 202 m 59 ch from Paddington*

Nowadays Port Talbot is almost entirely a steel town. Even the harbour, which once shared in the universal South Wales coal trade, is now devoted to imports of fuel and raw materials for the British Steel Corporation works. The town itself lies at the foot of the hills where the Afan river makes its way to the sea. It takes its name from the Talbot family of Margam Abbey which developed the metal industries here, a member of the family also being chairman of the South Wales Railway and, later, a director of the Great Western Railway.

Although of considerable importance to BR, both in business and operational terms, the railway facilities at Port Talbot are compact, the extensive freight activity connected with the steel works being part of the operation at nearby Margam. The main features of Port Talbot itself are the station and panel box. The latter lies on the four-track approach to the station on the Down side and there is a coal depot opposite. The barrier crossing between the panel box and the station is operated from the former.

Port Talbot station comprises a modern island platform with functional buildings and linked by footbridge to the car park and forecourt on the Up side, all adjacent to the town's main street. The old

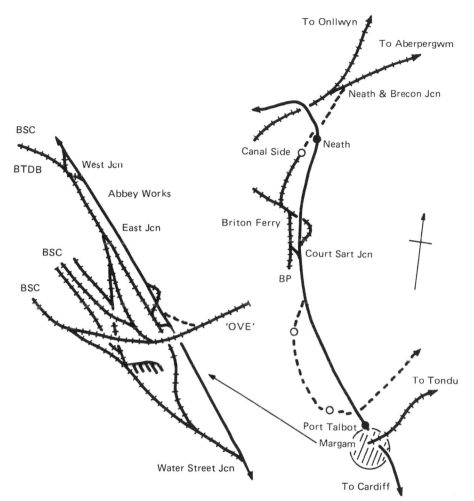

booking office on the platform was replaced in 1980 by an architecturally pleasing modern ticket office and travel centre on the Up side. Port Talbot is served by the hourly pattern of Inter-City 125 HSTs between Swansea and London and deals with a high level of passenger business, partly because of its good road links via the M4.

Beyond the station the main line climbs by a short, sharp rise to cross the Afan river alongside the modern Aberafan Shopping Centre. The climb involves a short stretch at 1 in 60 and there is a similar descent before the level section on to Briton Ferry and Court Sart Junction. The four lines become two immediately west of the station.

Port Talbot panel box was commission-ed in 1963 and over the next ten years its area of control expanded until it now covers the 45 m of main line from west of Llantrisant to a point between Llanelli and Pembrey. It also takes in the triangular layout at Swansea, Swansea passenger station and the 16¼ m Swansea District Line, plus the portion of Central Wales Line to Pantyffynnon (exclusive).

Port Talbot formerly had a considerable network of lines, mainly connected with its activities as a port. The Port Talbot Railway & Docks Company took over the harbour and docks of the old Port Talbot Company by an Act of 1894 and was authorised to make lines to join up with the Rhondda & Swansea Bay Railway and the GWR. These were constructed before the turn of the century

when new docks were brought into use. The half a million tons of traffic handled had risen to 3¼ million tons by 1923 and the dock was the first to tip the new 20-ton coal wagons introduced following the grouping of the South Wales railways under the GWR banner.

The PTR also operated passenger services from its Port Talbot Central terminus across the road from the GWR main line station. It was worked by the GWR from 1907, one year after the GWR had started working the R&SBR route down the Afan Valley, through a station at Port Talbot called Aberavon Town and across the main line on the level on the Briton Ferry side of Port Talbot General.

The only railway in Port Talbot docks now is the line over the BTDB to the BSC ore loading terminal. This is close to the deep sea harbour into which ore is shipped in bulk carriers and then placed in a stockpile for subsequent use at Port Talbot and Llanwern steelworks. Ore for the latter is taken by conveyor belt to the overhead bunker where it is loaded to trains of 30 BSC 101.5-tonne gross laden weight tippler wagons. The trains are positioned for loading by the train engines—two Class 56s—but these are detached while the train is propelled through the bunker,

Above *Class 47 locomotive and train near Port Talbot.*

Below *Britain's heaviest train runs regularly with a 3,304-tonne load of ore from Port Talbot to Llanwern.*

three wagon lengths at a time, by a ram-like lineside positioner. The line from the terminal is double track, becoming single on BR property and continuing single to the junction with the freight lines alongside the main line 2 m on the Margam side of Port Talbot. At the beginning of 1982 four trains were being operated every 24 hours, Mondays to Fridays.

P.28   Purton

Swindon-Gloucester line between Swindon and Kemble. 81 m 65 ch from Paddington

Purton Common level crossing stands at 81 m 65 ch and the miniature red/green warning light crossing at Purton Collins Lane at 81 m 9 ch. Between the two the old station site is still clear and a shelter still remains on the Up platform. Nearer Swindon Bremell Sidings ground frame (79 m) gives access to an oil terminal.

P.29   Pyle

Newport-Fishguard line between Bridgend and Port Talbot. 195 m 79 ch from Pad-dington*

Pyle was once an important main line junction but little now remains to indicate this, the station itself having closed in 1964. Pyle was originally the point at which the South Wales Railway intersected the tramroad of the Duffryn, Llynfi & Porthcawl Railway (of 1829) which carried traffic from the Llynfi and Ogmore valleys to the busy harbour at Porthcawl. With the conversion of the tramroad to a railway Pyle became a junction for Porthcawl and Tondu, but both lines closed to passengers in 1963 and to freight in 1965 and 1973 respectively. There was also a short lived and little used line linking Pyle with Waterhall Junction on the ex-PTR route from Tondu to Margam.

A spur opened in 1946 from the Porth-cawl line to the main line facing westwards can still be spotted.

Quaker's Yard—see Merthyr Branch

Quintrel Downs—see Newquay Branch

Q.1   Quedgeley

Birmingham-Bristol line between Glou-cester and Standish Junction. 97 m 1 ch from Derby

On the Up side, stretching from the gates of Brookthorpe crossing (97 m 1 ch)

north, is the vast government depot at Quedgeley. There are refuge and sorting sidings at the Bristol end and a connection to the main line at Tuffley Junction (94 m 60 ch). The siding complex also houses the Dow-Mac pre-stressed concrete firm.

R.1   Radley

Didcot-Birmingham line between Didcot and Oxford. 58 m 35 ch from Paddington

The Abingdon branch was extended to Radley and Abingdon Junction station closed on September 8 1873. The island platform provided to accommodate the branch trains is still used by the local Reading-Oxford services but, like the Up platform, now has only a waiting shelter. A ground frame at the London end of the station controls the crossover and the branch connection.

R.2   Radstock Branch

Reading-Taunton line, branch from Frome. 8 m 16 ch

A Frome-Radstock colliery line with a tri-angular junction at the Frome end opened on November 14 1954 but another 20 years were to pass before the line became a through route to Bristol. Passenger services, averaging about eight trains each way daily, then lasted until 1959. Freight traffic continued but the North Somerset coalfield production dropped as NCB rationalisation took effect and the northern section of the line ceased work in 1959. The Mells Road-Radstock portion had closed two years earlier but was re-opened to allow the last colliery, Writhlington, to be served from the Frome end.

Radstock is an area full of railway interest and was well served when it had both GWR and Somerset & Dorset stations. Their remains stand side by side with only the route of an old tramway between and the loco shed is now just a shell. The only remaining rail activity is that of the Marcroft Wagon Repair Co who have sidings for their wagon repair activity at Radstock and contribute to the retention of its last surviving rail link.

From Frome North via the sidings ground frame at Frome West (16 ch) and the one at Hapsford (2 m 20 ch) the single line is worked under the No Signalman Token regulations as far as Mells Road (4 m 71 ch) where Roads Reconstruction Ltd have a siding. An instrument is provided to mark the end of the token section and

the remainder of the line is worked on the one train basis.

The route to ARC's Whatley Quarry diverges at Hapsford and passes through three tunnels, the 275 yd Bedlam Tunnel (2 m 51 ch to 2 m 64 ch), the 319 yd Great Elm Tunnel (2 m 76 ch to 3 m 11 ch) and the 55 yd Murdercombe Tunnel (3 m 56 ch to 3 m 58 ch). BR traction brings the trains of incoming empties to the exchange sidings where they are handed over to the ARC locomotives. Outwards stone traffic passes to terminals in London, the Home Counties and the South-East.

R.3   Radyr

Merthyr-Cardiff line between Pontypridd and Llandaf. 5 m 32 ch from Cardiff

Radyr is on the ex-Taff Vale Railway main line and marks the point where, in 1859, the TVR made a facing junction with their 1840 line from the Valleys to Cardiff and carried a new branch round the city to the harbour and docks at Penarth. Radyr, originally known as Penarth Junction, is still a key point for freight activity on the ex-Taff Vale and Rhymney systems, its marshalling yard also feeding several installations in the Cardiff area. An Area Manager is located

there; it is an Area Freight Centre, TOPS Office, Train Crew Depot and a track pre-fabrication depot for the civil engineer.

There are four tracks on the approach to Radyr from the north with the main lines to the east and the relief lines to the west and the station platforms serving the former. There is a busy 'park-and-ride' car park on the Up side and a footbridge to the Up platform, access to the Down platform being from a narrow roadway beneath the line. The train service is that described in the Pontypridd entry.

At the south end of Radyr Down platform is Radyr Junction signal box, a modern WR timber framed manual box and with semaphore signals to control the sections to Walnut Tree Junction, Radyr Quarry Junction and Llandaf. The main line towards the latter continues as a double track but the two permissive relief lines have now become a single Up Relief line as the tracks cross the River Taff and head towards Llandaf Loop Junction. Flanking the east side of the double track, former Penarth Branch is Radyr marshalling yard with a smaller group of sidings on the Up side. Movements to and from the north end are controlled by Radyr Junction box (5 m 25 ch) and those at the south end by Radyr Quarry Junction box (4 m 2 ch), 39 ch away. This is an ex-TVR structure, on the Up side, and its semaphore signals also control the short Llandaf Loop back to the main line.

In the angle between the two lines at Radyr is the track prefabrication depot, which has its own departmental locomotive for internal movements. Shunting in Radyr

Yard itself is performed by Class 08s with services to and from the line almost exclusively the province of Class 37s. The yard functions mainly as a sorting point for traffic to and from the local collieries and yards, sidings and railway installations. It has links with Severn Tunnel Junction, Llandeilo Junction, Swansea Burrows Sidings and Margam and with such local points as Tidal Sidings, Penarth North Curve Sidings and the Cathays and Maindy shops.

Most of the trains going north from Radyr are conveying empty wagons to collieries but there are movements via the yard of coal from pits in the Gwent 'Western Valleys' to Nantgarw coke ovens and of coal to Abercwmboi. Similarly, most trains southwards into the yard come from collieries, Nantgarw coke ovens or Abercwmboi. Other movements are made up of coal to local yards, shipment coal to Newport or Swansea docks, shipment coke to Barry Docks and trains of coking coal to Llanwern steel works and to Llantrisant for the Coed Ely and Cwm coke ovens. Freight services passing through the yard include mgr services to and from Aberthaw and ballast trains from Penderyn quarry via Hirwaun, Aberdare and Abercynon.

From Radyr trains to and from points west of Cardiff run via Queen Street and the remainder run via the 'Penarth Branch'. The principal role of the latter is now to link Radyr with the Penarth Curves triangular layout west of Cardiff and Radyr Quarry Junction signal box on this route is a fringe box for the Cardiff panel. Between these two points is the site of Waterhall Junction where the ex-TVR line from Common Branch Junction, Llantrisant via Creigiau joined during its 1886-1964 lifetime. The route is also used by through passenger specials such as those serving the Scotland v Wales Rugby International at Edinburgh.

R.4 Rattery

Taunton-Penzance line between Totnes and Plymouth. 227 m 28 ch from Paddington*

Rattery Bank is the longest of the four inclines on the South Devon Railway section of the West of England main line, the line rising steadily for 5 m from Totnes to the Marley tunnels at gradients in the 1 in 46-95 bracket. The Rattery signal box, with a public siding opposite until 1938, lay on the Down side just east of the tunnels and even had its name in the telegraphic code book. 'Rattery' signified that the assistant engine from Newton Abbot was to be detached at Rattery rather than work through to Brent.

R.5 Reading

Paddington-Swindon line. 35 m 78 ch from Paddington

Reading was an important part of the original GWR scheme and remains a key centre in BR's Western Region. It has an excellent main line service to and from Paddington and on the four trunk routes leading to the West Midlands, South Wales and the West, a substantial business and commuter activity, and interchange

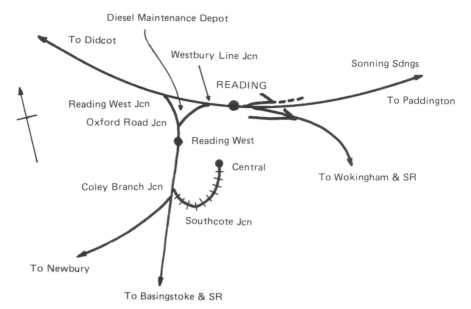

flows with the Southern Region via Wokingham and on the Basingstoke route. A number of cross-country passenger services are routed via Reading—Manchester to Gatwick/Brighton and Weymouth/Poole to Manchester/Liverpool—and it has a Railair coach link with Heathrow airport and a regular Gatwick service. The administrative offices of the WR's London Division are located in Western Tower, near the station.

The GWR linked Reading with London from March 30 1840. The station was built with platforms in tandem on the side nearest the town, a Brunel concept which made life easy for the passengers but very complicated for the traffic staff. Matters were made no easier by curves in the platform faces and eight years of coping with standard gauge trains at separate wooden platforms until mixed gauge lines were laid. It took a new station in 1899 and the present plan of three main platforms plus bays to improve matters.

Prior to 1899 the junction with the SER had been on the north side of the main line. When the Berks & Hants line to Hungerford (1847) was followed by the Basingstoke branch (1848), the possibilities of north-south movements eventually led to the building of the Reading West Loop (1856) and to powers to the Staines, Wokingham & Reading Railway for a link therewith. The GWR installed this as a separate line north of the main line, with a

separate platform and then under the main line again and away south-east. This arrangement lasted from 1858 until the new connection was put in during 1899.

The importance of Reading continued to increase. A new goods depot was opened at Reading Central, operational from May 4 1908, and in addition to the gas and electricity works sidings a considerable volume of business was derived from Huntley & Palmers who used fireless locomotives in their sidings and provided biscuits for the GWR dining cars. The firm's products gave the title 'The Biscuit' to the 10.30 pm fast freight service to Plymouth. On the other side of the line the vast goods shed amalgamated outwards loads and broke down inwards ones for transfer across the bench and delivery by a succession of horses, so-called 'Mechanical Horses' and conventional lorries. This era also produced huge numbers of passengers for the station ranging from parties heading for a Co-op lunch and a trip on the river to night journeys to Bristol or Birkenhead or early morning 'locals' to Leamington Spa or Southampton via Newbury.

Reading station comprises a mixture of early buildings, the 1899 basic platform layout and such later changes as the 1962 closure of Reading South (SR) in favour of a platform (now two) connected to the main Down platform with the consequent release of land for car parking. From Down to Up side the lines are Down

Above *The Up and Down stations at Reading in 1842.* Below *A Down HST passes the Metal Box headquarters at Reading.*

Main, Up Main and No 5 Platform Line; Down Relief, Loop, Up Relief; Down Reception, Up Reception and Pilot Line, with the panel box then standing in front of the low level yard. Bay platforms 1, 2 and 3 provide for the Newbury line and Basingstoke locals, and the Up bays for the Waterloo/Gatwick/Tonbridge trains and the London line slower services. All the main functions, except the Railair lounge, are in the narrow main buildings on the Down side and include ticket offices, refreshment and parcels facilities and staff accommodation. The recently modernised subway has separate exits towards the river on one side and to the bus interchange area, and travel centre across the road, on the other.

On the London side of the station the goods shed, now in the hands of National Carriers, stands below the Up Relief line from which connection is then made to Sonning Up Sidings and the CEGB private siding and oil discharge line. The SR line on the opposite side runs parallel to and makes connection with the Up and Down Main Lines, into No 4 Platform and, at one time, to the Up side. At the country end three lots of engineer's and S&T sidings lie north of the Main, Relief and Goods/Reception lines. Opposite, ie, south, is the triangle made by Reading West Curve and, within it, further engineer's sidings, the diesel depot and its fuelling plant. Sonning ground frame lies at 34 m 2 ch, Westbury Line Junction at 36 m 17

Attention to points at the London end of Reading station.

ch, Reading West Junction at 36 m 76 ch and the Scours Lane crossovers at 37 m 55 ch.

Just along the Westbury line lies the spartan Reading West station (36 m 75 ch), two high brick bridges precede Coley Branch Junction (37 m 59 ch) which gives access to the 1 m 55 ch line round to Reading Central, and Southcote Junction (37 m 52 ch) for the double line to Basingstoke.

Reading is a busy parcels centre handling some 85,000 Red Star packages annually. Reading Central, formerly a freight concentration depot for the whole area, now accommodates a coal concentration depot for Western Fuels and the Transtec container forwarding firm. There is a lot of Signal & Telecommunication Department activity at Reading, too. It continues the tradition of housing the Western's S&T headquarters while the outdoor work makes use of accommodation in the old signal boxes made redundant by the panel box. The diesel traction depot also maintains the Reading motive power tradition and, with the help of its subsidiary location at Southall, maintains the whole of the WR London suburban dmu fleet.

Redland—see Severn Beach Branch

R.6 Redruth

Taunton-Penzance line between Truro and Camborne. 309 m 68 ch from Paddington*

Serving part of the busy Redruth-Camborne area of Cornwall, Redruth

today is a functional station with the main brick buildings, single storey and including a buffet, on the Up side. Opposite, the Down platform has simple wooden buildings with a sloped canopy. The short, 47 yd Redruth Tunnel (309 m 62 ch to 309 m 64 ch) stands at the London end and a viaduct carries the line above the town. The original 1838 Hayle Railway terminus at Redruth lay west of this and to the north of the main line, with that company's Tresavean branch leading off to the south.

Reminders of the Cornish mining industry are apparent all around Redruth where an early 4 ft gauge mineral line was built out to Point Quay on the Fal estuary. The first section of this Redruth & Chasewater Railway opened on January 30 1826 and the route was very busy until the copper boom dwindled in the 1870s. The line struggled on for a while, with formal closure taking place in 1915.

Rhiwbina—see Coryton Branch

R.7   Rhymney Branch

Newport-Fishguard line, branch from Cardiff. 23 m 68 ch from Cardiff Bute Road

The Rhymney Valley branch was formerly the main line of the Rhymney Railway which obtained its initial Act in 1854 and was closely allied with the Bute interests in Cardiff. The route runs down the partly-industrialised valley of the Rhymney river as far as Caerphilly where the river swings east on its way to the Severn estuary at Cardiff. The railway, however, heads direct for Cardiff by tunnelling through the natural obstacle of the Caerphilly Mountain. The original RR line had avoided this problem when it opened by joining the Taff Vale at Taffs Well but the two companies were not the best of friends and the direct route to Cardiff, diverging at Aber Junction and including the tunnel, was opened in 1871.

The year 1871 also saw a northward extension of the RR from Rhymney to join the LNWR's line extending across the heads of the valleys from Abergavenny. From this time onwards there were close links between the two companies, including through long distance freight and passenger workings.

The Rhymney line is now single track and worked on the No Signalman Token system as far as Bargoed (18 m 7 ch) and double track onwards to Cardiff Queen Street (1 m 8 ch). There is two-way working over the Down line through Bargoed station to allow passenger facilities to be concentrated on a single platform and the signal boxes are located at Bargoed, Ystrad Mynach (an interesting RR structure set well back from the track up the side of a cutting), Aber Junction and Heath Junction, the latter a fringe box for the Cardiff panel area.

Diesel multiple units provide the passenger service on the branch with a basic pattern of through workings between Rhymney and Penarth. However, some journeys are shorter, starting or terminating in the valley at Bargoed, Ystrad Mynach or Aber, and some run to Central, Bute Road or Barry Island instead of Penarth. The Monday to Friday total of 26 trains each way is increased below Heath Junction by the addition of the Coryton line trains.

North of Ystrad Mynach freight workings are confined to 'as required' trips to serve the coal yard and private siding at Rhymney and the colliery at Bargoed. At Ystrad Mynach itself two important freight branches trail in but until 1982 the trains diverged again at Aber Junction over the 'old route' to Walnut Tree to reach Radyr Yard. A few, notably some mgr trains for Aberthaw, continue via the 'new route'. South of Aber Junction there is also a thrice-weekly freight working to serve the coal yard at Caerphilly, a clockwise circular trip from and back to Radyr via Aber Junction (reverse), Caerphilly and Cardiff.

An RR stone building housing station and ticket offices survives on the single platform remaining in use at Rhymney. Alongside, and reached by a short spur beyond the station, there is a run-round facility on the Up side, together with dmu stabling sidings and a train crew depot. On the Down side is a coal yard and a private siding serving a can factory. The intermediate stations on the section to Bargoed are Pontlottyn (22 m 65 ch), Tir-phil (20 m 40 ch) and Brithdir (19 m 31 ch), each with a brick shelter and using only the Up platform (although the Down platforms survive). There is a disused goods yard at Pontlottyn and on a bridge near Tir-phil, which also serves New Tredegar on the opposite side of the valley, a number plate of RR vintage and reading 'Main Line 73'.

Bargoed is approached over sharp

curves and a viaduct. As at Rhymney, a stone building accommodates the station and ticket offices on the one remaining (Down) platform. There is evidence that the station used to be larger and signs of the now removed lines in the Bargoed Rhymney Valley (Up side, north) and to Newport (Down, south) which were used by B&M trains from Brecon to Newport.

The first station on the double track, absolute block section is Gilfach Fargoed (17 m 35 ch) which is not served by all trains and has only coach-length platforms, each with a small corrugated metal shelter. Pengam (16 m 30 ch) is preceded by the recently closed connection at Bargoed Pits (16 m 63 ch) to Bargoed colliery, and followed by Hengoed (14 m 53 ch). Both have modern shelters, ticket offices and an RR lattice footbridge. Crossing the valley on the Down side at Hengoed is the distinctive stone viaduct which carried the Pontypool-Neath line.

Ystrad Mynach North Junction (13 m 79 ch) with the line from Penallta colliery heralds the station at Ystrad Mynach (13 m 60 ch) which has staggered platforms, a modern brick building on the Up platform and a wooden shelter on the Down. There is also a Mid-Glamorgan County Council 'park-and-ride' car park on the Up side. Beyond the station is South Junction (13 m 33 ch) with its signal box and lower quadrant signals on tall posts and where the line from Dowlais, Cwmbargoed, Ocean & Taff Merthyr collieries joins. There is a recess loop on the Down side of the junction.

Llanbradach (10 m 71 ch), the intermediate station between Ystrad Mynach and Aber, also has staggered platforms, a RR footbridge and modern brick shelters. It is followed, on the Down side, by a surviving archway and abutment of the former Barry Railway viaduct which crossed the valley here to tap the B&M route. Its short working life lasted from 1905 to 1926, the main structure being dismantled in 1937.

There are sidings at Aber Junction (9 m 8 ch) where the old line to Walnut Tree diverges, and signs of the former branch to Windsor Colliery and Senghenydd on the Up side. A sharp curve through Aber

Above left *A Rhymney branch train emerges from the tunnel into Cefn Onn station.*
Left *One of the 'Valleys' dmus at Llanishen.*

station (8 m 69 ch)—a prefabricated concrete structure with corrugated metal shelters and on an embankment—marks the beginning of the 'new' approach to Cardiff, through Caerphilly where the trackbed of the erstwhile line from Pontypridd trails in on the Up side.

Caerphilly station (8 m 21 ch) was modernised in 1974 with a new ticket office and direct access to a new bus station on the site of former track and platforms. It has another park and ride car park and is followed, on the Down side, by the site of the former RR locomotive works. This was enlarged by the GWR after grouping and by the end of the 1920s was handling over 250 locomotive repairs annually. Closed in 1963, it is now part of an industrial estate although the Caerphilly Railway Society still has some track, signalling and rolling stock here. Wernddu ground frame (7 m 42 ch) serves a coal yard on the Down side.

From its terminus the Rhymney Valley line is on falling gradients to Llanbradach, mostly between 1 in 50 and 1 in 200 but with a section of 1 in 42 between Pontlottyn and Tir-phil. Then the tendency is to rise to a summit at the north end of the 1,941 yd Caerphilly Tunnel (7 m 14 ch to 6 m 6 ch), drop through the tunnel at 1 in 122 and then on to Cardiff mostly at 1 in 85 or 1 in 80. Through the tunnel the line is straight until it approaches the southern portal, immediately beyond which is the station at Cefn On (6 m) comprising short shelterless platforms and served only by occasional trains. The station can only be reached by footpath. Beyond Cefn On, at the site of the former Cherry Orchard sidings, the two tracks are at different levels as the descent towards Cardiff begins in earnest.

Llanishen (4 m 61 ch), a South Glamorgan park and ride station, retains some of its stone buildings but has a modern shelter on the Down platform. Heath High Level (3 m 52 ch) is a prefabricated concrete structure, on a high embankment, and equipped with corrugated metal shelters. Nearby is Heath Low Level on the Coryton branch which joins at Heath Junction (3 m 23 ch). Finally, immediately before Queen Street (1 m 8 ch) the line passes through the site of the former RR Cardiff Parade station closed after grouping. The mileage changes from 1 m 22 ch to 1 m 17 ch where the RR route to the docks joined, now submerged beneath the foundations of the 16-floor Brunel House where the divisional offices are located.

Roche—see Newquay Branch

R.8   Royal Albert Bridge

Taunton-Penzance line across the Tamar between Plymouth and Saltash. 250 m 64 ch from Paddington*

Bearing his name high on the approach arch, the Royal Albert Bridge is the Western Region's greatest surviving monument to Brunel. In terms of cold statistics the bridge is 730 yds long, has two main spans of 465 ft each, 17 approach spans and cost £225,000. The bowed tubular girders of the main span and the plate girders of the approach spans carry a single line section of the West of England main line from St Budeaux Ferry Road (250 m 15 ch) on the Devon bank of the Tamar over the river to Saltash (251 m 26 ch) on the Cornish bank. Movements are under the control of the Plymouth panel and are subject to a 15 mph speed restriction but the only other special operational feature is the require-

The Royal Albert Bridge over the Tamar at Plymouth.

ment laid upon guards of freight trains to examine them at the last previous stopping place.

When the main railway route through Cornwall was finally decided it involved crossing the Tamar where it is 1,100 ft wide and 70 ft deep at high water. Cost and Admiralty clearance requirements led to the choice of the present design which was also influenced by Brunel's Chepstow bridge and by the construction methods used by Stephenson in his Britannia Bridge over the Menai Straits.

Building the Royal Albert Bridge was a complex and difficult, but dramatic, period. Many borings were needed to establish the true shape of the rock which lay below the river's mud and this work was carried out behind a cylindrical coffer dam, 6 ft in diameter and lowered into place from two hulks in 1848. Excavation of the mud began in 1849 but the affairs of the Cornwall Railway then went into limbo for three years due to a shortage of money and progress on the bridge piers was halted.

By the time work resumed a decision had been taken to cater for a single track only to save £100,000 in costs. To support this a double cylinder of 35 ft diameter was set in posiltion, in the middle of 1854, and gradually settled into its place. After

the masons had done their work and the approach arches had been made ready, the time arrived for positioning the first of the two main trusses which had been built on the banks of the river nearby. Brunel had devised detailed plans for the elaborate and tricky operation. Via small approach channels cut into the bank, two pontoons were floated under the ends of the first truss and the water in them pumped out to raise the truss from the ground. Bearing their load of well over 1,000 tons the pontoons were then towed into position by hawsers using a detailed signalling system and in the complete silence Brunel had requested of the crowds of onlookers. Taking advantage of the high tide and completing the job with hydraulic jacks, the truss with its suspension chains was then raised to its final position.

At this period Brunel was overly occupied with his mammoth vessel *Great Eastern*, an enterprise that was slowly, but surely, ruining his health. His chief assistant at Plymouth, Brereton, raised the second main truss into position in July 1858 and then completed the remainder of the work on the bridge. Brunel attended the opening ceremony performed by Prince Albert in the following year but was so ill that he had to ride across the bridge on a special truck drawn by one of Gooch's locomotives.

Brunel was to live only for another few weeks but the Cornwall Railway trains had started to run to Truro on May 4 1859 and Cornwall had been linked with the rest of the country by his great bridge. Today it performs the same vital function even if the trains are Inter-City 125 sets and a modern road bridge has been added alongside.

St Andrew's Road—see Severn Beach Branch

S.1 St Austell

Taunton-Penzance line between Liskeard and Truro. 286 m 34 ch from Paddington*

This is the administrative centre of the china clay industry and an area of great contrast. Both before and after the station great pyramids of quartz stand out on the northern skyline yet palms grow on the Up platform and rhododendrons line the approach cutting that ends the long climb from Par.

The main station buildings are on the Down platform which also has a Travellers-Fare buffet and a selection of ex-GWR platform seats. Outside is the interchange area used by Western National buses. A footbridge with a GWR motif and the

Traffic from the china clay area passes by rail for shipment and to the Potteries; today's special services are successors to this Clayfreighter service of 1967.

date 1882 leads to the long Up platform where various wooden buildings cater for the needs of passengers and staff and the signal box stands at the end. St Austell is a Motorail terminal and there are sidings and a dock behind the Up platform. The main goods depot lies nearer London and stands at right angles to the main running lines. It is still in use for coal and clay traffic and includes a substantial shed and a long high loading bank.

Beyond St Austell two viaducts precede the summit at Burngullow.

S.2   St Blazey

Taunton-Penzance line, branch from Par. 282 m 19 ch from Paddington*

Although part of the Newquay branch and near the main line at Par, St Blazey has an identity of its own. This derives from its function as a wagon supply and marshalling point for the china clay traffic that arrives from the Newquay line and goes forward to the Potteries or to Carne Point for shipment.

St Blazey lost its regular passenger trains back in 1925 but the platforms can still be seen where the double line from Par becomes the single line of the Newquay branch under the windows of St Blazey's traditional signal box. Behind the box are extensive sidings, those on the

south, main line side eventually leading through St Blazey Yard, past the locomotive and weighbridge sidings, to Par Bridge level crossing and Par Dock.

St Budeaux Ferry Road—see Plymouth

St Budeaux Victoria Road—see Plymouth

St Columb Road—see Newquay Branch

S.3   St Erth

Taunton-Penzance line between Camborne and Penzance. 320 m 67 ch from Paddington*

When the Inter-City 125 set stops at St Erth's Down platform, with its small stone building and separate wooden shelter and canopy, the traveller from Paddington will have been on his journey for about five hours. If he is changing to go to St Ives he will cross to the Up platform where the station's main buildings, long, low and of Cornish stone with pleasant rounded window arches, spread at right angles from the main line across the ends of the two terminating lines of the branch. This opened on June 1 1877 and was the last line built to the 7ft gauge.

The extensive wooden canopy covers both the main portion of the Up platform and the adjoining branch platform, which is at a slightly lower level and reached by steps. At the country end a refuge siding rises to the Up main line and there are freight facilities beyond the branch proper, with a rusting private siding in the angle between the connection from the branch to the Up Main. The latter is a reminder of the extensive broccoli traffic which used to be forwarded from St Erth which also dealt, until recently, with large quantities of milk traffic.

The large yard includes loading docks, a loading gauge and a scrap metal business. The signal box stands nearby, with the Down Refuge Siding opposite.

S.4   St Germans

Taunton Penzance line between Saltash and Liskeard. 256 m 24 ch from Paddington*

Scene of the Cornwall Railway's first accident, St Germans might have been a junction if a 1935 scheme for a direct line to Looe had materialised. Instead it is a simple station of two platforms and modest buildings on the rising gradient towards Menheniot and with a superb view from its viaduct of the quay and old lime kilns by the river below.

S.5   St Ives Branch

Taunton-Penzance line, branch from St Erth. 4 m 13 ch

St Ives, managing still to combine its blue seas and white sands with its mining and fishing traditions, is served by a single line branch from the West of England main line at St Erth. The short railway along the edge of St Ives Bay once provided a regular portion for the Cornish Riviera Express and still leads a busy life in the summer months when the dmu service is strengthened by using three-car sets and the 12 daily services each way rises to 19. In addition the sets fit in extra trips between Lelant Saltings and St Ives to provide a park and ride facility which helps to reduce road congestion in the town's narrow streets.

The St Ives line opened on June 1 1877 as a broad gauge line, the last piece of 7 ft railway in Britain. By 1885 the Cornwall Railway was pressing the GWR to convert to narrow gauge so that when the Tyringham Estates had a third line laid along the branch as far as Lelant Quay there was provision in the agreement for some reimbursement if conversion took place within ten years, as it did in 1892; and they were. In its busy years St Ives station consisted of a main platform face with platform and run round lines, plus a short bay platform and a line to the shed. This and the single storey station building

were of Cornish stone and working on the line was by electric token.

In 1971 the former station at St Ives was released to provide more car parking space and a new simplified station opened just east of Porthminster Viaduct. Goods facilities had already been withdrawn, including the arrangements for dealing with smalls consignments over the platforms at Lelant and Carbis Bay.

After leaving the branch platform at St Erth (320 m 77 ch) the line picks up the estuary at Lelant Saltings (321 m 51 ch), opened as part of the park and ride scheme in 1978, continues to Lelant (322 m 6 ch) and then takes to the coast proper at Carbis Bay (323 m 78 ch), all three stations being of the minimum facilities type. The route operates on the One Train Working basis with the train set and crew provided from Penzance. The Sunday service finishes at the end of summer when schoolchildren, commuters and shoppers repossess their local railway from the influx of summer visitors.

St James' Park—see Exmouth Branch

St Keyne—see Looe Branch

S.6   Saltash

Taunton-Penzance line between Plymouth and Liskeard. 251 m 26 ch from Paddington*

Saltash got its first station in 1859 when the rail route to the West was extended as far as Truro. Not that the GWR did much for local traffic until the Plymouth suburban services were developed in the early years of this century, creating a considerable volume of travel which was to continue right up to the opening of the Tamar road bridge. The first station at Saltash was rebuilt in 1880 and extended following the 1908 route alteration.

This is the point at which the route again becomes double after the single line section over the Royal Albert Bridge. It curves through the station, which is crossed midway by a road bridge, passes over Saltash Viaduct and heads for Forder Viaduct via the remains of Defiance Platform. The Cornwall Railway's original route, still visible on the Down side, was nearer the coast and involved five viaducts compared with three on the re-alignment, plus the 451 yd Wiveliscombe Tunnel (254 m 7 ch to 254 m 27 ch).

The main buildings at Saltash are on the

Up side and include a separate entrance for the once busy flower traffic. A ground frame provides access to a rusting Up siding at the country end where the stone goods shed is now in private hands.

S.7   Saltford

Swindon-Bristol line between Bath and Bristol. 111 m 57 ch from Paddington

The short, 176 yd tunnel (111 m 57 ch to 111 m 65 ch) is still faced in its original style. Nearer London are the former yard area and goods shed of Saltford station.

S.8   Sapperton Tunnels

Swindon-Gloucester line between Kemble and Stroud. 94 m 50 ch from Paddington

Like the earlier canal which is its companion in the Stroud Valley, the Gloucester to Swindon line needed the help of a tunnel through the main Cotswold ridge. Two tunnels, in fact, the 352 yd Short Tunnel (94 m 50 ch to 94 m 66 ch) at the top of the 1 in 100/94 rise from Swindon and the 1,864 yd Long Tunnel (94 m 70 ch to 95 m 74 ch) on the 1 in 90 down gradient beyond the summit. This is an area of vintage catch point notices and of the exhortation 'Whistle Frequently When Passing Through Tunnel'.

The tunnels and viaducts on this route made it dificult to build and hard to work. The Sapperton bores had to be made through a rock mixture intersected by fissures thus rendering lining necessary. However, the work was completed in less than two years and the public service through the tunnels began on May 12 1845.

Sapperton Siding site can be spotted at the London end. Frampton Crossing signal box stood on the Gloucester side.

Saundersfoot—see Pembroke Dock Branch

S.9   Savernake

Reading-Taunton line between Hungerford and Westbury. 70 m 7 ch from Paddington

The broad gauge branch from Savernake to Marlborough opened on April 14 1864 and Marlborough High Level, the GWR station, closed on May 19 just a century later. In between the Swindon, Marlborough & Andover Railway (later the M&SW Junction) had come along and paralleled the branch with its section from Savernake High Level to Marlborough Low Level. Following the GWR's absorbtion of the M&SWJ after the 1923 grouping various stages of rationalisation involved restoring the connection at Marlborough, abandoning the northern

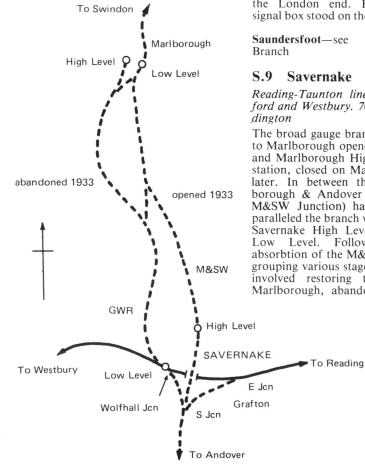

Western Chieftain and its Down train alongside the Kennet & Avon Canal near Savernake.

end of the GWR branch and working the southern end at times as two single lines.

The two routes and junctions at Savernake meant that for many years the start of term return to Marlborough College could be made from either Waterloo or Paddington but now the significance of the location is as the summit of the steady climb from Newbury and equally steady descent to Lavington and as the site of a crossover. At this point the Kennet and Avon Canal passes beneath the railway in Bruce Tunnel, the ventilation shafts of which are visible near the western end. Crofton Pumping Station, with its restored beam engines, lies north of the railway between Savernake and Bedwyn.

The GWR station approach road is visible on the Down side with some platform remains at the London end of the site. Grafton Curve, from the M&SWJ towards London on the south side of the main line, is still visible but the connection westwards at Wolfhall Junction is less easy to spot.

Sea Mills—see Severn Beach Branch

S.10 Seaton Junction

Waterloo-Exeter line between Axminster and Honiton. 148 m 5 ch from Waterloo

Passenger services were withdrawn from Seaton Junction (once Colyton) and from its branch line to Seaton proper in 1966, part of the great rationalisation of the former LSWR main line between Salisbury and Exeter. The approach from the branch to the station has now returned to its farming origins but the station itself remains largely intact. The triangular Down platform is now two track widths away from the running lines and the two-storey station house on the Up platform is in private hands, as is the former goods accommodation although a supplementary loop has been formed from one of the goods sidings and a loading gauge hangs forlornly over the trackbed of the dock line.

The station once handled milk business counted in millions of gallons but the lamp room now gathers cobwebs, the signs are fading and the two footbridges which span the site lead to nowhere in particular.

S.11   Severn Beach Branch

*Branch from Bristol Temple Meads. 13 m
50 ch*

The first line along the north bank of the
River Avon, from Bristol towards the
Severn Estuary, was that of the Bristol
Port Railway & Pier Company. It was
born at the time of the first concrete
proposals for shipping facilities at Avonmouth and opened its 5 m 52 ch line
quietly on March 6 1865. Trains took half
an hour for the journey from a terminus
beneath the shadow of Brunel's Clifton
Suspension Bridge to a station near the
new pier at Avonmouth.

Several schemes were proposed for
connecting this isolated passenger line
with the main line system and although
the owning company received authorisation for a link from Sneyd Park, under
Clifton Downs, to join the GWR/South
Wales Union line at Stapleton Road and
the MR at Lawrence Hill it ran out of
funds and work had to cease. The GWR
and MR took over the task by an act of
Parliament on May 25 1871 and opened to
Avonmouth for goods traffic on February
24 1877, the day the new dock there came
into service. After many problems with
the insolvent BPR&PC, passenger traffic
over the Clifton Extension Railway began
in 1885, operation of the Temple Meads-
Avonmouth service being the responsibility
of a GWR & MR Joint Committee from
1894. The BPR line between Hotwells and
Sneyd Park Junction closed in 1922 to

*The New Passage Hotel remained in use
long after the opening of the Severn Tunnel
ended the ferry service across to Portskewett.*

make way for a widened A4 route along
the Avon Gorge but traces of the route
and of the steamer quay and Clifton
Rocks Railway which, with the old tram
terminus, made up a major Bristol traffic
interchange point, can still be seen.

In 1901 a scheme for new dock facilities
at Avonmouth received Parliamentary
approval. The construction work involved
a realignment of the GWR single line
which had been opened on February 5
1900 from Avonmouth north along the
estuary and across the entrance to the
Severn Tunnel to join the main line at
Pilning. This remained a goods only line
for many years but passenger services
were eventually extended to the present
terminus at Severn Beach which was to
have been the Blackpool of the west. The
other major route into Avonmouth was
that from Filton to Hallen Marsh
Junction which opened on May 9 1910 but
there were extensive networks of docks
lines to serve the considerable industrial
activity which grew up within the docks
area and around it.

Passenger services on the Avonmouth
line in the 1930s were numerous and
varied. In addition to the generous main
service from Temple Meads to Avonmouth Dock and St Andrew's Road,
trains operated on a circular route to
Pilning via Avonmouth and back via
Filton and on the line via Henbury. From
Clifton Down trains to Mangotsfield and
Bath gave access to the LMS system and
included a through service to and from
Bournemouth.

Closures in 1964 and 1968 left the
present Temple Meads-Severn Beach
trains as the sole passenger survivors on
the   route.   Some   important   bulk
movements of freight remain, to and from

ICI Severnside, Fisons and ISC, but wagon load business is now negligible and the dock lines which once held wagons of bananas, meat, animal feed and a dozen other commodities are now fewer and rustier.

The route diverges from the main line through Stapleton Road at Narroways Hill Junction (2 m 3 ch) just beyond which lay the junction with the MR line. Following the 288 yd Montpelier Tunnel (2 m 61 ch to 2 m 47 ch) comes Montpelier station (2 m 68 ch) where the Down platform is in use although the generous stone buildings are closed and shuttered. At Redland (3 m 25 ch) the Down platform is bare and the Up one is used and the closed buildings are of brick. A passing loop section with three overbridges brings the

Hallen Marsh Junction with the Port of Bristol Authority lines to the left and a track maintenance machine heading towards Avonmouth.

A scene from the days when Avonmouth docks were busy with rail traffic.

route to the generous station at Clifton Down (3 m 72 ch) where the high stone walls, massive station buildings and ornamental supports to the footbridge still give an impression of the former grandeur of the place. A shopping development on the main road and a housing development in the former goods yard encircle the station on one side while the 1,751 yd Clifton Down Tunnel (4 m 7 ch to 5 m 6 ch) helps to complete this process on the other.

Clifton Down Tunnel was cut through a mixture of conglomerate, red sandstone and the harder central limestone. It leads under Bristol's protected area of parkland known as 'The Downs' to emerge at an elevated level in the Avon Gorge, the single line then dropping down towards the site of the junction with the BPR (still visible) and into Sea Mills station (6 m).

The bridge beyond spans an inlet where
traces can be seen of a very early dock
after which the line rises again to Shirehampton (7 m 50 ch), the passing point on
the original line. Now only the Up platform is used although a ground frame
gives access to the small oil terminal in the
former goods yard. The river and the M5
bridge which crosses it come into view as
the route continues to the inland end of
the docks complex where it becomes
double at Avonmouth Dock Junction (8
m 29 ch) where there is a signal box and
level crossing.

Avonmouth Dock station (9 m 2 ch) has
substantial buildings of red brick with
stone facings on its main platform. On the
side nearest the docks is a siding serving a
Rowntrees depot, and at the seaward end
a level crossing with closed circuit television, across the main entrance road to
the docks. A short distance further on
(9 m 32 ch) is St Andrew's Junction where
the route from the north ran into the docks,
a fact recognised by the change of mileage
(to 16 m) and the line on the seaward side
becoming the Up line. There is also a
signal box and level crossing.

The former Avonmouth Town Goods
Yard, again with signal box (15 m 50 ch),
lies on the Down side where Fison's tank
wagon traffic is also dealt with. Then
comes St Andrew's Road (15 m 37 ch)
with just two platforms, a shelter and a
footbridge   followed   by   successive

Above *A trainload of nitrogen liquor
tanks pulling away from Fison's discharge
sidings at Avonmouth.*

Above right *Avonmouth, with the mills
of the dock area straight ahead.*

junctions—Holesmouth. Junction (14 m
61 ch) where the Port of Bristol Authority
lines (or Up and Down Corporation lines)
join and Hallen Marsh Junction (14 m 41
ch) where the Henbury line leaves. A link
from the PBA lines at the former leads via
the latter to the Chittening Estate storage
area which is still provided with sidings,
albeit rarely used. There is also a
connection to the lines serving the ISC
works.

Beyond Hallen Marsh Junction the line
is single and worked under the No Signalman Token system. Severn Beach ground
frame (12 m 35 ch) controls the access to
the ICI Severnside Works internal rail
complex worked by the firm's own
locomotive. Then comes Severn Beach
station (11 m 62 ch) where only one of the
two platform faces is used and the red
brick terminal buildings are closed and
shuttered. The ICI connection headshunt
leads to sidings adjacent to Severn Beach
station beyond which the old trackbed
towards Pilning is still visible. Along this
there are traces of the branch which led to
the Severn Tunnel Pumping Station and
of the 1863 Bristol & South Wales Union

Railway route from Lawrence Hill to New Passage and the steam ferry on to Portskewett. This became redundant when the Severn Tunnel was opened but the first section westwards from Pilning was incorporated in the Pilning-Avonmouth line of 1900.

S.12 Severn Tunnel

Swindon-Newport line between Bristol (Parkway) and Severn Tunnel Junction. 11 m 60 ch from Bristol (Temple Meads)

The Severn Estuary, at the point where the tunnel passes beneath it, is nearly 3 m wide. It has a very high rise and fall of the tide and its depth varies from the hard rocks which are exposed at low water to 55 ft of water flowing fast through the channel known as The Shoots. It took 12 years to bore the 4 m 628 yd tunnel which carries the two tracks of the main line to South Wales from the Avon shore to the Gwent shore, but the tunnel saves 26 m compared with the route via Gloucester. To pass 35 ft below The Shoots there is a drop of 1 in 100 from the eastern portal, a level section of 12 ch and then a rise of 1 in 90 to the western portal.

The first railway travellers crossing at this point used a line built under GWR auspices by the Bristol & South Wales Union Railway and authorised by an Act of 1856. Physical work began two years later under Brunel's assistant, R.P. Brereton, and was completed in time for opening in 1864 despite the difficulties of a deep cutting at Horfield and the tunnel at Patchway. Rail passengers could then travel from Bristol to New Passage, along the 546 yd pier and via stairs or lifts to the steam ferry which carried them to the 258 yd pier at Portskewett and the short connection to the main line into Wales. This arrangement continued until the tunnel opened, the hotel at New Passage having closed only in recent years.

Charles Richardson had also been involved in the B&SWU scheme and had surveyed the estuary at that time. From this work sprang the one idea for crossing the Severn at this point which was actually to be carried into reality. Following the enabling Act of 1872 work under Richardson started on the Monmouth side, with a shaft at Sudbrook, in March 1873. Adding contractors to the direct labour brought additional shafts and steady progress until October 16 1879 when a massive flow from a fresh water spring overcame the pumps and flooded the workings. At this point Sir John Hawkshaw was placed in charge of the work and appointed T.A. Walker as his contractor based on a tender of £948,959.

Hawkshaw felt it necessary to reprofile the tunnel at a level 15 ft lower than before and Walker's later book *The Severn Tunnel: Its Construction and*

Difficulties (1872-1887) graphically describes the difficulties of first getting rid of the water, which took until the end of 1880. Walker also recounts the heroic achievements of diver Lambert in closing a flood door using an early form of compressed air diving bag. But more problems were to come, a salt water flooding in 1881, another period of progress, and then the heartbreak of October 1883 when the Great Spring again broke in, the Sudbrook pump broke down and finally a tidal wave completed the devastation.

Fortunately the worst was over and from this point the progress was rapid. The water was pumped out, activity resumed and by the following year much of the basic work on the main bore was complete, apart from the section in which the Great Spring had been caged. Imaginatively Hawkshaw overcame this last barrier by having a new heading prepared to siphon off the waters to the waiting pumps and soon the lining work had started in a dry tunnel. Other finishing work was sufficiently well advanced for Sir Daniel Gooch and a small party to make the first official journey through the tunnel on September 5 1885. Regular goods traffic started on September 1 and passenger trains on December 1 of the following year.

The opening of the tunnel helped the growth of GWR business and the main line via Chippenham became so congested

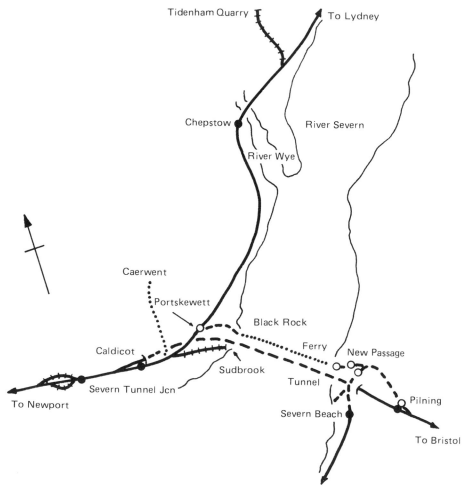

that quadrupling was considered. The alternative was a direct line from Wootton Bassett, the option chosen in 1895 and opened in 1903.

The waters of the Great Spring where harnessed by six pumps and six Cornish beam engines supplied by Harveys of Hayle and housed in the Sudbrook Pumping Station. Only in 1961 were they replaced by more modern machinery and today the 20 million gallons of water which the spring provides (for commercial use) is controlled by submersible electric pumps of the axial flow impeller type. The drainage system in the tunnel also copes with water soaking in from the surrounding land mass, the other main problem being that of ventilation. As it is not possible to have ventilation shafts in the main underwater section a single horizontal tandem compound steam engine was used to drive a 27 ft × 9 ft fan capable of displacing 800,000 cu ft of air per minute, forcing it into the tunnel and thus expelling the stale air from the tunnel mouth at each end. Today the power source is supplied by two 300 hp 3,300-volt two-speed electric motors installed in 1963.

The pumping and ventilation machinery

The great beam engines which used to contain the waters of the Severn Tunnel's Great Spring.

for the tunnel, plus the various monitoring devices, is controlled from the central control room at Sudbrook. There are many safety precautions including drawing electrical supplies from two grids and supporting them with alternator sets. The whole of the tunnel is inspected daily and the track has been given continuous welded rail and a deeper ballast but with factors like 70,000 sq yds of brick work to keep pointed, the WR civil engineer has constant employment for his tunnel staff.

The Severn Tunnel presents few operating problems these days although at one time a signal box inside the tunnel was considered to ease the congestion problems. With faster speeds, more powerful and cleaner traction and continuous track circuiting, traffic passes without fuss although very comprehensive regulations still remain in force to ensure safety and to cover any emergency which might arise. Emergency telephones are provided and white lights warn of the point at which the gradient changes.

S.13 Severn Tunnel Junction

*Swindon-Newport line between the Severn Tunnel and Newport. 148 m 61 ch from Paddington**

Severn Tunnel Junction and its marshalling yard is the freight traffic gateway to the WR's Cardiff Division, one of the busiest freight areas on BR. For passengers travelling from the London direction it is also the entry point into Wales as they emerge from the Severn Tunnel, travellers on the line from Gloucester having already crossed into the Principality, at Chepstow. The community in the area owes its original existence to the establishment of Severn Tunnel Junction and is based on the village of Rogiet.

The layout at Severn Tunnel Junction reveals its history. The straight through route is from the Gloucester direction, formed of the South Wales Railway's main line of 1850 which made a junction at Grange Court with the GWR's route from London. The later line out of the Severn Tunnel, opened in 1886, climbs at 1 in 90 to join the Gloucester line on the Up side at Severn Tunnel Junction where the two tracks become four. At this natural traffic junction marshalling yards have been established on both sides of the main line and are still the focal point for nearly all the long distance freight services into and out of South Wales, except for through company trains and a few others. The yards have a future, too, in the air-braked Speedlink age and there is a diesel locomotive servicing depot and a train crew depot nearby.

The station at Severn Tunnel Junction has four tracks, with outer platforms and a centre island. Although the forecourt is on the Up side, the northernmost line is a route to and from the diesel depot and yard and passengers pass by footbridge to the island platform for Up trains to Bristol on the north face, Gloucester on the south and to the southern outer platform which is used by Down trains on both routes. Steel and glass waiting shelters are provided. The service is provided by the Gloucester line dmus and stops by some trains on the Bristol route.

Although the humps remain, hump shunting was replaced by flat shunting in Severn Tunnel Junction's Up and Down yards in 1981. The latter, preceded by reception lines, extends westwards from behind the station and a Down loop behind the Down platform continues the length of the yard to become the Down Relief Line towards Newport. The Up yard, further west, is approached via the Up Relief Line and the former reception sidings for the Up hump, these now being used for the exchange of wagons between Speedlink services. The main yard, also known as the Bristol yard, then lies alongside the main line with its departure roads ending near the station. Shunting in the two yards is carried out by Class 08 locomotives.

There is much evidence of Severn Tunnel Junction's traditional wagon load traffic past, including the Down Hump (148 m 62 ch) and the Up Hump (149 m 60 ch) but it also has a busy modern function. It is a key point in the national Speedlink network and exchanges wagons passing between South Wales, Bristol and the West of England on the one hand and London and the other four regions on the other. Long distance wagonload services operate between Severn Tunnel Junction and SR and WR yards via the Severn Tunnel, to LMR yards via Gloucester and Hereford and to ER yards in London and Sheffield. Shorter workings run to and from yards in the Bristol area and there are links to all the main yards in South Wales. Local services operate to and from Caerwent, Tidenham, Glascoed, Hereford, Machen, Bedwas, Ebbw Vale and collieries in the Western Valleys and there are local trips to Llanwern and Newport (East Usk and Alexandra Dock Junction). Numerous long distance block trains pass through Severn Tunnel Junction, some stopping for crew changing purposes or to await a path in the timetable. Also, a company train operates from Ravenscraig, Scottish Region, to Severn Tunnel Junction conveying semi-finished steel from the BSC plant there for BSC plants in South Wales. Trains conveying wagons of rail ballast from Machen and Tidenham quarries are worked forward from Severn Tunnel Junction to destinations specified and as required by the civil engineering department.

To support all this activity there is, on the Up side at the station end of the yard, a diesel locomotive fuelling and servicing depot, also a building housing the Area Manager's organisation, Train Crew Depot, Area Freight Centre and TOPS office. On the Up side at the London end of the station a siding leads to the terminal at which motor vehicles brought in on Speedlink services are unloaded for distribution to dealers. This is on the site of the former steam locomotive shed. Another siding, behind the former Up platform, is used to stable the Severn Tunnel emergency train which includes water tank wagons and flat vehicles capable of conveying fire engines.

All movements on the main line, including the junction and the crossovers for the exchange of traffic between the Up and Down yards, are controlled from Newport panel box.

On the Up side of the main line, some 2½ m west of Severn Tunnel Junction, can be seen some of the former buildings of Magor station which was closed to passengers in 1964. Following Magor is the flyover at Bishton which carries the Up Relief Line from the south side of the main lines to the north. Bishton also has a level crossing controlled from a substantial GWR signal box which now acts as a ground frame.

S.14 Sharpness Branch

Birmingham-Bristol line, branch from Berkeley Road Junction. 4 m 17 ch

Until the night of October 25 1960 Britain's third longest railway bridge spanned the Severn from Lydney to Sharpness. Then an oil tanker searching for Sharpness docks in the thick fog collided with a pier and brought down two of the 21 spans to end the outlet originally built to connect the Forest of Dean coal output with a branch of the MR main line at Berkeley Road.

In GW & LMS hands around eight trains a day ran each way on the branch but the collision ended all services and the route is now truncated to the single line on the Gloucester bank, from a junction facing Bristol at Berkeley Road to the British Waterways Board docks at Sharpness. In between are the remains of Berkeley station (2 m 8 ch) where there is a ground frame for the connection to the small, secure terminal and gantry crane used for traffic to and from Oldbury nuclear power station.

The line curves into Sharpness at the south of the docks area and a connection from the sorting sidings leads to the lines on which a scrap metal firm uses an 0-6-0 diesel to marshal wagons. Beyond the sidings at the north end it is possible to trace the course of the high and low level routes into the docks and of the line towards the old bridge. Nearby stands the Severn Bridge and Railway Hotel where

The massive bridge across the Severn from Sharpness to Lydney is remembered in this hotel sign at Sharpness Docks.

188 RAILWAYS OF THE WESTERN REGION

the talk is of ships, waterways and seamen and the windows look out on the docks and the Gloucester & Berkeley Ship Canal.

Services on the branch are provided by a trip from Gloucester and the line is under the control of the Gloucester signalman.

S.15 Shelwick Junction

Oxford-Hereford line between Great Malvern and Hereford. 148 m 11 ch from Paddington

Shelwick Junction stands 1 m 11 ch on the Cardiff side of the boundary with the West of England Division and comprises a conventional double line junction, subject to a 20 mph speed restriction, linking the Worcester line with that from Craven Arms towards Hereford.

S.16 Sherborne

Waterloo-Exeter line between Salisbury and Yeovil. 118 m 4 ch from Waterloo

Just inside the regional boundary at milepost 117½, Sherborne station still shows evidence of its SR origins. The main station buildings are on the Up side, as are the former goods yard, dock and shed, and the signal box controlling the level crossing at the London end of the station.

Shiplake—see Henley Branch

S.17 Shipton

Oxford-Hereford line between Oxford and Kingham. 81 m 59 ch from Paddington

Gone are the days when Shipton was busy with traffic from the steam mills or brought in by the carrier from Burford. Now it is just a simple station of Up and Down platforms and shelters with a total service of four trains a day. Bruern CCTV level crossing lies on the section of line towards Kingham at 83 m 15 ch.

Shirehampton—see Severn Beach Branch

S.18 Slough

Paddington-Swindon line between Paddington and Maidenhead. 18 m 36 ch from Paddington

Although the GWR opening luncheon ceremony took place at Salt Hill, just west of Slough, pressures from Eton College delayed the provision of a station until June 1840. Then it was the Brunel arrangement of separate Up and Down buildings on the same (Down) side of the line. In the same month two years later Queen Victoria made her first railway journey, leaving Slough at noon with both Gooch and Brunel on the footplate of the 7 ft single Firefly class engine *Phlegethon*. By 1843 Cooke's electric telegraph franchise had linked Slough with Paddington and in the following year it carried the glad news of the birth of the Queen's second son.

Slough has always been important in railway terms, not just for royal trains—functional and funeral—but also for the volume of its passenger and freight business and as the headquarters of the GWR road motor activity. Freight business is limited now but the line into the Lloyd George inspired Slough trading estate is still there on the Up side, followed by the large goods yard and multi-section goods shed, the latter still with some corrugated portions and traditional colours. There is an Up Goods Line in this area.

The original passenger station at Slough was replaced in 1884 and the present twin-domed main buildings on the Down side lead to the three (island and outer) platforms, each with extensive brick buildings and conventional facilities, including refreshments. There is a bay on the Down side for the Windsor branch trains, another for parcels opposite and an Up bay to facilitate the working of the all-stations dmu service to Paddington. Slough also acts as an interchange point between these trains, those that stop from Reading and then run fast to Ealing Broadway and the main line services which stop here.

An unusual feature at Slough is the memorial on the Up side to 'Station Jim'. Station Jim was a notable doggy character who collected some £40 for the GWR Widows and Orphans Fund before his death in 1896. He had, so the inscription says, 'an armoury of tricks' and also made the occasional rail journey, including Paddington and Leamington Spa in his travellings.

S.19 Somerton

Reading-Taunton line between Castle Cary and Taunton. 125 m 62 ch from Paddington

The gradients on the fast stretch through Somerton are kept easy by the succession of cutting, viaduct, cutting and then the 1,053 yd tunnel (126 m 59 ch to 127 m 27 ch). Somerton station buildings, in the 1906 construction style, are still evident on the Up side, together with a crossover and some rusting sidings. But Long Sutton and Pitney, at the west end of the tunnel, is marked only by a slight widening in the cutting.

S.20 Sonning

Paddington-Swindon line between Maidenhead and Reading. 35 m 2 ch from Paddington

There is an oil discharge facility and a connection to the CEGB siding here on the Up side, also Up Refuge Sidings and a Down Goods Line. Towards London lies Sonning Cutting, a 2 m section through Sonning Hill beloved of railway photographers but not of those who originally built the line. For the 1,220 men at work in the wet winter of 1838/9 life was hard and some might have wished that the original route further north had been used for the tunnel involved there would at least have provided a little shelter.

Sonning Cutting was also the scene of the infant GWR's first bad accident when, on Christmas Eve 1841, the engine *Hecla* and its mixed train ran into a landslip and eight passengers were killed. This sad accident led the Board of Trade to examine the railway's treatment of third class passengers and was also the subject of a 'deodand' award, a Common Law provision for an instrument of a man's death to be forfeited to the Crown.

S.21 Southall

Paddington-Swindon line between Paddington and Slough. 9 m 6 ch from Paddington

From 1863 to 1915 a Southall to Victoria passenger train service existed and a morning and evening service operated along the branch to Brentford until 1942. Now the importance of the station is mainly to the commuters to and from Paddington whose diesel multiple unit trains may well be based, maintained and/or staffed at the Southall maintenance depot.

The main station buildings, twin-towered and at street level, give access to outer and island platforms serving the Main and Relief lines. At the London end the traction maintenance depot is on the Down side and on the Up a Shell oil terminal and scrap sidings. The Brentford branch veers off behind the depot complex

which includes sheds, offices, fuelling facilities and even a turntable pit from the steam era.

Adjacent to the station a preservation group is now housed in the former Walls private siding area and beyond it there are crossovers between the Main and Relief lines at Southall West Junction (9 m 57 ch) and a Tarmac private siding on the Up side.

S.22 Standish Junction

Birmingham-Bristol line between Gloucester and Westerleigh Junction. 99 m 68 ch from Derby

Standish Junction unites the line from Swindon with the former MR main line in a conventional double line junction towards Gloucester. There is a double crossover on the Gloucester side and the Haresfield Down Goods Loop ends just north of the junction.

Stapleton Road—see Bristol

S.23 Starcross

Taunton-Penzance line between Exeter and Newton Abbot. 202 m 36 ch from Paddington*

Starcross has the one remaining complete atmospheric railway pumping station building. The two-section structure of worn red sandstone, used for many years as a chapel, stands beside the Up line at the country end of the station.

Catering mainly for summer visitors, the station at Starcross comprises Up and Down platforms, shelters and a footbridge. A short path leads from the Down platform to the pier used by the ferry to and from Exmouth. Now operated by the Devon Dock, Pier & Steamship Co, the ferry was purchased by the GWR in 1898 to tap the Exmouth trade and for many years the legend 'Starcross for Exmouth' enhanced the small station's importance.

S.24 Steventon

Paddington-Swindon line between Didcot and Swindon. 56 m 42 ch from Paddington

Little remains at Steventon now apart from the overbridge and a very attractive stone house on the Up side but for four years after the broad gauge arrived on June 1 1840 it was the railhead for Oxford. Then, for a short period in 1842-3, board meetings were held in that house on the Up side in place of the former separate

Behind the pier used by the ferry service from Exmouth can be seen the Starcross pumping house, used during the South Devon Railway's atmospheric traction period.

meetings of the London and Bristol Committees. In 1872 the section became mixed gauge and finally standard gauge in 1892.

There are crossings to the west of the station site, the CCTV one at Stocks Lane (56 m 58 ch) and one at Causeway (56 m 72 ch), and to the east the Up Goods Line and a Down Goods Loop.

S.25   Stoke Canon

Taunton-Penzance line between Tiverton Junction and Exeter. 190 m 16 ch from Paddington*

The approach from the London direction is heralded by the Down side signal box and the barrier crossing it controls. This was the site of the original station which closed in 1894, and of the goods yard. Traces of the later station, served by loops as a result of 1930s' remodelling, can be seen nearer Exeter. There is a pleasant, centre-gabled station building surviving on the Down side and from the end of the bare Up platform opposite the trackbed of the 1885 Exe Valley branch can be seen curving off northwards.

S.26   Stoke Edith

Oxford-Hereford line between Great Malvern and Hereford. 142 m 22 ch from Paddington

Only the signal box, crossing and cross-over remain of this former station, closed

in 1965. Even less remains of the preceding Ashperton and following Withington but the former private railway road from Tarrington to Stoke Edith still has its ghost legend.

S.27   Stoke Works Junction

Birmingham-Bristol line between Barnt Green and Cheltenham. 57 m 43 ch from Derby

Here the line from Worcester and Droitwich Spa joins the former MR main line in a junction towards Birmingham. The former, single at the junction end, originated as a branch of the Oxford, Worcester & Wolverhampton Railway in 1852 but was worked as a loop off the MR. This resulted in the MR station becoming goods only from October 1855, the OWW (later GWR) station on the other fork of the junction remaining open until 1966 and a platform still surviving. The name of the location may well derive from the Salt Union Works which was served by one of the sidings here.

S.28   Stonehouse

Swindon-Gloucester line between Stroud and Gloucester. 104 m 74 ch from Paddington

Stonehouse, formerly with the suffix Burdett Road, now consists of simple Up and Down platforms with a shelter on each. The red brick signal box on the Down side is used by the permanent way staff.

Half a mile to the west on the converging Bristol-Birmingham line is the former MR junction station of Stonehouse

Bristol Road (101 m 47 ch from Derby), still retaining a railway activity in the form of a small coal concentration depot shunted by i/c locomotive *Dougal*. The old station house remains and there are Down refuge sidings used as a headshunt and for coal wagon storage, a footbridge, and a CCTV barrier crossing at Olds End (101 m 27 ch).

From the Down, junction platform a service operated over the 5¾ m line to Nailsworth, with a short spur from Dudbridge Junction to Stroud (Cheapside). The course of the line is still visible south of the A4096 and along the A46.

S.29   Stoneycombe

Taunton-Penzance line between Newton Abbot and Totnes. 216 m 74 ch from Paddington*

The ECC quarry at Stoneycombe lies halfway up the climb from Aller Junction to Dainton summit and is served by a trailing siding on the Down side and with the buffer stops end raised to permit wagons to descend to the loading point by gravity. The Up side signal box, switched in as required, is protected from blasting dangers by a strengthened roof and window grill.

Stormstown—see Abercynon

Stormy—see Bridgend

S.30   Stroud

Swindon-Gloucester line between Kemble and Gloucester. 102 m 13 ch from Paddington

One year after the Cheltenham & Great Western Union Railway was amalgamated with the GWR, the tracks reached Stroud, a centre of the Gloucestershire woollen industry. The opening, from Kemble to Gloucester on May 12 1845, completed the direct route between Cheltenham and London via Swindon. Stroud got its second railway on November 16 ten years later by a link to Dudbridge on the Nailsworth to Stonehouse Junction line. In the 1930s this gave the LMS terminus at Stroud (Cheapside) seven trains each way daily but the main station enjoyed a service of some 40 stops by the rail motors operating between Gloucester and Chalford plus the locals to Swindon and stops by the expresses to and from Cheltenham and Cardiff.

Although light industry has taken the place of the broadcloth which once uniformed the British Army and the halts served by the rail motors have closed, Stroud is still busy with passenger business. Its service is provided by the Swindon-Gloucester/Worcester dmus plus some trains through to Paddington, which can be reached in about 1½ hours.

Much of the former goods yard on the Up side is now devoted to car parking but the stone goods shed and its tall office on the end remain a pleasing architectural sight. The single storey station buildings, on the same side and accommodating a modern ticket office and parcels facilities, are also of warm Cotswold stone and baskets of flowers hanging from the platform canopies add further to the effect. Also on the Up side there is a double bay at the London end and a ground frame for access to the dock and three remaining sidings. At the country end a high bridge lifts the line over the town and the old Stroudwater Canal.

The Hill Paul & Co mill adjacent to the station typifies Stroud's past. Beyond it, the former Cheapside station is now in private hands, having closed to passengers in 1947 and to goods in 1966.

S.31   Sudbrook Branch

Gloucester-Newport line, branch from Caldicot Crossing. 1 m 1 ch

This single track freight line leads to the Severn Tunnel Pumping Station located on the shore of the Severn Estuary immediately above the line of the tunnel, but the main traffic flow is oil to a paper mill private siding just short of the end of the branch.

The community at Sudbrook originated from the building of the tunnel and until the Sudbrook pumps were converted from steam to electric power coal was taken to the pumping station by rail. Although the paper mill now uses oil, taken as block loads from Milford Haven, it also consumes in the production process large quantities of high quality fresh water pumped from the Severn Tunnel's Great Spring.

The short branch is operated on the One Train Working system and has three intermediate level crossings which have to be operated by the trainmen. There is a run round facility at the end of the line near the paper mill private siding.

S.32   Sugar Loaf Tunnel

Shrewsbury-Llanelli line between Lland-rindod Wells and Llandovery. 50 m 79 ch from Craven Arms

From Llanwrtyd the Central Wales line climbs at 1 in 70 via Berthddu Crossing towards the summit, 820 ft above sea level. A small, marshy plateau leads to a cutting containing the platforms which once served a few isolated railway houses and the line then plunges into the damp-ness of the 1,000 yd Sugar Loaf Tunnel (50 m 79 ch to 51 m 44 ch). Lined partly in brick and partly by masonry, the tunnel is over 100 ft below ground level at the mid-way ventilation shaft.

For Up trains the climb to the tunnel from Cynghordy Viaduct is at 1 in 60 and northbound journeys provide a dramatic view of the mountain itself.

S.33   Swansea

*Newport-Fishguard line. 216 m 7 ch from Paddington**

The city's terminal station at Swansea (at one time officially and still colloquially known as High Street) leads to a triangular layout enclosing Landore traction depot and from which the main lines east to Cardiff and west to Fishguard diverge. The triangle permits through east-west running without calling at Swansea but in practice through trains normally use the Swansea District Line.

Originally Swansea was at the end of a branch line from Landore, the South Wales Railway arriving in 1850 and pushing westwards from Landore two years later. Many main line trains then continued into West Wales after calling at Landore for a Swansea connection but this pattern changed with the completion of the western leg of the triangle in 1906 and the remodelling of Swansea station to accept larger trains in 1934. Landore station closed in 1964, the year in which it became the practice to terminate main line trains at Swansea and operate a separate service westwards.

To get from the Neath valley to the Swansea (or River Tawe) valley the double track main line climbs to Skewen summit and then descends at 1 in 91 and 1 in 106 towards Landore Viaduct over the Tawe. On the way it passes the site of Llansamlet station and the 'flying arches', bridge-like buttresses built to stabilise the sides of the cuttings. It also crosses the ex-MR lines at Six Pit and leading to Morriston.

Landore Viaduct, on a curve and 405 yds long, comprises two approach spans, a central river span and then 19 more spans, all carried on masonry piers. The structure dates from 1888 when it replaced a longer Brunel timber viaduct and in 1978-9 it was the subject of a £1¾ million scheme which involved 1,500 tons of new steelwork and resulted in the viaduct now being able to carry the heaviest axle loads. The opportunity was also taken to ease the curve at the Swansea end and this enabled the previous 20 mph speed rest-riction to be raised to 40 mph. The western end of the viaduct also bridged the 1881-1965 GWR line through Landore Low Level and extended in 1914 to Felin Fran but the course of this is now occupied by a new road, visible from the viaduct.

At Landore Junction (214 m 65 ch) the access lines to Landore diesel depot and a single line towards Swansea Loop West Junction (215 m 14 ch) diverge while the main line parallels the west bank of the Tawe for the descent into the terminus. It is joined at Swansea Loop East Junction (215 m 43 ch) by the double track from West Wales. On the Down side, at a lower level, are Maliphant carriage depot and High Street carriage sidings separated by the particularly inconvenient Maliphant level crossing. The sidings, which include a carriage washing machine, rejoin the main line immediately outside the station at a point opposite the former goods depot.

The station itself consists of four platform lines, numbered 1 to 4 from east to west and wherever possible the London HSTs are put into No 2 to facilitate inter-change with the West Wales trains in No 3. A few pre-1934 buildings survive along-side No 1 platform but the station mostly dates from that year. The booking hall was remodelled to give South Wales its first travel centre in 1972/3 and a current scheme provides for enlargement and enclosure from the station forecourt, the tracks being shortened by 60 ft in the process. At the rear of platform 4 is the stub of the line which led by viaduct to the LNWR at Swansea Victoria and the docks.

Leaving Swansea for West Wales the double track from Swansea Loop East Junction curves and climbs to Swansea Loop West Junction (a distance of 52 ch) and then steepens to 1 in 52 to a summit at the former Cockett station (closed 1964) beyond the 786 yd Cockett Tunnel (216 m 28 ch to 216 m 63 ch). This has two more

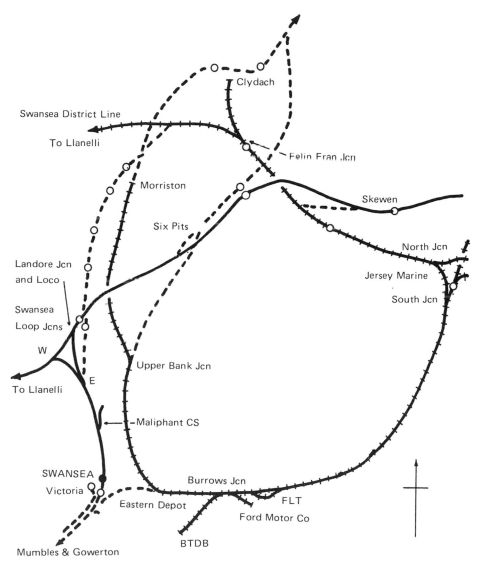

flying arches at the east end, provided when the tunnel was shortened.

Other railway hardware in the triangle area includes the recently closed Hafod goods yard, at a higher level and reached from East Junction, the Down loop from Landore towards the station and the former Hafod Junction where the Morriston line trailed in by a junction facing Swansea.

The main train service at Swansea is the near-hourly Inter-City 125 HST service to and from Paddington which has a turn-round time at Swansea of approximately 45 minutes. Five HSTs berth at Swansea overnight. There is also a service to and from the North-East, a few local workings to Cardiff and good connections there with other services. On the route west from Swansea dmus form the mainstay of the services to Pembroke Dock and to Shrewsbury via the Central Wales line and locomotive hauled trains of the principal services to Milford Haven. Some locomotive and carriage services also run to Fishguard Harbour, almost entirely in connection with the Sealink services to and from Rosslare. There are also local

services between Swansea and Carmarthen
and a few movements over the direct lines
to/from Milford Haven, Fishguard and
Carmarthen. Not all trains to the west call
at Gowerton.

Swansea station also handles some
parcels trains, notably the 'Premium
Parcels' trains from and to Paddington.
All the movements in, to and from the
station are controlled from the Port
Talbot panel box.

By a complex and intricate process of
history the freight lines of Swansea,
closely associated with the metal industries
and port trade of the city, have become
largely separated from the passenger lines
centred upon the station and the South
Wales main line. The freight lines are
based on a route along the foreshore of
Swansea Bay, east of the Tawe river and
reached from the Swansea District Line.
They serve the docks, the Freightliner
depot, a marshalling yard and several
private sidings.

At one period there were some 500
works and collieries within 20 m of
Swansea and 621,000 tons of tinplate and
black sheet went through the docks for
export in one year. There was a large
patent fuel works and Swansea was one of
the first ports used for oil piped to
Llandarcy for refining. The GWR fish

market at South Dock was a scene of
constant activity and in a good year might
land, auction and transport inland 15,000
tons of fish. The pattern has altered a
great deal but Swansea is still a busy
industrial area with a significant BR
freight activity.

There are two junctions between the
Swansea District Line and the freight
route into Swansea. Trains from the east
pass via Dynevor Junction (19 m 13 ch) to
Jersey Marine South Junction (20 m 18
ch) and those from the west via Jersey
Marine North Junction (1 m 24 ch) to join
at South Junction (2 m 22 ch). The former
leg of the triangle is single track with a
long passing loop. Nearby, on the Down
side, is the private siding to the premises
of Steel Supply Co (Western) Ltd at Neath
Abbey wharf who deal in scrap metal.
There are also train load movements of
coal from private mines inland from
Neath, brought in by road and then
forwarded from the siding as mgr trains to
Aberthaw power station. The line from
Neath & Brecon Junction also joins at
Jersey Marine South.

Jersey Marine Yard, a once extensive
area on the Up side of the line at Jersey
Marine Junction South, is now much
reduced in size and is used for reversing
and locomotive run-round purposes in

connection with mgr movements between Aberthaw power station and Blaenant colliery.

From Jersey Marine South Junction a busy section of double line leads to Burrows Junction (46 m 66 ch), 2 m 54 ch further on and the focal point of Swansea's freight operation with a nearby Area Freight Centre and TOPS office. Here Burrows Sidings signal box, a typical large GWR structure with semaphore signals, takes over from the Port Talbot panel. On the approach to the junction, on the Down side, is Danygraig Freight-liner Terminal equipped with two Goliath 0-4-0 Morris cranes spanning the three lines and forwarding a daily train of wagon sets to the Cardiff terminal for re-marshalling there. The terminal also undertakes the transhipment of freight conveyed by conventional, eg, Speedlink, services.

Between the Freightliner terminal and Burrows Junction is Burrows Sidings marshalling yard and, in the same area, the private siding of Gower Chemicals, another for Wagon Repairs Ltd, the line to Assembly Sidings, Danygraig wagon servicing shops, the private siding of the Ford Motor Company plant and the double track line to the BTDB network via Kings Dock Junction signal box. The

wagon shops are housed in the ex-Rhondda & Swansea Bay Railway loco-motive depot but their future is uncertain following an extensive fire in 1980.

On from Burrows Junction a single track line continues westwards to Swansea Eastern Depot (48 m 8 ch) where there are locomotive stabling sidings and a train crew depot, also the mechanised coal depot of Gloda Distributors (South Wales) Ltd partly financed by a Welsh Office grant under Section 8 of the Railways Act 1974. The section from Burrows Junction is worked under the No Signalman Token system.

Beyond Eastern Depot the single track continues via Upper Bank Junction (1 m 34 ch) to serve several private sidings at Morriston (3 m 16 ch), changing from a course behind the docks to one parallel with the east bank of the river. Operation is on the One Train Working system and there are run-round facilities at Morriston. The line from the level crossing at Upper Bank Junction to Six Pit, Llansamlet closed in 1976 and is now largely dismantl-ed although there are plans for a private railway preservation project here.

The main docks traffic at Swansea is export coal arriving as block loads from Pantyffynnon, Llandeilo Junction and Pembrey yards, and from Onllwyn. There are also movements from Maesteg and Abercwmboi via Radyr yard and periodi-cal special trains conveying BSC steel. Class 08 locomotives do the shunting at the docks and at Burrows Sidings which undertakes sorting and distribution of local traffic, the return of empty coal wagons to the anthracite field and, until recently, forwarding of Onllwyn coal to the phurnacite plant at Abercwmboi. Burrows Sidings has services linking it with Merthyr, Radyr, Severn Tunnel Junction and East Usk yards and operates local trips to Morriston, Eastern Depot, Neath Abbey Wharf, Felin Fran, Clydach and the Vale of Neath line. Among the private siding flows, the most notable is the daily overnight company train between Swansea and Dagenham which forms a vital link in the Ford production process.

The basis of the route through Jersey Marine to Swansea is the Vale of Neath line from Aberdare and Merthyr and extended forward from Neath as the Swansea & Neath Railway in 1863. The

Left *Immaculate diesel depot at Landore at the time of opening in 1963.*

Vale of Neath became part of the GWR in 1865 but a public house on the main road parallel to the Burrows Junction-Eastern Depot section is still called the 'Vale of Neath Arms'. From Court Sart Junction through Dynevor Junction to Jersey Marine South the route is that of the Rhondda & Swansea Bay Railway originating in 1894, worked by the GWR from 1906 and absorbed by that company in 1922. VoN passenger services ran to East Dock and ceased in 1936, RSB trains to Riverside and ended in 1933, the route of the latter west of Jersey Marine now having gone except for the Danygraig depot referred to earlier. The docks and their rail system came into GWR ownership in 1923 but the docks management was separated from the railway activity with nationalisation 25 years later.

Beyond Eastern Depot is the ex-Midland Railway enclave, the line to Morriston passing through the site of the MR St Thomas terminus and the closed line from Upper Bank to Six Pit being part of the MR's main route out of Swansea towards the Neath & Brecon, with the Morriston loop rejoining it at Glais Junction. This MR network originated as the Swansea Vale Railway which the Midland took over in 1876. At

Reconstruction and renewal work on Landore Viaduct, Swansea.

one time there was a connection across the River Tawe to the GWR main line at High Street station, the LNWR route out of Swansea Victoria (to the Central Wales line) and even to the Swansea & Mumbles Railway. The latter, although descended from the world's first passenger-carrying railway (the Oystermouth Railway, 1807) and then finishing its career using electric tramcars, did at one time carry freight.

S.34   Swansea District Line
Newport-Fishguard line, from Court Sart Junction to Morlais Junction (Central Wales line). 11 m 13 ch

The Swansea District, or Avoiding, Line forms a double track alternative inland route between Court Sart Junction, on the South Wales main line east of Swansea, and Llandeilo Junction, near Llanelli to the west of Swansea. It was completed as a through route in 1915, the final fling of the GWR's expansion period at the beginning of the century. Although only half a mile is saved in distance terms, the gradients are much easier than those on the main line.

The GWR's objective in building the new route was to ease the flow of traffic to and from Fishguard, where the harbour had been opened in 1906, and to facilitate the movement of coal from the Amman Valley. For the latter there was to be a direct line through Clydach to Felin Fran

but this was never completed and the Swansea District Line serves primarily as a through west-east route for freight and for the Amman Valley coal but via the traditional line from Pantyffynnon. It also serves a number of particularly important industrial sites, eg, Llandarcy oil refinery, the BSC tinplate works at Velindre and Trostre and the NCB Brynlliw colliery.

Although now a through route, the origins of the line were piecemeal and this is reflected in the three changes of mileage. From Court Sart Junction (18 m 7 ch) the line descends at 1 in 105 towards the Neath river with Neath Canal Side ground frame (18 m 44 ch) giving access to the Canalside branch and the swing bridge (now fixed) over the river preceding Dynevor Junction (19 m 13 ch and 47 ch) where the freight line into Swansea diverges southwards. This section originated as the Rhondda & Swansea Bay Railway's 1894 extension into Swansea.

The link from Dynevor Junction to Jersey Marine Junction North (1 m 24 ch) crosses over the line from Neath and Brecon Junction to Jersey Marine Junction South and is part of the 1915 construction. The next section was built three years earlier and passes through a deep cutting after which the single track to Llandarcy diverges on the Down side. This is followed on the same side by a loop passing behind the typical GWR brick signal box known as Llandarcy Ground Frame (51 ch) and another connection to the refinery. Oil for the refinery arrives in trainloads from Furzebrook in Dorset, with block loads of the refined products going forward to a wide variety of destinations in England and South Wales. Groups of wagons for sorting into other trains are tripped to Margam yard.

There is another change of mileage (0 to 1 m 8 ch) at Lonlas Junction reached via another deep cutting, eloquently reflecting the bold engineering of the GWR's early cut-off ventures, and followed by the 925 yard Lonlas Tunnel (1 m 8 ch to 1 m 50 ch). The junction, which trailed in on the Up side, led to Skewen East Junction on the main line and was the only access from the Cardiff direction prior to the 1915 construction. This point marks the summit of the SDL's climb out of the valley of the Neath river before the modest descent to the Swansea, or Tawe, valley.

The Tawe valley is crossed mainly on embankment and the next location is Felin Fran (2 m 25 ch) where the junction for the Clydach branch is on the Up side and a coal yard on the Down, both controlled from the large GWR timber signal box now classified as a ground frame. The SDL scheme included the construction of a large marshalling yard at Felin Fran and the GWR's Swansea-Morriston branch was extended to this point. At one time a dozen trains ran each day from Swansea via Landore Low Level, Plas Marl, Copper Pit Platform, Morriston, Pentrefelin Halt and on to Llandarcy Platform, or to Neath, Briton Ferry or Port Talbot, but on closure in 1956 this was down to a single train Port Talbot to Swansea and back. The line closed completely in 1965 and Felin Fran is now left with its through services on the SDL and the two daily trips from Swansea Burrows Sidings, one of which continues 'as required' to Clydach. An interesting forward possibility is that of a branch from Felin Fran to the Swansea Enterprise Zone, an area of special industrial development just to the north of the SDL

The section on to Morlais Junction (10 m 67 ch), from the valley of the Tawe to that of the Loughor, dates from 1913. After the viaduct over the Tawe comes the 1,953 yd Llangyfelach Tunnel (4 m 4 ch to 5 m 12 ch) and then the junction (5 m 55 ch) on the Up side and into the BSC Velindre tinplate plant via a run-round and reversing neck. Five train 'paths' are available for conveying coil for coating from the BSC steel works at Port Talbot but the shuttle service of 100-ton gross laden weight bogie steel wagons is related to the BSC production levels. A service is also scheduled to convey outwards tinplate to Margam yard for attaching to Speedlink trains there.

Llangyfelach station, closed in 1924 after a very short career, marks the beginning of the descent at a ruling gradient of 1 in 120 to the valley of the Loughor. The 287 yd Penllergaer Tunnel (6 m 45 ch to 6 m 58 ch) is followed by Pont Lliw, another 1924 closure but still revealing its platforms once served by loops off the main lines. A mile further on, on the Up side, are the exchange sidings for coal brought over the NCB line from Craig Merthyr colliery.

A bridge carrying the M4 over the SDL separates Craig Merthyr Colliery Sidings (8 m 74 ch) from Grovesend Colliery Loop Junction (10 m 5 ch) and at the latter is the connection to the line to Brynlliw colliery and Gorseinon coal depot, on the Down side. The rest of the Pontarddulais-Swansea Victoria route is closed but its course is bridged by the SDL just before reaching Grovesend loop. The Grovesend complex, east to west, consists of the Gorseinon Goods Junction connection (9 m 30 ch), the loop, a brick viaduct over the Loughor and then Grovesend Colliery Loop Junction proper with a double track diverging on the Up side to link up with the Central Wales line towards Pantyffynnon and the SDL continuing to Morlais Junction and the Central Wales line connection towards Llanelli. The latter is now made on the Up side with the single track Central Wales line but there is evidence of the former separate Down line which burrowed beneath the SDL. The connections to Morlais colliery have now been taken up.

From Morlais Junction, the SDL completes its course to the main line at Llandeilo Junction over the Llanelly Railway's 1839 route via Genwen Junction, described elsewhere in this book. In addition to the traffic originating on the line it is used by through west-east freight trains; coal, wagonload and Speedlink from Llandeilo Junction yard, oil trains from Milford Haven and others such as the company train for fertiliser traffic between Ince and Carmarthen. In addition to the use of the western end by Central Wales line passenger trains, the Swansea District Line is used by seasonal trains between Paddington and Fishguard Harbour, some Tenby summer Saturday services, and such other workings as the Llanelli/Carmarthen portion of the London-South Wales newspaper train.

Signalling is by multi-aspect colour lights controlled from Port Talbot panel box.

S.35 Swindon

Paddington-Bristol line, between Didcot and Wootton Bassett Junction. 77 m 23 ch from Paddington

Present day Swindon owes much of its size and importance to its railway origins. For many years it was, like Crewe, a 'railway town' distinguishing between people according to whether they were 'inside' (ie, the Works) or not. Today much has ·changed, but BREL still has an important works at Swindon and the remodelled station has an excellent HST service towards London and westbound. The introduction of the latter brought

significant increases in business and commuter travel. The station also has a service to Gloucester/Worcester, parcels facilities, and an attractive Travellers-Fare buffet in place of the millstone of catering by contractor and a refreshment stop by all trains which the infant GWR ill-advisedly started off with.

As a junction with the Cheltenham line, a locomotive change-over point and the site of its locomotive works, Swindon was soon important in the early activities of the GWR. The locomotive works, established in 1843, still occupies the site in the angle of the two lines. The carriage shops, transferred from Paddington, lay opposite (on both lines) with saw mill, fitting and machine shop and carriage body building shop next to St Mark's Church and the site between there and the station formerly occupied by the finishing, polishing, sewing, trimming and painting activities. Some of the remains are still visible south of the main line but the site of the heavier activities—stamping, frame building, etc—has largely been redeveloped.

In the best traditions of 19th century paternalism the GWR provided its workers at Swindon with attractive railway housing in a comprehensively planned estate. The cottages were designed by Matthew Digby Wyatt and built with Bath stone recovered from the tunnel works area at Box. Now the Borough of Thamesdown has modernised the 'railway village' in an imaginative project which includes the furnishing of No 34 Faringdon Road as a reflection, open to public view, of the domestic life of the period. The same area includes the Great Western Railway Museum, in a building planned as 'a model lodging house', and the Mechanics Institute.

The present station complex stretches along the main line from the ground frame leading to the truncated Highworth branch at 76 m 30 ch to 78 m 31 ch where the Rushey Platt ground frame marks the point of access to a timber firm's former siding and the old connection to the

Top right *The old M&SWJ station at Swindon and the house once used as administrative offices.*
Centre right *Although the site of the GWR carriage works at Swindon has been used for light industry, the frontage remains intact.*
Right *Swindon station before its facelift.*

M&SWJ line. There is a Down Goods Line from the London end to the station, plus an Up Goods Loop and Down Refuge Siding at Highworth Ground Frame, and an Up Goods Line at the country end in front of the BREL works. Various siding areas lie on both sides of the main line, with the goods shed and depot standing on the Down side at the London end.

The station, remodelled in the 1970s, consists of an island platform linked by subway to the ticket and parcels offices on the town side. Waiting, toilet and refreshment facilities are all on this platform where the gaunt original buildings rise above and behind the facelift. To allow through running on the main lines, the two platform faces are served by bi-directional, permissive working platform lines and a bay is provided at the junction end for the Gloucester line trains.

Swindon Works still undertakes coach and dmu refurbishing plus work on locomotives, wagons and some jobs for outside parties. The site consists of a 'graveyard' at the country end and three main areas comprising the machine shop and its ancillaries, the engine shop with wagon and brake shops and the foundry behind and, in the angle of the junction, the carriage repair shop and the bogie and wheel shop.

The remains of Swindon's other lines are apparent at each end of the area. At the London end the former Highworth branch veers away on the Up side, near the small oil traffic terminal. Closed for passengers in 1953, although trains for works employees continued until 1962, the remains of the branch now serve the BL works and a scrap metal activity. At the Rushey Platt end the route used by the Swindon Junction-Swindon Town trains can be seen on the Down side where the trackbed of the M&SWJ swings round towards High Town. There the station site is still derelict and the curved platforms are still visible together with a house formerly used as the company's administrative offices. North from Rushey Platt the M&SW route remained open until 1975 to serve Moredon Power Station and the section beyond is now in the hands of the Swindon & Cricklade Railway Preservation Society.

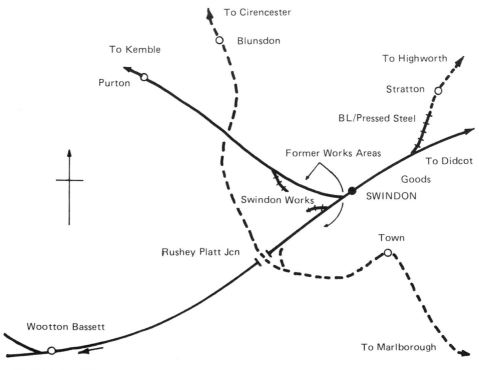

A Class 08 shunter at Swindon works.

T.1   Tackley

Oxford-Birmingham line between Oxford and Banbury. 72 m 50 ch from Paddington

A minimum facilities station with a basic weekday service of five trains each way and with a ground frame and emergency crossovers.

Taffs Well—see Pontypridd

T.2   Taplow

Paddington-Swindon line between Slough and Maidenhead. 22 m 39 ch from Paddington

By early in 1838 the GWR directors were taking trial trips out to a temporary wooden station west of the Bath Road bridge at Taplow. This became the station for Maidenhead, but disappeared after Maidenhead got its own station and the present Taplow site came into use in 1872, a quarter mile nearer London. As at Twyford, the main lines veer to accommodate the width of the central island platform; all platforms have buildings of red brick with faced double window arches and ornamental canopies in a development of a Brunel style. The footbridge has its own canopy and bears the date 1884.

At the London end there is an Up Refuge Siding, relief line crossover and a small coal depot.

T.3   Taunton

Junction of lines from Reading and Bristol towards Exeter. 163 m 12 ch from Paddington*

The Bristol & Exeter Railway was formally welcomed to Taunton on July 1 1842, the station then comprising two short sheds placed on the Down side and provided with overall roofs. This awkward arrangement had to be replaced as traffic through Taunton grew and branches were opened to Watchet (1862), Chard (1866) and Barnstaple (1871). The second station, to a Fox design, came into use in 1868 and comprised conventional Up and Down platforms, but again with an all-over roof. In 1895 the platforms were lengthened and an avoiding loop constructed on the south side of the site.

As the GWR traffic continued to grow the effect of the 7½ m bottleneck between Cogload and Norton Fitzwarren became increasingly unacceptable. The station still comprised two platforms and eight bays, even after the opening of the cut-off route, and although through trains went round the avoiding line at busy times the volume of train, locomotive and rolling stock movements made the working extraordinarily difficult.

In 1930 a contract was let for remodelling the whole area. This produced the flyover junction at Cogload, four tracks from there to Norton Fitzwarren and a revised station layout with three 1,200 ft and one 1,400 ft platform faces and incorporating

a small portion of the previous station in the present Down side. In this state Taunton continued until relatively recently.

Track preparation work at Taunton depot.

The approach to Taunton station is on the north side where the modest ticket office and new travel centre lead directly to the subway for platform access. The centre island platform is now out of use and as the Up and Down Main lines which flank it can now be used for through traffic the former avoiding lines have been relegated to the status of through sidings under local control. Passengers join and alight from trains at the remaining outer platforms which are served by the Up and Down Relief lines. With no branch services to Minehead or Barnstaple the bays at the country end are not needed, although the Up Bay at the London end is

still used for local stopping services to Bristol. There is a range of buildings on both sides of the station, the Roll of Honour on the Up side and the former telegraph office on the Down side providing a glimpse of a former era.

The locomotive depot, the remains of which can be seen beyond the two bridges at the country end of the platforms and on the Down side, once provided Castles and Stars for the main line workings, Bulldogs and 45XX tanks for local trains, Moguls for the Ilfracombe line and pilots for the many station shunting movements. At various times the station had such special workings as a slip carriage off the

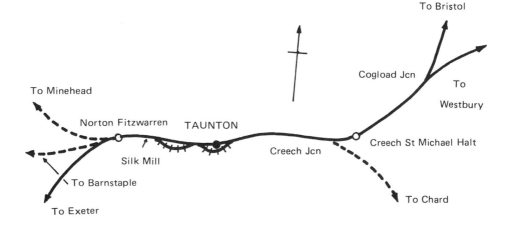

Taunton station looking west.

'Limited' and a Weymouth railcar running non-stop between Yeovil and Taunton. Nowadays HST sets from the west work to Paddington via Bristol and Lavington and on the North-East/South-West route. The wide catchment area brings good patronage and London lies within two hours, the Up Golden Hind taking 107 minutes for the 143 m journey.

Freight at Taunton comprises a coal concentration depot on the Down side at the London end; opposite is the civil engineer's concrete works. Adjacent and backing the avoiding line is the vast goods shed, now used by National Carriers.

Beyond Taunton towards London traces of the Chard line can be seen near the brickworks at Creech St Michael, with the former halt nearby. West of the station the civil engineer has an 8-siding depot with 204 hp locomotives for shunting and steam and internal combustion cranes. The headshunt for the depot terminates just short of Silk Mill level crossing (164 m 35 ch) where the signal box controls the crossing barriers. There is a good footbridge viewing on this side of the station.

T.4   Teignmouth

Taunton-Penzance line between Exeter and Newton Abbot. 208 m 78 ch from Paddington*

Winter gales delayed the building of the coastal section of the South Devon Rail-way but trains reached Teignmouth on May 30 1846 using locomotives borrowed from the GWR pending the introduction of the atmospheric system. Seven years later the sea brought down a massive section of wall and blocked the line for over a week. The waves have had their moments on many occasions since but the number of holidaymakers, excursionists and day outing parties brought by rail to the sea and sun at Teignmouth more than balance the account.

The present station lies on a curve behind the town centre and has cuttings on either side. The buildings and retaining walls are all of stone and create a pleasing overall effect. Originally the line was single and the station was rebuilt when the line was doubled in 1884. The old station area, on the landward side of the present one, then became the goods yard. At the same time the short East Cliff Tunnel was opened out.

Public freight facilities were withdrawn in 1967 although the rail access route to the yard is still obvious. The route taken by the old connection to Teignmouth Quay can also be traced on the Down side at the country end of the station, but Old Quay signal box no longer watches over the wagons of ball clay passing to the small ships for export or the movements of coal and timber in the opposite direction.

The walk along the sea wall east of the station, and a footbridge over the line there, provide good vantage points for viewing and photography. Further on are five tunnels, the 512 yd Parson's Tunnel (207 m 19 ch to 207 m 42 ch), the 66 yd Clerks Tunnel (206 m 72 ch to 206 m 75 ch), the 55 yd Phillot Tunnel (206 m 66 ch to 206 m 69 ch), the 224 yd Coryton Tunnel (206 m 53 ch to 206 m 63 ch) and the 209 yd Kennaway Tunnel (206 m 34 ch to 206 m 43 ch), the first two taking their names from the figures sculpted by the sea in the red sandstone of the adjacent headland.

Tenby—see Pembroke Dock Branch

T.5   Thatcham

Reading-Taunton line between Reading and Newbury. 49 m 51 ch from Paddington

This location consists of Thatcham station, level crossings on either side and a major area of private sidings. The station facilities are minimal but Thatcham, like Hungerford and Bedwyn, was still clinging to its period nameboards as late as 1981.

Travelling in the Up direction, the Ministry of Defence private siding is followed by the CCTV level crossing and the station by two connections to the Colthrop Reed paper works premises and Colthrop crossing. The private sidings are served via Thatcham ground frame (49 m 56 ch) and Colthrop ground frame (48 m 75 ch) and the former locking frame room of Colthrop Crossing signal box now serves humbly as the store for the tail lamps of trains placed in the paper firm's sidings.

T.6   Theale

Reading-Taunton line between Reading and Newbury. 41 m 22 ch from Paddington

Theale passenger station now consists of just Up and Down platforms, each with a basic waiting shelter, but there are extensive aggregate, cement and oil traffic sidings on the Up side of the line west of the station proper. In addition to the Down/Up Through Siding, No 1 and No 2 Down Reception Lines serve:
*ARC Stone Sidings 1 and 2 which receive five trains of aggregate traffic in tipplers each week from Tytherington.
*CMC Hopper Sidings taking cement in 100-tonne glw wagons.
*Foster Yeoman Sidings 1 and 2 serving a hopper house and taking a daily train of 37 × 51-tonne hopper wagons (which may increase to 60 wagons).
*Murco Sidings for receiving 3-5 trains of oil weekly from South Wales (11 × 100-

tonne wagons) and 'specials' from Ripple Lane, Barking.
*Holding and 'cripple' sidings.

The Dell—see Falmouth Branch

T.7   Thingley Junction

Swindon-Bristol line between Chippenham and Bath. 96 m 10 ch from Paddington

The first section of the Wilts, Somerset & Weymouth Railway was opened from Thingley Junction, on the GWR main line, to Westbury on September 5 1848. An early example of the railwayman's aversion to facing points showed up in the use of a reversing siding for trains proceeding from London towards Westbury. This line is now single, with a facing junction off the Down Main and the duties of Thingley Junction Signal Box have passed to Swindon panel under the Swindon area MAS scheme.

T.8   Thornford

*Westbury-Weymouth line between Yeovil and Dorchester. 144 m 35 ch from Paddington**

Thornford consists of an overbridge leading down to a short concrete platform and shelter on the west side of the single line and served by five trains each way daily.

Tidenham—see Wye Valley Branch

T.9   Tilehurst

Paddington-Swindon line between Reading and Didcot. 38 m 52 ch from Paddington

Comprising central island and two outer platforms, Tilehurst is the station for the western end of the Reading complex. It is served by the Paddington-Reading-Oxford local service using the Up and Down relief line platforms.

Tir-Phil—see Rhymney Branch

T.10   Tiverton Junction

*Taunton-Penzance line between Taunton and Exeter. 179 m 10 ch from Paddington**

Some 5 m east of the town of Tiverton, Tiverton Road station was opened on May 1 1844 on the Bristol & Exeter Railway's new route to Exeter. The branch linking the two opened four years later and the Culm Valley line east to Hemyock in 1876.

Above *Inter-City and ballast trains pass at Tiverton Junction. The route to Hemyock was on the right.*

Below *Tiverton has lost its link to Tiverton Junction, but the route was still visible in 1981.*

Now both branch lines have gone, although the station retains the word 'Junction' as part of its title and still has a spaciousness deriving from the interchange activity and from the quadrupling of the main line in the 1930s. The two long platforms are served by Up and Down loops with a second loop round the outer face of the Up platform. The long signal box on this platform has eight double windows on each side, curious in having three panes in the top portion but only two in the lower one. The ticket office, on the same platform, still has an impressive display of period wall tiles.

From the country end of the Up plat-

form the course of the line to Tiverton can be seen and there is a small oil storage installation at the London end. The Down side has fewer platform buildings, a timber firm using the old yard and dock and a short spur along the Hemyock line, once noted for its mixed trains and milk traffic. The last gas-lit carriages were at work on this branch because the mixed trains were unable to run at a speed sufficient to generate electric light.

Signalling is semaphore and the footbridge makes a good vantage point.

T.11 Tondu

Newport-Fishguard line; meeting point of lines from the Llynfi, Garw and Ogmore valleys and links to the main line at Bridgend and Port Talbot.

Near the small Mid Glamorgan town of Tondu, 3 m north of Bridgend, the rivers Llynfi and Garw join the Ogmore (Ogwr)

to flow through Bridgend to the sea. As so often happens in South Wales, railway lines in these three valleys also join at Tondu, from which point there are links to the South Wales main line not only at Bridgend but also westwards to Margam and Port Talbot. These lines, now largely devoted to coal traffic, originated mainly as horse-worked tramroads, although in the early days the main destination was the harbour at Porthcawl, with just a branch 'road' to Bridgend town.

From west to east the first valley is that of the River Llynfi which contains a single track branch from Bridgend via Tondu (2 m 69 ch) to Llynfi Junction (8 m 55 ch) where coal traffic from Maesteg Central Washery is transferred from NCB lines to BR. Just beyond Llynfi Junction signal box and the run-round and junction facilities is the physical end of the line at the site of Nantyffyllon station (9 m 12 ch). Returning southwards, ie, Down, the Maesteg layout on the Down side is followed by the platforms of the former Maesteg Castle Street station and then its coal yard lying deserted on the Up side. The sites of Troedyrhiew Garth and Llangynwyd stations come next, then the private siding for a factory making tissues and the disused sidings which once led to Llynfi power station and the location of the former Gelli Las signal box.

Mondays to Fridays the service on the Nantyffyllon line provides for up to four trips to bring empty wagons from Margam yard for the washery at Maesteg and take coal away, either to Ogmore Vale Central Washery or back to Margam. There is provision for one of these daily trips to serve the tissues factory on its return towards Tondu. The gradients on the line, descending to Tondu, are mostly between 1 in 110 and 1 in 50 and it is worked by the One Train Working system.

The railway in the Llynfi valley originated as a 4 ft 7 in gauge horse traction tramroad and developed through broad, mixed and standard gauge railway status, ownership mutating from Llynfi Valley Railway, through Llynfi & Ogmore Railway to GWR. From 1878 to 1970 the route extended northwards through a tunnel to the Afan Valley and in its later years the passenger service ran through the great Rhondda Tunnel to Treherbert. The NCB rail layout in the Maesteg area includes part of the Port Talbot Railway's erstwhile cross-valleys line from Port Talbot to the Llynfi and Garw valleys and

a PTR embankment is conspicuous on the northern outskirts of Maesteg.

The Garw valley lies east of the Llynfi and the single track freight line threads down from its head at Blaengarw (5 m 16 ch) to join the line from the neighbouring Ogmore valley at Tondu Ogmore Junction (66 ch), just outside Tondu. The route carries coal from the NCB Garw and Ffalddau collieries to Ogmore Vale Central Washery, the four daily trips reversing at Tondu and empty wagons being drawn from Margam or returning from the washery. The gradient drops towards Tondu, mainly between 1 in 69 and 1 in 87, but with a section of 1 in 39 at the top end. The One Train Working system is in operation.

Opened in 1876, this line has always been a standard gauge railway. It had a passenger service until 1953 serving stations at Blaengarw, Pontycymmer, Pontyrhyll, Llangeinor, Brynmenyn and Tondu. The line begins with an overhead loading bunker handling the output of both collieries, followed by the old station site and then the boundary between the BR and NCB tracks. There is a passing loop at Pontycymmer (4 m 48 ch) and at Pontyrhyll the junction with the PTR line which lost its passenger service in 1932 and was an early post-war casualty when closed to freight. From Brynmenyn the former double track section, now single, runs alongside the Ogmore Valley line. The old station lay in the vee between the two routes and a signal box still stands there, but no longer controlling signals.

Next east is the Ogmore Valley line from Nantymoel (7 m 10 ch) serving the Wyndham and Western collieries and the Ogmore Vale Central Washery. The first two are linked and reached via ground frames south of the run-round at the Nantymoel station site. Continuing south there are substantial remains of Ogmore Vale station with platforms, footbridge and derelict Up side buildings, complete with canopy, on the Nantymoel side of the level crossing. Semaphore signals and a busy level crossing are worked from Caedu signal box (4 m 79 ch) and this is followed by a long loop on the Down side leading to Ogmore Vale Central Washery. From Lewiston ground frame (4 m) at the end of the loop the route continues to the signal box at Tondu Ogmore Junction and then becomes double track to Tondu. Cardiff & Ogmore Junction, south of the washery, was the point of divergence of the 1876-1938 line which climbed the side of the valley and then ran east to Llanharan. The masonry piers of the viaduct which carried it over the Ogwr Fach valley can be seen from the present railway at Blackmill, where the line down the Ogwr joined until 1961 (1930 for passengers).

The gradients down the Ogmore Valley route are mostly between 1 in 41 and 1 in 99, easing at the lower end but with a section of 1 in 35 above Wyndham colliery. One Train Working applies above Caedu, between Caedu and Tondu Ogmore Junction movements are controlled by the Caedu signalman and Absolute Block Working applies between Tondu Ogmore Junction and Tondu.

Trips are worked as required between Ogmore Vale Central Washery and Wyndham Colliery, empty wagons going up, loaded down. Below Caedu movements are more frequent and include not only the loads from the adjacent branches but also outwards movements from the washery to Margam or direct to the sidings feeding the tippler for the coke ovens at the BSC Port Talbot steel works. There are empty wagon trains and some movements to Aberthaw and Newport.

This line originated in 1865 as a standard gauge railway opened by the Ogmore Valley company, later passing into Llynfi & Ogmore and later still GWR ownership. Passenger services to the stations at Nantymoel, Wyndham Halt, Ogmore Vale, Lewiston Halt, Blackmill, Brynmenyn and Tondu ceased in 1958.

The other line centred on Tondu is one which originated in 1877 as a direct route to the South Wales main line at Llanharan It ceased to be a through route in 1962 but continued to carry traffic on the portion at the western end between Wern Tarw colliery (3 m 17 ch) and Tondu Ogmore Junction (6 m 55 ch). Now the surviving portion is only that from Ynysawdre Junction, immediately adjacent to Tondu Ogmore Junction, to Raglan East opencast coal disposal point where there is a runround and connection into the NCB premises, with the 'End of Branch Board' just beyond. Wern Tarw colliery has closed, the plan to reactivate the line to serve its successor on the site has been abandoned and even the portion to Raglan East had fallen out of use by the beginning of 1982.

All these four lines meet at Tondu and then diverge into the two routes for Bridgend and Margam, the erstwhile passenger station being situated in the

angle between the two, where a footbridge spans the junction. The layout here includes sidings, run-round and passing facilities and a large GWR signal box controlling semaphore signals. It is busy with the coal movements to and from the adjacent branches, some of these involving reversals and others the detaching of wagons because of loading limitations on the climb up to Ogmore Vale. Tondu was the headquarters of the Llynfi & Ogmore system and very busy in the steam era and when it had passenger services from Bridgend up the valleys and over the Margam route to Pyle and Porthcawl.

The link between Tondu and Bridgend opened in 1861 as a broad gauge railway replacing an earlier tramroad branch but on a different alignment. It is sometimes used as a diversionary route when the main line is closed, the 2 m 69 ch being single and on a gradient easier than 1 in 100 rising towards Tondu.

The other line of this group, that from Tondu to Margam, also had tramroad origins. The section from Tondu to Cefn Junction (2 m 43 ch) was part of an 1829 tramroad to Porthcawl. This became a broad gauge railway in 1861 and beyond Cefn Junction there was a link with the main line at Pyle. The Tondu-Porthcawl passenger service ended in 1963 but the Cefn Junction-Pyle section survived, latterly as a one-way single line spur, until 1973. The other line from Cefn Junction, the surviving one to Margam, originated as the Port Talbot Railway's line of 1898 designed to tap the coal-bearing valleys and secure shipment of their traffic through Port Talbot docks. The route is still known as the OVE (Ogmore Vale Extension) and is measured from Copper Works Junction at Port Talbot to Cefn Junction where the PTR 7 m 41 ch changes to the Porthcawl line's 2 m 43 ch.

The route links Tondu with Margam yard, the BSC steel works and, by a west facing junction, the South Wales main line and it is used by the majority of the trains from the Tondu group of lines. A signal box and crossing loop at Cefn Junction divides the route and this is followed towards Margam by the connection to the Mill Pit opencast coal loading site (6 m 56 ch). Both sections, either side of Cefn Junction, are worked under the Electric Token system and the gradient profile involves a climb from Tondu to Cefn at 1 in 91 and then a drop westwards with substantial sections at 1 in 61 and 1 in 70.

At the Margam end the OVE bridges the main line and then joins the double track relief lines at Margam Abbey Works East (2 m 41 ch); there is also a direct line to sidings serving the BSC coke ovens. From 1960 a single line spur has linked Newlands Junction (3 m 50 ch) via Margam Moors sidings to an Up loop from the main line.

Tonypandy—see Treherbert Branch

Topsham—see Exmouth Branch

T.12   Torquay

Newton Abbot-Paignton line. 220 m 4 ch from Paddington*

Torquay's first station was the one at Torre to which a South Devon Railway branch, from a separate station shed at Newton Abbot, was opened on December 18 1848. An independent scheme, the Dartmouth & Torbay Railway, was conceived to link this to the estuary of the River Dart but encountered many dificulties. However, on August 2 1859 the first section of the D&T was opened from Torre to Paignton with a new station in Torquay and worked by the South Devon.
Torquay today is a simple, two-platform station with the main, very pleasant, stone buildings on the Down side. It is still busy with Torbay holiday-makers in the summer with through services to and from places like Sheffield,

Torquay station frontage.

Glasgow, Newcastle and Liverpool in addition to its local trains to Newton Abbot and Exeter. Today seat reservation arrangements have done away with the hectic scenes which used to characterise summer Saturdays but the station information and ticket offices and the privately-owned buffet still have their moments at the height of the season.

T.13   Torre

Newton Abbot-Paignton line. 219 m 10 ch from Paddington*

As described in the previous entry, Torre was the original station for Torquay. Like Torquay it has two platforms, the principal buildings on the Down side and a vacant space between the two tracks. The station is served by local trains only and is closed on Sundays. It is preceded on the Down side by the former goods shed and, at 216 m 34 ch, by the now closed Kingskerswell station. Torre signal box is on the Up side. Torre's atmospheric era pumping station was never commissioned.

T.14   Totnes

Taunton-Penzance line between Newton Abbot and Plymouth. 222 m 63 ch from Paddington*

Totnes is an ancient town standing at the

Above *Torre station showing clearly its South Devon ancestry.*
Right *The ornamentation on the footbridge at Totnes contrasts with the simple, functional lighting.*

head of the navigable portion of the River Dart and its station on a short level stretch of the West of England main line between the descent from Dainton and the climb to Marley tunnels. This section was opened on July 20 1847 and was designed to use atmospheric propulsion. The South Devon Railway abandoned the atmospheric principle in September 1847 but its mark remains in part of the buildings of the dairy behind Totnes Up platform.

Totnes station comprises two through lines with the long platforms served by Up and Down loops. There are wooden buildings on both platforms although these have been reduced on the Down side where there is now a separate booking-cum-parcels office. The adjacent footbridge carries GWR ornamentation and the date 1888. On the Up platform there is a typical GWR manual signal box, long and low in profile.

Loading docks still exist on both sides of the line at the country end of Totnes station and the former Ashburton branch is still connected, on the Up side beyond the bridge over the river, to allow the passage of special trains and movements to and from the Dart Valley Railway.

The traditional hardware of a semaphore signal provides the foreground in this view of Totnes. The creamery buildings incorporate parts of the engine house built for the atmospheric traction period.

Totnes was the station used by passengers who travelled up river from Dartmouth until the line to Kingswear was built. The goods branch to Totnes Quay was opened in 1873 and its route from a Down side connection just station side of the river bridge can still be seen. Timber was still passing from ship to rail this way as late as the 1950s and joined the bacon and dairy products forwarded and the coal, fertilisers and general merchandise received at this busy station.

T.15   Tram Inn

Shrewsbury-Newport line between Hereford and Abergavenny. 5 m 37 ch from Hereford

The Newport, Abergavenny & Hereford Railway acquired three old tramroads to make way for its own through route and this may well have given Tram Inn its name. Passenger services ceased in 1958 and the goods facilities were withdrawn in 1964, but a Down Goods Loop remains with the signal box at the Newport end.

Trecwn Branch—see Fishguard

Trefforest—see Pontypridd

Trefforest Estate—see Pontypridd

Trehafod—see Treherbert Branch

T.16   Treherbert Branch

Newport-Fishguard line, branch to Pontypridd and then Cardiff. 10 m 60 ch

There is a line in each of the Rhondda's twin valleys, the Rhondda Fawr from Treherbert and the Rhondda Fach from Maerdy. Where the rivers join at Porth so do the lines, and where the Rhondda joins the Taff, at Pontypridd, its railway joins the Merthyr-Cardiff line.

The principal line, from Treherbert, is single track to Porth and then double to Pontypridd and carries a passenger service. The Maerdy-Porth line is also single and carries coal from Maerdy colliery. Both lines follow the narrow valley floors in close company with river and road and where colliery villages, as they expanded, have formed almost continuous townships.

The lines were mostly opened between 1841 and 1856 by the Taff Vale Railway to serve the growing Rhondda coal industry. Freight services preceded passenger trains by several years although the coalfield was attracting workers in their thousands from all over England and Wales. The peak year for Rhondda coal was 1913 when there were 53 pits. Now there are two. However, the two lines represent the major part of the TVR system in the Rhondda, only short branches or extensions having closed. Competing lines have, however, all gone: the Rhondda & Swansea Bay through from the west to Treherbert to take coal to Swansea, the Barry Railway which tapped the TVR at Trehafod to take coal to its own port at Barry, and the GWR which had a branch from Llantrisant to Penygraig and the Cambrian Colliery, high above Tonypandy.

On the Rhondda Fawr line, Treherbert (23 m 75 ch) has a single open platform with an adjacent stone building housing station and train crew offices. Track beyond the station affords reversing and run-round facilities and there are dmu stabling sidings.

Intermediate stations on the single line section to Porth (16 m 10 ch) are Treorchy (22 m 2 ch), Ystrad (20 m 76 ch), Llwynpia (19 m 7 ch), Tonypandy (18 m 3 ch) and Dinas (17 m 41 ch). Singling took place to Cwmparc (21 m 50 ch) in 1972 and on to Porth in 1981 and the former Down track is now in use. The platforms remaining in use have vandal-proof shelters and some

The mural of local and railway themes at Porth.

have ticket facilities. The only other feature of this section is a ground frame at Treorchy leading to coal sidings but close examination reveals such items of interest as TVR mileposts, TVR monograms on the disused footbridge at Dinas and the latest BR bilingual trespass notices with the Welsh wording in green and English in black. Near Tonypandy the foot of the former 1 in 13 Pwllyrhebog branch incline can be seen on the Up side.

At Porth there are two platforms and a simple layout of crossover and junction with the Maerdy branch at the north end. This layout dates from the 1981 singling and involves a new, ground level signal box. There are brick shelters on both platforms, that on the Up incorporating parcels and ticket office. Here, too, is a 100 ft coloured mural depicting South Wales history—including railways—painted by teachers and children from a local school. The mural, erected in 1979, has won a Prince of Wales Award and a commendation from the Civic Trust.

Between Porth and Pontypridd, and beyond the bricked up Eirw Branch Junction signal box, is Trehafod station which is unstaffed and has shelters on each platform. Below Trehafod is Gyfeillon Upper signal box (14 m 35 ch), a TVR structure adjacent to the rail-linked Tymawr colliery which is alongside the running line.

The Maerdy branch is single track throughout and runs from Rhondda Fach Junction South (15 m 78 ch) just below

Porth to the boundary with the NCB at Maerdy Colliery (22 m 46 ch). It is steeply graded with nothing easier than 1 in 113 and one stretch at 1 in 37. The Treherbert line falls less sharply with gradients mostly less than 1 in 100 but with a short section of 1 in 68. Both routes are subject to mining subsidence which can lead to gradient changes.

Turning to services, there are 19 dmu services in each direction on the Treherbert line (eight each way on Sundays), mostly through trains to and from Barry Island. Coal from Maerdy is scheduled to be taken by two daily trains, one to Radyr yard, the other to Abercwmboi phurnacite plant. The Class 37s working the coal trains bring up the empty wagons. Treorchy domestic coal yard is served by a conditional overnight freight from Radyr which circulates via Treherbert and shunts the yard on the Down 'leg', while Tymawr colliery is served by a thrice-weekly working from Radyr.

The single line sections are operated by the No Signalman Token system (Treherbert-Porth) and One Train Working (Maerdy-Porth) with Absolute Block working applying on the Porth-Gyfeillon Upper and Gyfeillon Upper-Pontypridd Junction double line sections.

Treorchy—see Treherbert Branch

T.17   Treverrin Tunnel

Taunton-Penzance line between Lost-withiel and Par. 279 m 19 ch from Paddington*

This 564 yd, double line tunnel (279 m 19 ch to 279 m 44 ch) lies at the top of a minor summit between Lostwithiel and Par.

Troed-y-Rhiw—see Merthyr Branch

T.18   Trowbridge

Bristol-Weymouth line between Bradford-on-Avon and Westbury. 105 m 61 ch from Paddington

Today Trowbridge, as Wiltshire's county town, is served by the Weymouth line dmus and by the South Wales-Portsmouth route trains. But it is not quite the railway centre it used to be.

The town obtained its first railway facilities on September 5 1848 when the Wilts, Somerset & Weymouth Railway managed to get a section of 14 miles opened from Thingley Junction to

Westbury. This route from London to Weymouth lost its importance when the Stert Valley portion of the cut-off line was completed between Patney & Chirton and Westbury to cut 14½ m off the GWR passenger's journey from Paddington to Weymouth. The cut-off route also relegated Devizes to branch line status, but a service from Trowbridge to London continued via that town and the tunnel beneath its castle and calling at all stations to Newbury. In addition to its local services, the London and the Bristol trains, Trowbridge in the 1930s was a stop for through workings such as the Wolverhampton-Weymouth facility.

The stone buildings which form the main reminder of Trowbridge station's former standing are on the Down side, where a bay is also visible at the London end. Beyond this is the old goods shed, another stone structure with an office and dock at one end, a brick extension at the other and a wooden section on the former track portion. At one period a truck unloading machine was in use on the shed and the Sectional Appendix quite reasonably stipulated that 'no shunting movement is made which might move the wagons being unloaded'. On the Up side the platform has a modern shelter beneath an older canopy and at the Bradford end is the extensive area of the former yard.

T.19   Truro

Taunton-Penzance line between St Austell and Redruth. 300 m 57 ch from Paddington*

The first railway reached Truro from the west, to a temporary terminus at Higher Town, on August 25 1852 and then on to Newham on April 16 1855. Four years later the Cornwall Railway arrived from the east and laid a connection on to the earlier line at Penwithers Junction so that the West Cornwall Railway's trains could use a new joint station. The CR completed its Truro-Falmouth portion in 1863, crossing on the level the original WCR line to Newham which was then devoted to goods traffic. The break of gauge at Truro gave way to through broad gauge services for passengers from 1867.

After the drop from Buckshead Tunnel, two viaducts herald the approach to Truro from the east, giving excellent views of the city. Between them on the Down side stands the closed Cattle Pens signal box, the station signal box standing at the London end of the Up platform. The

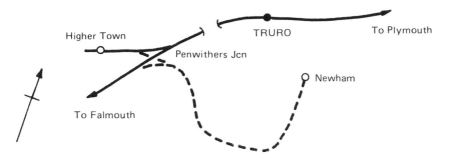

latter is a long island with a canopy over the several brick buildings and a wide yard beyond. Opposite, the long single-storey buildings on the Down platform include the Kenwyn Buffet. The Falmouth Bay stands at the country end and the Lee & Sons shed and siding beyond the level crossing at the London end.

Beyond the station a public footbridge crosses the whole complex and the line then passes through the 70 yd Higher Town Tunnel (301 m 10 ch to 301 m 13 ch). Further west still, the old connection from the Falmouth line to Newham, now closed, can be spotted at Penwithers Junction.

T.20   Turf

Taunton-Penzance line between Exeter and Starcross. 199 m 59 ch from Paddington*

Although this is now just a section of plain double line, the pond by the trees at SX 963 858 was the reservoir for the four Boulton & Watt engines in the South Devon Railway's atmospheric traction pumping station.

T.21   Twyford

Paddington-Swindon line between Maidenhead and Reading. 31 m 1 ch from Paddington

The GWR's infant main line crept forward to a temporary wooden terminus at Twyford on July 1 1839 and in 1857 it became the junction station for the branch to Henley-on-Thames. Today the latter is served from a double line bay at the country end of the Up Relief Line platform which also has a direct connection to the branch, with a facing crossover at the London end of the station completing the links with the secondary route. The main station buildings, in red brick and housing the ticket office, are on

this Up platform which also has a pagoda-style cycle shed.

The main lines at Twyford are slewed round the central island platform and both this and the Down side platform have simple brick buildings with canopies. The Reading 'locals' give Twyford an hourly service during the main part of the day but this is supplemented at peak times by stops in Oxford/Didcot/Newbury trains.

T.22   Tytherington Branch

Birmingham-Bristol line, branch from Yate. 6 m 24 ch

This was formerly the Midland Railway branch to Thornbury with intermediate stations at Iron Acton and Tytherington. Towards the end of the 1930s the train services were sparse—just three trains each way daily augmented by a fourth on Saturdays and an extra 4.50 pm departure from Thornbury on the second Wednesday in the month—and the passenger facilities were withdrawn in 1944.

Now, the single line is freight only and truncated at Tytherington Quarry. It exists to serve the extensive stone traffic forwarded in trainloads in ARC's privately-owned, high-capacity wagons to terminals in and around the London area. Operation is on the One Train Working system, the Yate Middle ground frame being released from the Bristol panel.

After leaving the junction at Yate the route runs west through Iron Acton, and the open station (1 m 66 ch) and trainmen-operated bypass (2 m 9 ch) level crossings, to pick up the course of the Ladden Brook. After another TMO crossing at Latteridge (2 m 47 ch) and the 224 yd Tytherington Tunnel (5 m 46 ch to 5 m 56 ch), the line terminates west of the bridge under the M5 at 6 m 24 ch. A little further on the remains of Thornbury station stand beside the B4061 road from Alveston.

U.1   Uffington

Paddington-Swindon line between Didcot and Swindon. 66 m 60 ch from Paddington

Uffington still has Up and Down Goods Loops but has been closed to passenger traffic since 1964. Apart from the dock and platform remains there is little trace of the station or of the 3½ m branch to Faringdon for which it was the junction. This was a small private enterprise, opened in 1864, bought out by the GWR for £9,250 in 1886 and closed in 1963. It was not exactly a hectic line, even in the 1930s when two journeys out from Uffington and back sufficed for the morning and then the evening demand.

Umberleigh—see Barnstaple Branch

V.1   Vale of Glamorgan Line

Newport-Fishguard line, from Barry to Bridgend. 18 m 75 ch

The Vale of Glamorgan line is a double track route serving the cement works at Aberthaw and Rhoose, the CEGB power station at Aberthaw and the Ford Motor Company's Engine Plant at Bridgend. In conjunction with the Cardiff-Barry line it is also used regularly as an alternative route to the South Wales main line between Cardiff and Bridgend.

The line originated as part of the grand end-of-century Barry docks project and was intended to bring coal from the Llynfi, Garw and Ogmore valleys to Barry for export. It was built by the Vale of Glamorgan Railway Company which, although its line was always worked by the Barry Railway, retained its independence until absorbed into the GWR in 1922. Opened in 1897, the route lost its passenger services in 1964 when the final intermediate stations were Rhoose, Aberthaw, Gileston, St Athan, Llantwit Major, Llandow (Wick Road) Halt, Llandow Halt and, until 1961, Southerndown Road. Aberthaw power station and its railway connection date from after the Second World War while the branch to the Ford plant at Bridgend opened as recently as 1980.

The route commences at Barry station as a straight continuation of the double track line from Cardiff, the Barry Island branch diverging on the Down side. There is a Down Goods Loop alongside the 'Vale' line as it commences a 2¼ m climb at 1 in 81 and 1 in 87 from just above sea level to the top of the cliffs overlooking

the Bristol Channel. On this climb are the two Porthkerry tunnels, the 543 yd No 1 (52 ch to 77 ch) and the 73 yd No 2 (1 m 73 ch to 1 m 76 ch), with the 18-arch masonry Porthkerry Viaduct in between. One of the piers of the viaduct subsided shortly after the line was opened and for almost two years a temporary diversion line, laid inland, had to be used.

From the summit beyond a deep rock cutting, the line drops at 1 in 165 and 1 in 200 for 3¼ m to beyond Aberthaw. On this section, at Rhoose (3 m 22 ch), the Aberthaw & Bristol Channel Portland Cement Co works and sidings are on the Down side, hard by a level crossing and the former station.

Aberthaw (5 m 3 ch) is the main point on the Vale of Glamorgan line. Immediately before the station, where the Down platform line remains as a loop and the ex-Barry Railway signal box is still in use, the double track line to the power station diverges on the Down side by a junction facing Barry. From here the power station line forms a continuous loop of 4 m via the double track discharge plant for automatic bottom door unloading of slow-moving (½ mph) merry-go-round coal trains. There are also sidings for discharging oil tank cars and others for the loading of periodical movements of pulverised fuel ash.

Beyond Aberthaw station, on the Up side, are the works of the Aberthaw & Bristol Channel Portland Cement Company. Cement is despatched by rail and, conveniently as it can be co-ordinated with the movements to the nearby power station, coal is also brought in by train. The conversion to coal is recent and the discharge facilities were partly paid for by a Welsh Office grant under Section 8 of the Railways Act 1974.

Absolute block working applies between Barry and Aberthaw signal boxes and again on the long section between the latter and Cowbridge Road signal box (18 m 53 ch). On this section the line reaches two summits, one at St Athan and one between Llantwit Major and Llandow. From the latter it descends at 1 in 140 to a crossing of the River Ewenny, via an area of stark limestone cuttings and quarries, and then rises at 1 in 100 towards Bridgend. The line to the Ford Motor Company plant diverges on the Up side, via a junction facing Barry, 1 m before Bridgend. Over the 1¼ m to the entrance to the Ford premises it rises and then falls at 1 in 83 to cross the A48 by means of an open level crossing which can only be used by trains between 21.00 and 07.00 in normal circumstances. There are sidings and run-round facilities within the Ford premises where the line terminates at a un/loading bay within the main plant building.

At the beginning of 1982 there were 22 paths every 24 hours for mgr trains between Aberthaw power station and its supplying collieries and opencast loading sites. The trains themselves consisted of 35 wagons hauled by two Class 37 locomotives, Class 47s with slow speed controls taking over for the circuit through the power station and the wagon discharge plant. Wagons or trains for scheduled maintenance or repair are worked to and from the wagon shops at Barry and the power station also receives a few trains of oil each week.

Cement in 'Presflo' wagons is despatched from Rhoose and Aberthaw to distribution depots in the south and west of England and at Carmarthen. The empty wagons are worked in from Barry, the Down service to Rhoose then taking loaded wagons to Aberthaw cement sidings from which point the loadings of both works are tripped to Barry, Radyr or Severn Tunnel Junction for onward movement on wagonload services. There are occasional block train loads of cement from Aberthaw to specific depots and a few Up main line trains are routed via the Vale of Glamorgan line to drop empty wagons from Carmarthen and take loaded ones forward.

The Ford plant at Bridgend has been serviced by Speedlink since its opening in 1980. The two services each day, Mondays to Fridays, run from Severn Tunnel Junction Yard with wagons of components inwards and then take complete engines away for both UK and Continental destinations.

W.1   Wantage Road

Paddington-Swindon line between Didcot and Swindon. 60 m 22 ch from Paddington

There is a ground frame for the crossovers between Up and Down Main and reversible working sections either side of the former station. The dock and platform faces can still be seen but little remains of the short line which used to bridge the 2½ m gap between the main line station and the town of Wantage.

The standard gauge Wantage Tramway started with a horse drawn tramcar in

1875 and introduced a Grantham Combined Steam Tramcar in the following year. Providing regular connections with the GWR main line trains and carrying substantial amounts of coal, other goods and parcels in its heyday, the line survived until the end of 1945 despite losing its passenger services 20 years earlier. The tramway's veteran England 0-4-0 *Shannon* is preserved at Didcot.

Wargrave—see Henley Branch

W.2   Warminster

Bristol-Portsmouth line between Westbury and Salisbury. 114 m 37 ch from Paddington*

After taking over the Wilts, Somerset & Weymouth Railway the GWR revived its halted construction and pushed forward from Westbury to Frome and also up to the 1 in 70/76 bank to Warminster, reaching the latter on September 9 1851. Another five years of conflict with LSWR interests and of financial stringency passed before local pressures were transformed into legal ones and the GWR was forced to renew its powers for completion to Salisbury and open the remaining 19½ m for traffic.

The arrival of the Army on Salisbury Plain in 1895 boosted traffic on the line and Warminster still enjoys a service of 12 trains each way daily. The main (wooden) buildings are on the Up side with a footbridge leading to the timber shelter and canopy on the Down side. There are two crossovers, a few remaining sidings and two ground frames. Four miles further on, just beyond the old stone building at Heytesbury, lies the Regional Boundary with the SR (118 m 40 ch).

W.3   Wellington

Taunton-Penzance line between Taunton and Tiverton Junction. 170 m 19 ch from Paddington*

Wellington bank involves a climb of some 10 m from just beyond Taunton, through Victory (166 m 4 ch) and Bradford (167 m 55 ch) level crossings, past the site of Poole Siding, through the former Wellington station and then at 1 in 90/86/80 to Whiteball Tunnel. The platforms at Wellington can still be seen, with buildings and signal box on the Up side, and the former goods yard is incorporated in the premises of a firm of

216   RAILWAYS OF THE WESTERN REGION

bed mattress manufacturers. There is a
little used Down Passenger Loop.

W.4   Wenford Branch

*Taunton-Penzance line, branch from
Bodmin Road. 13 m 7 ch*

Bodmin Road station nameboards still
invite the passengers to alight for Bodmin
and Wadebridge but these journeys must
now be made by bus and no longer using
part of the first Cornish line to be worked
by locomotives. The Bodmin & Wadebridge Railway opened to Wenford Bridge
with a branch to Bodmin as early as 1834
and part of its enterprise still survives to
serve the china clay industry at Wenford.

This single line BR freight branch is
now in two sections and under the control
of the signalman at Bodmin Road. The
first section is from that point to Boscarne
Sidings (280 m), made up of the GWR's
1887 branch to Bodmin General (277 m 44
ch) and the following year's link round
the town to join the LSWR recruit at Boscarne Junction. After the junction (where
the mileage changes from 280 m 10 ch to
5 m) there is a further 2 ch to Boscarne
level crossing, operated by the trainmen, a
reversal and then the journey northwards
to Wenford, tortuous, largely unfenced,
limited to 48 ft vehicles and worked
only during daylight. It has intermediate open
crossings at Dunmere (5 m 41 ch), Helland
(8 m 36 ch), Tresarrett (10 m 44 ch) and
Pooleys (11 m 25 ch) with the line terminating at 11 m 68 ch. There is a little agricultural traffic at Bodmin in addition to
the clay trips.

W.5   Westbourne Park

*Paddington-Swindon line between Pad-
dington and Acton. 1 m 20 ch from
Paddington*

From once having eight platform faces,
including a junction vee platform
embracing the Hammersmith & City Line,
and services along the Northolt Line as
well as the main line, Westbourne Park
since the remodelling of 1967 has just
been a single island platform station. The
station is the first out of Paddington and
its long ornamental brick frontage at
street level contrasts with the modest
wooden buildings on the platform,
standing below in the shadow of the
motorway as it crosses the main line. The
London Transport station is on the south
side of the WR route.

W.6   Westbury

*Reading-Taunton line and junction with
Bristol-Weymouth/Portsmouth lines. 109
m 64 ch from Paddington**

A market centre before the advent of the
railway and at one period a mining area
on a modest scale, Westbury has been
something of a railway town since it
became a junction in the 1850s. Although
still a junction between the West of
England main line and the route from
Bristol and Bath and on to Weymouth
and Southampton, Westbury's main
activity nowadays is in connection with
the heavy movements of aggregate traffic

Westbury station looking west.

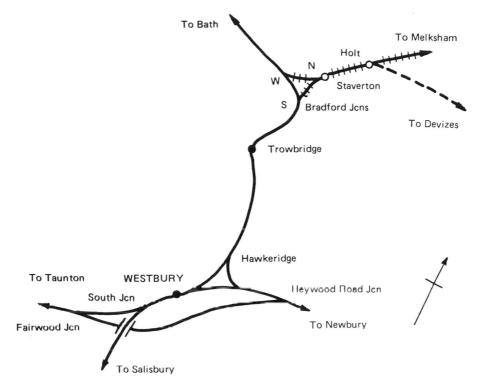

flowing from the Mendip limestone quarries.

Westbury acts as a staging point for the block train loads of aggregates heading east, providing motive power and crews and marshalling the returning empty wagons. Extensive siding accommodation exists at the country end of the complex for this purpose and Westbury has an allocation of Class 08 shunters. Further traffic originates from the Blue Circle cement works whose siding connects with the main line near milepost 92½ under the gaze of the Westbury White Horse which looks down from Westbury Hill to the south.

The railway came to Westbury from Thingley Junction in 1848 and probed forward to Frome in 1850 and Warminster in 1851. The milepost distances on to Castle Cary are still those from Paddington via the original route for the West of England main line was the late comer on the scene, only arriving from Lavington at the turn of the century. The station dates from this period and its two long island platforms serve the Down Salisbury/Down Main and Up Salisbury/Up Main in that order (from the south), access from the

separate ticket office at road level being by subway. All buildings are in red brick and there is a privately-owned refreshment room on the Down side.

Pending the introduction of the latest MAS scheme, North Signal Box controls the junction with the London line at one end of the station and South the junction towards Salisbury at the other. Hawkeridge, normally switched out, stands in the triangle formed by the Bristol-London line connection, while smaller wooden boxes at Heywood Road Junction (94 m 48 ch) and Fairwood Junction (111 m 16 ch) mark the two ends of the 2¼ m avoiding line which came into use at the beginning of 1933. This led to the Westbury slip coaches being detached at the former and brought into the platform by the station pilot.

There is a variety of buildings at Westbury, including those for the Area Manager and locomotive crews and the West of England Division training school. There is also much locomotive activity, locomotives being stabled here although allocated to Bath Road depot. Most trains on the north-south routes and some on the main line call at Westbury.

W.7   West Drayton

Paddington-Swindon line between Southall and Slough. 13 m 17 ch from Paddington

On the original GWR line West Drayton was one of the first stations and, for a time, had both an engine house and coke ovens. It was the scene of some early engine trials after *Premier* and *Vulcan* had arrived in 1837 following a sea and canal journey from Liverpool. The station became a junction on September 8 1856 with the opening of the line to Uxbridge Vine Street, closed in 1964, the branch to Staines West following in 1884-5.

The station today serves the WR's London commuter traffic and consists of the conventional centre island plus Up Relief and Down Main platforms, the former provided with waiting facilities and canopy. There are crossovers at the London end and two ground frames at the country end where the coal concentration depot lies in the loop formed by the truncated Staines branch which leaves West Drayton on the Up side and then turns to pass beneath the main line on its way to Colnbrook. There is a short section of Up Goods Line towards Iver and reverse curves where the Relief lines pass through the station.

W.8   West Ealing

Paddington-Swindon line between Acton and Southall. 6 m 41 ch from Paddington

West Ealing got its first station, called Castle Hill until 1899, in 1871. Today it is essentially a simple London suburban station with staggered Relief line platforms and reached from the severe station building at street level. It is also the point at which the Greenford branch diverges (6 m 56 ch). Between the station and the junction lies the once busy milk dock, and between the junction and the West Ealing Loop leg of the triangle the Engineer's Siding ground frame (6 m 53 ch) which gives access to three Up Refuge Sidings. The track maintenance machine firm Plasser & Theurer has a depot within the triangle.

W.9   Westerleigh Junction

Swindon-Newport line, junction with Birmingham-Bristol line. 107 m 12 ch from Paddington (121 m 26 ch from Derby)

This junction north-west of Bristol played a part in the GWR : MR rivalries. The direct GWR curve to the MR route was built in substitution for a proposal for a separate line to reach the Severn & Wye and the Midland went to court to confine the use of the junction to trains to and from the S&W via Berkeley Road. It lost and the GWR gained a new route to Birmingham via Gloucester and Honeybourne.

Now the direct Midland route into Bristol has been truncated, with the stub used for civil engineering department training, and trains run via the GWR Filton Junction route. The east loop at Westerleigh is long closed and steadily disappearing but the MR route beneath the GWR viaduct and the former GWR flyover for northbound traffic is still clear.

W.10   Western Valleys

Newport-Fishguard line, route to Ebbw Vale plus Rose Heyworth and Oakdale branches. 18 m 53 ch to Ebbw Vale and 17 m 30 ch to Rose Heyworth (from Newport) and 7 m 78 ch branch to Oakdale

Western Valleys is the name applied to the valleys of the River Ebbw and its tributaries, the waters of which flow into the Severn Estuary on the western side of Newport. Today the Western Valleys rail network comprises a line down the main Ebbw (Ebbw Fawr) valley from Ebbw Vale (Waunllwyd Sidings) to the main line at Newport and joining this lines down the Ebbw Fach valley at Aberbeeg and across from the Sirhowy Valley at Risca. The function of the lines is to serve collieries producing, mainly, coking coal for the steel industry: the Ebbw Vale line also serving the BSC tinplate and coating complex there.

The lines owe their origins to tramroads and canals from the early days of iron making and before the development of coal extraction demanded proper rail communication. The Ebbw Fawr and Fach lines were developed by the Monmouthshire Company which had so much influence on the areas around Newport. It was incorporated way back in 1792 and was amalgamated with the GWR in 1880.

The main line is that from Ebbw Vale (Waunllwyd) to Newport Gaer Junction, with the Cardiff Curve providing a link westwards between Park Junction and Ebbw Junction at the Newport end. In 1981 the route was reduced to single track except for the central section between Lime Kiln Sidings (6 m 15 ch) and

Aberbeeg Junction (14 m 22 ch) which remains double track.

The top end of the main line is now just beyond Waunllwyd sidings (17 m 75 ch) which are on the Up side. Here traffic is exchanged with the BSC and there is a junction with the BSC's own rail network serving the tinplate works. The main movement is that of steel coil made at Llanwern and conveyed to Ebbw Vale for coating, with up to five trains every 24 hours and made up of 100-ton gross bogie steel carrying wagons. Two other services link Ebbw Vale daily with Severn Tunnel Junction yard and take such forwardings as tinplate for attaching to Speedlink services or conveyance in ferry wagons to the Continent.

The former station of Cwm lay near Marine colliery and while the latter has not been closed, its intake of coal from Six Bells for washing has been lost to rail as a result of the two locations being linked underground.

The section from the end of the line to the junction at Aberbeeg is operated on the No Signalman Token system and is steeply graded. The gradient falls towards Newport, most stretches being steeper than 1 in 100 and the ruling gradient being 1 in 55. Aberbeeg itself used to be an important traffic centre with a station, yard and locomotive depot. Now it consists of the sizeable GWR gabled brick and timber signal box with colour light signals controlling the junction between the Waunllwyd and Rose Heyworth lines and a Down Goods Loop below the junction. Lying deep in the valleys of the Ebbw Fach and Fawr rivers as they join, Aberbeeg is dominated on the east, Down side by the hillside and substantial retaining walls supporting the main road along it.

On the long double track section south to Lime Kiln Sidings signal box (6 m 15 ch) there were formerly stations at Llanhilleth, Crumlin (Low Level), Newbridge, Celynen South Halt, Abercarn, Cwmcarn and Cross Keys. High on each side of the valley at Crumlin can be seen the stone abutments of the vast 1,658 ft long and 208 ft high iron and steel Crumlin Viaduct which from 1857 to 1964 carried the Pontypool Road-Neath line across the valley. A steep, 1 in 42, line used to link this with the Western Valley line permitting through running between Aberbeeg and Pontypool Road.

Below Crumlin is Celynen South colliery with rail connections (9 m 45 ch and 10 m 6 ch) on the Down side. It is served by a daily train bringing empty wagons from East Usk Yard and conveying loaded ones to BSC Llanwern or Severn Tunnel Junction. The Abercarn Tin Plate Works sidings nearby (9 m 30 ch) are currently out of use.

Lime Kiln Sidings signal box is on the Up side of the line. Its colour light and semaphore signals control a level crossing, the junction (facing Newport) with the line from the Sirhowy valley and the commencement of the long section of single line to Park Junction (1 m 2 ch). On this section there used to be stations at Risca (junction with the old, predominantly LNWR route from Nantybwch, Tredegar and the Sirhowy valley via Nine Mile Point), Tynycwm Halt, Rogerstone and Bassaleg Junction. Below Risca the traffic once warranted quadruple track.

For 1¼ m in the Rogerstone area the Western Valleys line follows a new alignment, financed by the Gwent County Council and opened in November 1981 to enable a new by-pass road and interchange to occupy the former course of the line and the site of Rogerstone marshalling yard. At the northern end of the diversion a rail connection to Rogerstone power station has been perpetuated and at the southern end, built into the brickwork of a new bridge, are 'betrothal bricks' recording the marriage of the Prince of Wales and Lady Diana Spencer in the year that the bridge was completed. From Bassaleg Junction (2 m 5 ch) the single track from Bedwas runs alongside the Western Valleys line, on the Up side, to join at Park Junction by a connection facing Newport. Until 1923 the railway between Bassaleg and Park Junction was the property of Lord Tredegar's estate and earned substantial tolls from the enormous coal traffic carried.

A passing loop precedes the junction and Park Junction signal box where the single line on to Gaer Junction passes through the 403 yd Gaer Tunnel (159 m 47 ch to 159 m 65 ch). The main route of the former Monmouthshire Railway, until it was taken up in 1981, went between the two links to the main line and on to Courtybella Junction and, eventually, Newport Dock Street. At one time the tracks of the independent Alexandra (Newport & South Wales) Dock & Railway Company ran from south of the line at Park Junction over the main line and into the same company's Newport docks.

Throughout from Aberbeeg gradients

Locomotive 37 185 takes eight 100-tonne bogie steel carrying wagons to Ebbw Vale over the new line diversion at Rogerstone.

are falling towards Newport in the 1 in 100 to 1 in 200 range although minor changes have occurred as a result of mining subsidence around Aberbeeg itself.

Turning now to the Ebbw Fach route, this single track now starts just above the Abertillery New Mine and then falls at gradients between 1 in 48 and 1 in 96 to the junction at Aberbeeg. At the top of the line there is a run-round and loop, together with a loading 'pad' from which coal is loaded to trains standing on the single line. In BR terms this point is still known as 'Rose Heyworth' after one of the collieries now embraced in the Abertillery New Mine complex. Two trains are scheduled each day, Monday to Friday, to bring empties in and then take coking coal to Llanwern or Port Talbot.

On the way to Aberbeeg the line passes through the, still traceable, site of Abertillery station and through Six Bells Halt. Six Bells colliery, alongside the line, has been linked below ground with Marine colliery in the Ebbw Fawr. The line originally ran through from Brynmawr (on the LNWR/LMS Merthyr-Abergavenny line) and until passenger services ceased in the Ebbw valleys in 1962 there were stations between Brynmawr and Abertillery at Nantyglo, Blaine and Bourneville Halt.

Brynmawr-Nantyglo was a joint LNWR/GWR line dating only from 1906 but replacing an earlier private railway.

The third line making up the Western Valleys group originates at Oakdale colliery in the Sirhowy valley and joins the main Western Valleys line at Lime Kiln Sidings signal box. Although it starts in the Sirhowy valley, after 2 m it strikes eastwards across the inter-valley ridge to the Ebbw valley and then gradually descends on its western side. It then crosses the Western Valley line, the river and the main road by a masonry and steel viaduct before joining the former on the Down, east side at Lime Kiln Sidings by a junction facing Newport.

At the colliery itself the line is double track and there is a modern overhead bunker rapid-loading installation for forwarding the output not only of the Oakdale pit but also of the Celynen North and Markham collieries which are all linked underground. Until 1979 coal was moved by rail from Markham, further up the Sirhowy valley, for washing at Oakdale but this is no longer necessary and the 2½ m of line involved have been closed. In addition to the trainload movements to the BSC at Llanwern and Port Talbot, one of the four trains scheduled daily is a 28-wagon mgr service taking coking coal to BSC Scunthorpe.

The gradients, falling from Oakdale, are easier than 1 in 100 for the first 2¼ m to Penar Junction (4 m 67 ch) where the line used to connect with and cross the Neath-Pontypool Road line. They then steepen to 1 in 86 or stiffer, with a 1 in 30 section approaching Lime Kiln Sidings signal box. Just below Penar Junction is the 239 yd Penar Tunnel (4 m 42 ch to 4 m 53 ch). Above it the line was double track until 1981 but is now single throughout and worked as one section using the Train Staff and Ticket system.

The present Oakdale line is built on the course of Halls Tramroad which was built in 1805 and leased by the GWR in 1877. Conversion to a normal railway took place north of Penar Junction in 1886 but the lower section was not converted until 1912. For three years from 1967 to 1970 the section below Penar Junction was closed, traffic passing via the LNWR route to Risca, but then the position was reversed. The line's only passenger service was one of trains from the Pontypool Road line via Penar Junction to Penmaen and Oakdale stations. This ceased in 1939 but a platform remains visible at Penmaen.

There is a change of mileage from 6 m 48 ch to zero just beyond the junction at Lime Kiln Sidings.

Weston Milton—see Weston-super-Mare

W.11 Weston-super-Mare

Bristol-Taunton line between Bristol and Bridgwater. 137 m 33 ch from Paddington

The flat Bristol & Exeter Railway route south from Bristol was not encouraged by the growing and fashionable resort at Weston-super-Mare and the railway passed it by slightly inland. A branch was provided from Weston Junction to a station where the floral clock is now located and worked by trains made up of four-wheeled carriages hauled by three horses harnessed in tandem. Locomotives took over from April 1 1851 and a new station was built on what is now the goods yard site in 1866. This in turn closed when the branch from the main line was converted into a loop and the present station brought into use in 1884.

Weston is approached via the CCTV crossing at Huish (132 m 11 ch), the Puxton & Worle crossing (133 m 79 ch) marking the remains of the former station there, Worle Junction (135 m 11 ch) where the loop diverges as a single line and Weston Milton (136 m 12 ch) serving the inland edge of the seaside resort. The

main station has two platforms provided with bi-directional lines to allow it to operate not only as a passing point but as a point at which some of the London and local dmu services originate or terminate. The main buildings, in attractive grey stone, are on the Up side and include the ticket office and travel centre and the supervisors' office with its subsidiary 'slave' signalling panel. This can be switched in to allow the loop to function in the event of equipment failure. The bay at the London end of the platform is little used, as is the goods yard. The latter still contains the signal box used at the time of the second station and nearby, but now converted to a coach park, is the site of the former Locking Road excursion station which catered for Weston's summer influx of trippers. There are a few sidings in this area, the one leading in the direction of the gasworks approximating to the route of the original branch.

The Weston loop rejoins the main line at Uphill Junction (139 m 5 ch—138 m 4 ch on the avoiding/direct line).

Whatley Quarry Branch—see Radstock Branch

W.12 Whimple

Waterloo-Exeter line between Honiton and Exeter. 163 m 2 ch from Waterloo

On the single line section approaching Exeter Central, Whimple still has both platforms with a shelter on the Down side and the main buildings, including the SR-style brick goods sheds, on the Up. The use of this by Showerings maintains a link with Whimple's past as a cider traffic station.

Whitchurch—see Coryton Branch

W.13 Whiteball

*Taunton-Penzance line between Taunton and Tiverton Junction. 173 m 13 ch from Paddington**

The 1,092 yd tunnel (173 m 13 ch to 173 m 63 ch), on the last 1 in 127 stretch to Whiteball summit, marks the boundary between Somerset and Devon. Beyond the tunnel are the Down Refuge Siding and Down Goods Loop and the small signal box (174 m). Once many a country signal box was supplied with its coal and water by train—sometimes officially, sometimes otherwise—and Whiteball is a surviving example, receiving its water by means of an early morning freight service.

Whiteball Tunnel, thickly lined with bricks, used to have a noise reputation blamed upon underground streams.

W.14   Whitland

Newport-Fishguard   line   between Carmarthen and Fishguard. 258 m 68 ch from Paddington*

This small market town on the River Taf, junction for the line to Tenby and Pembroke Dock, was reached by the South Wales Railway in 1854 with the opening of its Carmarthen-Haverford-west section. The Pembroke Dock line made Whitland a junction from 1866 and from 1873 to 1963 it was the transfer point for the Crymmych Arms and Cardigan branch which diverged from the main line 2¼ m to the west.

The approach to Whitland from Carmarthen is via the CCTV level crossing at St Clears (253 m 18 ch), a sweeping curve towards the 187 yd Whitland Tunnel (257 m 1 ch to 257 m 10 ch), two bridges over the meandering Taf and then the Unigate milk depot siding trailing into the Up line. The station itself is a post-war structure of brick and glass with long, flat steel verandahs and dating from 1958. The platforms flanking the double track main line each have a bay at the country end, the one on the Down side being used by trains on the Pembroke Dock line, that on the Up side formerly serving the Cardigan branch. The modern timber-framed, flat-roofed signal box at the London end controls the barrier crossing there and all movements in the area, with colour light signals for the main line and semaphore signals for the branch. There are calling on facilities from the main line and branch into the Up platform to enable portions of dmu trains to be joined. Alongside the face of the former Cardigan branch platform is the run-round and shunting neck for a group of engineer's sidings and opposite, in the area of the old steam locomotive depot, are freight and coal sidings.

Whitland is served by trains to and from Milford Haven and Pembroke Dock, some of the latter originating and terminating at Whitland. Most trains to and from Fishguard also call and a weekly freight service is scheduled from Carmarthen Junction to Whitland and back.

W.15   Wickwar

Birmingham-Bristol line between Glou-cester and Westerleigh Junction. 115 m 28 ch from Derby

The 1,401 yd Wickwar Tunnel (115 m 28 ch to 116 m 12 ch) lies on a 5 m down gradient of 1 in 281 northbound between the former Rangeworthy and Charfield boxes. The site of the former station, closed in 1965, lies north of the tunnel and is now marked only by the old platforms and the remains of the goods yard.

W.16   Windsor Branch

Paddington-Swindon line, branch from Slough. 2 m 63 ch

The Great Western was the first to arrive at Windsor, the branch from Slough being opened on October 8 1849 after the passage of the authorising Act in the previous year. The battle to get to Windsor—with the college, castle and London & South Western Railway—had been quite dramatic and the GWR's Act contained quite onerous provisions connected with the Thames waterway and for protecting Eton's privacy. The latter included screening the bathing place, access for recovering wayward scholars and policing of the line.

The branch route is on a raised embankment throughout, the original wooden approach to the 202 ft span bridge over the Thames being later reconstructed in brick. The double track route was of mixed gauge from 1862 to 1883 when the broad gauge disappeared and Slough and Windsor stations were rebuilt. The West (or Queen's) Curve at the Slough end has gone and, apart from a short section after leaving No 1 platform there, the route is now single throughout. It is controlled from the panel box at Slough.

The single track of the branch line runs into the remaining long Down platform at Windsor (21 m 19 ch), still officially Windsor & Eton Central to distinguish it from the SR's Windsor & Eton Riverside, past the ramp down to the former goods yard and terminating opposite the period refreshment room. At an angle to the end of the line are the main offices, including the rounded ticket office and its ticket hall filled with dark panelled woodwork and dull green marble. Towards the town and castle are GWR entrance gates and the clock, date (1897) and GWR coat of arms at the end of the substantial canopy. In the opposite direction stands the Royal

Above *The royal waiting rooms and great arcade at Windsor station in 1981.*

Right *The clock and GWR coat of arms surmounting the approach to Windsor station.*

Waiting Room with its coats of arms and the dates 1897 and 1907. In 1981 this was still being used by a wholesale newsagent but an agreement with Madame Tussaud's Ltd then provided for the area, including the Jubilee glass canopy, to become part of a new 'Royalty and Railways' exhibition including a full size royal train replica.

A dmu service on the branch gives it an excellent service of some 40 trains each way daily, 30 on Sundays.

W.17 Witham

Reading-Taunton line between Westbury and Castle Cary. 120 m 76 ch from Paddington*

Once the junction for the East Somerset Railway to Wells and the Cheddar Valley line on to Yatton, Witham remains important despite the loss of its passenger trains on October 3 1966. The old ESR remains open as far as Cranmore and the junction and its adjacent holding sidings are now part of the facilities for servicing the extensive limestone traffic emanating from the Merehead Stone Terminal. The branch junction is on the Up side where

there is also an Up Refuge Siding and
further sidings lie on either side of the
Down side signal box.

W.18   Woodborough

*Reading-Taunton line between Hunger-
ford and Westbury. 78 m 72 ch from
Paddington*

Up and Down Goods Loops are still in use
here but little of significance remains of
the former station.

W.19   Woofferton

*Shrewsbury-Newport line between Craven
Arms and Hereford. 32 m 2 ch from
Shrewsbury*

Until 1961 trains from Tenbury Wells had
been running over their 5¼ m railway to
join the main line at Woofferton Junction
for just 100 years. Woofferton station lay
south of the junction and its brick
buildings and goods shed survive there.
Today there is still a signal box on the
Down side with a Down Refuge Siding
and an Up Goods Loop immediately
north thereof.

W.20   Wootton Bassett Junction

*Swindon-Bristol/Newport lines just west
of Swindon. 83 m 7 ch from Paddington*

Here the routes to South Wales via
Badminton and to Bristol via Box divide
and a Foster Yeoman aggregate terminal
is located on the Down side. There is an
Up Goods Loop by-passing the physical
junction from the South Wales direction
and London side of this is the former
station, with an old dock and remains of
the platform from which workmen's
trains once carried the artisans to
Swindon Works. The original GWR
temporary terminus at Wootton Bassett
Road was 2¾ m nearer Swindon.

W.21   Worcester

*Oxford-Hereford line. 120 m 31 ch from
Paddington*

Worcester's railway origins derive from
the Oxford, Worcester & Wolverhampton
Railway, a line conceived with GWR
support as a trunk route from the West
Midlands to London but one which ran
into trouble early from the financial
difficulties of 1846 and from misunder-
standings with its sponsor. The first, short
line was not opened until 1850 when the
link was made between Abbotswood (then

Abbots Wood) Junction and Worcester,
the section to Droitwich and Stoke Prior
following in 1852. By the following year
Worcester was linked to Oxford, with the
line west to Hereford being built in stages
between 1859 and 1861.

For many years Worcester was a major
junction between the Bristol/Birmingham
and Oxford/Hereford line services, with
the trains of the 1930s running on via
Kidderminster to Wolverhampton and via
Hereford to South Wales. Now the north-
south services do not use the Worcester
loop and the town derives its train services
from the Paddington-Oxford-Hereford
line, the dmu service from Swindon via
Cheltenham and the local workings to and
from Birmingham via Kidderminster or
Bromsgrove.

Two stations still serve Worcester,
those at Boughton Halt, Henwick and
Rushwick Halt on the Hereford line,
Fernhill Heath on the Droitwich line and
Norton Halt at the junction of the
Evesham and Cheltenham lines having
closed some time ago. Shrub Hill is the
main station and administrative centre
and stands on the loop from Norton
Junction and on to Droitwich. Once joint
GWR and LMS it has Up and Down
Platform lines (the latter bi-directional)
with a centre siding between the two. The
north end bay is now filled in but the bay
at the other end remains in use for letter
mail traffic. The other station is Foregate
Street where the platforms are raised
above the town's main street ready for the
line's crossing of the River Severn.
Although now fairly functional, the
station once had refreshment rooms one
of which, on the Up side, had a
'suspended' cellar; its original lift system
was also interesting in that it used the
water balance principle now mainly
confined to cliff railways. There is a travel
centre at Foregate Street.

From the east the approach to
Worcester is via Norton Junction (117 m
26 ch) where the lines from Oxford, and
from Cheltenham via Abbotswood
Junction, meet. The signal box here
controls the junction and the section
towards the Shrub Hill Station box (120 m
31 ch). The Metal Box private siding and
the former LMS and GWR goods yard
and their buildings lie on this side of the
station which is followed by Shrub Hill
Junction (120 m 46 ch) where a single line
veers off to the Down platform at
Foregate Street (121 m 12 ch) and on to
Henwick (121 m 65 ch) where the signal

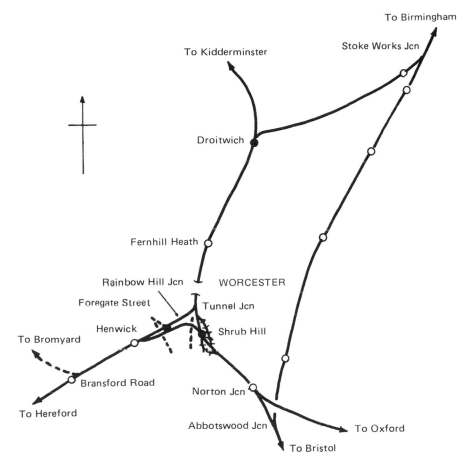

To Birmingham

Stoke Works Jcn

To Kidderminster

Droitwich

Fernhill Heath

Rainbow Hill Jcn   WORCESTER

Foregate Street   Tunnel Jcn

Henwick   Shrub Hill

To Bromyard

Bransford Road

To Hereford   Norton Jcn

Abbotswood Jcn   To Oxford

To Bristol

box controls the level crossing, access to the Up Refuge Siding and where the Acceptance Lever single line becomes double again. The main Worcester loop continues ahead from Shrub Hill Junction to the next signal box at Worcester Tunnel Junction (120 m 72 ch) where the single line from Foregate Street towards Droitwich joins. Then comes the 212 yd Rainbow Hill Tunnel (120 m 79 ch to 121 m 9 ch). To the east of the line approaching the tunnel are the sites of the former GWR sheet works and carriage works and, opposite, of the former locomotive depot, now just a stabling point without fuelling facilities.

Worcester has some attractive buildings and interesting features, including some decorative ironwork and tiling on Shrub Hill station. It also has a wide variety of signalling systems—absolute block, track circuit block, acceptance lever and some permissive working in the yard. It once

had a large collection of private sidings, among which was that of Hill Evans & Co and known as 'The Vinegar Works Branch'. This 900 yd Lowesmoor Tramway, opened in 1872, was worked by GWR 19XX 0-6-0PTs and used standard semaphore signals to control road traffic. The connection with the main line was near the locomotive shed and its course ran by the Great Western Hotel at the approach to Shrub Hill station.

W.22 Wrangaton

Taunton-Penzance line between Totnes and Plymouth. 231 m 58 ch from Paddington*

Completely closed since 1963, Wrangaton station was at the summit of the section between Totnes and Plymouth. There is a short, 69 yd tunnel (231 m 58 ch to 231 m 61 ch) and the Monksmoor Government Depot still has a rusting siding controlled by the ground frame (232 m 2 ch). Also on the Up side a small stone station building remains and the closed signal box can be seen at the country end of the Down platform. There were some adjustments in alignment when the original South Devon line was doubled and a previous alignment is visible on the Up side at the country end of the station area.

W.23 Wye Valley Branch

Gloucester-Newport line, branch from Wye Valley Junction. 2 m 60 ch

This single track branch is the surviving stub of the 1876 Chepstow to Monmouth line, originated as the Wye Valley Railway but worked by the GWR from opening until amalgamation in 1905. Today it runs to the quarries of T.S. Thomas & Sons (Lydney) Ltd at Tidenham and Walton Goody (Tintern) Ltd at Tintern but is out of use beyond Tidenham.

The passenger service on this highly scenic route ended in 1959 but Gwent County Council have captured some of its atmosphere at the centre established in the old station at Tintern. From the junction on the Gloucestershire side of the river at Chepstow the surviving line starts with a short gentle rise immediately after the site of Tutshill Halt at the junction. It then steepens to 1 in 66 to cross the A48 road and arrive at the site of Tidenham Halt where an overhead gantry now loads the railway limestone ballast from the quarry. After the run-round loop there are now stop blocks across the line although it is still intact as far as the run-round and sidings at Tintern Quarry. This section includes the 1,188 yd Tidenham Tunnel from a summit in which the route drops at 1 in 100 to Tintern.

The service on the branch is provided by two trips daily, Mondays to Fridays, from Severn Tunnel Junction. Empties are conveyed on the outward trip and loaded ballast wagons on the return, the ballast trains ultimately going forward from Severn Tunnel Junction to the sites stipulated by the WR Civil Engineer. The line is operated on the One Train Working system.

Y.1 Yate

Birmingham-Bristol line between Gloucester and Westerleigh Junction. 119 m 47 ch from Derby

Once a busy station and goods yard with signal boxes at Yate South Junction and Yate Main Line Junction, this former MR junction lost its branch passenger trains to Thornbury in 1944 and its main line stopping trains in 1965, freight facilities going one year later. Now its main significance is as the junction for the Tytherington branch which lies on the Up side, north of the road which divides the station site. South of the road bridge and on the Down side are the old red brick shed, an attractive building with a pleasant design and stone facings, and the gabled station house of warm stone.

The single line to Tytherington, used by ARC stone trains, leaves the main line at Yate Middle (119 m 54 ch). There are three ground frames, crossovers and a bi-directional Up line.

Y.2 Yatton

Bristol-Taunton line between Bristol and Weston-super-Mare. 130 m 28 ch from Paddington

Yatton was one of the original Bristol & Exeter Railway stations and carried the name Clevedon Road until the branch to the coast at Clevedon opened in 1847. The Cheddar Valley line heading inland was opened to Cheddar in 1869 and on to Wells in 1876. This came to carry through services to Witham and also had its own branch from Congresbury to Blagdon (the Wrington Vale Light Railway).

The present station still uses the single storey B&E stone buildings on each of the platforms and is still an important railhead despite the closure of its branches. Substantial numbers of Bristol commuters use Yatton which is served by local dmus and by some longer distance trains.

There are still traces of Yatton's junction facilities and, although the days of slip coaches and track quadrupling plans have gone, the station retains 80-wagon Up and Down Goods Loops at the country end. The old coal yard and loco area can be seen at this end of the station.

Yeoford—see Barnstaple Branch

Y.3 Yeovil

Yeovil Junction is on the Waterloo-Exeter line 122 m 48 ch from Waterloo and Yeovil Pen Mill on the Westbury-Weymouth line 141 m 22 ch from Paddington*

Yeovil benefited in terms of its railway facilities from lying in an area bitterly contested by Great Western and London & South Western Railway interests.

Above *Yatton station, with cars standing where the Clevedon branch trains once stood.*
Below *A Class 50 waits to leave Yeovil Junction with its Waterloo-Exeter train.*

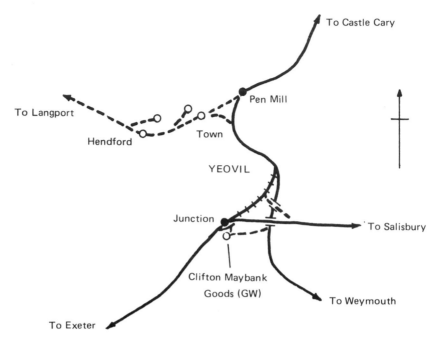

The first arrival, on October 1 1853, was the Bristol & Exeter branch from Durston, then east to a terminus at Hendford. More broad gauge metals appeared when the Wilts, Somerset & Weymouth line arrived at Pen Mill from Frome on September 1 1856, the extension on to Dorchester and the link through the town to Hendford following a few months later. In 1860 came the L&SW in the guise of the Salisbury & Exeter which laid a narrow gauge line into Hendford until a new, shared Town station was opened just one year after the first narrow gauge train had reached Yeovil on June 1 1860. Meanwhile the main line had been extended to Exeter to contribute the station at Yeovil Junction to the town's railway facilities. A curve led from Yeovil Junction to Pen Mill and Town stations, with a second connection from the GWR goods transfer point at Clifton Maybank (adjacent to Junction station but on the Down side) under the L&SW line to the Pen Mill one.

Former railway buildings still exist at Hendford but little remains at the Town station site to recall the era of trains to Seaton and Exeter, trains from Pen Mill via Town to Paignton and Penzance, and other trains constituting the shuttle service up to Junction. The area is now Old Town Station Car Park but has some reminders of the past in adjacent street names like Old Station Road and South Western Terrace, and a fading legend across the street which reads 'Refreshment Rooms. Horses to Let or Hire'. A railway bridge is still there, and the route to Pen Mill is now a pleasant walkway.

Although the former L&SW main line has been partially singled, the Class 50 motive power used on the route gives a 2½-hour timing from Yeovil Junction to Waterloo. The trains use the two faces of the Up platform, the Down platform retaining its buildings and canopy but now being used as offices in connection with the engineer's tip on the Up side and the sleeper depot on the Down. Pen Mill is also a single line passing point using two platforms with a single line between them and a second line round the outer face of the Down island. At Junction the ticket office is on the platform itself and the adjacent privately-run buffet offers secondhand books and floral tile surroundings as well as home cooking. The single storey building at Pen Mill is unimposing although there is an interesting stone portion at the south end. The Down semaphore starting signal still has its ancient route indicator.

The Pen Mill lines and sidings diminish to a single line on leaving the station southbound and then divide into parallel

Weymouth and Junction lines. The curves to and from Town station can still be seen on the Up side as well as the links, opposite, to the Salisbury line in the Up direction and to Clifton Maybank. The 1 m 42 ch link between the two stations is electric token worked and signal boxes remain at both.

Y.4 Yetminster

Westbury-Weymouth line between Yeovil Pen Mill and Dorchester West. 145 m 46 ch from Paddington*

Only the Up platform is now in use although the Down one still exists. The brick station building is out of use and a shelter has been provided instead.

Y.5 Ynysybwl Branch

Merthyr-Cardiff line, branch from Storms-town Junction. 1 m 41 ch

This single track freight only line ascends the Nant Clydach valley, mostly at 1 in 40 to 1 in 60, to serve the NCB's Lady Windsor colliery. The junction at Storms-town faces north, operation is on the One Train Working system and at the end of the line there is a loop and the connection with the NCB colliery lines.

Each day, Mondays to Fridays, three trains are scheduled to bring in empties from Radyr yard and take away coal from Lady Windsor, and from Abercynon colliery with which it is linked underground, either to the Phurnacite plant at Abercwmboi or other destinations. Because of the gradient, inwards trains may need to be split at Stormstown sidings with the train locomotive returning for a second trip on the branch.

This line originated as the Ynysybwl branch of the Taff Vale Railway, opened for freight in 1886 and for passengers four years later. In 1900 a triangular junction was completed with the Pontypridd-Abercynon line, by Ynysybwl South Curve, and passenger services then ran mainly from Pontypridd to serve stations going up the valley at Clydach Court Halt, Ynysybwl New Road Halt, Robertstown Halt, Ynysybwl and Old Ynysybwl Halt. Passenger trains ceased in 1952.

The route originally extended to collieries beyond Ynysybwl but the present end of the line is below the Ynysybwl station and halts and the spur for through running from or to Pontypridd has been removed.

Ystrad Mynach—see Rhymney Branch

Ystrad Rhondda—see Treherbert Branch

SECTION 4

Route summaries

Paddington-Swindon-Bristol (Temple Meads)-Taunton

The original main line of the Great Western Railway was authorised by Acts of Parliament passed in 1835 and 1837. The first section, between Paddington and a station east of the Thames at Maidenhead, was opened on June 4 1838 and the last gap in the route to Bristol was closed three years later on June 30 1841. A few days earlier the associated Bristol & Exeter Railway had reached Weston-super-Mare and Bridgwater, with opening to Taunton following on July 1 1842 and through to Exeter on May 1 1844.

Today the Western Region main line, after leaving Brunel's station at Paddington and the magnificent bridges which follow, heads for Old Oak Common where the complex of HST shed, diesel maintenance depot and carriage servicing facilities is followed by the junction with the Wycombe line and Acton marshalling yard. The busy main line with its crossovers and the junctions to cross-London routes is controlled by the panel box at Old Oak Common. Multi-track so far, beyond the Ealing Broadway interchange point with London Transport and the Greenford branch there are two pairs of

5022 Wigmore Castle *approaches Paddington with a long train in December 1936 (Paddington-Swindon).*

running lines, Main and Relief, and these continue all the way to Didcot.

An 1838 Brunel viaduct carries the route over the Brent valley at Hanwell as the Inter-City 125 sets accelerate to their line speed of 125 mph and the three-car suburban dmu sets serve the suburban stations from the Relief lines. The freight branch to Brentford then departs behind the dmu maintenance depot at Southall and the Colnbrook branch behind the coal concentration depot at West Drayton. On through Slough for Windsor, Maidenhead for Marlow and Twyford for Henley-on-Thames the line passes through Sonning Cutting to the important interchange station at Reading, junction for the SR and where the West of England route parts with the main line.

Still nearly level, the line now follows the course of the Thames Valley, crossing the river twice before the two part company just before Cholsey and the now closed freight line to Wallingford. The four lines become two after Didcot, junction for the Oxford route and formerly for the Didcot, Newbury & Southampton Railway, home of the Great Western Society and of a huge power station. This is Vale of White Horse country with a view, south, of the Uffington White Horse to prove it. The gradient steepens slightly but this is no more noticeable than the remains of the old Wantage Tramway or the branch to Faringdon.

Although much reduced in size Swindon Works still dominates the railway complex and the remains of the Highworth branch and the Midland & South Western Junction lines are hard to spot. Although the station buildings are original, passengers changing for the Gloucester line can forget about the notorious catering concession Brunel so much disliked and enjoy the modern Travellers-Fare buffet.

At Wootton Bassett Junction the original main line parts company with the later, direct route to South Wales and drops down the short 1 in 100 bank to Dauntsey, the first junction for Malmesbury. Beyond Chippenham and Thingley Junction, where the diversionary route via Melksham veers off, another 1 in 100 drop through the oolite ridge is achieved by courtesy of Box Tunnel and then Bathampton Junction with the line along the Avon valley

A scene from the era of the Blue Pullmans (Swindon-Bristol).

heralds the approach to Bath. By inspired design the railway here harmonises well with its surroundings. Ornamented tunnels, a view of the old Midland line north across the river, and a section clinging to the north bank of the Avon via further tunnels complete the approach to Bristol.

Bristol is so full of railway interest that it seems sad to leave it behind via the commuter and excursion section to Weston-super-Mare. There is a good view of the city and the Clifton Suspension Bridge—another Brunel project—as the line rises through the dampness of Flax Bourton cutting and tunnel and descends again to the coastal plain and Yatton, once a busy junction for the small resort of Clevedon and the services west towards the Mendip hills. A single line loop serves Weston-super-Mare, the main line passing behind the town and on to Highbridge where the Somerset & Dorset had its works and crossed the Great Western on the level to get to its pier at Burnham-on-Sea. The route keeps company with the Bridgwater & Taunton Canal from the town of Bridgwater, where a Brunel dredger worked in the docks less than 15 years ago, to the flyover junction at Cogload just beyond Durston, former junction for the Langport branch. Now reunited with the West of England main line, the short section into Taunton is marked only by a few, barely discernible traces of the (Creech) junction with the line to Chard.

Paddington-Swindon

P.1	Paddington
O.3	Old Oak Common (2 m 64 ch)
A.6	Acton (4 m 21 ch)
E.1	Ealing Broadway (5 m 56 ch)
W.8	West Ealing (6 m 41 ch)
G.10	Greenford Branch
H.3	Hanwell (7 m 28 ch)
S.21	Southall (9 m 6 ch)
B.18	Brentford Branch
H.6	Hayes/Harlington (10 m 71 ch)
W.7	West Drayton (13 m 71 ch)
C.27	Colnbrook Branch
I.1	Iver (14 m 60 ch)
L.1	Langley (16 m 18 ch)
S.18	Slough (18 m 36 ch)
W.16	Windsor Branch
B.33	Burnham (20 m 77 ch)
T.2	Taplow (22 m 39 ch)
M.1	Maidenhead (24 m 19 ch)
M.8	Marlow Branch
T.21	Twyford (31 m 1 ch)
H.11	Henley-on-Thames Branch
S.20	Sonning (34 m 2 ch)
R.5	Reading (35 m 78 ch)
T.9	Tilehurst (38 m 52 ch)
P.3	Pangbourne (41 m 43 ch)
G.4	Goring and Streatley (44 m 60 ch)
C.19	Cholsey and Moulsford (48 m 37 ch)
M.19	Moreton Cutting (51 m 20 ch)
D.5	Didcot (53 m 10 ch)
S.24	Steventon (56 m 42 ch)
W.1	Wantage Road (60 m 22 ch)
C.10	Challow (63 m 20 ch)
U.1	Uffington (66 m 60 ch)
S.35	Swindon (77 m 23 ch)

Swindon-Bristol (Temple Meads)

S.35	Swindon (77 m 23 ch)
W.20	Wootton Bassett Junction (83 m 7 ch)
D.2	Dauntsey (87 m 67 ch)
C.17	Chippenham (93 m 76 ch)
T.7	Thingley Junction (96 m 10 ch)
C.31	Corsham (98 m 41 ch)
M.11	Melksham
B.14	Box Tunnel (99 m 12 ch)
B.4	Bathampton Junction (104 m 45 ch)
B.3	Bath (106 m 71 ch)
S.7	Saltford (111 m 57 ch)
K.2	Keynsham (113 m 63 ch)
B.22	Bristol Temple Meads (118 m 26 ch)
S.11	Severn Beach Branch

Bristol (Temple Meads)-Taunton

B.22	Bristol Temple Meads (118 m 26 ch)
P.25	Portishead Branch
F.7	Flax Bourton (124 m 38 ch)
N.1	Nailsea and Backwell (126 m 33 ch)
Y.2	Yatton (130 m 28 ch)
W.11	Worle Junction (135 m 11 ch)
W.11	Weston-super-Mare (137 m 33 ch)
W.11	Uphill Junction (138 m 4 ch)
B.11	Bleadon and Uphill (138 m 49 ch)
H.14	Highbridge (145 m 25 ch)
H.21	Huntspill (147 m 5 ch)
D.13	Dunball (149 m 21 ch)
B.21	Bridgwater (151 m 47 ch)
D.15	Durston (153 m 60 ch)
C.26	Cogload Junction (158 m 32 ch)
T.3	Taunton (163 m 12 ch)

Reading-Taunton-Penzance

The West of England main line has piecemeal origins. Until 1906 the route to the far West was via Bristol but in that year the last of the cut-off construction was completed to provide a more direct line between Reading and Taunton. The new construction first linked the Reading-Newbury-Devizes route from Patney and Chirton to Westbury and then connected the Westbury-Castle Cary portion of the Weymouth line to Langport on the Taunton-Yeovil branch, with a junction at Cogload instead of Durston.

West of Exeter, the South Devon Railway limped forward from Teignmouth which it reached on May 30 1846 to Plymouth Millbay, opening to the latter on April 2 1849—despite a disastrous flirtation with atmospheric propulsion. The standard gauge West Cornwall Railway linked Penzance with Truro from 1852 and the broad gauge Cornwall Railway reached that city from the east seven years later. Through broad gauge running did not commence until 1867 and ended in 1892 with the mammoth railway event which finally converted Brunel's 7 ft gauge to the standard 4 ft 8½ ins.

The West of England line leaves Reading and the junctions for Reading Central branch and the line to Basingstoke and passes through a mixture of commuter and industrial stations, keeping in increasingly close company with the River Kennet and the Kennet and Avon Canal. It rises imperceptibly through Newbury with its Racecourse station and traces of old routes to Didcot, Lambourn and Winchester and then steepens on the approach to the summit at Savernake, former junction with the M&SWJ and which took its name from the nearby forest. Down into the Vale of Pewsey brings the first of the Wessex White Horses and the first cut-off portion from Patney and Chirton to Westbury, stone traffic centre and junction with the Bristol-Portsmouth and Bristol-Weymouth lines.

A Down HST passes through Newbury at speed (Reading-Taunton).

There is an avoiding line round Westbury and a second one by-passes the overall roof station at Frome as the route climbs to Brewham summit and drops again, past the point where the old Somerset & Dorset crossed and into Castle Cary where the single line to Weymouth veers off south. Now comes the long cut-off portion through the Somerset lowlands with King Arthur's Castle to the south and a view of Glastonbury Tor away to the north. After the old Durston trackbed departs on the Up side, the West of England line rejoins the via Bristol line at Cogload and becomes quadruple track into the county town of Taunton.

The departure from Taunton is by way of Norton Fitzwarren, memorable as the site of accidents and of the branches to Minehead and Barnstaple. Past the 160 ft Wellington Monument the gradient steepens to 1 in 80 at the top of Whiteball summit. The descent to Tiverton Junction (formerly for Tiverton and Hemyock) is in company with the Grand Western Canal and the M5, and the water meadows increase as the line passes the old junction at Stoke Canon and the present one at Cowley Bridge where the Barnstaple line joins the main one on the outskirts of Exeter.

The important junction at Exeter, where trains for Central and the Salisbury/Waterloo line originate, is followed by a course along the Exe estuary, along the coast through Dawlish and Teignmouth and then up the estuary of the Teign to Newton Abbot. Not quite its former self, Newton Abbot still has a stub of the former Teign Valley line to Heathfield and it is the interchange point for the Torbay line trains which veer off south just beyond the station at Aller Junction. This section was the scene of Brunel's flirtation with atmospheric traction which must have made hard work of the steep climb to Dainton summit and tunnel which precede the drop into Totnes, on the beautiful Dart River and where GWR traditions are still cherished by the Dart Valley Railway on the old Ashburton branch. Up Rattery bank, past the remains of Brent station and its junction with the Kingsbridge branch, the main line now twists and turns among the hills of South Dartmoor, calling for the first of the Brunel viaducts to bridge the valleys of small rivers heading for the sea. The approach to Plymouth is down the 1 in 42 of Hemerdon bank to Tavistock Junction and Laira Junction where the newly-remodelled diesel maintenance depot lies in the triangular junction with the route to Friary.

Plymouth North Road is a busy modern Inter-City station and has suburban services to the stations lying on the elevated main line westwards. Along this some traces remain of the once busy connections to Millbay and the Ocean Terminal, Devonport SR and the naval dockyard. The lovely route up the Tamar to Calstock and Gunnislake veers off before the dramatic passage over the Royal Albert Bridge to Saltash, the first station in Cornwall. The present onward route through Shillingham Tunnel replaced the original one nearer the coastal creeks and leads to St Germans and the climb to the first of the Cornish high lands around Doublebois. Others follow at Burngullow and finally Redruth. On the Cornwall Railway portion alone, these called for some 30 viaducts and five tunnels.

The Looe line departs at Liskeard, the Wenford freight branch at Bodmin Road, the Carne Point clay line at Lostwithiel and the Newquay branch at Par. In the process the countryside changes from green hills and valleys to the china clay dominated coastal area and another link with the china clay lines leads off north at Burngullow. More viaducts and tunnels precede the cathedral city of Truro and its subsequent junction for the Falmouth branch and the countryside then changes once more, this time to the tin and copper mining landscape either side of Redruth and Camborne. Former branches departed at Chacewater for Perranporth, Redruth for Tresavean and Portreath and Gwinnear Road for Helston, the present St Ives line making junction at St Erth. Across the peninsula towards St Michael's Mount brings the West of England main line to the long embankment along the shore of Mount's Bay and finally the terminus at Penzance.

Reading-Taunton

R.5	Reading (35 m 78 ch)
T.6	Theale (41 m 22 ch)
A.7	Aldermaston (44 m 63 ch)
M.15	Midgham (46 m 56 ch)
T.5	Thatcham (49 m 51 ch)
N.4	Newbury (53 m 6 ch)
K.5	Kintbury (58 m 42 ch)
H.20	Hungerford (61 m 47 ch)
B.7	Bedwyn (66 m 29 ch)
S.9	Savernake (70 m 7 ch)
B.30	Burbage (70 m 75 ch)
P.17	Pewsey (75 m 26 ch)
W.17	Woodborough (78 m 72 ch)
P.8	Patney and Chirton (81 m 7 ch)
L.4	Lavington (86 m 55 ch)
W.6	Westbury (109 m 64 ch)
F.10	Frome (115 m 44 ch)
R.2	Radstock Branch
W.17	Witham (120 m 76 ch)
C.33	Cranmore Branch
M.13	Merehead Quarry Branch
B.19	Brewham Bank (122 m 54 ch)
B.27	Bruton (126 m 13 ch)
C.8	Castle Cary (129 m 54 ch)
S.19	Somerton (125 m 62 ch)
L.2	Langport (129 m 73 ch)
A.13	Athelney (134 m 79 ch)

Change of mileage 137 m 69 ch to 158 m 9 ch

C.26	Cogload (158 m 32 ch)
T.3	Taunton (163 m 12 ch)

Taunton-Penzance

T.3	Taunton (163 m 12 ch)
N.11	Norton Fitzwarren (165 m 10 ch)
W.3	Wellington (170 m 19 ch)
W.13	Whiteball (174 m)
B.31	Burlescombe (174 m 62 ch)
T.10	Tiverton Junction (179 m 10 ch)
H.9	Hele and Bradninch (185 m 41 ch)
S.25	Stoke Canon (190 m 16 ch)
E.5	Exeter (193 m 72 ch)
B.1	Barnstaple Branch (also C.35)
E.6	Exminster (198 m 59 ch)
T.20	Turf (199 m 59 ch)
S.23	Starcross (202 m 36 ch)
D.4	Dawlish Warren (204 m 34 ch)
D.3	Dawlish (206 m 7 ch)

T.4	Teignmouth (208 m 78 ch)
N.9	Newton Abbot (214 m 6 ch)
H.8	Heathfield Branch
A.9	Aller Junction (215 m 15 ch)
T.13, T.12, P.2	Paignton Line
S.29	Stoneycombe (216 m 74 ch)
D.1	Dainton (217 m 79 ch)
T.14	Totnes (222 m 63 ch)
R.4	Rattery (227 m 28 ch)
M.7	Marley Tunnels (227 m 62 ch)
B.17	Brent (229 m 60 ch)
W.22	Wrangaton (231 m 58 ch)
I.2	Ivybridge (235 m 19 ch)
C.30	Cornwood (237 m 44 ch)
H.10	Hemerdon (239 m 10 ch)
P.20	Plymouth (245 m 75 ch)

Change of mileage 246 m 29 ch to 247 m 42 ch

G.12	Gunnislake Branch
R.8	Royal Albert Bridge (250 m 64 ch)
S.6	Saltash (251 m 26 ch)
M.12	Menheniot (261 m 61 ch)
L.9	Liskeard (264 m 66 ch)
L.27	Looe Branch
M.18	Moorswater
L.3	Largin (270 m 1 ch)
B.13	Bodmin Road (274 m 3 ch)
W.4	Wenford Branch
L.28	Lostwithiel (277 m 34 ch)
F.8	Fowey Branch
T.17	Treverrin Tunnel (279 m 19 ch)
P.5	Par (281 m 69 ch)
N.8	Newquay Branch
S.2	St Blazey (282 m 19 ch)
S.1	St Austell (286 m 34 ch)
B.32	Burngullow (288 m 56 ch)
P.6	Parkandillack Branch
P.21	Polperro Tunnel (297 m 50 ch)
T.19	Truro (300 m 57 ch)
F.1	Falmouth Branch
C.9	Chacewater (306 m 9 ch)
D.12	Drump Lane (309 m 35 ch)
R.6	Redruth (309 m 68 ch)
C.7	Carn Brea (311 m 43 ch)
D.9	Dolcoath (312 m 52 ch)
C.3	Camborne (313 m 40 ch)
G.13	Gwinnear Road (315 m 73 ch)
H.7	Hayle (319 m 32 ch)
S.3	St Erth (320 m 67 ch)
S.5	St Ives Branch
M.5	Marazion (324 m 56 ch)
P.15	Penzance (326 m 50 ch)

An Up HST heads through Totnes (Taunton-Penzance).

Swindon-Newport-Fishguard

The South Wales Railway's main line opened from Chepstow to Swansea on June 19 1850. Two years later the Brunel bridge over the River Wye at Chepstow completed the link with the GWR at Grange Court and gave through rail communication between South Wales and London. The second route to South Wales was via the Bristol & South Wales Union Railway with a line opened on September 8 1863 to New Passage where a ferry then took passengers across the Severn to Portskewett to rejoin the main line. The two piers there closed on December 1 1886 with the opening of the Severn Tunnel which produced extra traffic and the doubling of the route to Bristol. This extra business, in turn, put pressure on the capacity of the main line via Box and the GWR's Bristol & South Wales Direct Railway scheme provided a line from Wootton Bassett Junction to Patchway to relieve this. It was opened on July 1 1903 and the link from Stoke Gifford to Hallen Marsh and Avonmouth Docks opened in 1910.

West of Swansea, the South Wales Railway's original objective of a port at Fishguard was abandoned in favour of a main line to Haverfordwest and Neyland, reached in 1854/6. It fell to an independent company to open to Fishguard in 1895/9, the present line and port dating from 1906.

After leaving the original main line at Wootton Bassett, the South Wales route drops to Little Somerford, to which the Malmesbury branch was once connected, and then climbs to pass through the Cotswold ridge via the Alderton and Sodbury tunnels and the once-extensive station at Badminton. Trains from Birmingham now join the main line at Westerleigh Junction, instead of taking the former MR route into Bristol, and the line continues to descend to Stoke Gifford and the station built at Bristol Parkway to compete with the M4 motorway. From Stoke Gifford Junction one line leads to Temple Meads and the

The traction workhorse of South Wales is the Class 37 locomotive, normally seen hauling coal or freight but here resplendent with a new name, Sir Dyfed, County of Dyfed *(Newport-Fishguard).*

other heads across North Bristol towards Patchway where the alignment of the tunnels on the Up and Down lines reveals their separate origins. At Pilning the line to New Passage and Severn Beach used to diverge.

Over its 4 m 628 yds the Severn Tunnel drops first at 1 in 100 and then rises at 1 in 90 to the western bank of the estuary and then the junction with the earlier route via Gloucester, at Severn Tunnel Junction, a major WR marshalling yard. Recognising the importance of the BSC at Llanwern the Relief lines run south of the main lines on the approach to Newport where the Uskmouth and docks branches diverge on the south side and a triangular junction is made with the North and West line to Shrewsbury on the north. Beyond Newport are further docks lines and the triangular link to the Western Valleys lines to Ebbw Vale, Rose Heyworth and Oakdale.

Cardiff, too, has its docks links and, to the north, passenger services on the 'Valleys' lines to Coryton, Rhmyney, Merthyr and Treherbert (with freight on the Dowlais, Ocean & Taff Merthyr, Nantgarw, Ynysybwl, Hirwaun Pond and Maerdy lines). West of the capital city the Penarth Curves triangle holds Canton diesel maintenance depot and leads to the suburban lines to Penarth and Barry Island and the Vale of Glamorgan freight route via Aberthaw to Bridgend. Between Cardiff and Bridgend the main line leaves the coastal plain by courtesy of the Ely valley which continues to be used by the Cwm and Coed Ely branches from Llantrisant as the main line rises to the summit at Llanharan and then descends to Bridgend. There it is reunited with the Vale of Glamorgan line and makes connection with the Tondu valleys lines.

The main line now passes through the Port Talbot industrial complex, making a second connection with the Tondu valleys coal via the Ogmore Vale

A dramatic 1972 maintenance scene showing work on Briton Ferry swing bridge (Newport-Fishguard).

Extension line which connects the latter with Margam yard. Beyond Port Talbot comes Court Sart Junction which leads, in turn, to the Swansea freight lines network east of the Tawe and to the Swansea District Line, South Wales' own cut-off line which takes an easier route (with branches to Clydach and Gorseinion) to Morlais Junction and back to the main line east of Llanelli. From Court Sart Junction the main line passes through Briton Ferry Yard and makes a great loop northwards through Neath and over the lines from Jersey Marine South to Aberpergwm and Onllwyn to reach Swansea via Landore Viaduct and the west bank of the Tawe. Landore diesel maintenance depot lies in the triangle formed by the line into Swansea terminus, the line out through Cockett Tunnel to West Wales and the link between the two.

After crossing the Loughor estuary by the viaduct of the same name the route from Central Wales, combined with the western end of the Swansea District Line, joins the main line at Llandeilo Junction. Llanelli station follows the Llandeilo Junction yard with a branch then departing north to Cynheidre, another from Pembrey/Kidwelly to Cwmmawr and then an estuarial section into the triangular layout at Carmarthen. The line north from Carmarthen to Newcastle Emlyn and Lampeter has gone as have those from Whitland to Cardigan and the old route from Clunderwen to Letterston but West Wales is still served by the coastal route from Whitland to Pembroke Dock and the line from Clarbeston Road to Milford Haven. There are minor summits at both these junctions and one more near Letterston Junction (connection for the short branch to Trecwn) before the final drop of 1 in 50 to Fishguard Harbour.

Swindon-Newport

S.35 Swindon (77 m 23 ch)
W.20 Wootton Bassett Junction (83 m 7 ch)
H.19 Hullavington (94 m 10 ch)
A.8 Alderton Tunnel (97 m 34 ch)
C.18 Chipping Sodbury (104 m 40 ch)
W.9 Westerleigh Junction (107 m 12 ch)
B.22 Bristol Parkway (111 m 62 ch)
H.1 Hallen Marsh Branch
Change of mileage 112 m 72 ch to 5 m 64 ch
P.7 Patchway (5 m 77 ch)
P.18 Pilning (9 m 43 ch)
S.12 Severn Tunnel (11 m 60 ch)
S.13 Severn Tunnel Junction (148 m 61 ch)
L.24 Llanwern (153 m 5 ch)
N.7 Newport (158 m 47 ch)

Newport-Fishguard

N.7 Newport (158 m 47 ch)
W.10 Western Valleys
B.6 Bedwas Branch
C.5 Cardiff (170 m 30 ch)
C.32 Coryton Branch
R.7 Rhymney Branch
D.10 Dowlais Branch
O.1 Ocean and Taff Merthyr Branch
M.14 Merthyr Branch
H.15 Hirwaun Pond Branch
M.1 Maerdy Branch
Y.5 Ynysybwl Branch
T.16 Treherbert Branch

N.2 Nantgarw Branch
P.12 Penarth Branch
B.2 Barry Branch
V.1 Vale of Glamorgan Line
L.23 Llantrisant (181 m 43 ch)
C.38 Cwm Branch
C.25 Coed Ely Branch
L.21 Llanharan (184 m 32 ch)
B.20 Bridgend (190 m 45 ch)
T.11 Tondu Lines
P.29 Pylle (195 m 79 ch)
M.6 Margam (198 m 35 ch)
P.27 Port Talbot (202 m 59 ch)
B.23 Briton Ferry (206 m)
S.33 Swansea District Line
A.4 Aberpergwm Branch
O.5 Onllwyn Branch
N.3 Neath (208 m 20 ch)
S.32 Swansea (216 m 7 ch)
G.6 Gowerton (219 m 49 ch)
L.29 Loughor (221 m 49 ch)
L.16 Llanelli (225 m 20 ch)
C.41 Cynheidre Branch
P.9 Pembrey and Burry Port (228 m 70 ch)
C.39 Cwmmawr Branch
K.3 Kidwelly (234 m 23 ch)
F.3 Ferryside (238 m 47 ch)
C.6 Carmarthen (245 m 55 ch)
W.14 Whitland (258 m 68 ch)
P.10 Pembroke Dock Branch
C.23 Clunderwen (264 m 22 ch)
M.16 Milford Haven (also H.5 and J.1)
F.6 Fishguard Line.

Didcot-Birmingham

The GWR reached Oxford by courtesy of the Oxford Railway on June 12 1844 and the Oxford & Rugby Railway's line from Banbury arrived on September 2 1850, the present station site replacing the original wooden station two years later. The through route on to Birmingham and Wolverhampton came into use in 1869.

Past the Great Western Society depot at Didcot the line commences a near-level course northwards, crossing the Thames twice before Radley where the Abingdon branch joins. It is to have river and then canal companionship through the flat, green countryside all the way to the Regional Boundary just south of Banbury. At Oxford, the main location on the stretch within the WR, the short Morris Cowley branch joins just south of the station, the Bicester line then departing from Oxford North Junction and the Worcester line from Wolvercot Junction. Little remains of the line that linked these two or of the short branch from Kidlington to Blenheim.

D.5 Didcot (53 m 10 ch)
A.10 Appelford (55 m 16 ch)
C.37 Culham (56 m 17 ch)
R.1 Radley (58 m 35 ch)
A.5 Abingdon Branch
M.22 Morris Cowley Branch

O.6 Oxford (63 m 41 ch)
B.8 Bicester Line
B.12 Bletchington (70 m 34 ch)
T.1 Tackley (72 m 50 ch)
H.13 Heyford (75 m 21 ch)
Regional Boundary (76 m 40 ch)

Oxford-Hereford

The troubled Oxford, Worcester & Wolverhampton Railway started construction at the Worcester end and had reached Evesham by May 1 1852, the link to Wolvercot Junction (Oxford) following on June 4 1853. The line west from Worcester was made by the Worcester & Hereford Railway which, with the Newport, Abergavenny & Hereford Railway, was amalgamated into the OWW which then became the West Midlands Railway. Opening between Worcester and Shelwick Junction was in four stages between 1859 and 1861.

Immediately on leaving Wolvercot Junction the Witney branch trackbed departs on the Down side and the main route takes up a winding course through a countryside of wheat and woodland which brings it to Kingham. Here two branches eventually became linked to form the Banbury & Cheltenham Direct line. Climbing on through Moreton-in-Marsh, from which a short branch once ran to Shipston-on-Stour, the line reaches a summit near milepost 92½ and then dips and curves, at 1 in 100, down Campden Bank to the Vale of Evesham.

At the foot of the drop is Honeybourne where the main line developed by the GWR from Bristol to Birmingham via Cheltenham, Stratford and Bearley crossed beneath the OWW route. A portion survives as a freight spur to Long Marston but at Evesham the former Midland branches are marked only by surviving trackbed and station. Crossing the River Avon twice here, the route then passes over the Birmingham-Bristol main line and enters Worcester Shrub Hill via Norton Junction. From Shrub Hill one route forks to Droitwich and the other through Foregate Street towards the Malvern hills. These are skirted through the long Malvern township and then pierced by the Colwall and Ledbury tunnels after which the line continues through long-closed stations to the junction with the Shrewsbury line just north of Hereford. Three former branches along this section, to Bromyard, Tewkesbury and Newent, have all gone.

O.6	Oxford (63 m 41 ch)	E.4	Evesham (106 m 55 ch)
H.2	Handborough (70 m 39 ch)	P.16	Pershore (112 m 50 ch)
C.29	Combe (71 m 44 ch)	W.21	Worcester (120 m 31 ch)
F.5	Finstock (75 m 10 ch)	N.5	Newland (126 m 22 ch)
C.13	Charlbury (76 m 60 ch)	M.3	Malvern Link (127 m 75 ch)
A.11	Ascott-under-Wychwood (80 m 36 ch)	G.9	Great Malvern (129 m 6 ch)
		M.4	Malvern Wells (130 m 13 ch)
S.17	Shipton (81 m 59 ch)	C.28	Colwall (131 m 72 ch)
K.4	Kingham (84 m 59 ch)	L.5	Ledbury (136 m 6 ch)
M.20	Moreton-in-Marsh (91 m 56 ch)	S.27	Stoke Edith (142 m 22 ch)
C.4	Campden (94 m 78 ch)	S.15	Shelwick Junction (49 m 26 ch)
H.16	Honeybourne (101 m 48 ch)	H.12	Hereford (51 m 14 ch)

Swindon-Gloucester-Newport

This was the original route to South Wales, the Swindon-Gloucester section authorised to the Cheltenham & Great Western Union Railway, the Gloucester-Grange Court section to the Gloucester & Dean Forest Railway and that from Grange Court onwards to the South Wales Railway. On its own the Cheltenham & Great Western Union only managed the opening of the portion from Swindon to Kemble/Cirencester (May 31 1841) and amalgamation with the GWR was necessary to secure the completion of the Cheltenham-Gloucester section for

Kemble station, with the stub of the Cirencester branch curving away right (Swindon-Gloucester).

opening on July 8 1844 and of the central section on May 12 1845. The two sections west of Gloucester were opened together on September 19 1851.

From the junction at Swindon the route is through open Wiltshire countryside, the gradients then steepening from Kemble until the summit between the Sapperton tunnels is approached by a 1 in 94 section and followed by 1 in 90. Road, river, canal and railway keep company through the winding curving section past Chalford and into Stroud, an area full of history and beauty and once served by a busy timetable of rail motors. At Standish Junction the route joins the main line for the approach to Gloucester and now follows its original course via Gloucester Yard Junction, into the modernised Gloucester Central and out via Over Junction where the Newent line used to depart and the Llanthony docks branch still does so.

The route now follows the west bank of the Severn from which the GWR lines from Bullo Pill and Awre tapped the Forest of Dean coal and the Severn & Wye's line probed west from Lydney and, later, east across the Severn Bridge. The stub of the Wye Valley line still serves a quarry at Tidenham and joins the main just before its crossing of the river outside Chepstow. On the section on to join the main line at Severn Tunnel Junction there is the site of Portskewett station and the trackbed of the route to the ferry pier and two remaining branches to Caerwent and Sudbrook. From Severn Tunnel Junction the dmu service continues on the main line to Newport and Cardiff.

Swindon-Gloucester

S.35 Swindon (77 m 23 ch)
P.28 Purton (81 m 65 ch)
M.17 Minety (86 m 74 ch)
K.1 Kemble (90 m 79 ch)
S.8 Sapperton Tunnels (94 m 50 ch)
S.30 Stroud (102 m 13 ch)
S.28 Stonehouse (104 m 74 ch)
S.22 Standish Junction (106 m 74 ch)
G.3 Gloucester (114 m 4 ch)

Gloucester-Newport

G.3 Gloucester (114 m 4 ch)

G.8 Grange Court (121 m 4 ch)
N.6 Newnham (125 m 8 ch)
A.15 Awre (129 m)
L.31 Lydney (133 m 37 ch)
W.23 Wye Valley Branch
C.15 Chepstow (141 m 33 ch)
P.26 Portskewett (145 m 77 ch)
S.31 Sudbrook Branch
C.1 Caerwent Branch
C.2 Caldicot (148 m 2 ch)
S.13 Severn Tunnel Junction (148 m 61 ch)
L.24 Llanwern (153 m 5 ch)
N.7 Newport (158 m 47 ch)

Bristol-Westbury-Weymouth/Portsmouth

These routes were primarily the enterprise of the Wilts, Somerset & Weymouth Railway which opened from Thingley Junction to Westbury on September 5 1848 and struggled on to Frome on October 10 1850 and to Warminster on September 9 1851. Finances were a major problem and the enterprise was vested in the Great Western Railway by an Act of Parilament of 1851 but that company was almost as reluctant to complete the original plans and it was 1856 before the line through to Salisbury was opened, with trains running via Yeovil to Weymouth from January 20 of the following year. Bradford-on-Avon had a station a long while before it had a railway, the line up the Avon valley to Bathampton Junction not opening until February 2 1857.

The Up direction is southbound along the Avon valley and the trains from Bristol and Bath leave the main line at Bathampton and take the route of the river southbound, although to add to the confusion this is upstream. The Kennet and Avon Canal, now being restored, takes the same route which passes through Limpley Stoke, former junction for the line to Hallatrow, and Bradford-on-Avon to the triangular layout at Bradford Junctions. Here the original WS&W line joins from Thingley and the route continues through Trowbridge to the second triangle at Hawkeridge on the outskirts of Westbury.

From Westbury to Castle Cary the original WS&W line is now part of the West of England main line but at the latter point it takes up its original course as a single line via Yeovil Pen Mill to the Regional Boundary between Maiden Newton and Dorchester West. At Yeovil the WS&W passes beneath the Waterloo-Exeter line and then climbs, finally at 1 in 51, to Evershot Tunnel and summit. From Maiden Newton on the long descent towards the sea, there was formerly a branch to Bridport.

The other route from Westbury, to Salisbury where the GWR had its own station, lies inside the WR only for a short distance. Within this it encompasses a 1 in 76/75/70 climb through the tiny Dilton Marsh station and the station at Warminster.

Bristol-Westbury

B.4	Bathampton Junction (0 m)
L.8	Limpley Stoke (4 m 28 ch)
F.9	Freshford (4 m 70 ch)
A.14	Avoncliff (5 m 63 ch)
B.16	Bradford-on-Avon (7 m 9 ch)
B.15	Bradford Junctions (8 m 64 ch and 9 m 11 ch)
T.18	Trowbridge (105 m 61 ch)
W.6	Westbury (109 m 64 ch)

Westbury-Weymouth

W.6	Westbury (109 m 64 ch)
C.8	Castle Cary (129 m 54 ch)
Y.3	Yeovil Pen Mill (141 m 22 ch)

T.8	Thornford (144 m 35 ch)
Y.4	Yetminster (145 m 46 ch)
C.16	Chetnole (147 m 50 ch)
E.3	Evershot (149 m 49 ch)
M.2	Maiden Newton (154 m 12 ch)
G.11	Grimstone and Frampton Tunnel (156 m 70 ch)
	Regional boundary (160 m 20 ch)

Westbury-Portsmouth

W.6	Westbury (109 m 64 ch)
D.6	Dilton Marsh (111 m 11 ch)
W.2	Warminster (114 m 37 ch)
	Regional boundary (118 m 40 ch)

Waterloo-Exeter

The origins of this route lie deep in the rivalry between the Great Western and London & South Western companies. After some bitter Parliamentary battles in 1847 the post-Railway Mania shortage of money kept matters quiet until 1851 when the whole process began again, but eventually the route was completed by the Salisbury & Yeovil which opened to the latter point on June 1 1860 and the L&SW's Yeovil-Exeter line which opened on July 19 of that year.

From Waterloo to beyond the former Templecombe junction with the Somerset & Dorset route the line is part of the Southern Region, the first WR station being Sherborne. Then comes Yeovil Junction, high above the Westbury-Weymouth line and well south of the town both routes serve. From here to Pinhoe the route is single, with passing loops and block posts at Chard Junction and Honiton and worked on the Tokenless Block system. This derives from the 1967 rationalisation but with the Class 50 motive power now in use on the route the passenger service is quite a reasonable one.

The scenery is pastoral as the route heads west, just within the Somerset border, to Chard Junction and its former line to Chard, Ilminster and Taunton. The first main summit lies on this stretch, just west of Crewkerne, and it is followed by a 13 m descent as the line follows the River Axe to Axminster and Seaton Junction and then rises again towards Honiton, at 1 in 80 on the final stretch to the tunnel. The Devon branches from Axminster to Lyme Regis, Seaton Junction to Seaton and Sidmouth Junction to Sidmouth and Budleigh Salterton are all now closed but the one from Exmouth Junction to Exmouth remains busy with commuters and summer holiday traffic. Queens Street at Exeter, now Central, remains an interesting station and leads on, via a short tunnel and a steep gradient, to Exeter St Davids.

	Regional boundary (117 m 40 ch)		S.10	Seaton Junction (148 m 5 ch)
S.16	Sherborne (118 m 4 ch)		H.17	Honiton (154 m 60 ch)
Y.3	Yeovil Junction (122 m 48 ch)		F.2	Feniton (159 m 24 ch)
C.36	Crewkerne (131 m 33 ch)		W.12	Whimple (163 m 2 ch)
C.11	Chard Junction (139 m 32 ch)		E.7	Exmouth Branch
A.16	Axminster (144 m 41 ch)		E.5	Exeter (171 m 18 ch)

Birmingham-Bristol

The coal-producing area north of Bristol attracted thoughts of a railway as early as 1803 and from the local lines built between 1831 and 1835 sprang the idea of a Bristol and Gloucester Railway intended to join the Cheltenham & Great Western Union at Standish Junction. By the time the latter had been taken over by the Great Western and the routes from Bristol and Swindon had reached Gloucester in 1844/5 the Birmingham & Gloucester Railway was already open and operational arrangements had been agreed between the companies involved, despite the fact that the B&G was a narrow gauge line and the other two routes were broad gauge. After the two B&G companies had agreed upon amalgamation they were invited to share in the Great Western's ambitions for the extension of the broad gauge to Birmingham but the Midland stepped in when terms could not be agreed and the route became an important MR main line.

The WR takes over the Birmingham-Bristol route at the summit preceding the 1 in 37 down the Lickey Bank. After this dramatic descent the gradients are modest all the way to Bristol.

At Stoke Works Junction the line to Droitwich and Worcester veers off south-west to rejoin at Abbotswood Junction and the route then takes a straight and easy course down the wide valley of the Severn, crossing in the process the

Stratford Avon which joins the Severn at Tewkesbury. The Malvern Hills can be seen to the west but the line which led there from the triangular station at Ashchurch has closed as has the other branch along the Vale of Evesham. All the stations along this section are now just barely-discernible sites but there are still several examples of the unusual and attractive gate-keepers' cottages to be seen.

Into the Vale of Gloucester, with the Cotswolds showing to the east, the line comes to Cheltenham and just beyond the present station the former junction with the independent main line the GWR created for itself via Honeybourne to Birmingham. Just a short distance further south is the site of Hatherley Junction used by the trains to Banbury and those of the Midland & South Western Junction Railway to Swindon. Along here the route still reveals that the Midland and Great Western railways once had separate tracks but the former's route through Gloucester went in a piece of BR rationalisation which retained the through lines to South Wales and Bristol but meant a reversal for those Birmingham-Bristol trains which call at Gloucester. The four pairs of tracks used to continue on, with branches to Gloucester's docks and canal, as far as Standish Junction where the line to Swindon via Stroud climbs away south-east.

On the remaining section to Bristol the route keeps to the flat land along the Severn estuary, between the widening river and the Cotswold hills which run parallel to it. At the nearest point to the former the single line to Sharpness departs and after passing through Wickwar Tunnel another such line runs from Yate to Tytherington quarry. On the east side of the route former branches ran from Stonehouse to Stroud and Nailsworth and from Coaley to Dursley. The main line to South Wales is joined by a conventional junction, facing Bristol, at Westerleigh, trains then reaching Bristol via the GWR route instead of over the old MR line via Mangotsfield, from which the connection to Bath and the S&D was made.

	Regional Boundary (52 m 40 ch)	C.14	Cheltenham (86 m 58 ch)
B.10	Blackwell (52 m 57 ch)	G.3	Gloucester (93 m 18 ch)
L.7	Lickey Incline	Q.1	Quedgeley (97 m 1 ch)
B.25	Bromsgrove (55 m 30 ch)	H.4	Haresfield (98 m 64 ch)
S.26	Stoke Works Junction (57 m 43 ch)	S.22	Standish Junction (99 m 68 ch)
D.14	Dunhampstead (62 m 12 ch)	S.28	Stonehouse (101 m 47 ch)
O.2	Oddingley (62 m 60 ch)	C.24	Coaley (105 m 36 ch)
A.1	Abbotswood Junction (68 m 60 ch)	S.14	Sharpness Branch
P.19	Pirton (70 m 51 ch)	C.12	Charfield (113 m 13 ch)
E.2	Eckington (74 m 51 ch)	W.15	Wickwar (115 m 28 ch)
N.10	Northway (78 m 76 ch)	Y.1	Yate (119 m 54 ch)
A.12	Ashchurch (79 m 47 ch)	T.22	Tytherington Branch
C.21	Cleeve (82 m 60 ch)	W.9	Westerleigh Junction (121 m 26 ch)

Shrewsbury-Newport

The Shrewsbury & Hereford Railway was incorporated on August 3 1846 and opened its route to Ludlow on April 20 1852 and on to Hereford on December 6 1853. On January 2 of the following year the Newport, Abergavenny & Hereford Railway, which had been incorporated on the same day as the S&H, opened between Hereford and Coed-y-gric where it linked with the Monmouthshire Railway & Canal Company's route to Newport until that of the Pontypool, Caerleon & Newport Railway was opened in 1874.

From the dramatic scenery south of Shrewsbury the line descends unevenly but steadily from Church Stretton summit pretty well all the way to Hereford. The Central Wales line veers off right at Craven Arms but the old branches from Ludlow to Clee Hill and Woofferton to Tenbury Wells failed to survive the rationalisation process. Leominster, once with branch lines in either direction, is now but a shadow of its former self but the surrounding country-side remains most pleasant as the line uses two tunnels to penetrate the ridge at Dinmore and then pick up the course of the River Lugg, through Shelwick Junction with the Worcester line and into Hereford.

At Hereford only the stub of the line towards Barton and Eardisley remains, serving private sidings and Bulmers Railway Centre. The route used southwards is that of the former Ross-on-Wye branch with a return to GWR metals via a short stretch of former LNWR line between Rotherwas and Red Hill Junctions. Traces of the Golden Valley route to Hay can still be seen as the 'North and West' line makes its 6 m climb to Llanvihangel in company with the River Monnow, and then drops for the next 7 m, coming finally to Abergavenny where once a dramatic line cut across the heads of the valleys to Neath. Now only the main line remains, the branch from Little Mill Junction to Monmouth being now truncated at Glascoed.

On the final stretch the route is one of woods and tumbling streams on the way to the next summit at Pontypool after which the line drops for 6 m at 1 in 95/106/120. Pontypool, once Pontypool Road the second gateway to the valleys of South Wales, is now just a bare platform with all its neighbouring junctions submerged beneath new road works. The links with the original route have gone, as have the intermediate stations, and today's Shrewsbury/Crewe-Newport/Cardiff trains pass unhindered to the triangular junction at Maindee and then into Newport station.

Regional boundary (18 m 10 ch)		H.12	Hereford (51 m 14 ch)
C.34	Craven Arms (19 m 27 ch)	Change of mileage 52 m 19 ch to 0	
O.4	Onibury (22 m 68 ch)	T.15	Tram Inn (5 m 37 ch)
B.24	Bromfield (25 m 20 ch)	P.22	Pontrilas (11 m 14 ch)
L.30	Ludlow (27 m 42 ch)	A.3	Abergavenny (22 m 75 ch)
W.19	Woofferton (32 m 2 ch)	G.2	Glascoed Branch
L.6	Leominster (38 m 60 ch)	P.23	Pontypool (32 m 19 ch)
D.7	Dinmore Tunnels (42 m 67 ch)	L.22	Llantarnam Junction (36 m 26 ch)
M.21	Moreton-on-Lugg (46 m 65 ch)	N.7	Maindee West Junction (41 m
S.15	Shelwick Junction (49 m 26 ch)		66 ch)

Shrewsbury-Llanelli

The southern end of this route was built first with the Llanelly Railway opening to Pontarddulais in 1839, on to Tirydail in 1841 and then to Llandeilo in 1857. That company leased the Vale of Towy Railway which opened the section on to Llandovery in 1858. Backed by LNWR influence the northern section started with the Knighton Railway's portion from Craven Arms to Knighton in 1860-1, continued with the Central Wales Railway portion from Knighton to Llandrindod Wells in 1862-5 and the link was completed via the Central Wales Extension Railway which opened the Llandrindod-Llandovery section in 1866-8. Through an LNWR lease of the Vale of Towy and running powers over the Llanelly Railway it became that company's route into Swansea and West Wales and eventually a shared route with the GWR.

From Craven Arms the line swings south-west through pastoral lowlands to

Central Wales line dmu heading for Shrewsbury (Shrewsbury-Llanelli).

Knighton where the town is in Wales and the station in England. Using the River Teme it then makes a long loop to reach the summit at Llangynllo by way of the 13-arch Knucklas Viaduct and a 645 yd tunnel. The descent is via a shelf on the north side of the Lugg valley to the delightful scenery around Dolau and Pen-y-bont and then the spa resort of Llandrindod Wells. This is one of the passing loops on the light railway portion of the line which extends to Pantyffynnon.

At Builth Road the route crosses that of the old Cambrian Railways and it then accompanies the infant Wye to pass between the Mynydd Eppynt range and the edge of the Cambrian Mountains, through the spa country and on to the next summit, pierced by the 1,000 yds of Sugar Loaf Tunnel. With a new river companion, the Bran, the line dashes down from the mountain and over the 18 spans of Cynghordy Viaduct into the next passing point at Llandovery.

The next section means several crossings of the River Towy and on to the passing loop at Llandeilo where the trackbed of the line to Carmarthen is still visible south of the station. There is a final summit before the route drops to Pantyffynnon where the junction with the Gwaun-cae-Gurwen and Abernant branches is followed by the link with the Swansea District Line. The route is then double track to Llandeilo Junction and along the main line where the dmus operating the service reverse to complete the journey to Swansea.

C.34	Craven Arms (0 m)	S.32	Sugar Loaf Tunnel (50 m 79 ch)
B.26	Broome (2 m 46 ch)	C.40	Cynghordy (54 m 55 ch)
H.18	Hopton Heath (5 m 9 ch)	Change of mileage 59 m 14 ch to	
B.34	Bucknell (8 m 4 ch)	29 m 40 ch	
K.6	Knighton (12 m 23 ch)	L.13	Llandovery (29 m 24 ch)
K.7	Knucklas (14 m 69 ch)	L.25	Llanwrda (25 m 40 ch)
L.20	Llangynllo (18 m 57 ch)	L.17	Llangadog (23 m 59 ch)
L.10	Llanbister Road (21 m 55 ch)	L.12	Llandeilo (18 m 9 ch)
D.8	Dolau (25 m 26 ch)	F.4	Ffairfach (17 m 19 ch)
P.14	Pen-y-bont (28 m 21 ch)	L.15	Llandybie (13 m 4 ch)
L.14	Landrindod Wells (31 m 36 ch)	P.4	Pantyffynnon (10 m 8 ch)
B.29	Builth Road (37 m 40 ch)	S.34	Swansea District Line
C.20	Cilmeri (39 m 39 ch)	L.19	Llangennech (3 m 1 ch)
G.1	Garth (42 m 69 ch)	B.34	Bynea (1 m 7 ch)
L.18	Llangamarch (44 m 47 ch)	L.16	Llandeilo Junction (0 m)
L.26	Llanwrtyd (47 m 77 ch)		

SECTION 5

Traffic and operation

The key to the Western Region passenger business lies in the public timetable and the activity is open to public view especially at the main stations in the region (P.1 Paddington, R.5 Reading, O.6 Oxford, S.35 Swindon, B.22 Bristol Temple Meads, N.7 Newport, C.5 Cardiff Central, S.35 Swansea, T.3 Taunton, E.5 Exeter and P.20 Plymouth). The interchange activities at places like Reading, Bristol and Cardiff are of special interest, and the branch services provide an opportunity to study the train planning operation in its simplest form since many of the elements—market requirements, train capacity and line constraints—are easy to appreciate. Within the region the range of passenger traffic operations is enormous with simple lines like the St Ives branch (S.5) contrasting with the North-East/South-West service where the trunk route makes connection with so many other routes. In South Wales, too, there are situations of unique interest and complication; Cardiff where there are both main line services and suburban services on six branches (B.2 Barry, C.32 Coryton, M.14 Merthyr, P.12 Penarth, R.7 Rhymney and T.16 Treherbert) and Swansea where the main line HST pattern has to be linked with the services in West Wales.

The support services for the passenger business are also both fascinating and easy to study, whether it be the information offered in the travel centres or the physical tasks involved in train servicing, many of which take place on the station platforms. As night approaches many stations become busy with mails, newspapers and parcels traffic and most of the big ones offer much of interest to the observer. There are also many non-standard operations such as the service to Fishguard to connect with the Sealink service to Rosslare, the Motorail trains and the links from Reading to Heathrow and Gatwick airports.

The WR freight business is equally varied. The stations in the London area tend to be receiving points, especially for aggregates from the Mendips (M.13) or Tytherington (T.22), cement from Westbury (W.6) coal from South and oil from West Wales (M.16). Theale (T.6) is a good example of this business mix. Passing outwards from the London area is an efficient and complex operation which conveys GLC compacted refuse (B.18, A.10) using nine sets of 60 ft Freightliner-type wagons each loaded with three 20 ft containers.

The West of England Division originates the Mendip stone trains, servicing Merehead (M.13) and Whatley Quarry (R.2) from Westbury (W.6) and Witham (W.17) and then providing traction with Class 37 locomotives allocated to Bath Road (B.22) and such back-up facilities as regular wagon maintenance carried

out at Barton Hill shops (B.22). It also deals with an appreciable volume of
china clay originating on the Meeth (M.9) and Heathfield (H.8) branches and on
the Cornish china clay lines (N.8, P.6) and conveyed to Fowey (F.8) for shipment or by special working to the Potteries.

The major part of the WR's freight activity occurs in South Wales where the
movement of coal is of very great importance. Many of the single line, freight-
only branches in the area exist solely to carry coal, major examples being those
in the Western Valleys (W.10), in the valleys above Cardiff (D.10, H.15, M.14,
N.2, O.1, P.11, R.7, T.16, Y.5), the Ely (L.23) and Tondu (T.11) valley lines,
the routes to Onllwyn (O.5) and Aberpergwm (A.4), to Gwaun-cae-Gurwen and
Abernant (P.4) and the branches west of Llanelli (C.39, C.41). Movements take
place between NCB installations, to power stations, to BSC works and to other
industrial users, for shipment and to the domestic market. Among the principal
flows are the mgr movements to Aberthaw power station where the loading and
discharge are part of a continuous movement process.

Despite the contraction of the steel industry, the BSC plants in South Wales
provide large volumes of freight for BR. There is coal and limestone being
brought in to feed the steel-making process, steel going out for coating, and
finished products being sent to a variety of UK and overseas destinations.
Britain's heaviest train conveys ore from Port Talbot (P.27) to the BSC Spencer
works at Llanwern (L.24) and the Corporation is also an extensive user of the
WR's Speedlink network of express airbraked freight services. Aberthaw
cement (V.1), Ford Motor Company traffic (B.20, S.33), oil from West Wales
(M.16) and chemicals (B.29) are among the other vital South Wales traffics.

In addition to the originating freight business, the WR receives inwards flows
from the other regions including such movements as the UKF fertiliser traffic
from Ince and Elton to purpose-built distribution depots (B.21, C.6). It has
specialised terminals for aggregates (A.6, T.6, W.20), cement (B.22, C.6, C.9),
vehicles (M.1, S.13) and oil (L.1, S.20, T.6, T.10) as well as numerous coal
concentration depots (B.22, C.14, T.3, W.7). Other traffics range from railway
ballast (B.6, M.10, W.23) to scrap metal (C.27, H.17, S.14, S.35) and from

High capacity vans are used on the Speedlink air-braked service network.

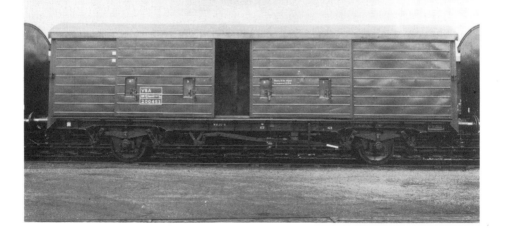

Above *A train of empty hopper wagons rattles through Newport and into the tunnel.*
Below *One of the eight Class 56 locomotives allocated to Canton depot, Cardiff.*

Left *As multiple aspect signalling schemes are extended sights like this will become increasingly rare.*

Below *Trainload freight traffic is an important part of the WR activity.*

Below right *The panel box at Temple Meads, Bristol, with the original station in the background.*

government department business (B.8, F.6, S.20, Q.1) to Red Star parcels (P.1, R.5).

At the beginning of the decade the Western Region had 316 stations and 1,259 vehicles for its passenger business, 603 vans for parcels and similar traffics and 64 stations and 319 sidings dealing with freight. Much of the 1,772 m annual freight tonne miles of the latter now moves in privately-owned high capacity wagons, although a new design of BR van is used on Speedlink services and BR mineral wagons are used for some coal and stone movements. Wagonload business of the traditional type has given way to block train loads and specialised movements such as the Speedlink and Freightliner trains (B.22, C.5, S.13, S.33). These changes have been reflected in the pattern of freight marshalling yards where the total numbers have decreased and those which remain (A.6, E.5, L.16, M.6, R.3, S.13) tend to have special functions.

For its haulage requirements the WR had a 1982 allocation, in round terms, of 47 HST sets, 350 main line locomotives, 125 shunting locomotives and 440 diesel multiple units. There were also rail-mounted cranes, independent snowploughs, vans for parts movements and other departmental equipment. Mileage-based maintenance of the traction is carried out at five main depots (B.22, C.5, P.20, O.3, S.33) and some specialised subsidiary locations (G.3, M.6, N.7, P.15, R.5, S.21) and there is usually some traction activity evident at most of the main traffic centres. Activities of special interest include banking on the Lickey Incline (L.7) and the use of Class 03 shunters on the Cwmmawr branch (C.39). Double heading is quite common in South Wales and for many of the stone trains into the London area.

Much of the main line route mileage has now been laid with continuous welded rail track and on the HST routes speed limits have steadily been raised until significant stretches can now be traversed at 125 mph. The braking characteristics of the Inter-City 125 sets are such that the Multiple Aspect Signalling schemes, already well advanced when the HSTs were introduced, have been able to handle the higher speeds involved without major alteration. The existing panel boxes (O.3, S.18, R.5, S.35, B.22, N.7, C.5, S.33, O.6, G.3

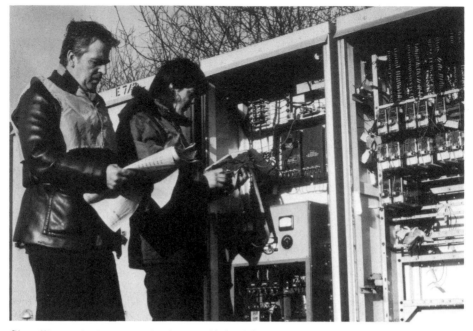

Signalling and telecommunications staff check lineside equipment near Didcot.

and P.20) cover some 700 miles of route and when the £30 million scheme for
the West of England main line is completed it will add a further 107 route miles
to the total and provide additional panel boxes at Westbury and Exeter.

Places like Swindon provide an interesting study in track configuration,
signalling and traffic operation using the latest techniques in colour light
signalling and with such refinements as reversible working over the platform
lines. The semaphore signalling strongholds at Taunton, Exeter and Newton
Abbot will be converted to a similar pattern but major pockets of conventional
signalling will still remain (H.12, W.21, Y.3). Similarly, traditional absolute
block working continues to apply to the double line sections in Cornwall, on the
North and West line, on some Welsh routes and, mixed with Acceptance Lever,
Tokenless Block and Electric Token systems, on lines like those from Oxford to
Hereford and Salisbury to Exeter. Worcester (W.21) is especially endowed with
signalling variety. Further west, the 'Lock and Block' signalling between
Malvern Wells and Ledbury is unique on the WR. It works on the principle of a
locked single line entrance signal, with line clearance released by treadles
worked by the passage of trains.

Most of the WR routes provide interesting studies in train planning, the
process which reconciles market requirements and operational feasibility/
economy and translates the results into timetables, equipment diagrams and
staff rosters. Despite the high speed capability and minimum of two tracks on
the main lines complications can still arise in pathing at major junctions (C.26,
D.5, N.7, R.5, W.9) and the routes with single line sections (L.3) provide
another set of complications. The Cornish branch lines may seem simple enough
in isolation but when their service has to be dovetailed in with main line
connections at the junction points (L.9/L.27, T.19/F.1, P.5/N.8, S.3/S.5),

The modern travel centre at Exeter.

then the complications start to arise.

The Central Wales line embraces some interesting operational facets. In the interests of economy the 78¾ m between Craven Arms and Pantyffynnon are operated under a Department of Transport Light Railway Order which allows signalling and other simplifications in return for a limitation on train numbers and speeds. Between the block posts and crossing loops (L.12, L.13, L.14) train regulation is by telephone and many of the level crossings have been simplified to a 'stop and proceed' or 'open with warning lights' basis. Journey times have been kept acceptable by making many of the stations request stops.

This sort of simplification has been extensive in the sphere of level crossings and single line operation. In the case of the former many traditional sets of gates have been replaced by full or half barriers, some crossings are user-operated, others closed circuit television monitored and many are now completely open. On single lines where traffic is light working may be on a 'one train' basis or just under the control of 'the person in charge'.

In addition to the equipment and working interest to be found on the WR, many of its passenger routes are very attractive scenically. Outstanding in this respect are the Shrewsbury-Newport and Shrewsbury-Llanelli lines, the Golden Valley route through Stroud and the branches to Exmouth (E.7), Barnstaple (B.1), Gunnislake (G.12), Looe (L.27), Falmouth (F.1) and Newquay (N.8). Other attractive sections occur between Kidwelly and Carmarthen, along the Exe and Teign between Starcross and Newton Abbot, down the Avon Valley from Bathampton to Bradford-on-Avon, along the banks of the Tamar and across the Callington Viaduct from Plymouth to Gunnislake, through the wooded areas of Cornwall from Saltash to Truro and through the Oxfordshire countryside towards Evesham.

SECTION 6

Civil engineering

The Western Region has nearly 2,000 route miles of railway which, in turn, involves some 3,500 track miles. To cross or be crossed by the routes of its main lines and branches calls for 2,000 assorted public and private level crossings and over 7,600 bridges, ranging from major civil engineering structures like the Royal Albert Bridge across the Tamar at Plymouth to humble farm crossings deep in the countryside. The routes also involve embankments and cuttings, and the WR Chief Civil Engineer has to maintain 45 m of tunnels and 3,800 m of boundary fencing. Add 400 stations and depots and countless individual buildings and the size of the civil engineering task in the region becomes apparent.

Much advantage still accrues from the fact that much of the WR was originally built to accommodate a gauge of 7 ft and the main line to Bristol, with its gentle gradients and broad, sweeping curves, made an ideal route for the introduction of the first High Speed Train services in 1975/6. However, many of the other routes are neither straight nor level. The South Devon line is an outstanding example in this category. The four main banks (D.1, R.4, H.10) have sections as steep as 1 in 37-47 and the route also curves and twists through the foothills of South Dartmoor, reflecting both Brunel's excessive optimism about the capabilities of atmospheric propulsion and the financial stringencies of the building period. In contrast to the short, sharp inclines west of Taunton and Newton Abbot, the climb either side of milepost 146½ on the Salisbury-Exeter line involves 13¼ m in one direction and 7 m in the other.

Other significant gradients on the region include the Lickey (L.7), Whiteball (W.13), Evershot (E.3) and Cockett (S.33) banks. The climb from Honeybourne through Campden Tunnel (C.4) involves 4 m of 1 in 100, on the main line through Cornwall there is a lot of climbing and descending (including 3 m of 1 in 80 west of Truro), two major peaks occur between Newport and Hereford and the Cotswold (A.8, C.18, S.8) and Malvern (C.28, L.5) barriers necessitate eight tunnels in total. Gradients and tunnels in combination produce some very scenic journeys on the Central Wales and Gunnislake lines, crowned in the former case with the views south of Sugar Loaf Tunnel (S.32) and in the latter with views over the Tamar valley (G.12).

The WR has six tunnels over a mile long: Severn (4 m 628 yds), Sodbury (2 m 926 yds) (C.18), Box (1 m 1,452 yds), Llangyfelach (1 m 193 yds) (S.34), Caerphilly (1 m 181 yds) and Sapperton (1 m 104 yds). Others are notable for reasons other than those of length. Some are double bores such as the Marley

Above *A modern bridge just outside Newport station.*
Below *Multiple aspect signalling for Bristol also meant track simplification and a major programme of alterations to be fitted in without too much disruption of traffic.*

(M.7), Newport (N.7), Dinmore (D.7) and Patchway (P.7) examples, the last two having quite different levels and gradients. Ledbury (L.5) is a very narrow tunnel, a nightmare for footplatemen in the days of steam when the only way to avoid choking was to wear a wet handkerchief over the mouth and nostrils and to crouch down out of the direct line of the acrid fumes. The tunnel at Pontarddulais (P.4) is quite small owing to its tramroad origins and this has brought the problem of maintaining an adequate depth of ballast; the use of slab track may be the answer. Some tunnels, like the one approaching Kemble (K.1), were not really necessary in the first place and some have been converted to cuttings (B.22) or reduced in length (S.33). Most of the longer tunnels caused headaches for the original builder and even today call for special maintenance skills as varied as the massive tasking of pointing the brickwork in the Severn Tunnel (S.12) or of just getting to high, lonely places like Llangynllo (L.20).

Wherever possible the original railway builders preferred to avoid a direct confrontation with severe gradients and frequently achieved this by using a convenient river valley. The River Ely helps the main line westwards out of Cardiff, the Tawe helps it into Swansea and the Tywi gives it access to Carmarthen. The same process shows very clearly on the Central Wales line which is rarely without a river companion and on the West of England main line it produces the scenic stretch down the estuary of the Exe and up that of the Teign. But rivers had to be crossed as well as used and the challenge of this shows up not only in structures like the Royal Albert Bridge (R.8) but also in the work involved in the high level approach from the Plymouth side (P.20). It is also nowhere more evident than on the main line east and west of Plymouth where Brunel built so many viaducts in that near-classical trestle form for the South Devon and Cornwall railways (C.30, F.1, I.2, L.9, L.3, S.4, S.6, T.19).

The variety of bridges seems infinite. They take WR lines across the Somerset levels and beneath countless roads outside Paddington. Wood, bricks, metal and concrete all figure in their construction which can be as traditional as the original bridges still to be found on the Bristol main line (B.3) or as modern as

Permanent way involves many complications, including points, curves and bridges as in this view of the approach to Carmarthen.

the crossings of and by the motorways of the region. The former double deck bridge can still be seen at Ashton, Bristol (B.22), the bridge at Haverfordwest (H.5) was once one of the lifting type, there are eye-pleasing examples like those at Maidenhead (M.1) and across the Brent Valley (H.3) and great, dramatic edifices like the Calstock (G.12). Cynghordy (C.40) and Knucklas (K.7) viaducts. Chepstow (C.15) is in a fine setting and skew examples like the bridge at Cogload (C.26) make an interesting study.

The track itself has received a great deal of attention in recent years. Prior to the introduction of the High Speed Trains on the routes to Bristol and South Wales a major three-year programme of engineering work was undertaken between Acton and Box/Bristol Parkway, the line between Wootton Bassett Junction and Westerleigh Junction being closed for five months in 1975 to facilitate this. In 1978 and 1979 the process was extended to the West of England route where track was relaid, ballast cleaned and renewed and certain formation and embankment stretches strengthened. By casing curves and simplifying layouts (N.4) it was possible to raise line speeds, the Theale-Newbury section, for example, being lifted to a 110 mph limit from the previous 90 mph restriction.

The special attention preceding HST operation plus the results of the normal permanent way renewal programme have brought a position where most of the main line track is now continuous welded rail. The constituents of this are flat bottomed rail weighing 113 lb per yard, affixed to concrete sleepers using Pandrol rail clips and the whole laid on a 300-400 mm bed of ballast. Jointed track still exists on many secondary routes and branches and consists of bullhead rail laid in chairs and resting on jarrah hardwood sleepers. Softwood sleepers are now rarely used and limestone has given way to hard sedimentary rocks for ballast purposes.

Relaying with continuous welded rail is now a highly mechanised process. Using pre-planned operations in pre-timetabled periods the old track is prepared for removal and then replaced by pre-assembled sections of new track. The

Dawlish platform suffered badly from severe gales early in 1974 as this picture of the repair work shows. Taken on May 24, the train is the 9.55 am Paignton to Paddington.

temporary rails are removed from these sections and replaced by 60 ft rails welded into 600-900 ft lengths and stressed with hydraulic tensors. New or cleaned ballast will be used and a final corrective tamping and lining will allow the track to be returned to the normal maintenance cycle. The latter also uses a high degree of mechanisation and tamper/liner machines used in squadron service can produce a good level and correct alignment deficiencies at up to 500 metres per hour. Machine ballast cleaning is commonplace but gauging, the control of curves and cant and the maintenance and renewal of switches and crossings still demands high professional skills from the permanent way staff.

For his track maintenance activities the WR civil engineer has a number of quarries (M.10), siding areas, tips and specialist depots (N.5, T.3) throughout the region. He also has a number of mobile cranes, departmental shunting loco-motives and a large wagon fleet still rejoicing in such code names as Walrus, Dogfish, Salmon and Sea Lion.

British Rail is very conscious of its rich architectural heritage and, despite the cost and operational problems of using period structures for modern traffic activities, has paid a great deal of attention to retaining and maintaining those buildings which are of real historic significance, and to adapting stations of the past to a present day role with the least possible detriment to their architectural character. The Western Region is no exception to this situation and, like the rest of BR, it has a considerable variety of buildings ranging from original to modern, from large to small and from ornate to functional.

The styles and materials of the WR buildings are equally varied. Some stations, especially the modern ones, are essentially simple, others are highly ornamental. Some are single-storey, squat or flat-roofed, others rise high with gables, towers or spires. Timber still appears in many places. Quite a few timber signal boxes remain, plus a few stations (F.10, H.3), and quite a few of the

Typical of the North Devon line stations, these buildings at Kings Nympton are a reminder of the variety of railway architecture.

One of the track maintenance machines used by the WR civil engineering department.

modern, simple shelters are built of wood. Dilton Marsh (D.6) provides a reminder of the GWR's halt building period.

Stone is much in use on the WR and stations like Kemble (K.1) and Stroud (S.30) on the Golden Valley route are a delight to the eye and an inspiration to the camera. Some measure of the amount of stone excavated from Box Hill in the building of Box Tunnel and subsequently can be gauged from the amount put to use in stations and bridges on and near the Bristol main line. Bath (B.3) and its approaches provide the most notable example but there are many others. Brick construction, of course, appears everywhere but a careful examination will reveal many varieties of the traditional, standard red brick. Early construction in particular depended heavily on local brick supplies. In a number of cases blue engineer's bricks have been used to add variety and pattern to building work, and to relieve the plainness otherwise associated with brick construction. Ironwork and steelwork also appears everywhere, especially in footbridges and canopy supports, and the more recent construction shows an increasing use of modern materials such as plastics, reinforced concrete and composite blocks.

Surprisingly, perhaps, quite a few original stations still survive. Among the outstanding examples is Culham (C.37) which has simple 1844 buildings in the original Brunel tradition and with steep gables and tall chimneys. Menheniot (M.12) is a good example of the so-called 'chalet' style and is a reminder of the extent to which the Brunel and Great Western influence spread throughout the associated railways. The South Devon window pattern is, in fact, still well represented west of Exeter where its rounded arches are unmistakable. Outstanding examples of wooden station buildings are now rare but an example of the GWR overall roof station has been retained at Frome (F.10) and there are some interesting wooden canopies among the London suburban stations.

Many examples of early railway buildings are no longer BR property. Among those in South Wales are the Barry Railway's headquarters building at Barry Docks (B.2) and the Taff Vale Railway offices in Cardiff (C.5). Cardiff is also interesting in providing comparisons with the 1930s approach to station building, as demonstrated by Cardiff Central, and with a more modern treatment as revealed in the recent modernisation of Queen Street. Of course, many stations are a mixture of different building and rebuilding exercises, and attempting to understand and date the changes can be quite a fascinating activity. Highbridge (H.14) is one example. A small part of the remaining GWR building may well date back to the B&E era and this contrasts with the strong SR influence still apparent in what is left of the S&D line platform and footbridge.

The Western Region's most dramatic stations are, of course, Paddington and Bristol. Despite all the changes which have taken place at the former the great roof spans still give the station its unique character and maintain a sense of space and grace despite the intense activity of trains and passengers below. The approach to the station at Bristol is surely without equal. The view from the foot of the approach road is of the graceful main station straight ahead, the Jacobean style of the Bristol & Exeter Railway offices on the right and the long, historic buildings of the original station on the left. The character of the latter, which includes the bow window of the old boardroom in the street frontage, is now being maintained by the Brunel Engineering Centre Trust which has taken over the care of.part of the area.

Some of the WR's smaller stations are equally pleasing and high on the list of these is Hereford which, curiously, was not built as a station but taken over for this purpose. Slough has substantial and pleasing buildings on the Down side, the twin domes providing a reminder of several other examples in the London area where twin towers have been used to make relatively simple buildings more imposing (S.18, S.21, W.7). Great Malvern (G.9) is a very attractive station and Pontypridd (P.24) can also be counted among the dramatic, partly because it is so evocative of busier days.

Quite a few traditional country stations remain, mostly on branch lines, although Castle Cary (C.8) is an interesting main line example. On the main line in the far west the country stations remain but there are hardly two alike, while on other routes, eg, the North Devon line (B.1) the origins show up quite clearly in the common architectural style used in the station buildings.

Of course, many of today's stations are essentially functional and many of their buildings are based on standard, easy to maintain designs and prefabricated construction methods. Some consist only of platforms plus shelters of wood, brick, stone or glass and metal, and numerous examples of these occur on the Cardiff 'Valleys' routes where the commuter function of the lines warrants no more elaborate provision. A problem here, and elsewhere, is that of vandalism but despite this some imaginative developments have brightened up what would otherwise be very plain stations (P.24, T.14). Many modern stations are pleasing in looks and effective in passenger handling; Bristol Parkway (B.22) and Kingham (K.4) are good examples. Neath (N.3) has been very effectively rebuilt and includes very attractive buffet premises.

Local authorities are empowered to make a contribution towards transport facilities and in a number of cases this has taken the form of a station development with BR. South Wales has several examples. Other station development schemes have had a commercial input (G.10, S.11, S.35). The result of such a variety of periods, influences and other factors is a vast treasury of interest for those who find pleasure in this aspect of civil engineering.

This same interest is available over the whole range of civil engineering on the WR and not all the sources of it are obvious. Subsidence is a major concern for the civil engineer but—fortunately—finds little tangible expression (L.21, S.1). In contrast, the lineside furniture of mileposts, gradient posts, etc, are rather a routine matter for the civil engineer but can still offer much of interst for the railway devotee. Such byways as crossing keepers' houses can provide a great deal of interest, and a careful scrutiny will usually turn up something of interest whether it be a surviving period drinking fountain (B.27) or a piece of non-standard ornamentation (W.21).

SECTION 7

Early and closed lines

Throughout Great Britain the growth of industrial activity at the end of the 18th century and the beginning of the 19th put increasing pressure on transport resources. An increase in the size of the canal network was the main response but early railways and tramroads also grew in numbers, usually in the form of short feeder lines to a port or the nearest navigable waterway.

The exploitation of the coal resources of South Wales produced a concentration of early tramroads in that area, many built by port or canal companies and most bringing coal down the valleys to the Severn Estuary. Some perished as the main line system took over; others, like the Bridgend Railway and the Llanelly Railway, became part of it; and some, like the three early tramroads between Pontypool and Hereford, were acquired to avoid them causing problems for their main line successors. Quite a few traces of these early lines remain (A.2, B.6, C.41, P.28, W.6). Indeed, the tunnel at Pontarddulais is still making its presence felt because of the small bore which derives from its tramroad ancestry. The Forest of Dean also contains a number of surviving traces of early lines serving the coal mines of the Free Miners there.

The other major area for early lines was the South-West. They served the ore and granite wrested from Dartmoor, the arsenic, lead and copper mines around the Tamar and the copper and tin industries of Cornwall. Most have left traces—best discovered from a detailed history of the line and the earlier ordnance survey maps—and some examples are the Plymouth & Dartmoor (P.20), the Liskeard & Caradon (M.18), the Redruth & Chasewater (C.9, R.6), the Bodmin & Wadebridge (W.4) and the Hayle Railway (H.7). Most of these were early railways rather than tramways and they dealt with considerable volumes of business during their peak years. Other early lines in the South-West served the china clay industry (N.8).

Elsewhere the early railways were less numerous and existed for specific local purposes. Examples include the tramway from Ralph Allen's quarry at Bath (B.3) and William James' 4 ft gauge Stratford & Moreton Railway (M.20), although the latter was conceived as part of a trunk route from the Midlands to London.

The rationalisation of railways since the war has closed many miles of track. The longest of the various closed routes are described separately below but many branch lines also succumbed to the twin enemies of rising costs and falling receipts. These factors bore most heavily on the lines which were not part of the

After closure the station at Blagdon became a very attractive private dwelling.

national main line system and some such railways were among the first to close, for example:

The Bideford, Westward Ho! & Appledore Railway
Opened from Bideford to Northam on May 20 1901 and extended, as a light railway, to Appledore on May 1 1908. Services lasted only until March 27 1917.

The Lynton & Barnstaple Railway
Essentially a local enterprise, this 1 ft 11½ in gauge line opened on May 6 1898 but was never a financial success. The Southern Railway bought it for £30,000 but closed the route on September 30 1935. Many signs of the route remain and ideas of partial re-opening have been gathering momentum.

The West Somerset Mineral Railway
Built to provide an outlet for the iron ore of the Brendon Hills, this line opened on September 28 1859 and closed in 1910. Remains are still visible near Raleigh's Cross.

The Weston, Clevedon & Portishead Railway
The route across the flat coastal plain from Weston-super-Mare to Clevedon opened on December 1 1897 with the extension to the third coastal town on September 1 1907. Only the light railway operational skills of Colonel H.F. Stephens and the indulgence of the line's creditor kept the highly individualistic railway going until final closure on May 19 1940.

Swansea & Mumbles Railway
This was the first public passenger carrying railway in the world, authorised by an Act of June 29 1804 and in the passenger business from March 25 1807.

Above *The West Somerset Mineral Railway has long since closed but the engine house at the top of the incline lingers on.*

Left *Passengers for the North Somerset line at one time obtained their tickets from the local pub at Farrington Gurney.*

Although the line became, to all intents and purposes, an electric tramway, it survived until January 5 1960.

The major stretches of closed line within the Western area are:

The Somerset & Dorset Railway system

Living up to its title, the Somerset & Dorset network comprised the route from Burnham-on-Sea, Highbridge and Bridgwater to Evercreech where junction was made with the Bath Extension which had climbed to Masbury summit to surmount the Mendip hills. From Evercreech Junction the line ran south-east, connecting with the L&SW main line to the West at Templecombe, and then on through the heart of Dorset to further junctions with the L&SW outside Bournemouth.

The system originated with the Somerset Central Railway's broad gauge line from Highbridge Wharf to Glastonbury, opened on August 28 1854 with a short line to Wells following in 1859. Earlier close relationships with the Bristol & Exeter Railway deteriorated and with them the plans for connection with the Wilts, Somerset & Weymouth line. Soon the Somerset Central was planning, instead, to link up with the Dorset Central Railway which opened from Wimborne to Blandford on November 1 1860, the union between the two eventually taking place at Cole on February 3 1862. Using the pier at Burnham and running powers over the LSW to Poole, the Somerset & Dorset as the amalgamated railways became from 1862—saw itself as providing a steamer-rail-steamer route from South Wales to France.

Despite many financial problems the Somerset & Dorset opened its extension to Bath on July 20 1874 but the additional business to and from the north was not enough to keep the S&D out of the hands of the Midland and LSW companies whose offer for the enterprise was better than that made by the GW and B&E railways.

The S&D main line closed on March 7 1966 although various other bits lingered on until 1972. Much of the route can still be found, some locked in the glorious countryside south of Bath, more at Radstock, viaducts survive at Shepton Mallet and Cole and much of interest is still to be seen in the Highbridge area (H.14).

South Wales

It would not be possible in this short section to cover adequately the closed lines of South Wales but a number of routes warrant mention for the sheer drama of their origins and course. Chief among these are the cross-valley lines like that by which the LNWR secured access to the rich industrial traffic of the Principality. By a lease of the Merthyr, Tredegar & Abergavenny Railway it secured a route from Abergavenny Junction to Merthyr which opened slowly westwards between 1862 and 1879. Via Brynmawr, Nantybwch, Rhymney Bridge and Dowlais the route ran via gradients, mountain sides and tunnels, rising to 1,400 ft above sea level at Waenavon and needing up to 110 minutes for the 24½ m journey. Most of the route was closed in 1968.

Another great east-west route in South Wales was that from Pontypool Road to Neath, started from the west by the Vale of Neath Railway in 1851-3 and from the east by the Taff Vale Extension scheme in 1855. An outstanding feature of the eventual 41¾ m line was the great Crumlin Viaduct over the valley of the Ebbw, ten spans of 150 ft each rising to a height of 208 ft built by T.W. Kennard. It was demolished following the closure of the through route in 1964.

In the north-south direction West Wales had the long meandering line from Carmarthen to Aberystwyth, with branches to Aberayron and Newcastle Emlyn, and the 27 ½ m branch from Whitland to Cardigan. In South Wales the three lines to Brecon have all gone although the southern end of the Neath & Brecon—part of the Midland Railway's South Wales probe—remains in use as the Onllwyn coal line (O.5).

The Withered Arm

This was the title bestowed by T.W.E. Roche on the former SR lines in Devon and Cornwall. From Exeter the system ran through the Devon heartland to Meldon Junction (B.1, M.10) where the line to Tavistock and Plymouth separated from the route on to Launceston, Wadebridge and Padstow and the branch from Halwill Junction to Bude.

For nearly 60 years prior to opening GWR and LSWR interests had sparred with one another in the counties of the South-West, especially after the latter's illegal acquisition of the Bodmin & Wadebridge Railway in 1847. It achieved nothing to fill the gap until, through the instrument of the Devon & Cornwall Railway, narrow gauge metals reached Okehampton in 1871 and Lydford, en route for Plymouth, in 1874. A line to Holsworthy served Bude from 1878 to 1898 with the North Cornwall Railway limping L&SW interests to Wadebridge between 1886 and 1895.

Although this was the route of the SR's Atlantic Coast Express, it took six hours of the night to cover the 260 m from Waterloo and local trains on the meandering route needed four hours for the 88¾ m between Exeter and Padstow. But even this must have been better than nothing, the situation which applied west of Okehampton from October 3 1966 when this 'main line' became

These stone blocks, just visible, are a reminder of the many early tramroads in the Forest of Dean.

just long stretches of trackbed, a collection of old stations and a few redundant bridges and viaducts.

Midland & South Western Junction Railway

This 62½ m route left the Cheltenham-Kingham line at Andoversford and passed via Cirencester, Swindon, Marlborough and Savernake to join the LSW at Red Posts Junction, near Andover. It derived from the Swindon, Marlborough & Andover Railway which opened the southern portion in 1881-2 and from the Swindon & Cheltenham Extension Railway which reached Cirencester on December 18 1883 and Andoversford on August 1 1891. To avoid using GWR metals between Marlborough and Grafton an independent link was opened in 1898 and the M&SWJ also had an important branch from Ludgershall to Tidworth Camp.

In addition to such through workings as a Liverpool-Southampton service the route had Cheltenham-Andover stopping trains and local workings either side of Swindon. The former M&SWJ offices at Swindon, closed after the line passed to the GWR under grouping, are still visible as is the Town station there. The line closed on September 11 1961 although odd sections remained open for freight, the last to go being that from Swindon to Moredon power station. Much of the trackbed remains visible (S.9, S.35).

Didcot, Newbury & Southampton Railway

The 34 m of this company's line used a portion of GWR metals between junctions either side of Newbury (N.4) and a bay platform at Didcot (D.5) as part of its route from the latter to Winchester. The northern section opened on April 13 1882 and the southern portion on May 1 1885, and although local traffic was sparse, the route did carry a Paddington-Winchester/Southampton service. The southern section was closed first, on March 7 1960, and the rest followed on September 10 1962.

Despite the bleak terrain, a number of railways and tramroads penetrated Dartmoor as this trackbed shows.

Top *Demolition has already started in this view of the Midland station at Gloucester and was soon to level the site.*

Above *For a long while after closure the Midland station in Bath remained in use as a car park.*

Left *Cheltenham Racecourse station was once on the GWR main line from Bristol to Birmingham but now lies deserted in its cutting.*

Cheltenham (Lansdown Junction) to Stratford-upon-Avon

In the first decade of the century the GWR's policy of shortening and improving its routes produced a new main line between Bristol and Birmingham. Using Westerleigh Junction north of Bristol and the newly-reopened avoiding line at Gloucester, the package consisted of a new line from Honeybourne to Cheltenham (1904-6), doubling the Bearley-Honeybourne branch and a new line (1907-8) from Tyseley Junction to Bearley. The Midland failed in its bid to confine the use of the Westerleigh spur to trains for the Severn & Wye and a number of GWR express services, eg, Wolverhampton-Penzance, used the new line. However, local traffic was not great and closures took place piecemeal in the 1960s, the line then lingering on as a diversionary route for many years. Now only the short freight spur to Long Marston (H.17) remains operational but most of the route can be traced without difficulty.

Banbury & Cheltenham Direct Railway

By lines from Cheltenham to Bourton-on-the-Water (1881) and Chipping Norton to Kings Sutton (1887) this company completed a route from Banbury via Kingham to Cheltenham. Although the lines either side of Kingham were provided with a connecting loop in 1906 they continued to be operated primarily as two branches and through workings were few. Closure was piecemeal between 1951 and 1969, leaving Kingham (K.4) with surplus platforms.

In aggregate the lines on the west bank of the Severn represented a significant closed mileage. In addition to the GWR and Severn & Wye systems in Dean—perhaps the most fascinating of all groups in the region—the three routes from Ross-on-Wye have gone, as have those from Monmouth. Of great nostalgic regret is the loss of the route down the Wye Valley to Chepstow, although a stub remains at the southern end (W.23) and Gwent County Council has a recreation centre on the line at Tintern where the signal box is an information point and the active days of the line are recalled in display material in the former station buildings.

Another long stretch of closed railway is the cross-Somerset route from Yatton, along the edge of the Mendip hills to Wells and then on to Witham (Y.2, C.33, M.13, W.17). It had its own branch from Congresbury to Blagdon, built under the Light Railway legislation. Through trains could take over two hours for the 31½ m journey but the scenery was delightful. Many of the station buildings can still be located.

References to closed lines in the Gazetteer section are normally included with the nearest and appropriate operational location, eg, the Calne branch is referred to in the Chippenham entry as this is where it made junction with the main line.

SECTION 8

Preservation and non-BR lines

The area covered by this book is as rich in preserved lines and equipment as it is in other aspects of railways. And the range is again extraordinarily varied, from the dramatic operational ventures like the Dart Valley and Torbay & Dartmouth railways to such fascinating miniature lines as those at the Bird Paradise at Hayle and along the quay at Kingsbridge. The same can be said of static preservation, whether it be the impressive collection at the Great Western Railway Museum at Swindon or the exhibits incorporated in mining museums at Wheal Martyn, Redruth and Wendron in Cornwall. Some of the ventures are especially imaginative and the development centred on the royal waiting rooms at Windsor will add to their number. Others are unique, and among these is the Pendon Museum of Miniature Landscape and Transport at Long Wittenham where the enjoyment of the model railway scenes is enhanced by the work being done on the accurate recreation of Vale of White Horse scenes in miniature.

The major locations of railway interest comprise:

Bicton Woodland Railway
Bicton Gardens, East Budleigh, Budleigh Salterton, Devon. This 1¼ m, dual-route railway runs through delightful grounds where André le Notre laid out notable landscape gardens in 1735. Of 18 in gauge, it was opened in 1963 using equipment from the former Woolwich Arsenal system.

Bitton Railway Centre
Bitton Station, Bristol, Avon. The Bitton Railway Company has built up a preservation centre at the former Bitton station on the old MR route from Mangotsfield to Bath. In addition to the station buildings, goods shed and a signal box brought from Painswick Road Crossing at Gloucester, the preservation body has a short length of operational line towards Warmley and plans more. The locomotives at Bitton include interesting representatives of the Bristol industrial locomotive builders.

Brecon Mountain Railway
Pontsticill Station, Merthyr Tydfil, Mid-Glam. The combination of a narrow gauge railway and a National Park area makes a visit to this 1 ft 11¾ in gauge line a very attractive outing. From Pant station the line runs for 2 m, mainly along the route of the old Brecon & Merthyr Railway to Pontsticill on the shore of the Taf Fechan reservoir. A further extension into the park is envisaged.

Operation is daily from May to September plus some subsequent weekends, using a variety of industrial steam locomotives.

Dart Valley Railway

Buckfastleigh Station, Devon. The Dart Valley Railway is a commercial venture with enthusiast support, started in 1969 and now operating each summer over a 7 m section of the former BR Ashburton branch from Buckfastleigh to Totnes (Riverside). The former is the main station and accommodates the railway's collection of GWR and industrial steam locomotives and its rolling stock which includes such special items as GWR auto trailers, directors/engineers saloons, a Pullman observation car and a sizeable GWR wagon/van fleet. As might be expected, the railway has a strong GWR flavour.

Dean Forest Railway Society Ltd

Norchard Steam Centre, Nr Lydney, Glos. After nearly 12 years of waiting for the closure of the Lydney-Parkend line the society was able to begin final negotiations with BR for its takeover in 1981. During the waiting period the society's collection of GWR and industrial locomotives and rolling stock had been moved from the initial depot at Parkend to Norchard where a steam centre and short operational line were established.

Dowty Railway Preservation Society

Northway Lane, Ashchurch, Tewkesbury, Glos. The society has a mixed and interesting collection of standard and narrow gauge equipment ranging from 0-4-0 industrial steam locomotives to GWR passenger and freight stock. Visitors are welcomed on Sunday afternoons and open days are held from time to time.

Two locomotives in steam at the Bicton Woodland Railway in Bicton Gardens.

4-6-0 7827 Lydham Manor *and 2-6-2T 4588 head a BR special on Torbay & Dartmouth metals near Greenway Tunnel.*

East Somerset Railway

Cranmore Station, Shepton Mallet, Somerset. This is the home of David Shepherd's engines and the former signal box at Cranmore is used as a gallery for the work of this notable railway and wildlife artist. In addition to the restored station, there is an engine shed built in the Victorian tradition and summer train services are operated along the line westwards. Among the locomotives and rolling stock at Cranmore are 2-10-0 92203 *Black Prince* and 4-6-0 75029 *The Green Knight.*

Forest Railroad Park

Dobwalls, Liskeard, Cornwall. Daily from mid-April to early October each year visitors can find in Cornwall a miniature of the Union Pacific Railroad in Wyoming and of the Rio Grande's Colorado forest routes. They are part of the 11 acres of railway fascination at the Forest Railroad Park where there are tunnels, lakes, forests, 1 in 65 gradients, trestle bridges, canyons and many other aids to realism, as well as supplementary exhibitions and attractions. The lines are worked by 4-8-8-4 *William Jeffers*, 4-8-4 *Queen of Wyoming*, 2-8-2 *General Palmer*, 2-8-2 *Otto Mears*, 2-6-2 *David Curwen* and internal combustion locomotives.

Great Western Railway Museum

Faringdon Road, Swindon, Wilts. Located in the heart of the 'village' created by the GWR at Swindon and now restored by the local authority, the twin-towered museum building was first a lodging house for railway workers and later a Wesleyan chapel. Since 1962 it has been a museum with a collection of five locomotives, including *City of Truro*, and a range of smaller items—models, prints, photographs, signalling and traffic equipment—helping to bring to life the era of the Great Western Railway.

Great Western Society Ltd

Didcot Railway Centre, Didcot, Oxon. The society celebrated its 20th anniversary in 1981 with the operation of the first steam train on the second of its lines at Didcot, although the official opening took place as part of the 21st anniversary weekend celebrations in March 1982. That year also provided the 50th birthday of the Didcot engine shed, now part of the railway centre complex sited in the angle between the Bristol and Oxford lines. In addition to its superb collection of over a hundred locomotives and rolling stock items, the society has a typical GWR small station and such paraphernalia as lineside mail exchange equipment. Some items are outbased with groups at Swindon and Taunton.

Below *A quiet moment on the East Somerset Railway at Cranmore with 92203* Black Prince *on the right.*
Bottom *One of the splendid steam locomotives on the Union Pacific line at the Forest Railroad Park, near Liskeard.*

Above *Open Day activity at the Great Western Society's Didcot Railway Centre.*
Above right *Substantial civil engineering on the line that conveys visitors to the World of Models at Oakhill Manor.*
Right *Scene on the West Somerset Railway. 0-6-0T 6412 is now back in traffic.*
Below right *A good example of smaller steam traction at the Beer Modelrama with locomotive* Dickie *and a train of holidaymakers.*

Gwili Steam Railway

Bronwydd Arms, Nr Carmarthen, Dyfed. The preservation company has a Light Railway Order covering 8 m at the southern end of the ex-BR line from Carmarthen to Aberystwyth. The summer weekend passenger services operate over 1¾ m from Bronwydd Arms along the course of the River Gwili.

Lappa Valley Railway

St Newlyn East, Newquay, Cornwall. This 1 m, 15 in gauge railway operates over part of the GWR Newquay-Perranporth branch trackbed, between Benny Mill and East Wheal Rose. The ruins of the engine house and chimney at the latter point, where the trains have a turning circle, are a reminder of the mineral traffic origins of the route.

Morwellham Quay

Morwellham, Tavistock, Devon. In a beautiful Tamar Valley setting a project of the Dartington Amenity Research Trust has brought life back to the inland port and mining complex which once served Europe's richest copper lodes. Included in the Morwellham site are two railways, a raised system on the great dock and a 2 ft gauge tramway for taking visitors into the George & Charlotte Copper Mine.

Oakhill Manor

Oakhill, Bath, Somerset. This 1 m, 10¼ in gauge railway conveys visitors over a landscaped and fully engineered route to the manor itself. This houses a remarkable collection of railway, ship, aircraft and other models.

Seaton & District Electric Tramway

Riverside Depot, Harbour Road, Seaton, Devon. Coming from Eastbourne

in 1970, the 2 ft 9 in gauge tramway now operates on a 2½ m section of the former BR Seaton branch as far as Colyton. The seven trams in the fleet use an overhead current supply and services operate during the main summer holiday period.

Torbay & Dartmouth Railway
Paignton Park Station, Paignton, Devon. A companion venture to the Dart Valley Railway, the T&D was taken over with local authority assistance after the BR Paignton-Kingswear line closed in 1972. Now, each summer, GWR tank and tender engines haul trains over the 7 m route from a station backing on to the BR one at Paignton to the estuary of the River Dart at Kingswear. The route is scenic and offers steep gradients, viaducts and a 429 yd tunnel.

West Somerset Railway
Minehead Station, Minehead, Somerset. Despite all sorts of problems this preservation project opened its first section of line, from Minehead to Blue Anchor, in 1976 and has since extended its services to Watchet, Williton and Bishops Lydeard. The avowed intention is the restoration of services over the whole 24¾ m to Taunton. The WSR uses GWR and industrial steam traction plus dmus for off-peak services. The Somerset & Dorset Railway Museum Trust is based on the WSR line at Washford.

A location of a slightly different kind is the Bulmer Railway Centre at Whitecross Road, Hereford run, in conjunction with the cider firm, by the 6000 Locomotive Association and several preservation societies. It is not only the home of such famous locomotives as 6000 *King George V,* 35028 *Clan Line* and 6201 *Princess Elizabeth*, but also acts as the base for steam tours. The centre is open at weekends and on special open days.

Museums in the area include the Bristol Industrial Museum (Princes Wharf, Bristol), the South Devon Railway Museum (Dawlish Warren Station, Devon), Tiverton Museum (St Andrews Street, Tiverton) and the growing industrial and maritime museums in Cardiff and Swansea. Other locations of special railway interest are the Tintern Station Picnic Area, the Bugle Railway and the Plymouth Railway Circle's exhibits at Saltram House, Plympton, Plymouth.

The Caerphilly Railway Society undertakes restoration work in the yard of the former Rhymney Railway works at Caerphilly and the Railway Club of Wales is developing a steam centre in association with the Swansea Industrial & Maritime Museum. Line re-opening schemes include those of the Swindon & Cricklade Railway Society (Moredon-Cricklade), the Vale of Teifi Narrow Gauge Railway (9 m of 2 ft gauge line along the Newcastle Emlyn branch) and schemes for the Lynton & Barnstaple, Cheltenham-Honeybourne and Yelverton lines.

The Western Region since 1983

The original introduction of InterCity 125 High Speed Trains on the Western Region produced a golden opportunity for breaking speed records. This was duly taken but more records fell in 1984 when a world speed record for diesel electric traction was established on a run from Paddington to Bristol (Temple Meads) on August 30. The journey was covered in 62 minutes 33 seconds to produce an average speed of 112.8 mph, beating the 111 7 mph set up on April 10 1979 on a Paddington Chippenham run. On arrival at Temple Meads, power car 43002 of the new record breaking train was named *Top of the Pops* by Jimmy Savile OBE.

Another record fell in the following year, this time on a Paddington-Plymouth run. On March 21 a charter train covered the 225.7 miles in 2 hours 31 minutes 47 seconds to produce an average speed of 89 mph, a record for the route.

The two routes are, of course, quite different. On the Bristol line HSTs can now run at 125 mph from Acton to Box Tunnel apart from an 80 mph section at Reading, 100 mph at Swindon and a short 120 mph spot on the Up line at Cholsey. On the West of England main line the maximum speed between Reading and Taunton is 110 mph, with 90/100 mph to Exeter and around 70 mph on the South Devon section on to Plymouth.

InterCity traffic growth in the Region has been substantial, 26 per cent over the last three years on the West of England route and 37 per cent on the main line to Bristol and South Wales. The number of HST sets available remains at 31 but their utilisation has been improved to lift the availability figure from 81 per cent to 87 per cent and the total daily mileage of the fleet from 20,755 to 22,790 miles. Even so, overcrowding has been a problem on the WR but some easement is likely from the use of 2 + 8 car sets in the place of the present 2 + 7 combination when the delivery of new Mk 4 stock throws up some extra trailer vehicles from the East Coast Main Line.

Contrasting with the modern face of the WR was the celebration in 1985 of 'GWR150', the 150th anniversary of the Great Western Railway. A mammoth exhibition at Swindon had to be cancelled because of reactions to the announcement of the closure of Swindon Works, but a number of worthwhile events did take place. Among them was the operation of an exhibition train which toured major locations and admitted some 130,000 people to its display and art gallery coaches.

New services from the South Coast to the North West via Kensington Olympia and Reading were inaugurated with the May 1986 timetables, just before the emergence of the new Network South East business sector on June 10 of that year. The Chiltern Lines routes out of Marylebone fall under the latter's jurisdiction and are now part

With the opening of the new panel signal box at Exeter St Davids, modern multiple aspect signalling now covers the West of England main line as far as Totnes.

of the WR, which also controls the experimental service introduced between Oxford and Bicester Town from May 11 1987.

The 'park and ride' philosophy was extended on the WR by adding more 'Parkway' stations to the original Bristol Parkway. In addition to the elevation of Port Talbot and Didcot to Port Talbot Parkway and Didcot Parkway, a brand new station was opened at Tiverton Parkway in place of the old Tiverton Junction. A further such development is in mind for the Iver area.

South Wales suffered a setback when severe storms resulted in the collapse of a bridge on the Central Wales line while a dmu was passing over it. Tragically four lives were lost and the gap had to be operated with buses until a new bridge was installed. In contrast, the Cardiff Valleys network has been a scene of considerable expansion with two new lines and several new stations being added.

In the freight sphere the yards at Severn Tunnel Junction have been closed and Margam reorganised to fulfil a more compact purpose. Movements of Mendip aggregates have continued to increase, with Foster Yeoman purchasing their own locomotives for main line use and adding to their wagon fleet. Another major freight development was a 15 year contract between BR and Avon County Council for the movement of containerised refuse from the former Barrow Road steam depot site to London Brick Company claypits at Calvert. In Cornwall the future of the china clay business was assured with an agreement for the provision of new purpose-built wagons to replace the old Medfit fleet.

From May 16 1988 more Pullman services were added to the Golden Hind and Red Dragon pair already operating. These were the West Country Pullman running to Paignton via Bristol and the Stratford-upon-Avon Pullman, both summer services aimed specifically at the tourist and leisure market. The 'St David Pullman' to and from Swansea was added in 1989.

Stations on the Western Region have also received attention, a major reconstruction taking place at Reading to give it a new car park and a complete restyling of the forecourt and entrance facilities. Roof renovation work has begun at Paddington and at Bristol (Temple Meads).

Further changes lie ahead for Paddington. An agreement signed between Network South East and Heathrow Airport Ltd provides for the building and operation of a new, electrified rail link to the airport and this will use Paddington as its London terminal. Two platforms there will be dedicated for the use of the new 100 mph Heathrow Express trains which are due to start running in 1993.

The Paddington-Heathrow electrification will require alterations along the WR main line as far as Hayes and the opportunity is to be taken to bring the remodelling of Paddington planned for 1995 forward and to introduce a new track layout concurrent with the Heathrow scheme changes. After completion of the various alterations Paddington will have no further locomotive-hauled services, just InterCity 125s, Heathrow Express trains and Networker Turbos.

As this book goes to press, latest developments are the opening of a new station at Islip following the successful reinstatement of passenger services on the Oxford-Bicester line, and the commencement of work on a new £3.5 million scheme to replace Oxford's relatively modern station, scheduled for completion in the first half of 1990. Yate station on the Gloucester-Bristol line has also been reopened, following a vast increase in the population of the area north-east of Bristol. Costing £140,000, the new station came into use from May 10 1989 with a service of seven trains a day.

Gazetteer update

Aberdare Branch

A passenger service was resumed on the Aberdare branch on October 3 1988. The development was part of a £2 million Mid Glamorgan County Council scheme and provided for new, single-platform stations at Abercynon North, Penrhiwceiber, Mountain Ash, Fernhill, Cwmbach and Aberdare.

Barnstaple Branch

Track lifting beyond Barnstaple on the line to Bideford was undertaken in 1985. In its latter days the line had carried Meeth clay traffic, Torrington milk and coal via Fremington.

Lower down the Barnstaple branch, colour light signalling has been installed on the portion from the junction with the main line to the diversion of the Meldon line. That work was carried out in December 1984 and subsequently the former double track portion south of Crediton was converted to single line operation.

Bicester Line

In a joint venture with local councils, BR restored a passenger service to the Oxford-Bicester line on May 11 1987. A special train from Oxford to Bicester Town (the former London Road, closed on January 1 1968) and back formed part of the special celebration of the event on May 9.

Box Tunnel

The West Portal of the 1 mile 1,452 yard Box Tunnel was given a thorough clean in 1986. On completion, a viewing platform was provided nearby with the assistance of the Railway Heritage Trust.

Right *After this official opening in the previous week, passenger services were restored to the Aberdare 'Valleys' branch from October 3 1988.*

Below *Bicester London Road station, closed in 1968, began to deal with passenger trains once again in 1987, under the name Bicester Town.*

Bristol

Changes at Bristol include the demolition of the old Temple Meads goods depot to permit development of the waterside site. An original Bristol & South Wales Union Railway commemorative plaque has been moved to the station which is also undergoing major roof renovation. The single-span, Gothic arch roof, now having £1.25 million spent on it, was the work of Francis Cox and has 26 individual spans supported on the curve by brick walls and cast-iron columns.

Another change at Bristol is the enlargement of the HST depot at St Philips Marsh. This is a £3 million project to enable the depot to deal with the longer trains needed because of overcrowding on the main line.

Cardiff-Radyr Line

This ex-Taff Vale Railway line rejoined the passenger network from October 5 1987 with new stations at Danescourt, Fairwater and Ninian Park (previously used for major events at the nearby stadium). Another new station, Waungron, opened the next month.

Cathays

A new station was opened at Cathays on October 3 1983. The old 1846 Taff Vale works area nearby was, at that time, suffering from a reduction in its coal wagon repair activities and the future looked far from hopeful. However, the location now has a new lease of life specialising in high grade rolling stock refurbishment and repair. Perhaps the decision was influenced by the calibre of the special work done by Cathays in fitting out the 'GWR150' exhibition train.

Central Wales Line

Work took place during 1986 to implement an £815,000 scheme of alterations designed to provide more efficient and cost effective operation. Under a new Light Railway Order, the loops on the line were converted to a self-acting basis, permitting the transfer of control from local signal boxes to the one at Pantyffynnon. At Llandrindod Wells the passing loop was moved to the station.

In the following year disaster struck the Central Wales Line. On October 19 1987, after a period of heavy rain, the bridge over the River Tywi at Glanrhyd, near Llandeilo, collapsed under an early morning dmu service, plunging the train into the swollen river with the loss of four lives. On October 16 of the following year a 200 ton replacement bridge was erected on new concrete abutments to permit normal through working to be resumed on the route.

Chipping Sodbury

At the west end of the tunnel the track has been raised to lessen the accumulation of flood water which tends to drain from the tunnel and cause permanent way faults. At the same time the 7 ft wide aqueduct carrying the River Frome over the track was raised by a similar amount.

Coryton Branch

May 11 1987 brought the full opening of a new station at Ty Glas, although trains had been calling on request from April 29.

Cwmbran

Cwmbran lost its station on the Eastern Valley line from Newport to Blaenavon in 1962 but got a new station, between Newport and Pontypool, on May 12 1986. Costing £215,000, the new station serves the Cwmbran Development Corporation area and consists of two 400 ft platforms with a Down side ticket office.

Dawlish

In mid-November 1986 new colour light signalling was introduced on the stretch of coastal line through Dawlish. The scheme was part of the overall resignalling of the West of England main line with five boxes closing and their work being concentrated on the new Exeter panel.

As part of the Dawlish alterations, the Up line was made bi-directional to permit its use when heavy seas make the Down line impassable.

Didcot

With its change of name to Didcot Parkway from July 19 1985, Didcot also got a 600 space free car park, a new station building and a plaque to commemorate these events.

Eastbrook

A new station was opened at Eastbrook, on the Barry Island line between Dinas Powys and Cogan, on November 24 1987.

Exeter

The new signalling centre at Exeter St

Davids was opened on the site of the old water tank on April 13 1988. Controlling 100 route miles between Athelney and Totnes, the new installation replaced 31 mechanical frames.

Fowey Branch

The continued use of the branch for china clay shipment traffic has been aided by a Railfreight investment of £4 million in new hopper wagons. As part of an overall scheme, the English China Clay Company is also refurbishing its discharge area at Carne Point.

Frome

Fourteen passengers were injured in a head-on collision at Frome North Junction on March 24 1987 between an empty stone train and a loaded passenger train.

Gloucester

Following the closure of Severn Tunnel Junction, Gloucester's freight yard has been upgraded to handle some 80 freight movements daily. Speedlink trains are now separated and marshalled at the New Yard, alongside the Avoiding Line, the CCE having moved to a new site where the old Barnwood loco shed used to be.

Great Malvern

The main station buildings were badly damaged by fire on April 11 1986 but were subsequently restored with the help of the Railway Heritage Trust and English Heritage. A plaque was unveiled to mark the completion of the works which included a new booking hall. A 'Clockwatch' appeal has been launched to restore the original clock tower.

A subsequent development affecting the 1862 Hereford & Worcester Railway station has been the restoration of what was originally a private waiting room provided for Lady Foley in recognition of the amount of land she provided for the original railway construction. It is now back in use as a tearoom after being elegantly refurbished in Victorian style and winning a 1989 Railway Heritage Trust award.

Henley-on-Thames Branch

The 1892 building at Shiplake and the 1900 example at Wargrave were demolished in 1985 and replaced by simpler modern structures.

Kidwelly

A new freight line, one mile long, was brought into use between Kidwelly and the coal washery at Coedbach on September 19 1983 with a formal opening ceremony following on October 27. The new line enabled the 5¼ miles of the old Burry Port & Gwendraeth Valley Railway between Coedbach and Pembrey & Burry Port to be closed.

Lickey Incline

The reduction in banking requirements has permitted the move of the banking engines from Bromsgrove to Gloucester where they can do other work. Only night banking assistance is now required.

Llandeilo

The signal box has been closed consequent upon the alterations in the working of the Central Wales Line (see that entry).

Llandovery

The signal box has been closed consequent upon the alterations in the working of the Central Wales Line (see that entry).

Llandrindod Wells

The 1986 scheme of alterations on the Central Wales Line (see that entry) included moving the passing loop at Llandrindod to the station area.

Llanwrtyd

The signal box has been closed consequent upon the alterations in the working of the Central Wales Line (see that entry).

Lostwithiel

A new £90,000 station building was brought into use in November 1984. The displaced Brunel-design wooden buildings went to the Plym Valley Railway's site.

Margam

Changes at Margam have replaced the former hump yard with a purpose-built Knuckle Yard of 18 sidings. Operational from November 1987, the new yard handles coil and slab steel from the local British

Steel works plus inwards movements of coal and lime. Railfreight will use four of the sidings for Speedlink wagon load traffic.

An additional crossover at Margam Moors East Junction plus local track simplification and the removal of Water Street Junction have achieved both easy access to the new yard and main line running improvements. All signalling, except within the new yard, has been concentrated on the Port Talbot panel.

Melksham

Originally closed on April 18 1966, Melksham was reopened on an experimental basis from May 13 1985 and has a modest Westbury-Swindon service.

Merehead Quarry Junction Branch

Now with its own locomotive fleet, the Foster Yeoman company took delivery of 50 new 67 tonne stone wagons between July and October 1988. The wagons were acquired from Tiphook Rail and will be used for 2,400 tonne trainloads from Merehead to South East England.

Newport

A new single line spur off the Uskmouth branch was opened on August 19 1988. This was a joint Railfreight Isinglink project, the new line leading to a mini terminal for delivering steel coil into British Steel's works.

Newquay

Following the withdrawal of locomotive-hauled trains from the branch, the station at Newquay has been simplified. The track at Platform 1 has been lifted and trains now use Platforms 2 and 3.

Newton Abbot

A simplication of the station layout has removed the Up Platform Loop to allow easier passenger access to the main platforms.

Removing the Up platform loop has created room at Newton Abbot for this car park, and has improved passenger access to the platforms.

Paddington

In 1987 work started on the 1930 portion of station roof above The Lawn, as part of a four-year plan which also embraced the original Brunel roof area.

Pantyffynnon

Operational changes on the Central Wales Line have resulted in the concentration of control of the southern portion on the signal box at Pantyffynnon.

Pinhoe

Previously closed on March 7 1966, Pinhoe station, 2¾ miles east of Exeter, was reopened on May 16 1983.

Port Talbot

Port Talbot station was renamed Port Talbot Parkway from December 3 1984 following the creation of a 100-space car park in the former goods yard.

Radstock

A clearance train ran to and from Radstock on June 19 1988 to remove items from Marcroft Engineering Works and permit the final closure of the line from Frome.

Reading

February 1988 brought the addition of a 1,000-space car park to the facilities at Reading, the first stage of a multi-million pound development scheme. The scheme also plans a new concourse in glass and steel with up-to-date ticket, information, Railair and other passenger facilities. In a third stage of the overall project, Reading's 1865 main block will be refurbished and a new station forecourt provided.

The last traffic over the Reading Central branch was on July 25 1983, the Coley Branch Junction connection being removed on January 20 1985.

Rhymney Branch

In 1984 the junction between the Rhymney and Coryton lines was remodelled. The single line connection from the latter to the double track route on to Cardiff was placed

nearer Heath station and a crossover provided between the Up and Down main lines.

In the following year the branch got a new station at Lisvane & Thornhill, located between Llanishen and Caerphilly and opened on November 4 1985. Costing £182,000, the new station consists of two 167 ft platforms linked by a footbridge.

Further changes took place in May 1987 when a new small panel was installed in the 1984 Heath Junction signal box. Under the same scheme a crossover was provided at Caerphilly to allow more trains to turn round there, and the old Aber Junction signal box was closed.

St Blazey

A Railfreight investment of £4 million in 124 32 tonne hopper wagons for china clay means the replacement of 477 old wooden wagons. As part of the overall scheme, English China Clays undertook the refurbishment of its discharge area at Fowey and BR the modernisation of St Blazey depot where the china clay locomotives and rolling stock are maintained.

Severn Tunnel Junction

The rationalisation of Speedlink activities in South Wales led to the decision to close Severn Tunnel Junction yard, train crew depot and locomotive servicing point in July 1987. By the end of 1988 track lifting had

been completed, leaving only the lighting towers, a hand crane and a scattering of buildings to mark the once extensive freight activity.

Swansea

Kings Dock Junction signal box, unusual in being operated by Associated British Ports, closed on May 29 1987 as a result of a decline in coal traffic movements.

Swindon

The site of the closed Swindon Works was sold by BR in 1987 to Tarmac Properties for around £9 million.

Thorney Mill

A new, automated aggregate unloading depot was opened at Thorney Mill on the former West Drayton-Staines West branch on October 6 1986.

Tiverton Parkway

Work began on the new railhead for the Tiverton area in 1985 in readiness for its introduction with the May 1986 timetables. The modern Tiverton Parkway took over

This new station has opened at Tiverton Parkway on a site convenient to the M5 motorway and with adequate car parking for its railhead function.

from the old Tiverton Junction from that date.

Treherbert Branch

A new Ystrad Rhondda station, with self-acting passing loop and two 300 ft platforms with shelters, opened on September 28 1986 and the old Ystrad Rhondda was renamed Ton Pentre. On the same day there was a formal opening of a single platform station at Ynyswen, between Treorchy and the Treherbert terminus, public services beginning on the following day.

Trowbridge

Trowbridge was provided with a new station building in 1988. This replaced the old Brunel-style stone building which was unsafe.

Westbury

The new signal box is now in operation, controlling 107 route miles and taking over from 12 older boxes.

West Ealing

Rebuilding of the station, including a new footbridge and improved waiting areas, was completed in May 1987.

Windsor & Eton Central

The Tussaud 'Royalty & Empire' exhibition now encloses about half of the station, including the former royal waiting room and leaving just a single platform for the dmu shuttle service to Slough. The main station buildings are also part of the exhibition area, and a number of access improvements have been made.

Routes, operation, closures and preservation since 1983

The Western Region passenger network has been affected by the transfer of control of the Chiltern Lines out of Marylebone and by two experimental passenger services. The first of these involved the revival of Melksham station with a modest Westbury-Swindon dmu service. Subsequently an experimental passenger service was restored to the Oxford-Bicester route.

Most of the physical changes in route mileage have, however, been in South Wales. On the freight side, a new link between Kidwelly and the National Coal washery at Coedbach permitted the closure of the 5¼ mile restrictive route of the old Gwendraeth Valley Railway between Coedbach and Pembrey & Burry Port. A number of coal-carrying lines have been affected by the trend towards pit rationalisation in the South Wales coalfield.

The South Wales 'Valleys' network of the BR Provincial Services sector experienced some operational problems when Sprinters were first introduced but these were resolved and two more lines have been added to those already operational in the Cardiff area. The first of these was the ex-Taff Vale line between Cardiff and Radyr. This had its passenger service restored from October 5 1987, adding four new stations to the Valleys network. Six more new stations then came into use from October 3 1988 with the introduction of a passenger service on the freight branch to Aberdare. Several other new stations have been added to existing lines.

There were also some operational changes on the Valleys lines. The Treherbert branch, for example, got a self-acting passenger loop at the new Ystrad Rhondda location, and a new panel was installed at Heath Junction signal box on the Rhymney branch. A 1984 remodelling there was altered again in 1987 and a new crossover provided at Caerphilly to allow more trains to run round there.

On the Barnstaple line the southern portion of the route, below the junction with the Meldon line, was given colour light signals. At the same time the double track section south of Crediton was reduced to single. Further west, on the West of England main line in Cornwall, a fourth section to be singled was the stretch between Burngullow and a point near the old Probus & Ladock Platform. This arrangement became operational from October 6 1986.

When the new panel box was opened at Exeter it brought modern signalling to the West of England main line as far as Totnes, linking with the companion installation at Westbury and with the Reading panel to the east to control 175 miles of the route. Even so, its technology is already being challenged by the concept of integrated electronic control centres. These are based on a system of trains routing themselves from computerised control data, and with information being fed to signalmen, for overall regulation, via visual display TV screens. An installation of this sort is being planned for the Marylebone lines, with subsequent extension to the first generation of WR panel boxes at Old Oak Common, Slough, Reading, Oxford, Gloucester, Swindon and Bristol.

Closures on the Western Region include the Pembrey-Coedbach line mentioned earlier and also the portion of the old North Somerset line which had survived to serve a wagon works at Radstock. A special clearance train removed materials from the Marcroft Engineering Works at the end of June 1988. Much trackwork has also gone following the closure of the yards at Severn Tunnel Junction and the alterations at Margam to produce a small purpose-built freight yard from the old hump yard area.

In the Bristol area the line to Portishead survives and could have an interesting future. At one stage there were plans to use it to move Scottish stone shipped into Royal Portbury Dock, but a subsequent development has been the announcement of a private rapid transit scheme for Bristol which would encompass the line to Portishead. The plan, by ATA (Advanced Transport for Avon), is to provide a circular underground system for the centre of Bristol with links to BR lines, including the dormant Portishead branch.

There has been a fair amount of preservation activity in the WR area. Major

Civil engineering equipment has been steadily improved in recent years. An innovation is this combined tunnel inspection vehicle and personnel carrier.

developments have included:

Bath Stone Quarry Museum This developing activity at the Pickwick Quarry site includes 2 ft 5½ in and 1 ft 9 in gauge lines, the former to preserve aspects of the old Corsham Tramway system.

Bodmin & Wenford Railway Three societies are now cooperating in this venture and have a short line operational within the station limits of the old Bodmin General station.

Cholsey & Wallingford Railway The first steam train ran over a ½ mile line south from Wallingford on April 17 1988.

Dean Forest Railway In addition to its passenger trains, the Parkend-Norchard line has prospects of carrying the coal production of a new opencast coal mine at Oakenhill, near Parkend.

Gloucestershire Warwickshire Steam Railway There was a ceremonial reopening of Winchcombe station on August 2 1987 marking a further extension of the route from Toddington.

Gwili Railway This railway plans to extend from Llwyfan Cerrig to Cynwyl Elfred which will add a further 1½ miles to its operational route.

GWR Preservation Group After a period of difficulties, the Group's collection was moved to a new site at Southall diesel depot on September 18 1988.

Stroud Preservation Trust The Trust's members are restoring the old GWR stone goods shed at Stroud.

Teifi Valley Railway By 1987 there was an operational 2 ft gauge line at Henllen with work taking place on extension westwards towards Newcastle Emlyn.

The principal preserved railways and steam centres in the Western Region area are now:

Avon Valley Railway, Bitton Railway Station, Willsbridge, Bristol BS15 6ED. Standard gauge line of ¾ mile.

Bodmin & Wenford Railway, Bodmin General Station, Bodmin, Cornwall PL31 1AQ. The present station line is being extended.

Brecon Mountain Railway, Pant Station, Dowlais, Merthyr Tydfil, Mid Glam CF48 2UP. Two miles of 1 ft 11¾ in gauge.

Bristol Industrial Museum, Wapping Wharf, Bristol BS1 4RN. The museum also has a ¼ mile of quayside line.

Bulmer Railway Centre, Whitecross Road, Hereford. Locomotive centre with short standard gauge track.

Caerphilly Railway Society, Railway Centre, Harold Wilson Industrial Estate, Van Road, Caerphilly, Mid Glam. Centre includes ¾ mile of standard gauge track.

Cholsey & Wallingford Railway, Hithercroft Industrial Estate, Wallingford, Oxon OX10 0NF. Short standard gauge line.

Dart Valley Railway, The Station, Buckfastleigh, Devon. A 7 mile line to Totnes is part of the Buckfastleigh Steam & Leisure Park.

Dean Forest Railway, Norchard Steam Centre, Lydney, Glos. The steam centre includes a short line towards Parkend.

Didcot Railway Centre, Didcot, Oxon. This is a major centre for GWR preservation and includes both standard and mixed gauge track.

Dobwalls Theme Park, Dobwalls, Nr Liskeard, Cornwall. The park includes two miles of 7¼ in gauge line.

East Somerset Railway, Cranmore Station, Shepton Mallet, Somerset BA4 4DP. Two miles of operational standard gauge track.

Cardiff Canton traction maintenance depot, which caters for a large volume and variety of rail maintenance work in South Wales, has a new wheel lathe workshop to add to its facilities.

Gloucestershire Warwickshire Steam Railway, Toddington Station, Glos GL54 5DT. Standard gauge line being extended.

Great Western Railway Museum, Faringdon Road, Swindon SN1 5BJ. The museum includes five locomotive exhibits.

Gwili Railway, Bronwydd Arms, Carmarthen, Dyfed. Short standard gauge line currently being extended.

Lappa Valley Railway, Newlyn East, Newquay, Cornwall TR8 5HZ. 15 in gauge line on the trackbed of the old Perranporth branch.

Launceston Steam Railway, St Thomas Road, Launceston, Cornwall PL15 8DA. A standard gauge line of 2 miles.

Plym Valley Railway, Marsh Mills Station, Coypool Road, Plymouth PL7 4NL. Standard gauge line under construction.

Pontypool & Blaenavon Railway, Council Office, Lion Street, Blaenavon, Gwent. Standard gauge line of 1½ miles.

Slough Manor Railway Museum, Slough Station, Brunel Way, Slough, Berks. Short portion of standard gauge track.

Somerset & Dorset Railway Museum Trust, Washford Station, Washford, near Minehead, Somerset. Museum.

Swindon & Cricklade Railway, Blunsdon Station, Tadpole Lane, Blunsdon, Swindon SN2 4DZ. Short standard gauge line.

Teifi Valley Railway, Henllan Station, near Newcastle Emlyn, Dyfed SA44 5TD. One mile of 2 ft gauge line.

Torbay & Dartmouth Railway, Queens Park Station, Paignton, Devon. Seven miles of former BR line south from Paignton station.

Wales Railway Centre, Bute Street, Cardiff CF1 6AN. Collection adjacent to Welsh Industrial & Maritime Museum.

West Somerset Railway, The Station, Minehead, Somerset TA24 5BG. Twenty miles of standard gauge line towards Taunton.

In the former Southern Railway 'territory' between Weymouth and Exmouth, the 'Pecorama' complex at Beer includes a short 7¼ in gauge line, and the 2 ft 9 in gauge Seaton & District Electric Tramway runs for three miles northwards from Seaton along the trackbed of the old SR branch to Axminster.

Bibliography

A selection of books and booklets providing information on the area of the
Great Western Railway/Western Region of British Rail.

BR(WR)/Avon-Anglia publications
Paddington 1854-1979, C.R. Clinker (1979)
Rail 125 in Action, (1981)
Riviera Express: The train and its Route, G. Body (1979)
Western at Work Series:
 No 1 British Rail's Western Region, (1981)
 No 2 Western Motive Power, G. Body (1982)
 No 3 Heart of Wales Line, N. Sprinks & G. Body (1981).

Avon-Anglia publications
Clinker's Register of Closed Stations, C.R. Clinker (1979)
GWR: A Register of Halts and Platforms, C.R. Clinker (1979)
New light on the Gauge Conversion, C.R. Clinker (1979)

David and Charles publications
Forgotten Railways: Chilterns and Cotswolds, E. Davies & M.D. Grant
Forgotten Railways: South Wales, J.H.R. Page
Great Way West: The History and Romance of the Great Western Route to the West, D. St John Thomas
Great Western Railway: A New History, F. Booker
Regional History of the Railways of Great Britain:
 Vol 1 West Country, D. St John Thomas (1960/1981)
 Vol 12 South Wales, D.S. Barrie (1980)
 Vol 13 Thames & Severn, R. Christiansen (1981)

Oxford Publishing publications
An Historical survey of Great Western Engine Sheds, E. Lyons & E. Mountford
An Historical Survey of Great Western Stations Vols 1-3, R. Clark
A Pictorial Record of:
 Great Western Engines, J.H. Russell
 Great Western Absorbed Engines, J.H. Russell
 Coaches, Parts 1 & 2, J.H. Russell
One Hundred Years of the Great Western, D. Nicholas & S.J. Montgomery (1981)
Spirit of the Great Western, M. Esau (1980)

Ian Allan publications

GWR Country Stations, C. Leigh
History of the Great Western Railway
  Vol 1, E.T. MacDermot & C.R. Clinker (1927/1964)
  Vol 2, E.T. MacDermot & C.R. Clinker (1927/1964)
  Vol 3, O.S. Nock (1967/1982).
Rail Centres: Bristol, C. Maggs (1981)
Rail Routes in Devon & Cornwall, C. Leigh (1982)
The Western since 1948, G. Freeman Allen (1979)
This is Paddington, J.A.M. Vaughan

Oakwood Press Publications

Barry Railway, The, D.S. Barrie (1962/1978)
Bath to Weymouth Line, The, C. Maggs (1982)
Brecon & Merthyr Railway, The, D.S. Barrie (1957/1975)
Didcot, Newbury & Southampton Railway, The, T.B. Sands
Great Western London Suburban Services, T.B. Peacock (1978)
Midland and South Western Junction Railway, The, T.B. Sands (1959/1979)
Oxford, Worcester & Wolverhampton Railway, The, S.C. Jenkins & H.I.
Quayle (1977)
Plymouth, Devonport & SW Junction Railway, The, A.J. Cheesman
Rhymney Railway, The, D.S. Barrie (1952/1973)
South Devon Railway, The, R. Gregory (1982)
Taff Vale Railway, The, D.S. Barrie (1939/1969)

Other related publications

Gone With Regret, G. Behrend (Jersey Artists, 1964)
Guide to Light Railways, Transport & Industrial Preservation, G & I.G. Body
(Avon/Anglia, 1982)
Great Western Railway in the 19th Century, The, O.S. Nock (Ian Allan)
Great Western Railway in the 20th Century, The, O.S. Nock (Ian Allan)
Track Layout Diagrams of the GWR and BR(WR), R.A. Cooke

Other Sources of information

Bristol Industrial Museum
Great Western Railway Museum, Swindon
Great Western Society, Didcot
Industrial and Maritime Museum, Cardiff

Supplementary index

HST at speed.